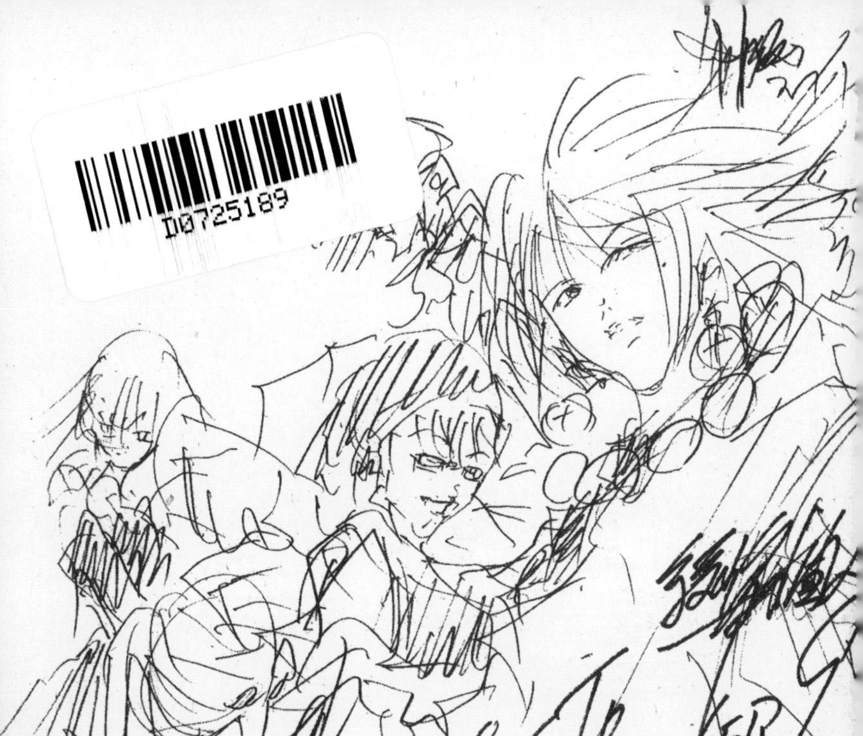
GETBACKERS
02.6.2.

16

GETBACKERS™

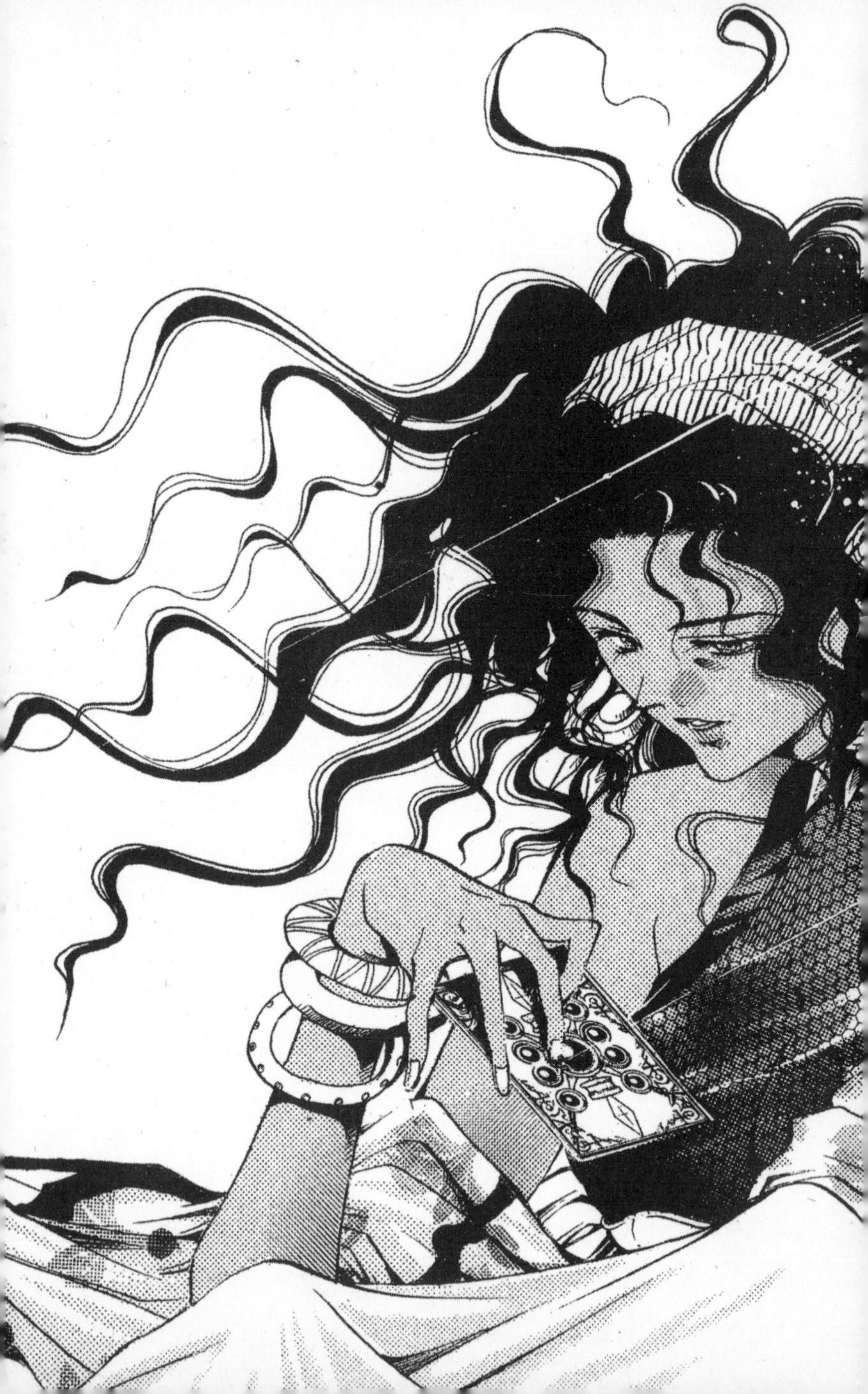

GETBACKERS

Volume 16

Art by Rando Ayamine
Story by Yuya Aoki

HAMBURG // LONDON // LOS ANGELES // TOKYO

GetBackers Vol. 16
Written by Yuya Aoki
Illustrated by Rando Ayamine

Translation - Alexis Kirsch
English Adaptation - Peter Ahlstrom
Retouch and Lettering - Lianne Ricci
Cover Design - Kyle Plummer

Editor - Alexis Kirsch
Digital Imaging Manager - Chris Buford
Pre-Press Supervisor - Erika Terriquez
Art Director - Anne-Marie Horne
Production Manager - Elisabeth Brizzi
Managing Editor - Vy Nguyen
Editor-in-Chief - Rob Tokar
VP of Production - Ron Klamert
Publisher - Mike Kiley
President and C.O.O. - John Parker
C.E.O. and Chief Creative Officer - Stuart Levy

A  Manga

TOKYOPOP Inc.
5900 Wilshire Blvd. Suite 2000
Los Angeles, CA 90036

E-mail: info@TOKYOPOP.com
Come visit us online at www.TOKYOPOP.com

ISBN: 1-59182-978-X

First TOKYOPOP printing: November 2006
10 9 8 7 6 5 4 3 2 1
Printed in the USA

Story Thus Far:

Ginji Amano can amplify and control electromagnetic waves. Ban Mido has the power to create illusions in people's minds for one minute. Together they are the GetBackers, a retrieval agency whose motto is "We get back what shouldn't be gone." For the right price, they'll recover anything that's been taken.

The students of a prestigious cram school have gone missing, and their parents are afraid this has something to do with the "Divine Design" card game they've been playing...which turns out to be a very dangerous game indeed! Ban, Ginji, Kazuki, Himiko, and Hevn discover cards that correspond to each of them, and when they see a man literally turn to crumbling stone, they realize the cards somehow have the power to affect reality. After meeting up with an old "friend" from the pre-Volts days who is none too happy to see him, Kazuki is spirited away right before Ginji's eyes, and though Ginji's electricity somehow manages to penetrate the field surrounding them, it's not enough to save Kazuki from going down in defeat.

The missing children, who are card masters, or "Dominators," believe themselves to be Archangels chosen to help reshape the world—chosen by the Angel Lord Lucifer himself, president of the game company. Ban trades blows with Lucifer but barely makes it out alive...and the GetBackers and co. realize they need to learn more about these cards! They seek help in the form of a blast from Ban's past—a beautiful, young...99-year-old witch named Maria who used to babysit him. Proving her skill at sorcery by pulling Ginji's heart from his chest and reinserting it with no ill effects, she starts training them to master the cards and become Dominators, but somehow even Hevn is having more success than Ban, who just can't believe the cards' power is anything more than a crappy trick...

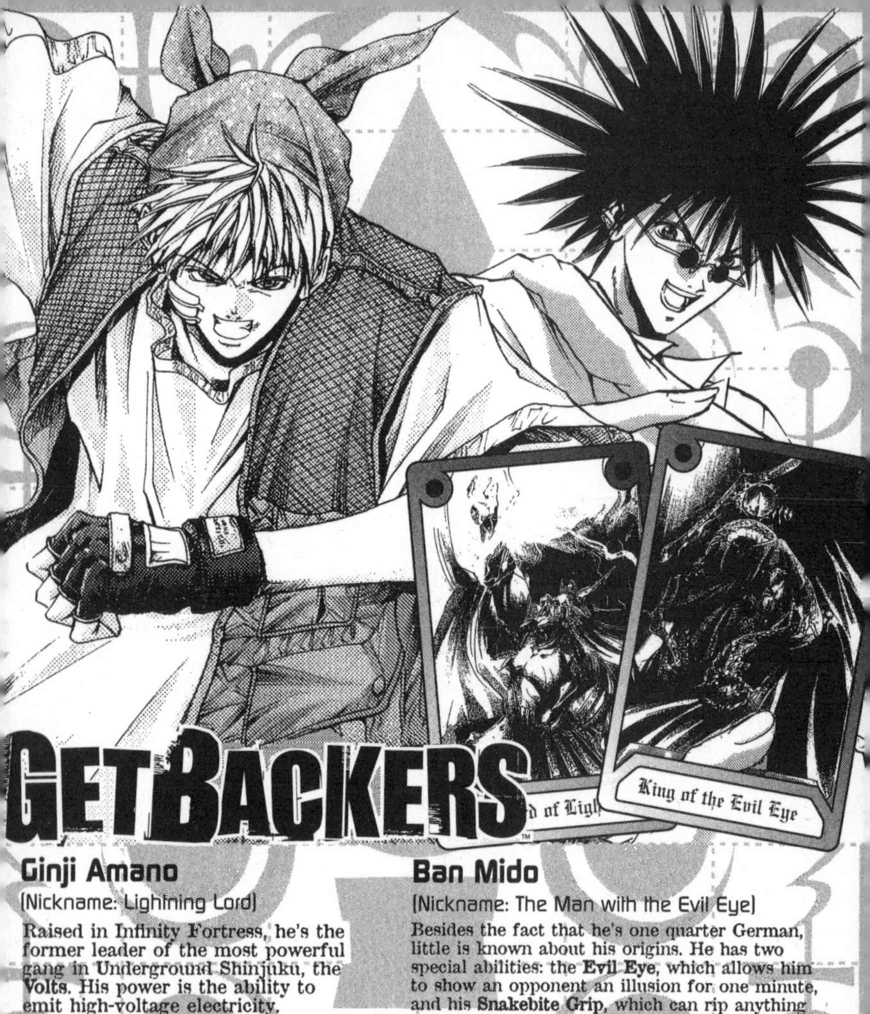

King of the Evil Eye
d of Ligh

GETBACKERS™

Ginji Amano

(Nickname: Lightning Lord)

Raised in Infinity Fortress, he's the former leader of the most powerful gang in Underground Shinjuku, the **Volts**. His power is the ability to emit high-voltage electricity.

Height: 176 cm (5'9"), Weight: 62 kg (137 lbs.), Blood Type: O.

Ban Mido

(Nickname: The Man with the Evil Eye)

Besides the fact that he's one quarter German, little is known about his origins. He has two special abilities: the **Evil Eye**, which allows him to show an opponent an illusion for one minute, and his **Snakebite Grip**, which can rip anything apart with its 200 kg per square cm force.

Height: 175 cm (5'8.5"), Weight: 58 kg (128 lbs), Blood Type: B.

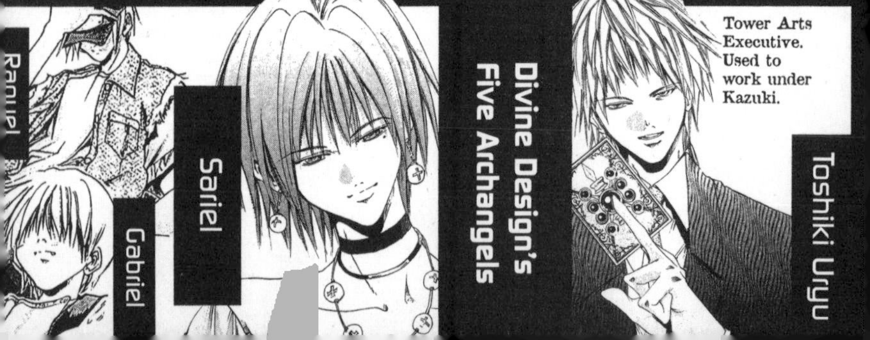

Toshiki Uryu
Tower Arts Executive. Used to work under Kazuki.
Divine Design's Five Archangels
Sariel
Gabriel
Raguel

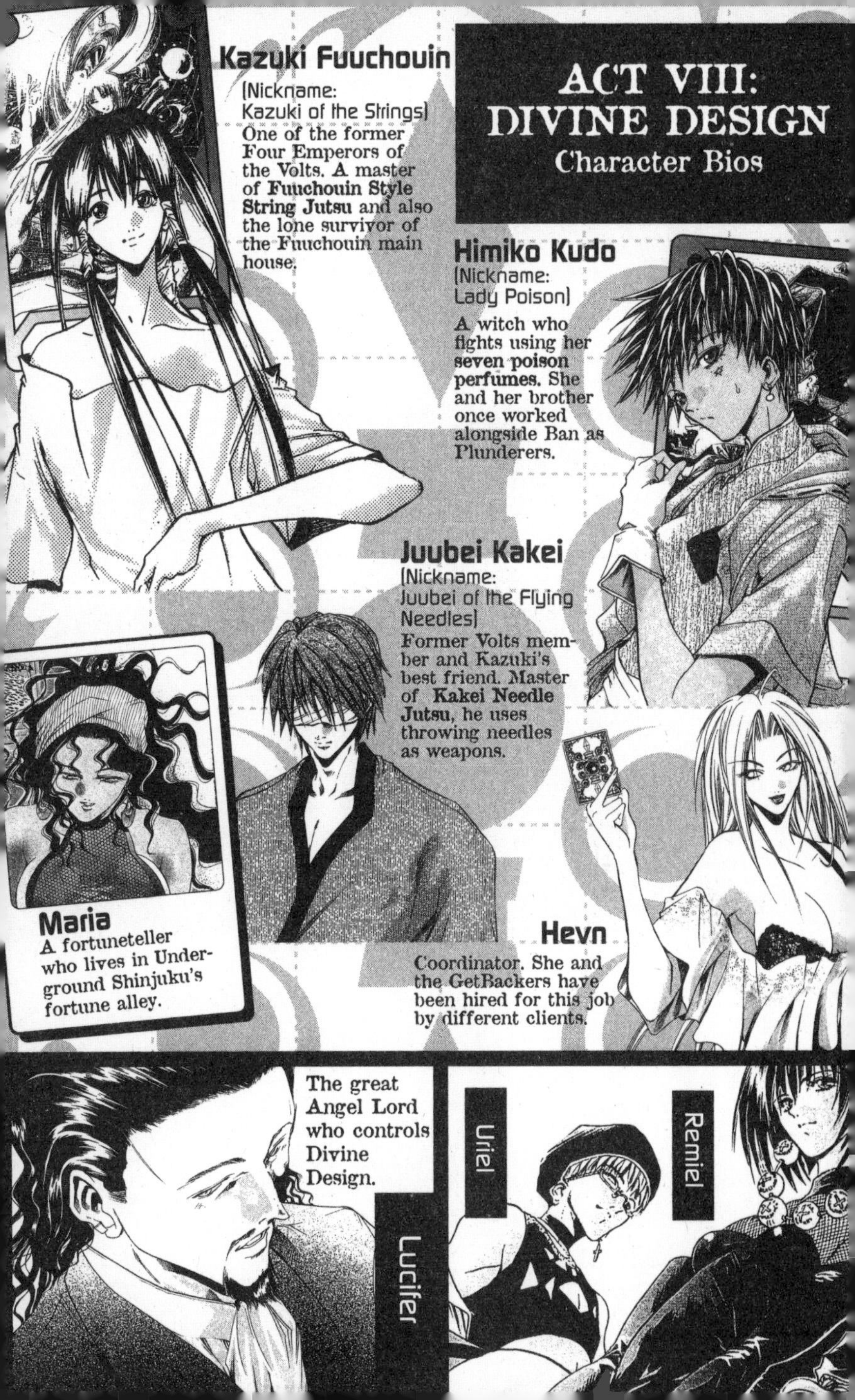
ACT VIII: DIVINE DESIGN
Character Bios
Kazuki Fuuchouin
(Nickname: Kazuki of the Strings)
One of the former Four Emperors of the Volts. A master of Fuuchouin Style String Jutsu and also the lone survivor of the Fuuchouin main house.
Himiko Kudo
(Nickname: Lady Poison)
A witch who fights using her seven poison perfumes. She and her brother once worked alongside Ban as Plunderers.
Juubei Kakei
(Nickname: Juubei of the Flying Needles)
Former Volts member and Kazuki's best friend. Master of Kakei Needle Jutsu, he uses throwing needles as weapons.
Hevn
Coordinator. She and the GetBackers have been hired for this job by different clients.
Maria
A fortuneteller who lives in Underground Shinjuku's fortune alley.
Remiel
Uriel
The great Angel Lord who controls Divine Design.
Lucifer

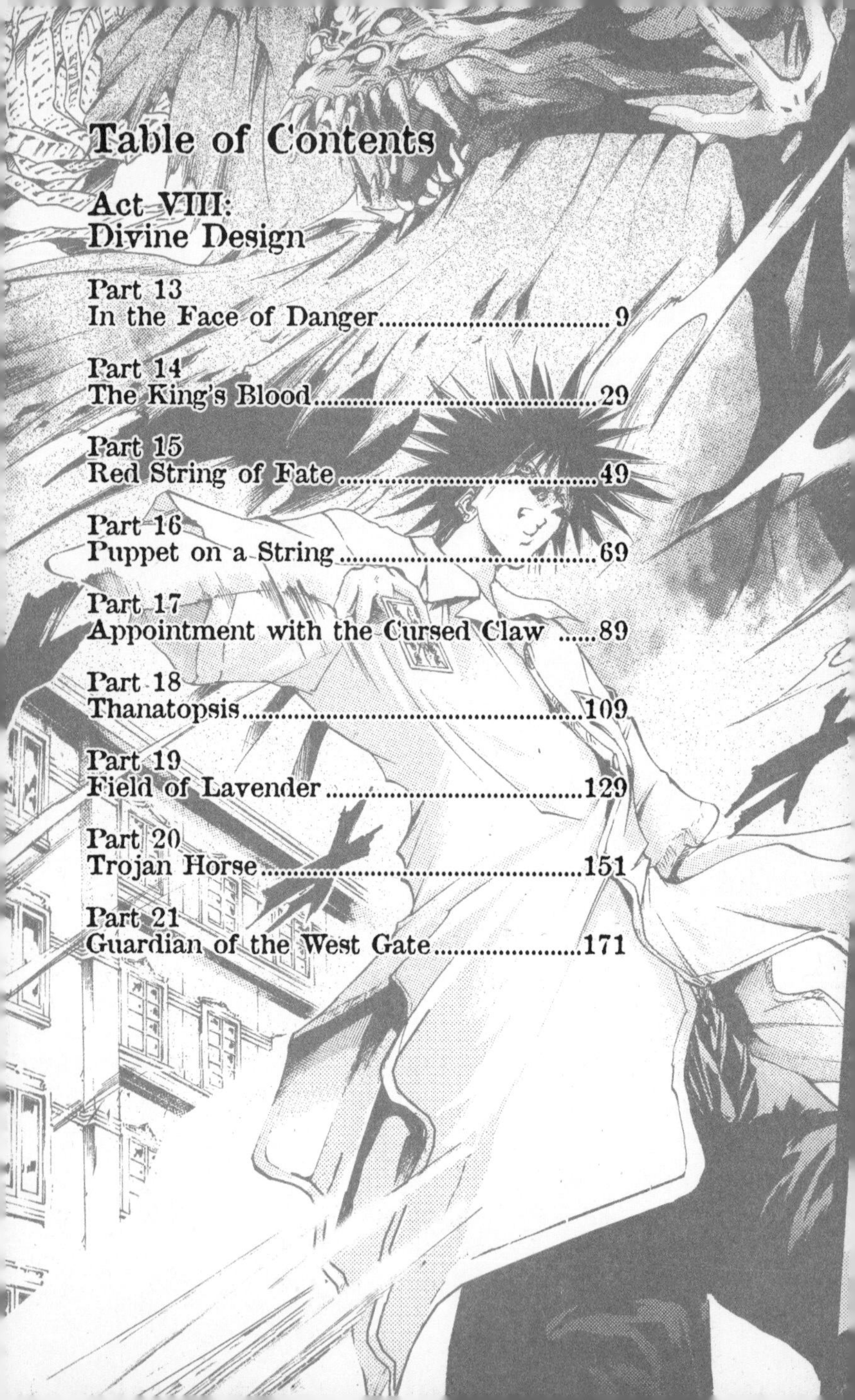

Table of Contents

Act VIII: Divine Design

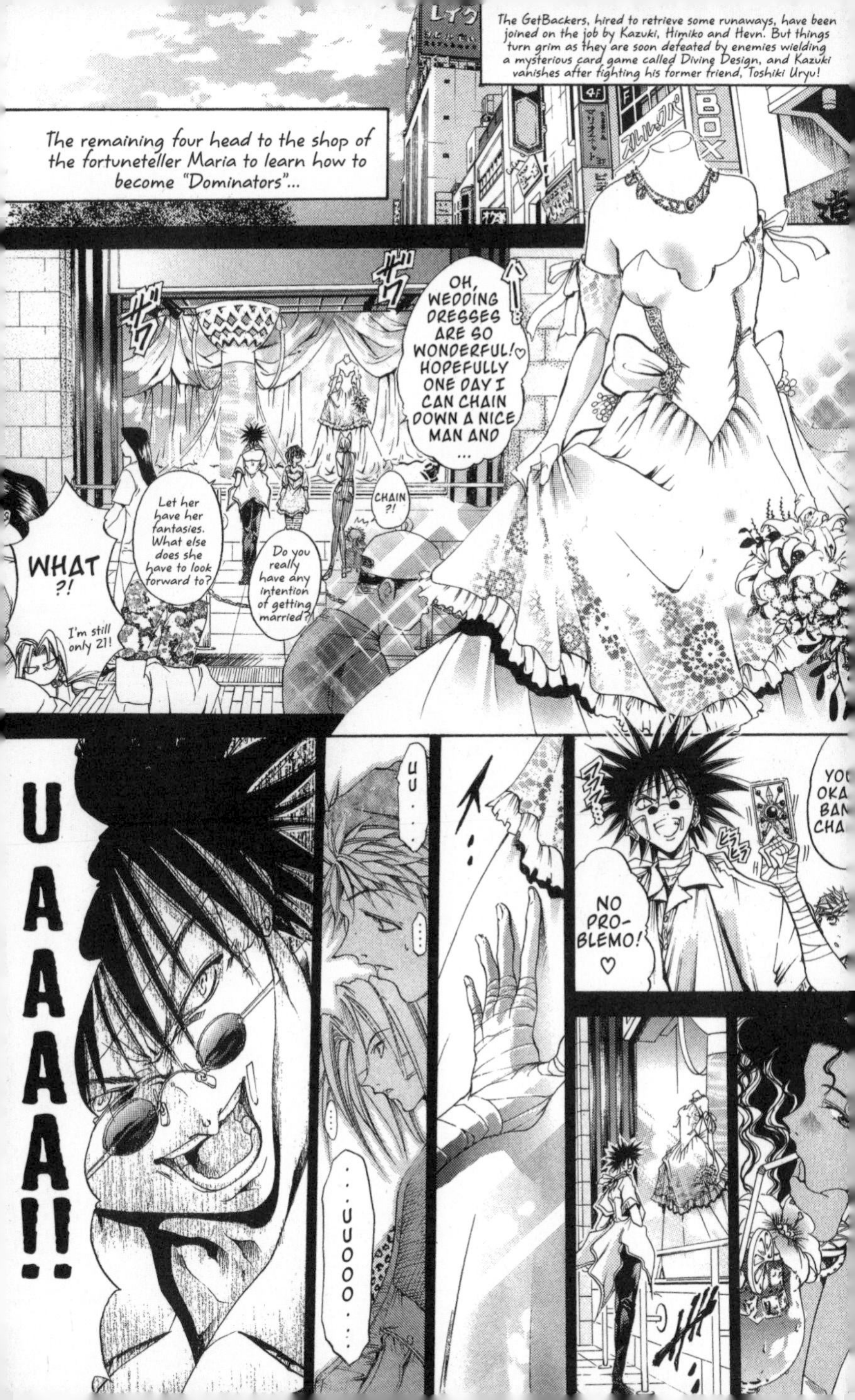
The GetBackers, hired to retrieve some runaways, have been joined on the job by Kazuki, Himiko and Hevn. But things turn grim as they are soon defeated by enemies wielding a mysterious card game called Divine Design, and Kazuki vanishes after fighting his former friend, Toshiki Uryu!
The remaining four head to the shop of the fortuneteller Maria to learn how to become "Dominators"...
OH, WEDDING DRESSES ARE SO WONDERFUL!♡ HOPEFULLY ONE DAY I CAN CHAIN DOWN A NICE MAN AND ...
CHAIN ?!
Do you really have any intention of getting married?
Let her have her fantasies. What else does she have to look forward to?
WHAT ?!
I'm still only 21!
YOU OKA BAN CHA
NO PRO-BLEMO! ♡
UU . . .
. . .
. . .
. . . UUOOO . . .
UAAAA!!

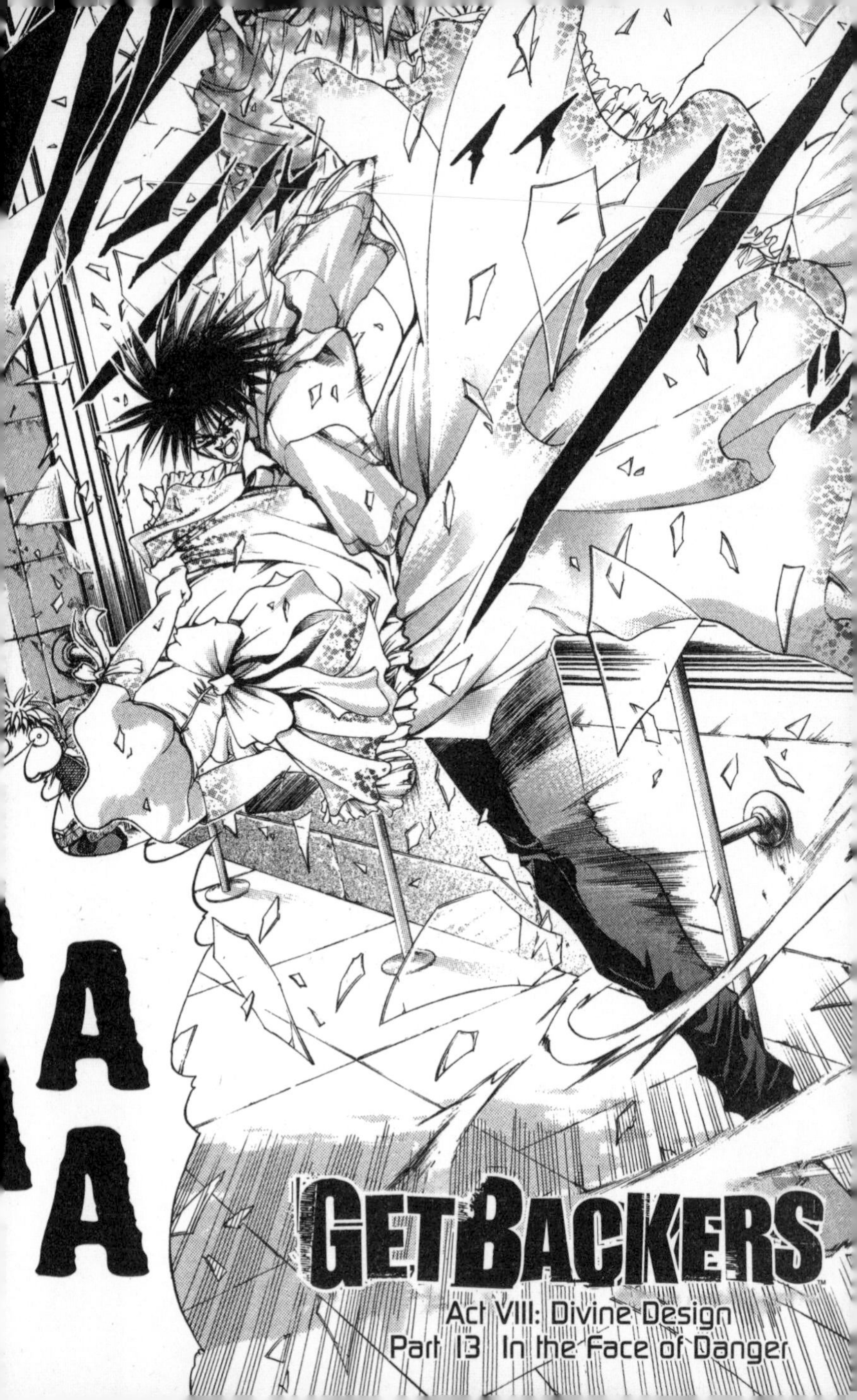
AAA
GETBACKERS
Act VIII: Divine Design
Part 13 In the Face of Danger

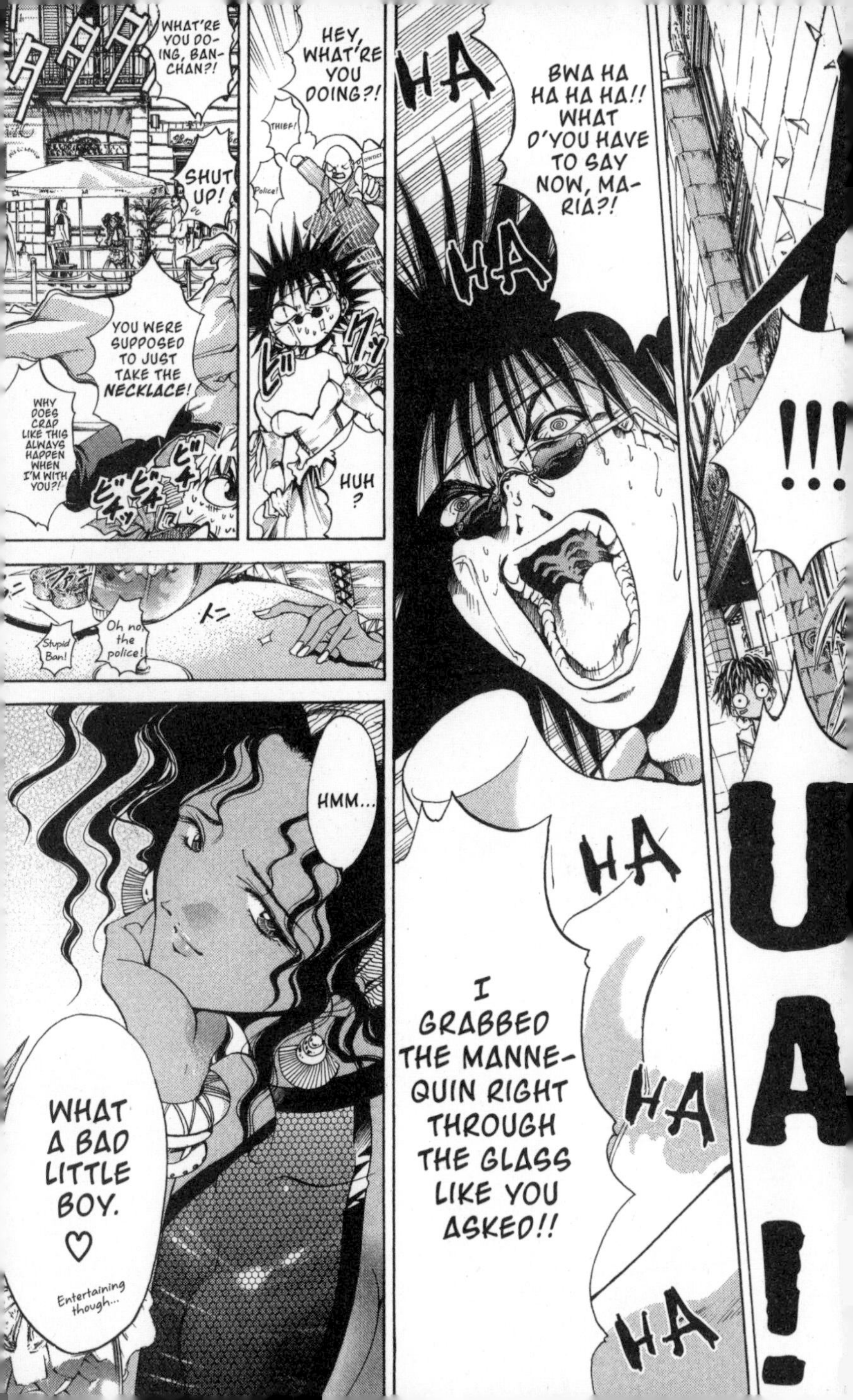
!!!
UAA!
BWA HA HA HA HA!! WHAT D'YOU HAVE TO SAY NOW, MA-RIA?!
HA
HA
HA
HA
HA
I GRABBED THE MANNE-QUIN RIGHT THROUGH THE GLASS LIKE YOU ASKED!!
HEY, WHAT'RE YOU DOING?!
THIEF!
owner
Police!
HUH?
WHAT'RE YOU DO-ING, BAN-CHAN?!
SHUT UP!
YOU WERE SUPPOSED TO JUST TAKE THE NECKLACE!
WHY DOES CRAP LIKE THIS ALWAYS HAPPEN WHEN I'M WITH YOU?!
Oh no, the police!
Stupid Ban!
HMM...
WHAT A BAD LITTLE BOY. ♡
Entertaining though...

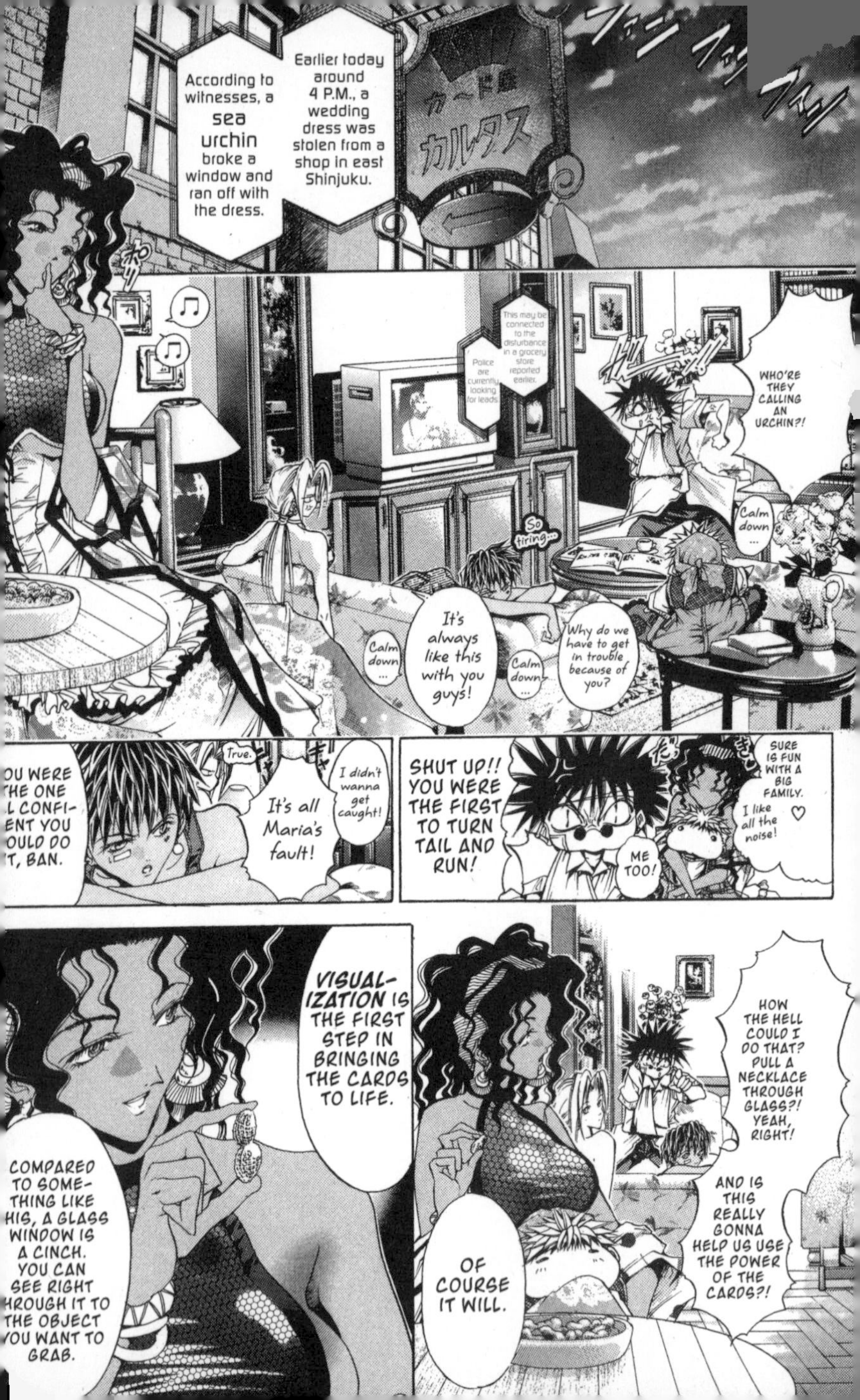
Earlier today around 4 P.M., a wedding dress was stolen from a shop in east Shinjuku.
According to witnesses, a sea urchin broke a window and ran off with the dress.
カルタス
WHO'RE THEY CALLING AN URCHIN?!
Calm down ...
This may be connected to the disturbance in a grocery store reported earlier.
Police are currently looking for leads.
So tiring...
Why do we have to get in trouble because of you?
Calm down ...
It's always like this with you guys!
Calm down ...
SURE IS FUN WITH A BIG FAMILY.
I like all the noise! ♡
SHUT UP!! YOU WERE THE FIRST TO TURN TAIL AND RUN!
ME TOO!
I didn't wanna get caught!
True.
It's all Maria's fault!
OU WERE THE ONE L CONFI- ENT YOU OULD DO T, BAN.
HOW THE HELL COULD I DO THAT? PULL A NECKLACE THROUGH GLASS?! YEAH, RIGHT!
AND IS THIS REALLY GONNA HELP US USE THE POWER OF THE CARDS?!
OF COURSE IT WILL.
VISUAL- IZATION IS THE FIRST STEP IN BRINGING THE CARDS TO LIFE.
COMPARED TO SOME- THING LIKE HIS, A GLASS WINDOW IS A CINCH. YOU CAN SEE RIGHT HROUGH IT TO THE OBJECT YOU WANT TO GRAB.

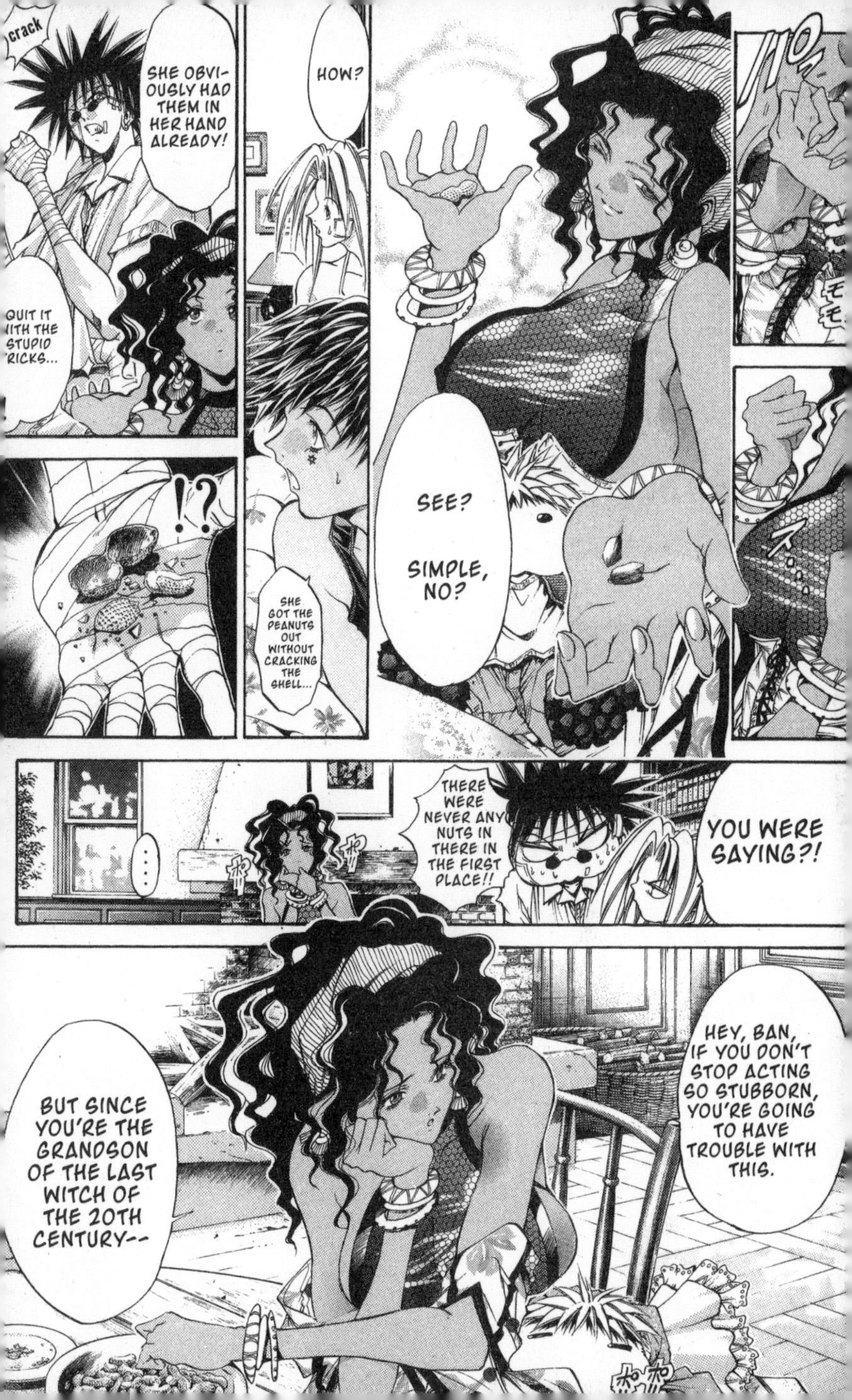
SEE?
SIMPLE, NO?
HOW?
SHE GOT THE PEANUTS OUT WITHOUT CRACKING THE SHELL...
crack
SHE OBVIOUSLY HAD THEM IN HER HAND ALREADY!
QUIT IT ITH THE STUPID RICKS...
!?
YOU WERE SAYING?!
THERE WERE NEVER ANY NUTS IN THERE IN THE FIRST PLACE!!
...
HEY, BAN, IF YOU DON'T STOP ACTING SO STUBBORN, YOU'RE GOING TO HAVE TROUBLE WITH THIS.
BUT SINCE YOU'RE THE GRANDSON OF THE LAST WITCH OF THE 20TH CENTURY--

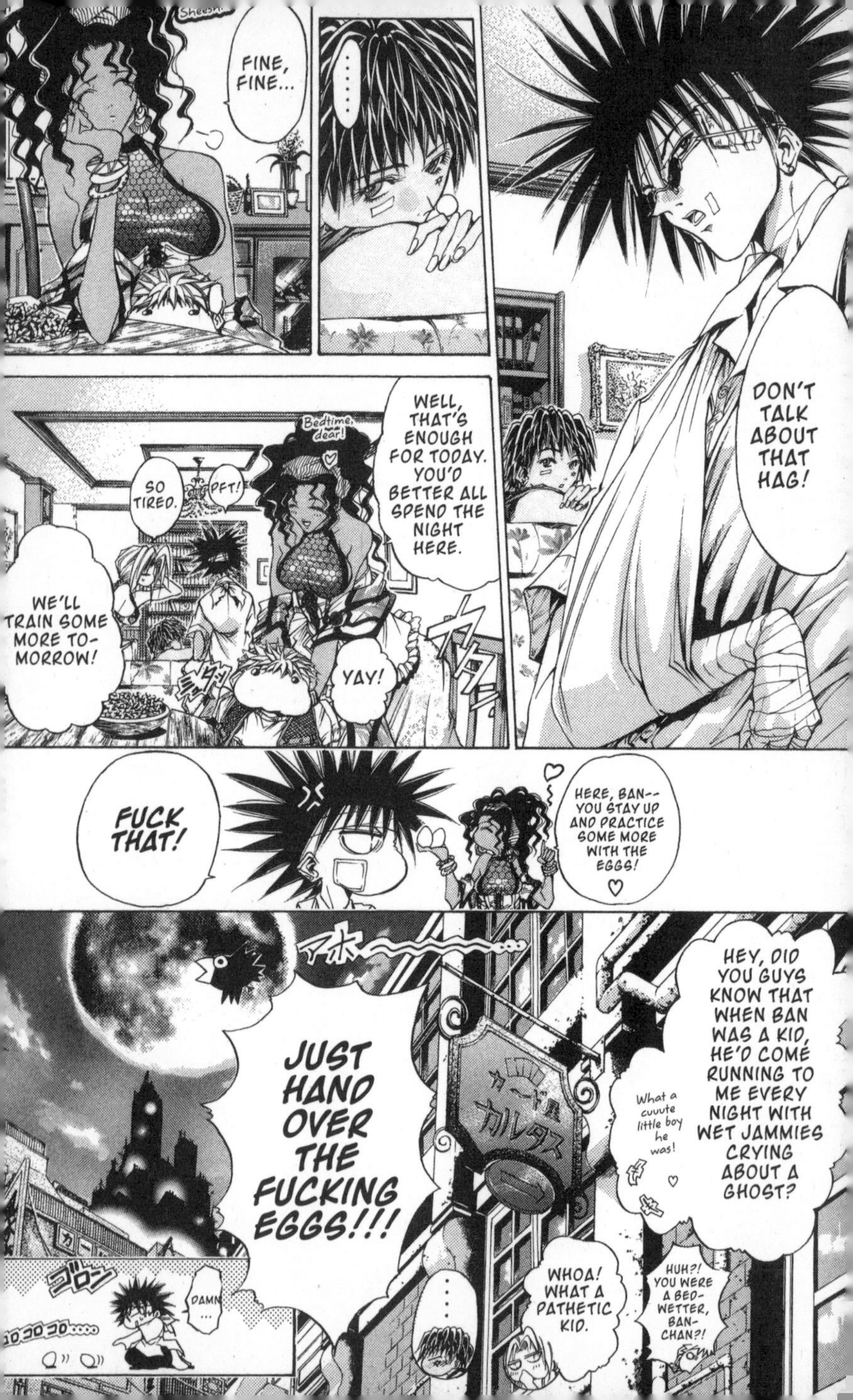
DON'T TALK ABOUT THAT HAG!
......
Sheesh...
FINE, FINE...
Bedtime, dear!
WELL, THAT'S ENOUGH FOR TODAY. YOU'D BETTER ALL SPEND THE NIGHT HERE.
YAY!
PFT!
SO TIRED.
WE'LL TRAIN SOME MORE TO-MORROW!
HERE, BAN-- YOU STAY UP AND PRACTICE SOME MORE WITH THE EGGS!
FUCK THAT!
HEY, DID YOU GUYS KNOW THAT WHEN BAN WAS A KID, HE'D COME RUNNING TO ME EVERY NIGHT WITH WET JAMMIES CRYING ABOUT A GHOST?
What a cuuute little boy he was!
HUH?! YOU WERE A BED-WETTER, BAN-CHAN?!
WHOA! WHAT A PATHETIC KID.
......
アホ〜〜〜
JUST HAND OVER THE FUCKING EGGS!!!
DAMN...
ゴロン
コロコロコロ

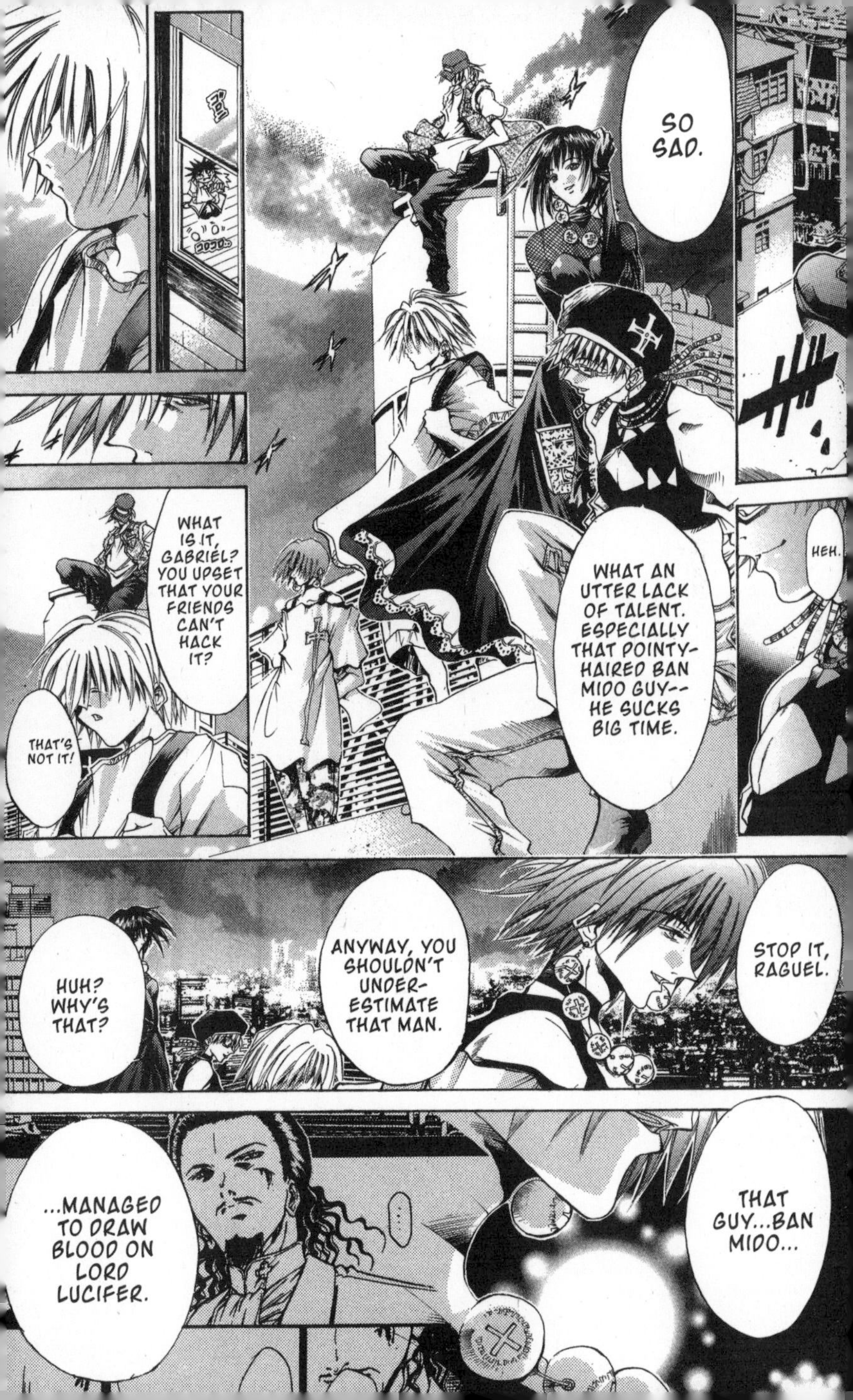
HEH.
SO SAD.
WHAT AN UTTER LACK OF TALENT. ESPECIALLY THAT POINTY-HAIRED BAN MIDO GUY--HE SUCKS BIG TIME.
WHAT IS IT, GABRIEL? YOU UPSET THAT YOUR FRIENDS CAN'T HACK IT?
THAT'S NOT IT!
STOP IT, RAGUEL.
ANYWAY, YOU SHOULDN'T UNDER-ESTIMATE THAT MAN.
HUH? WHY'S THAT?
THAT GUY...BAN MIDO...
...
...MANAGED TO DRAW BLOOD ON LORD LUCIFER.

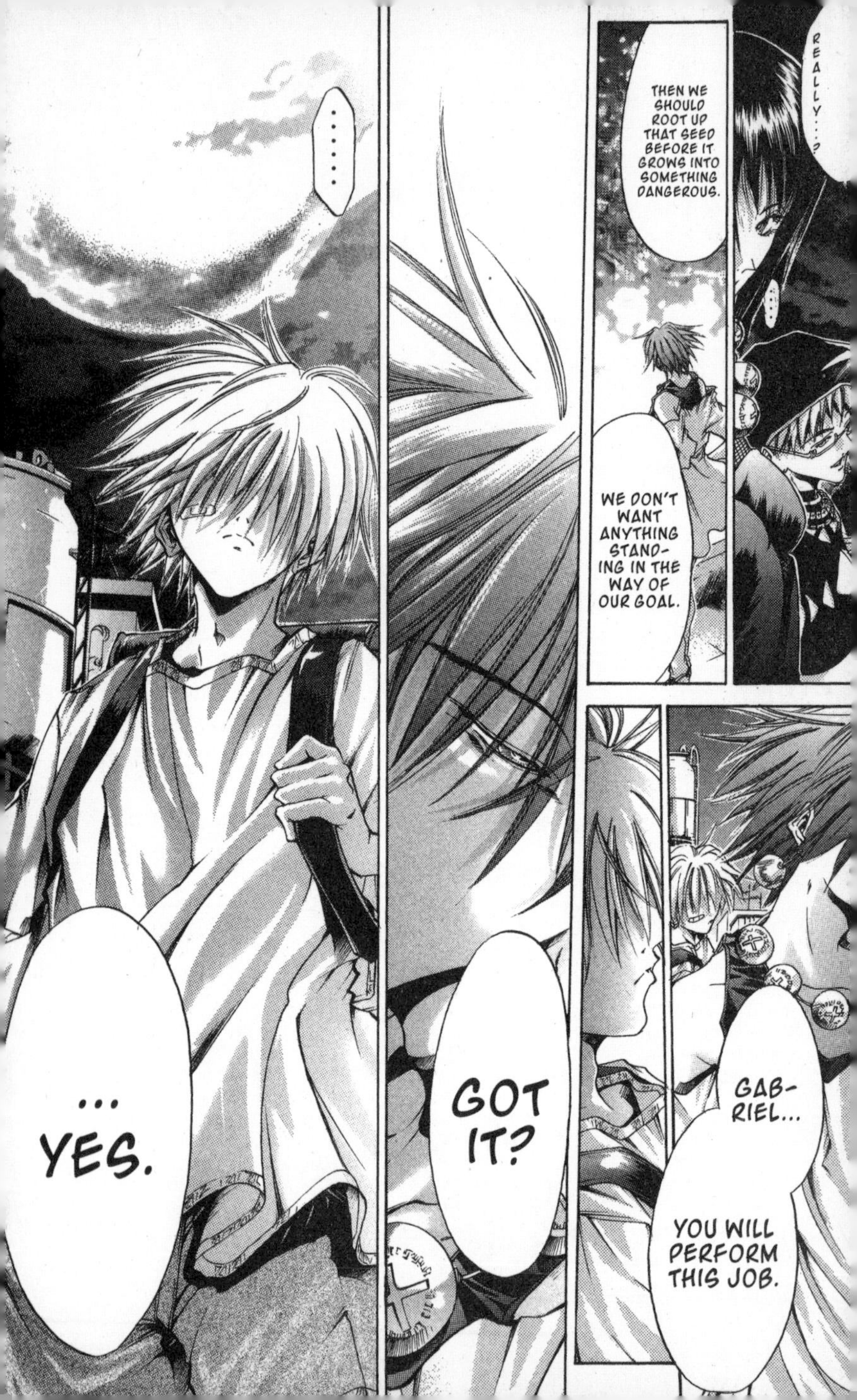
REALLY...?
THEN WE SHOULD ROOT UP THAT SEED BEFORE IT GROWS INTO SOMETHING DANGEROUS.
...
WE DON'T WANT ANYTHING STANDING IN THE WAY OF OUR GOAL.
GABRIEL...
YOU WILL PERFORM THIS JOB.
GOT IT?
......
...YES.

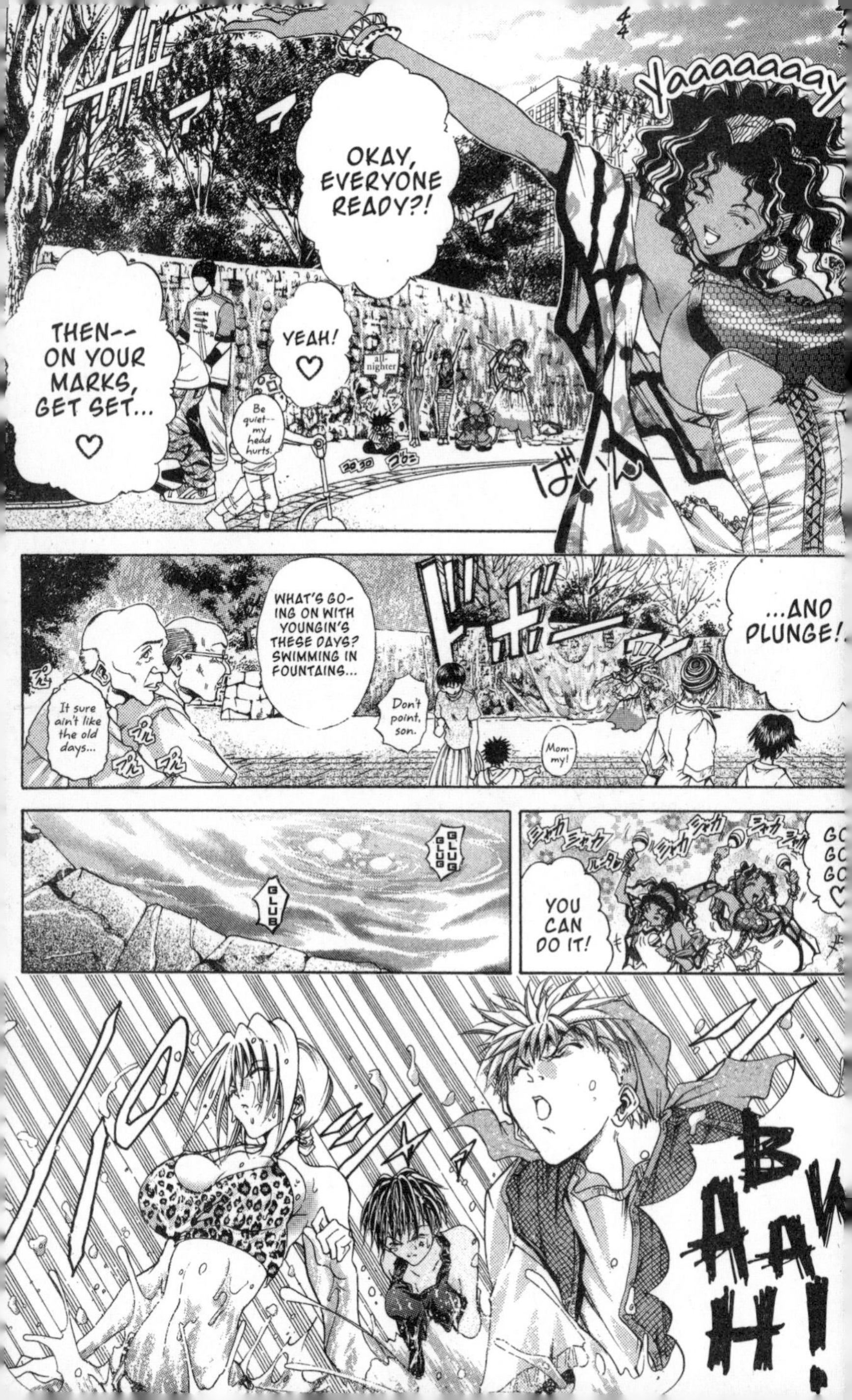
Yaaaaaaay
OKAY, EVERYONE READY?!
YEAH! ♡
all-nighter
THEN-- ON YOUR MARKS, GET SET... ♡
Be quiet--my head hurts.
...AND PLUNGE!
Mommy!
Don't point, son.
WHAT'S GOING ON WITH YOUNGIN'S THESE DAYS? SWIMMING IN FOUNTAINS...
It sure ain't like the old days...
GO GO GO ♡
YOU CAN DO IT!
GLUB GLUB
GLUB
BWAAH!

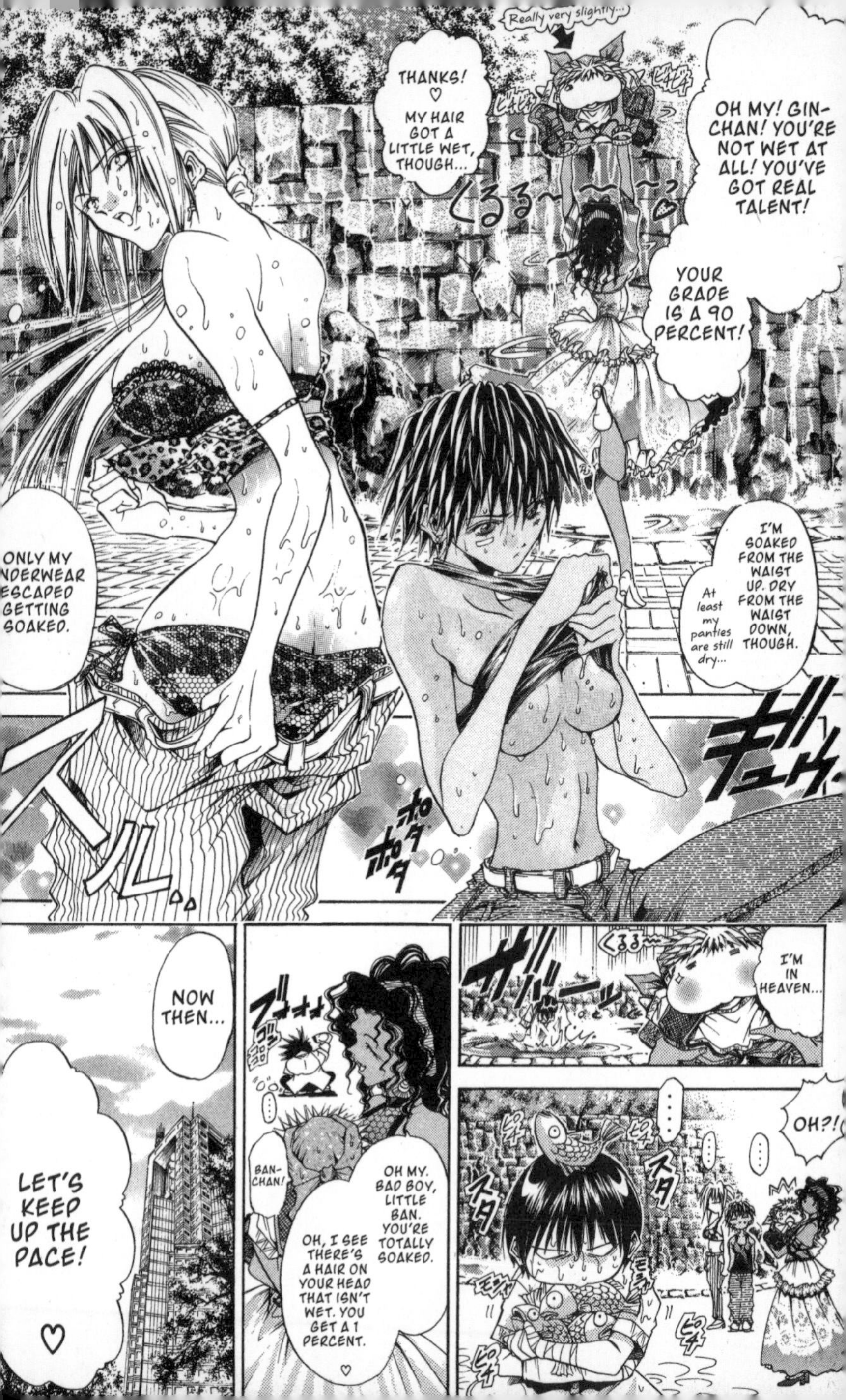

Really very slightly...
OH MY! GIN-CHAN! YOU'RE NOT WET AT ALL! YOU'VE GOT REAL TALENT!
YOUR GRADE IS A 90 PERCENT!
くるる〜〜
THANKS! ♡ MY HAIR GOT A LITTLE WET, THOUGH...
I'M SOAKED FROM THE WAIST UP. DRY FROM THE WAIST DOWN, THOUGH.
At least my panties are still dry...
ONLY MY NDERWEAR ESCAPED GETTING SOAKED.
くるる〜
I'M IN HEAVEN...
OH?!
...
...
...
OH MY. BAD BOY, LITTLE BAN. YOU'RE TOTALLY SOAKED.
BAN-CHAN!
OH, I SEE THERE'S A HAIR ON YOUR HEAD THAT ISN'T WET. YOU GET A 1 PERCENT.
♡
...
NOW THEN...
LET'S KEEP UP THE PACE!
♡

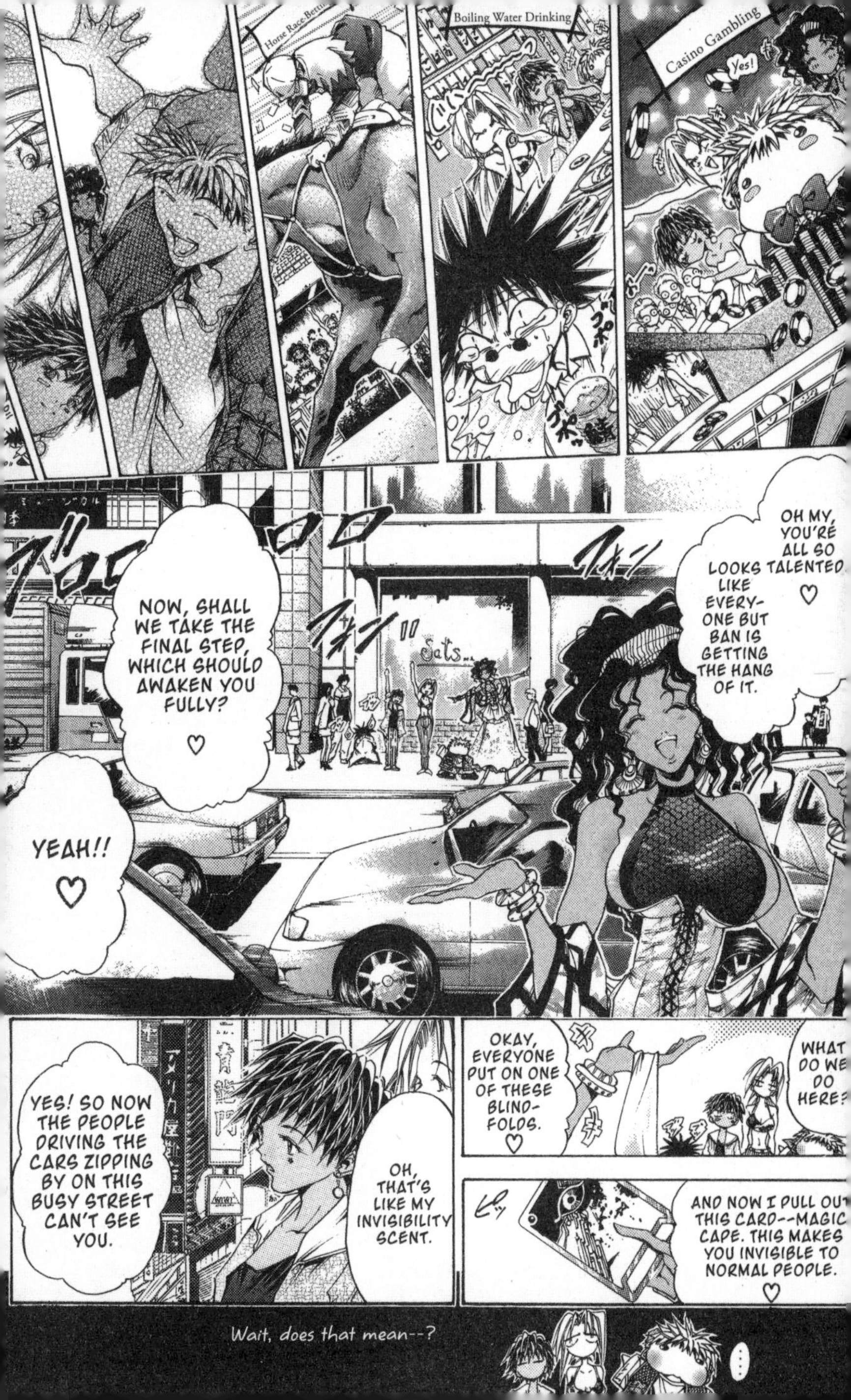
Casino Gambling
Yes!
Boiling Water Drinking
Horse Race-Betti
OH MY, YOU'RE ALL SO TALENTED ♡
LOOKS LIKE EVERYONE BUT BAN IS GETTING THE HANG OF IT.
NOW, SHALL WE TAKE THE FINAL STEP, WHICH SHOULD AWAKEN YOU FULLY? ♡
YEAH!! ♡
WHAT DO WE DO HERE?
OKAY, EVERYONE PUT ON ONE OF THESE BLINDFOLDS. ♡
AND NOW I PULL OUT THIS CARD--MAGIC CAPE. THIS MAKES YOU INVISIBLE TO NORMAL PEOPLE. ♡
OH, THAT'S LIKE MY INVISIBILITY SCENT.
YES! SO NOW THE PEOPLE DRIVING THE CARS ZIPPING BY ON THIS BUSY STREET CAN'T SEE YOU.
Wait, does that mean--?
...

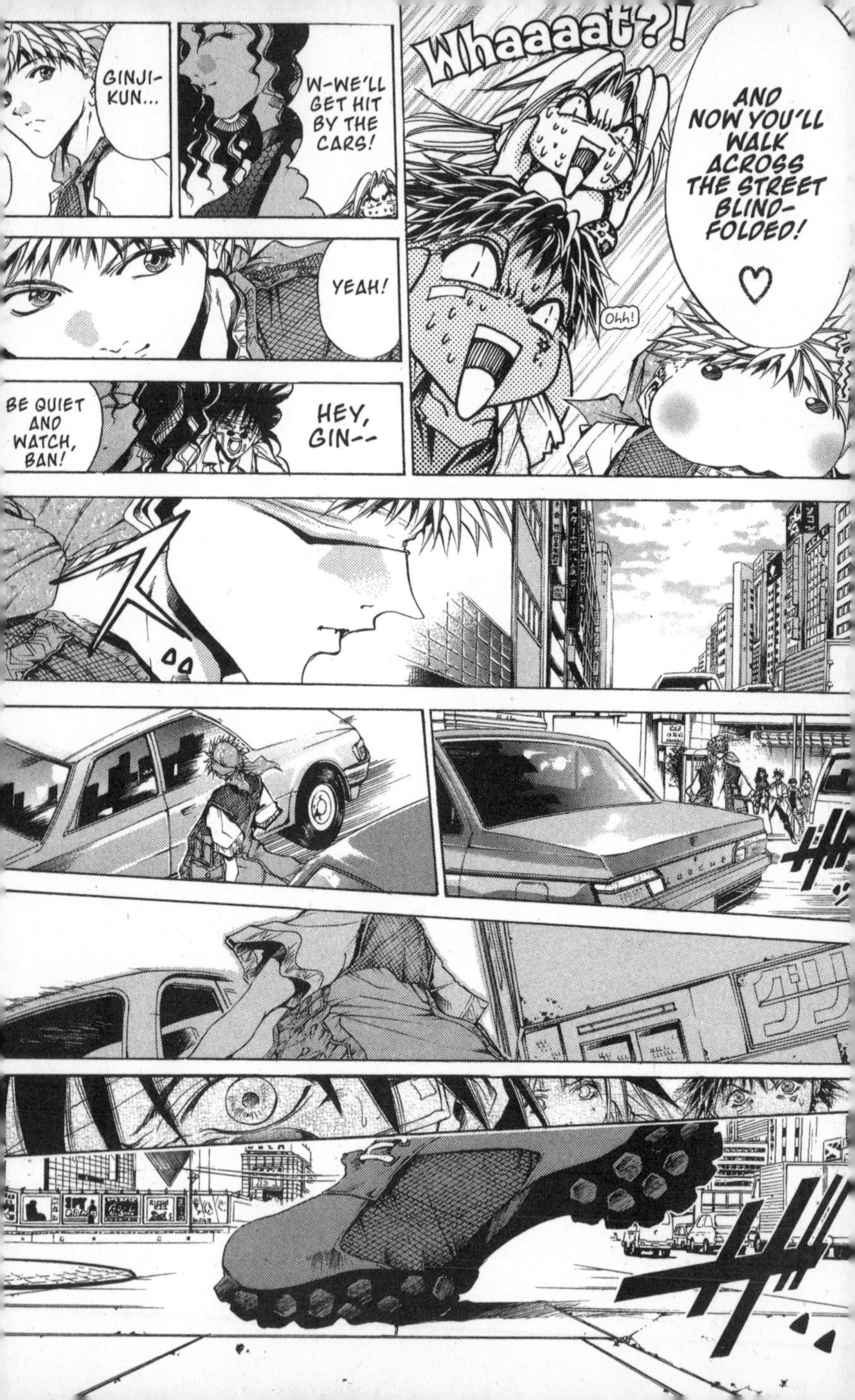

AND NOW YOU'LL WALK ACROSS THE STREET BLIND-FOLDED! ♥
Whaaaat?!
Ohh!
W-WE'LL GET HIT BY THE CARS!
GINJI-KUN...
YEAH!
HEY, GIN--
BE QUIET AND WATCH, BAN!

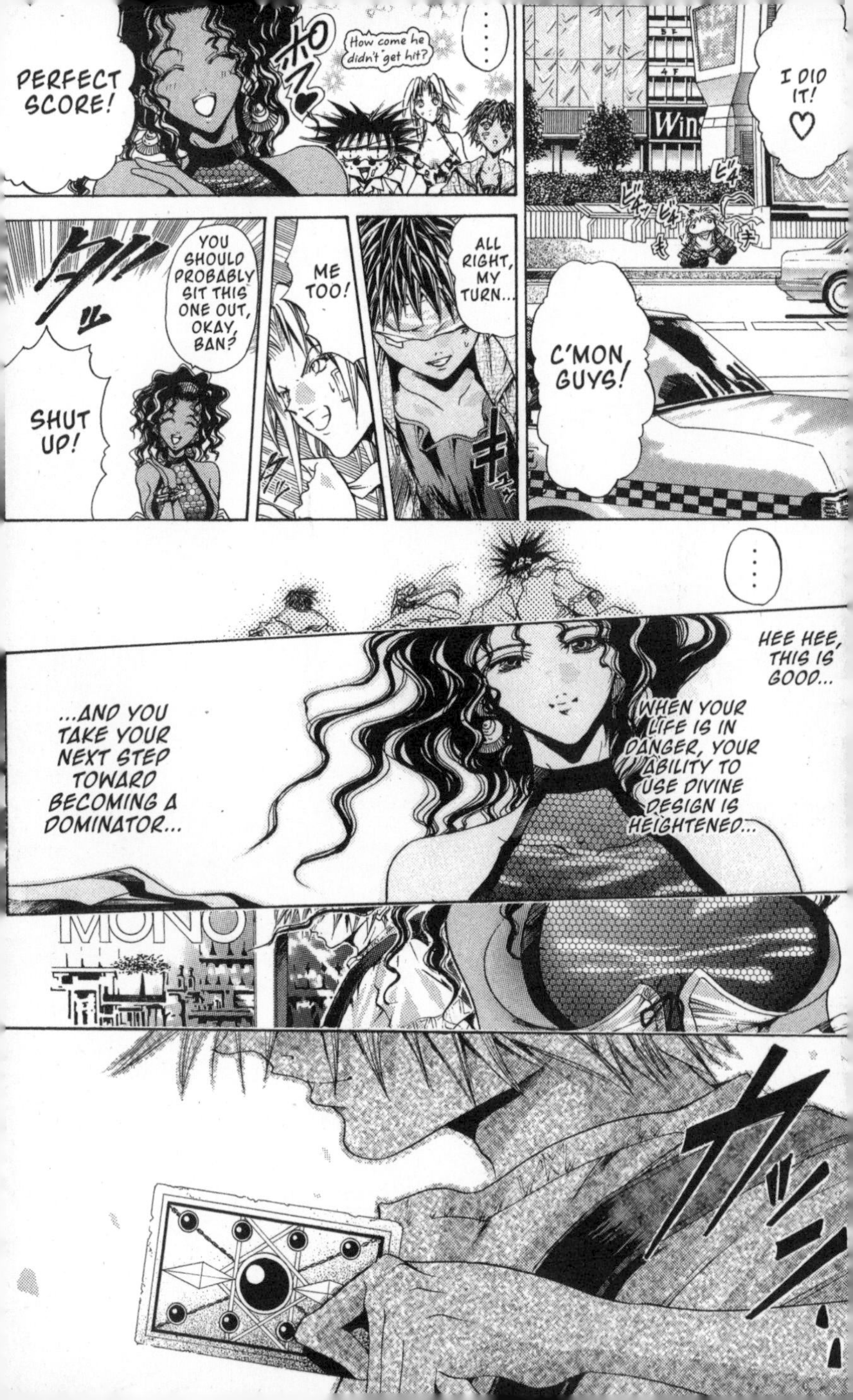
I DID IT! ♡
C'MON GUYS!
....
How come he didn't get hit?
PERFECT SCORE!
ALL RIGHT, MY TURN...
ME TOO!
YOU SHOULD PROBABLY SIT THIS ONE OUT, OKAY, BAN?
SHUT UP!
....
HEE HEE, THIS IS GOOD...
WHEN YOUR LIFE IS IN DANGER, YOUR ABILITY TO USE DIVINE DESIGN IS HEIGHTENED...
...AND YOU TAKE YOUR NEXT STEP TOWARD BECOMING A DOMINATOR...

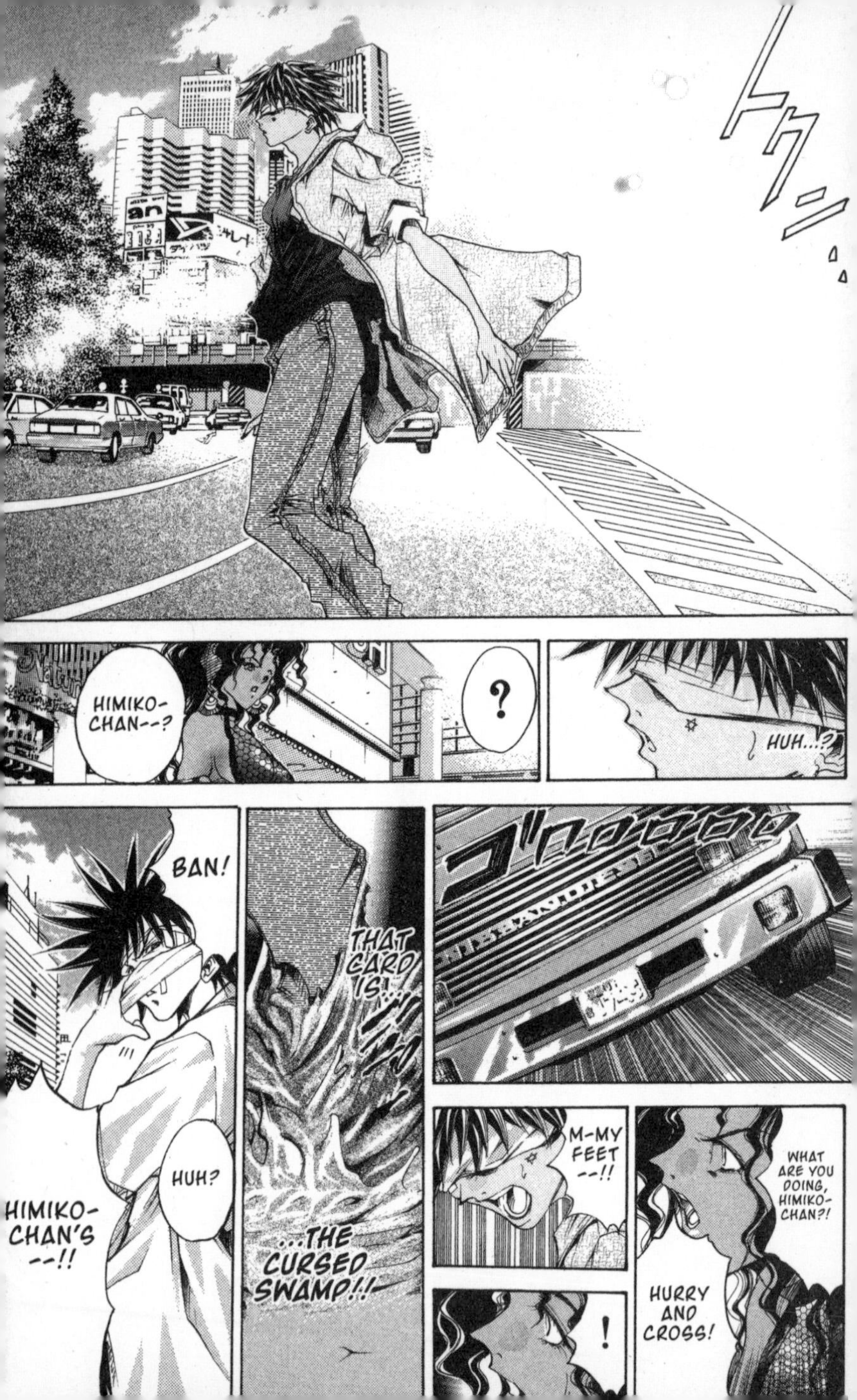

HUH...?
?
HIMIKO-CHAN--?
WHAT ARE YOU DOING, HIMIKO-CHAN?!
HURRY AND CROSS!
M-MY FEET--!!
!
THAT CARD IS...
...THE CURSED SWAMP!!
BAN!
HUH?
HIMIKO-CHAN'S--!!

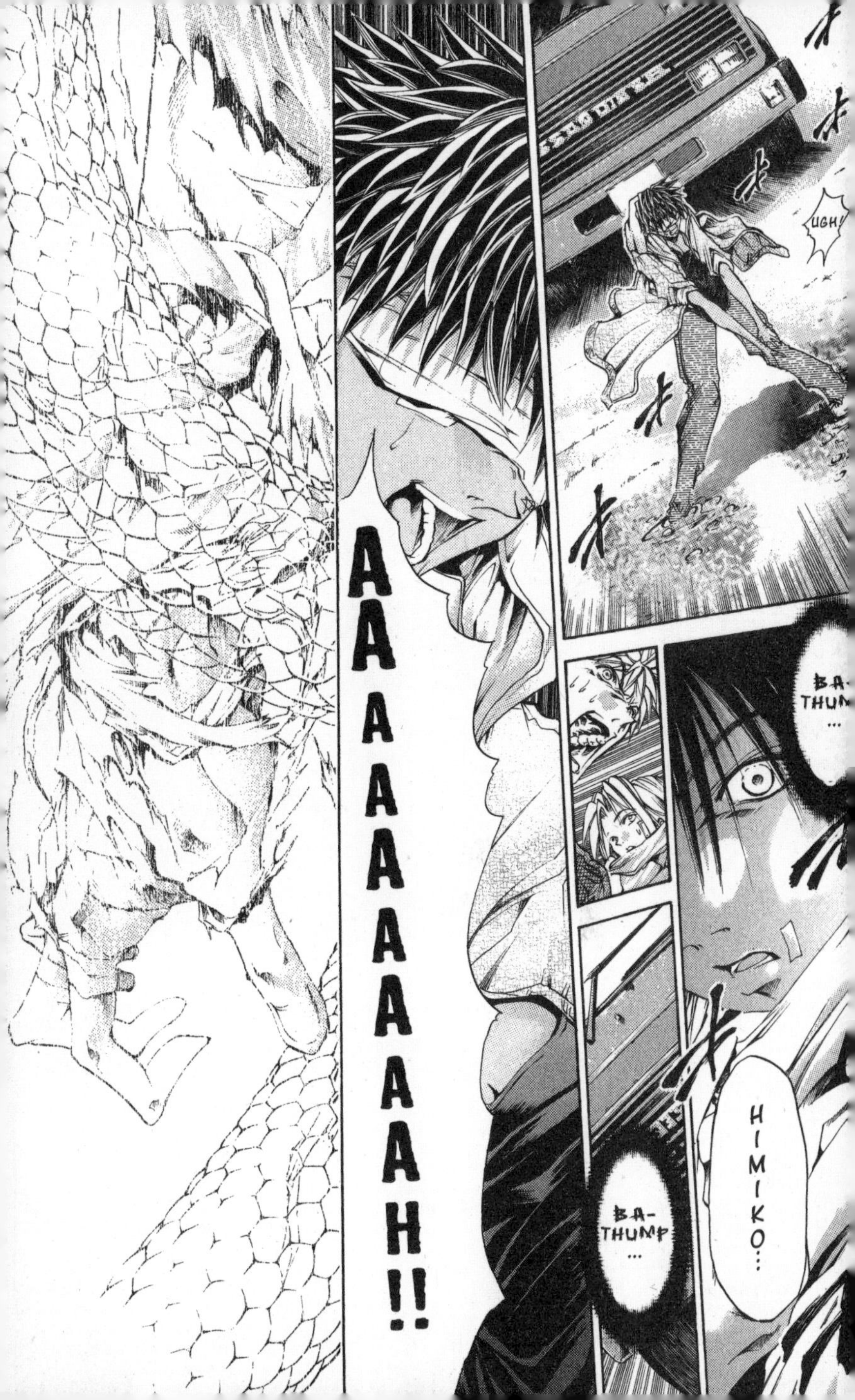
UGH!
BA-THUM…
HIMIKO…
BA-THUMP…
AAAAAAAH!!

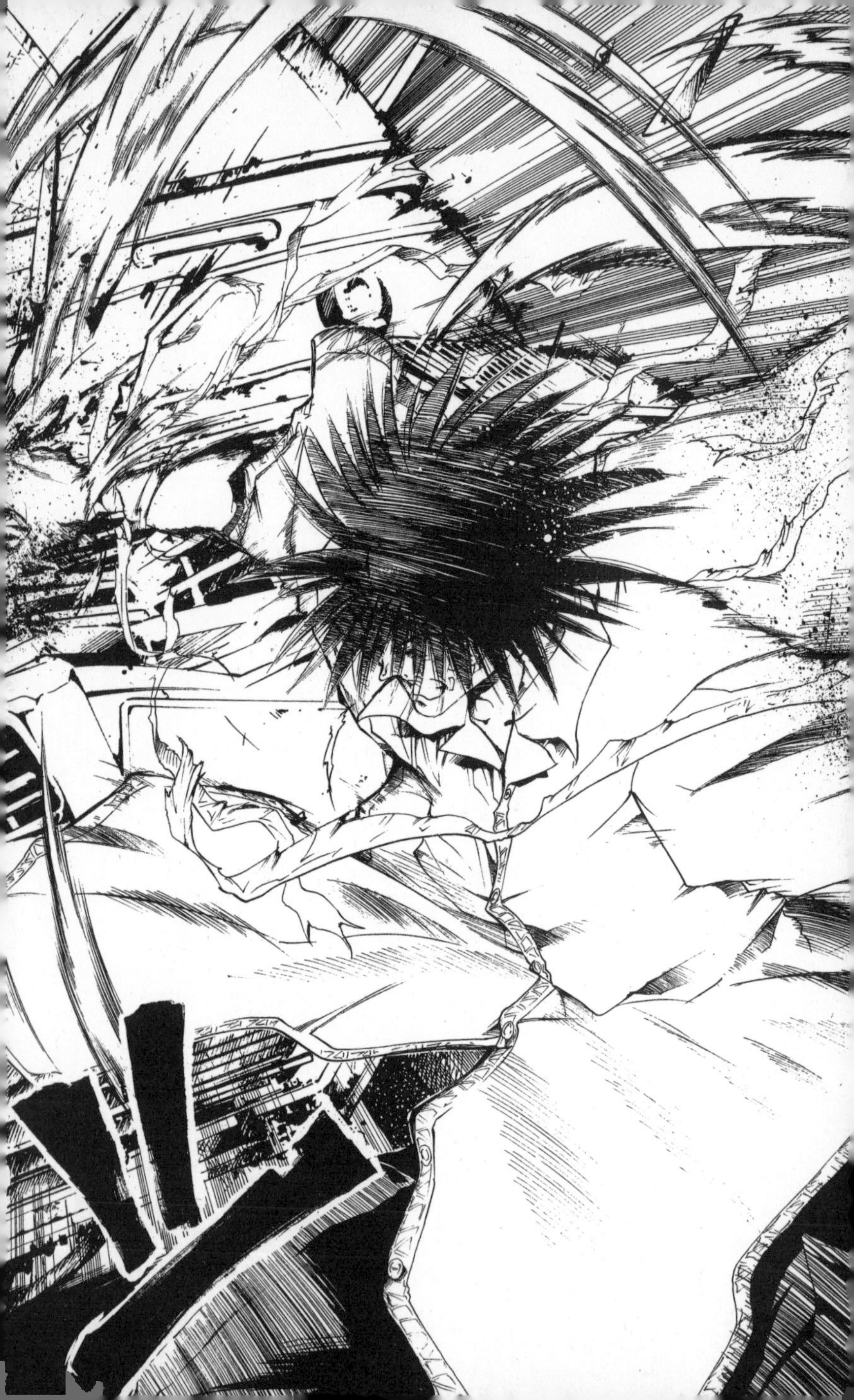

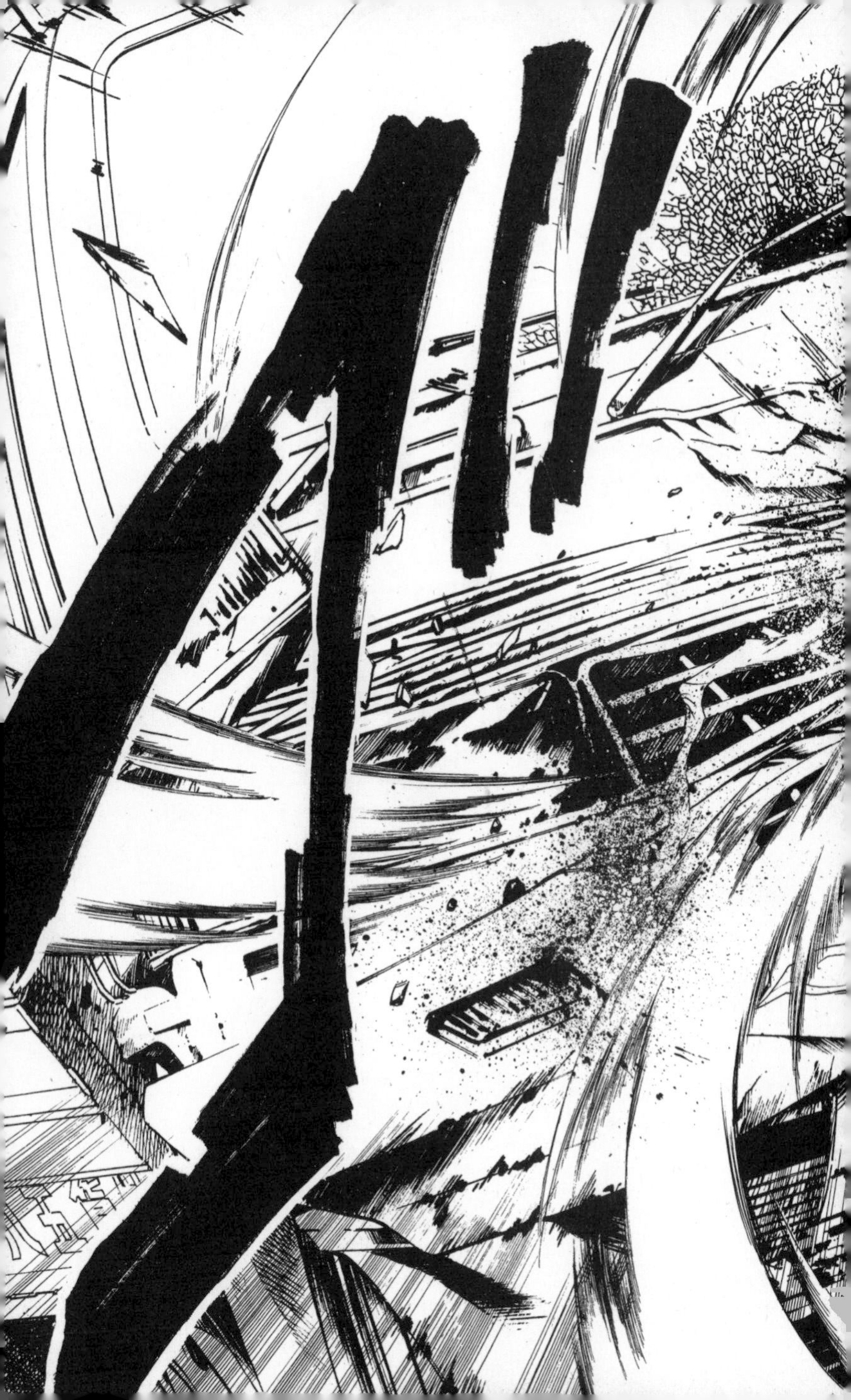

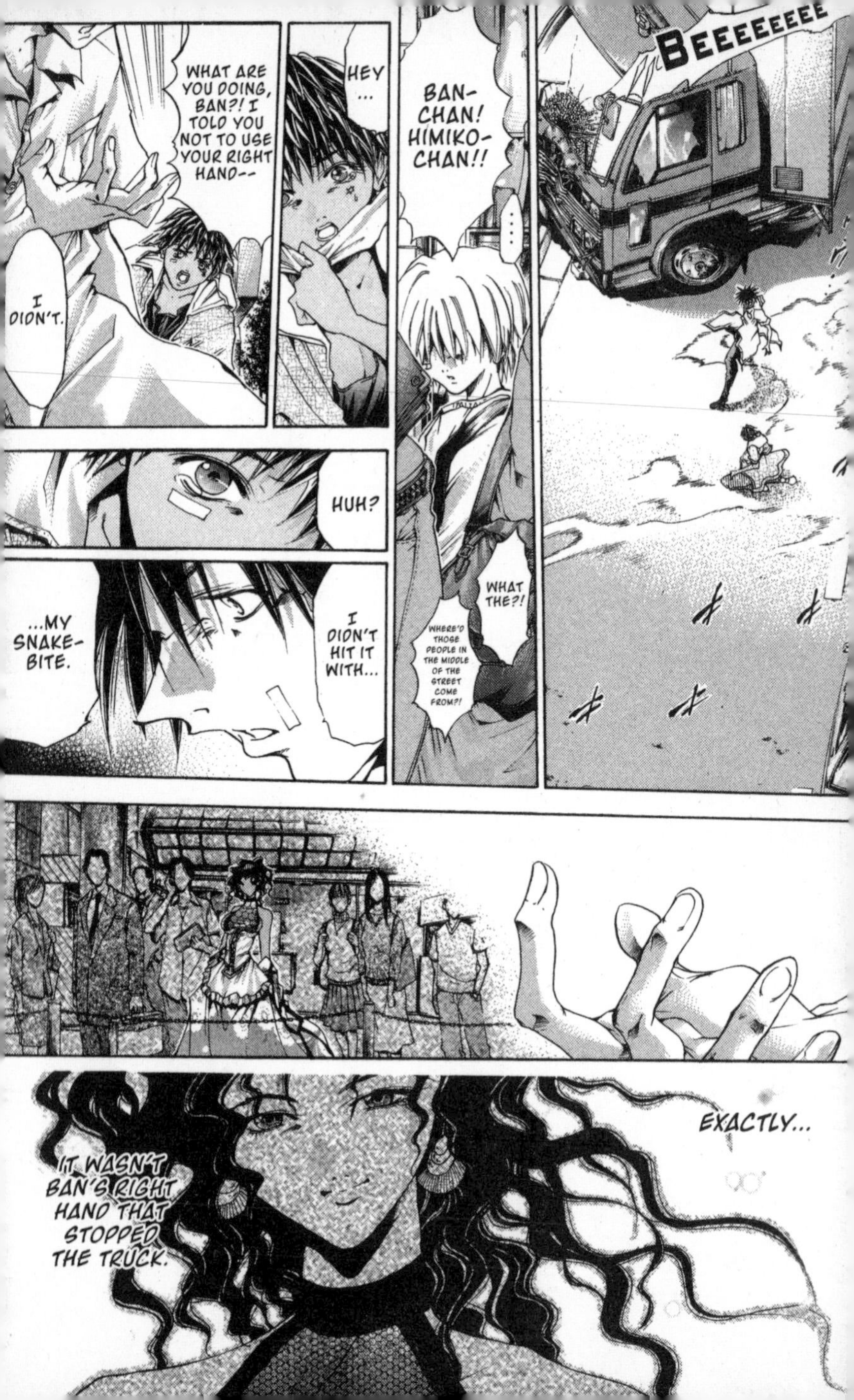
BEEEEEEEE
BAN-CHAN! HIMIKO-CHAN!!
....
WHAT THE?!
WHERE'D THOSE PEOPLE IN THE MIDDLE OF THE STREET COME FROM?!
HEY ...
WHAT ARE YOU DOING, BAN?! I TOLD YOU NOT TO USE YOUR RIGHT HAND--
I DIDN'T.
HUH?
I DIDN'T HIT IT WITH...
...MY SNAKE-BITE.
EXACTLY...
IT WASN'T BAN'S RIGHT HAND THAT STOPPED THE TRUCK.

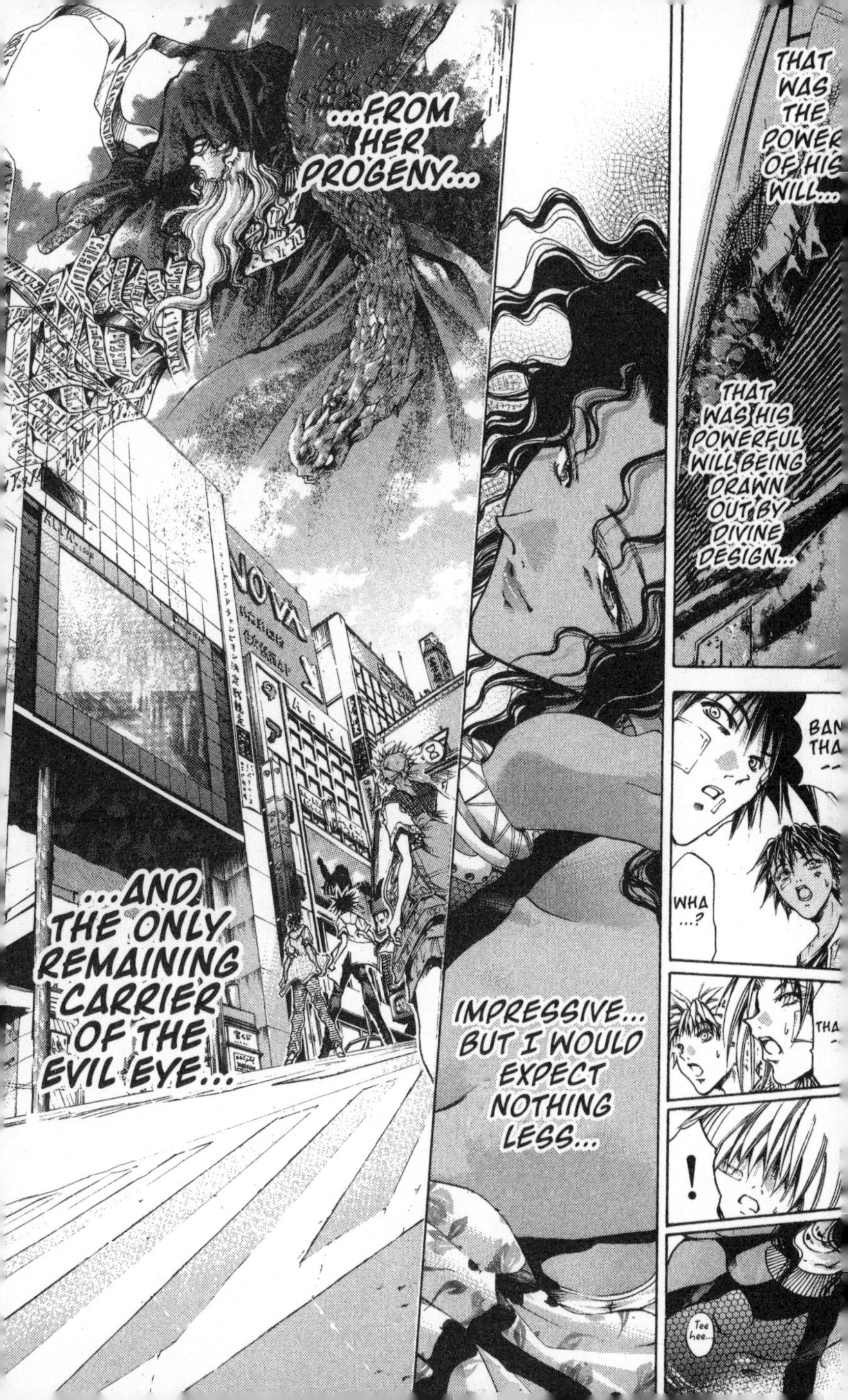
THAT WAS THE POWER OF HIS WILL...
THAT WAS HIS POWERFUL WILL BEING DRAWN OUT BY DIVINE DESIGN...
BAN THA --
WHA ...?
THA -
!
Tee hee...
IMPRESSIVE... BUT I WOULD EXPECT NOTHING LESS...
...FROM HER PROGENY...
...AND THE ONLY REMAINING CARRIER OF THE EVIL EYE...

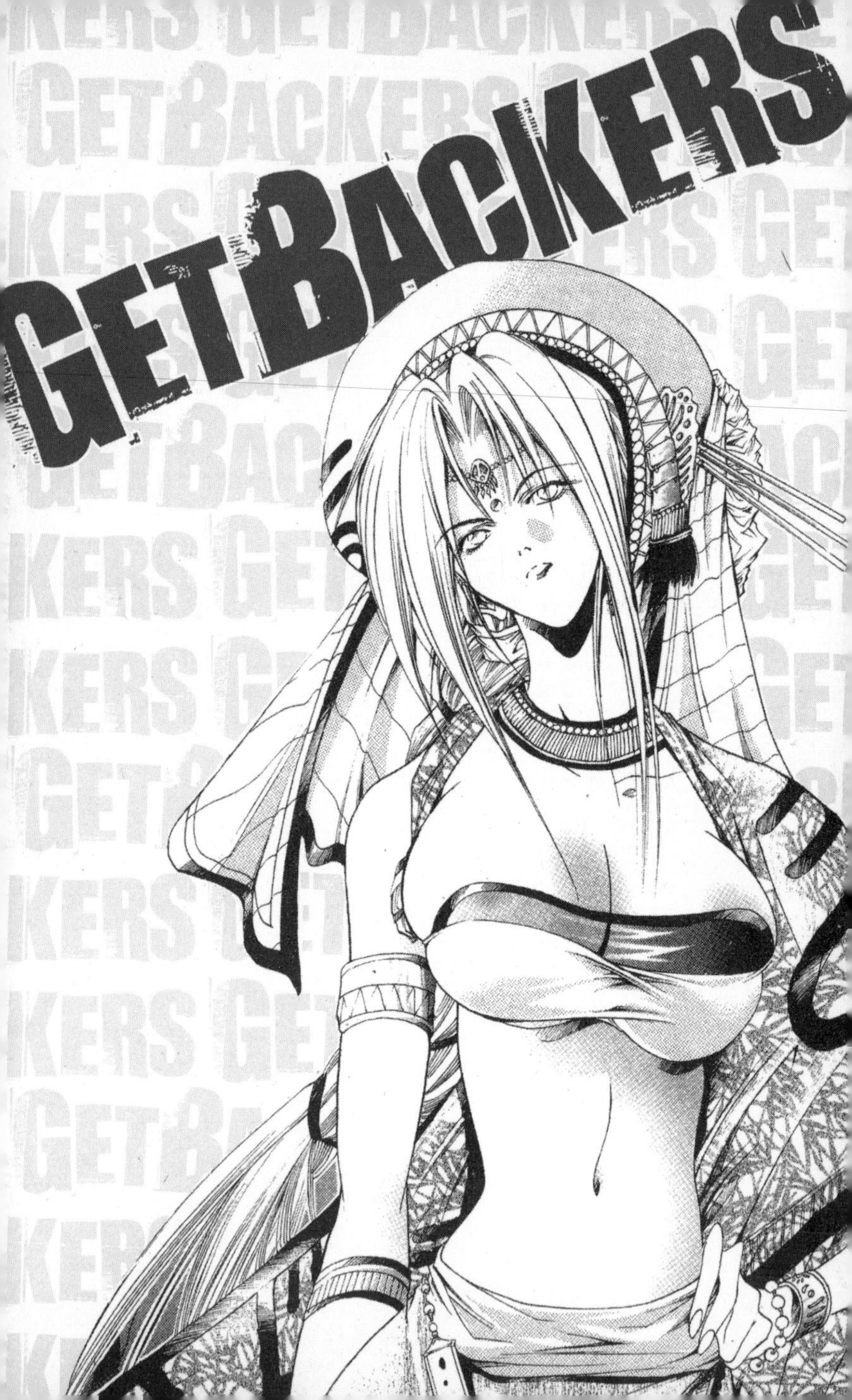
GETBACKERS

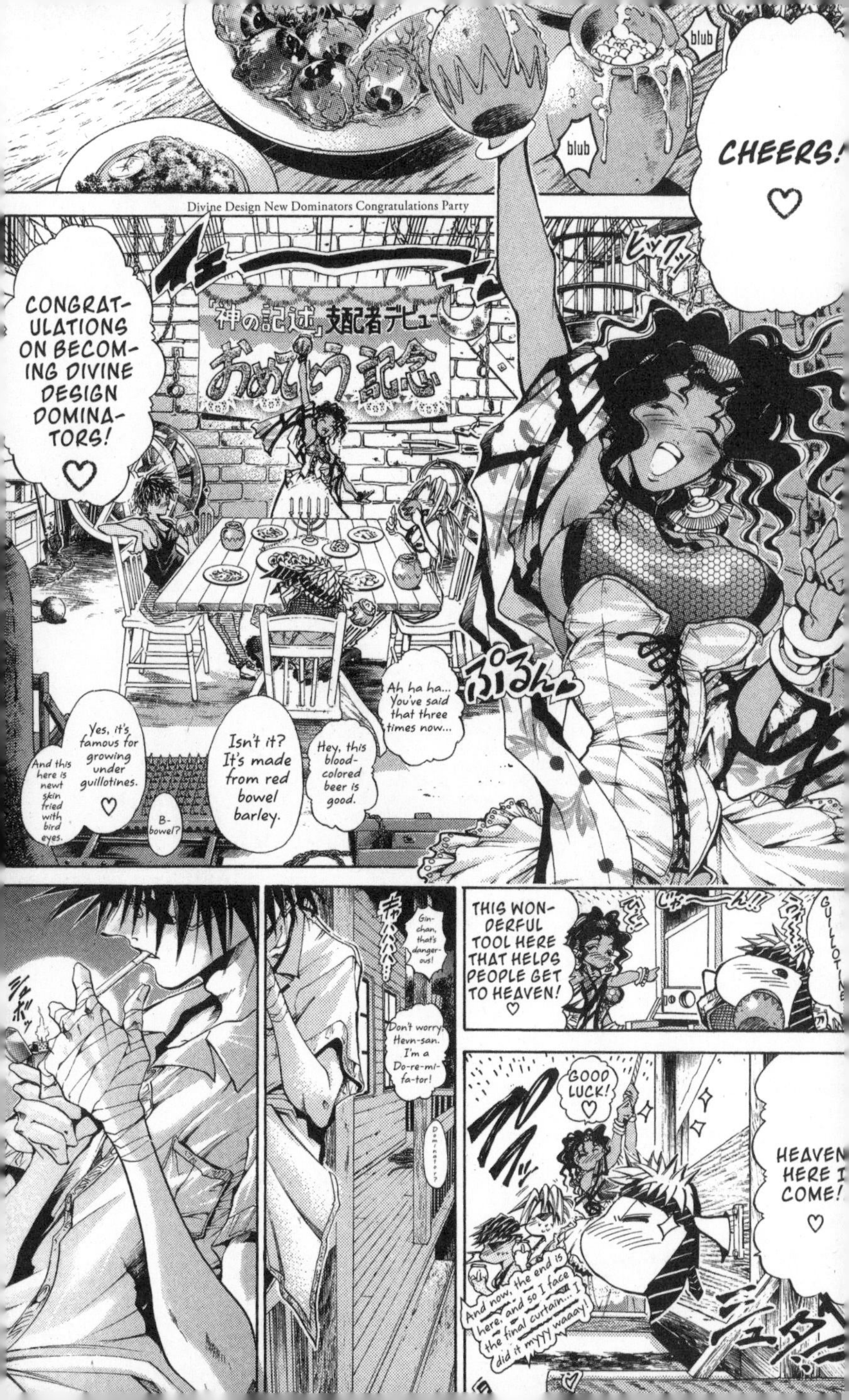
blub
blub
CHEERS! ♡
Divine Design New Dominators Congratulations Party
「神の記述」支配者デビュー
おめでとう記念
CONGRATULATIONS ON BECOMING DIVINE DESIGN DOMINATORS! ♡
Ah ha ha... You've said that three times now...
Hey, this blood-colored beer is good.
Isn't it? It's made from red bowel barley.
Yes, it's famous for growing under guillotines. ♡
B-bowel?
And this here is newt skin fried with bird eyes.
THIS WONDERFUL TOOL HERE THAT HELPS PEOPLE GET TO HEAVEN! ♡
GUILLOTINE
HEAVEN HERE I COME! ♡
GOOD LUCK! ♡
And now, the end is here, and so I face the final curtain... I did it myyy waaay!
Gin-chan, that's dangerous!
Don't worry, Hevn-san. I'm a Do-re-mi-fa-tor!
Dominator?

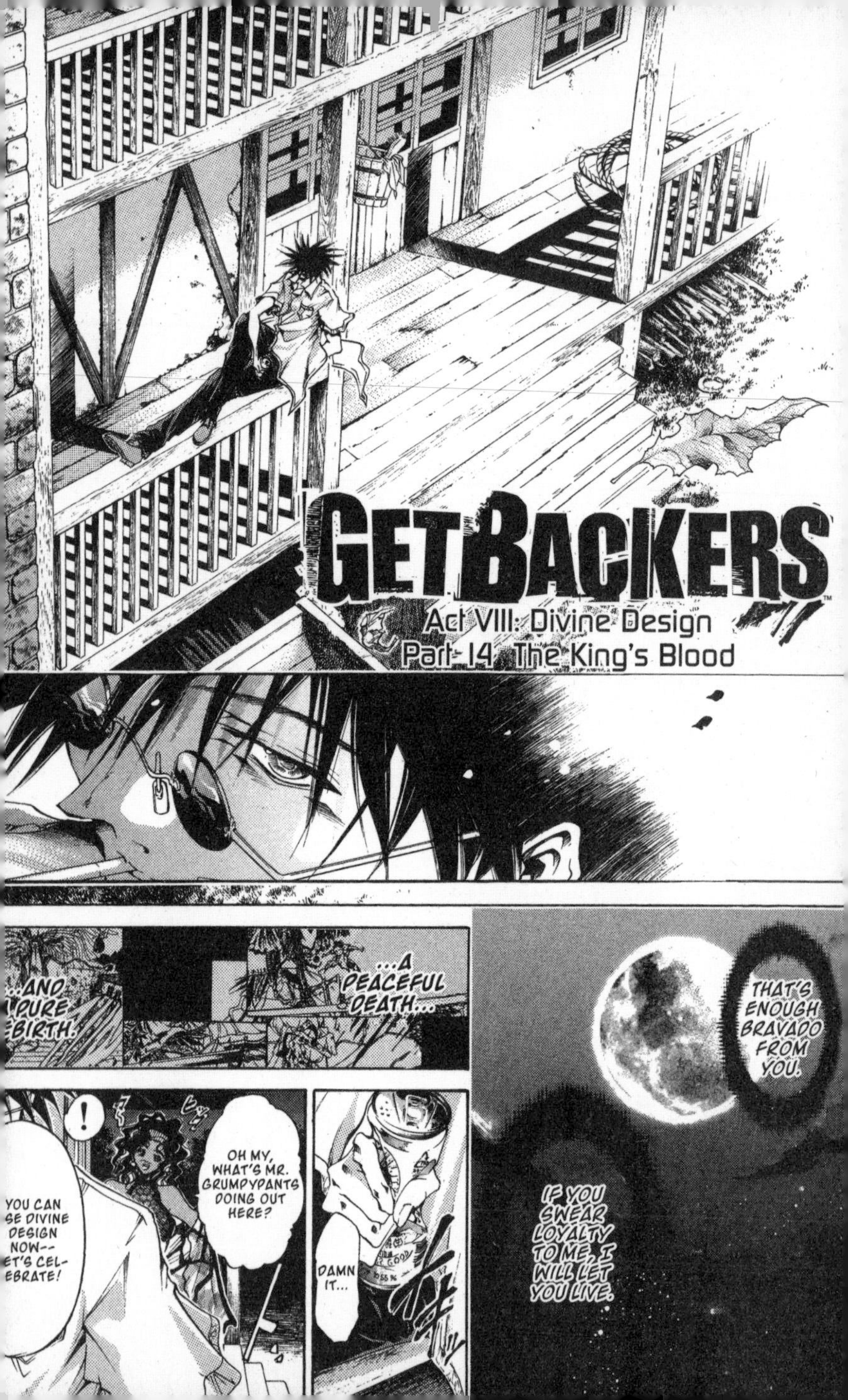
GETBACKERS™
Act VIII: Divine Design
Part 14 The King's Blood
THAT'S ENOUGH BRAVADO FROM YOU.
IF YOU SWEAR LOYALTY TO ME, I WILL LET YOU LIVE.
...A PEACEFUL DEATH...
..AND PURE EBIRTH.
DAMN IT...
OH MY, WHAT'S MR. GRUMPYPANTS DOING OUT HERE?
!
YOU CAN SE DIVINE DESIGN NOW-- ET'S CEL-EBRATE!

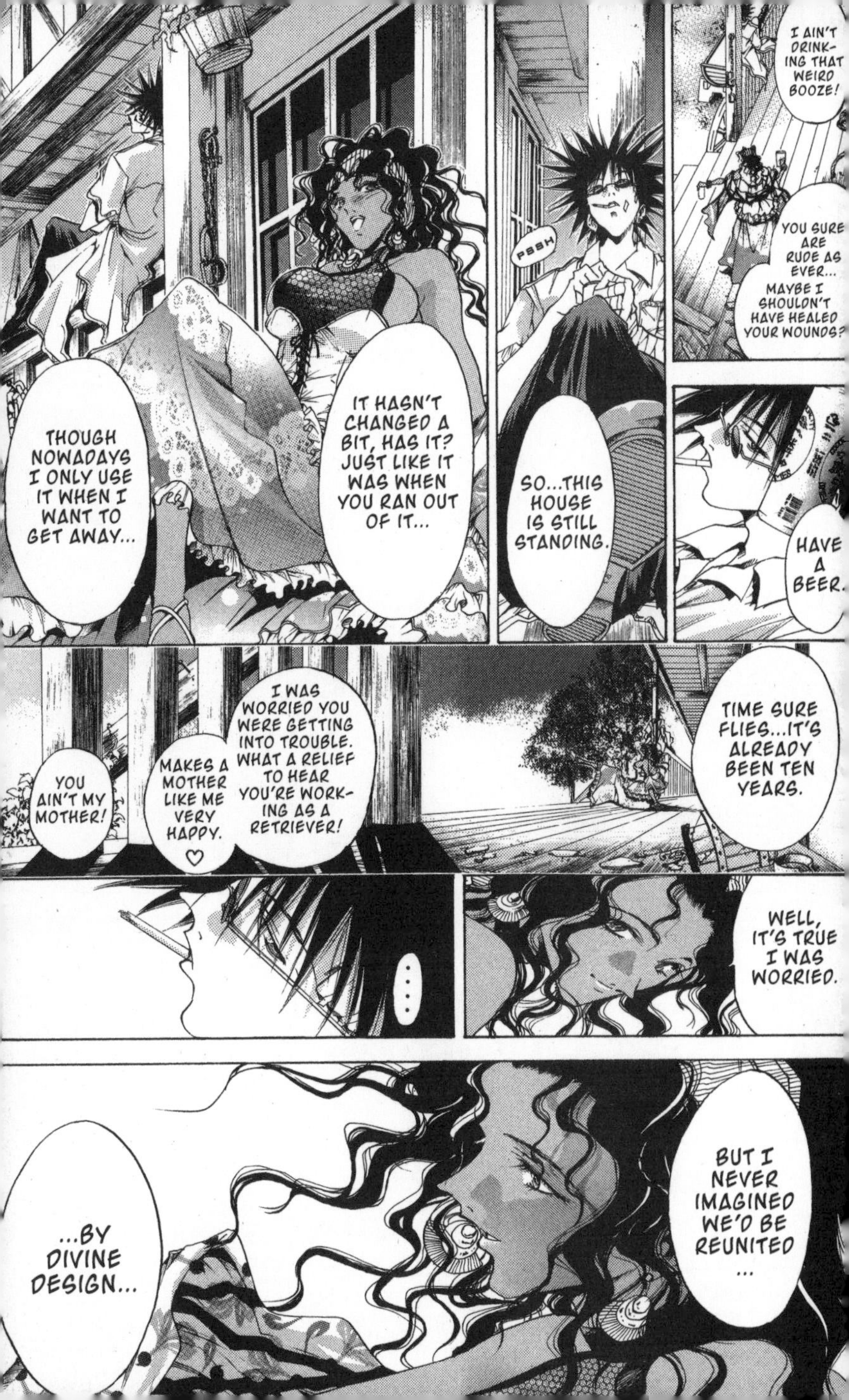
I AIN'T DRINKING THAT WEIRD BOOZE!
YOU SURE ARE RUDE AS EVER... MAYBE I SHOULDN'T HAVE HEALED YOUR WOUNDS?
HAVE A BEER.
PSSH
SO...THIS HOUSE IS STILL STANDING.
IT HASN'T CHANGED A BIT, HAS IT? JUST LIKE IT WAS WHEN YOU RAN OUT OF IT...
THOUGH NOWADAYS I ONLY USE IT WHEN I WANT TO GET AWAY...
TIME SURE FLIES...IT'S ALREADY BEEN TEN YEARS.
I WAS WORRIED YOU WERE GETTING INTO TROUBLE. WHAT A RELIEF TO HEAR YOU'RE WORKING AS A RETRIEVER!
MAKES A MOTHER LIKE ME VERY HAPPY. ♡
YOU AIN'T MY MOTHER!
WELL, IT'S TRUE I WAS WORRIED.
...
BUT I NEVER IMAGINED WE'D BE REUNITED...
...BY DIVINE DESIGN...

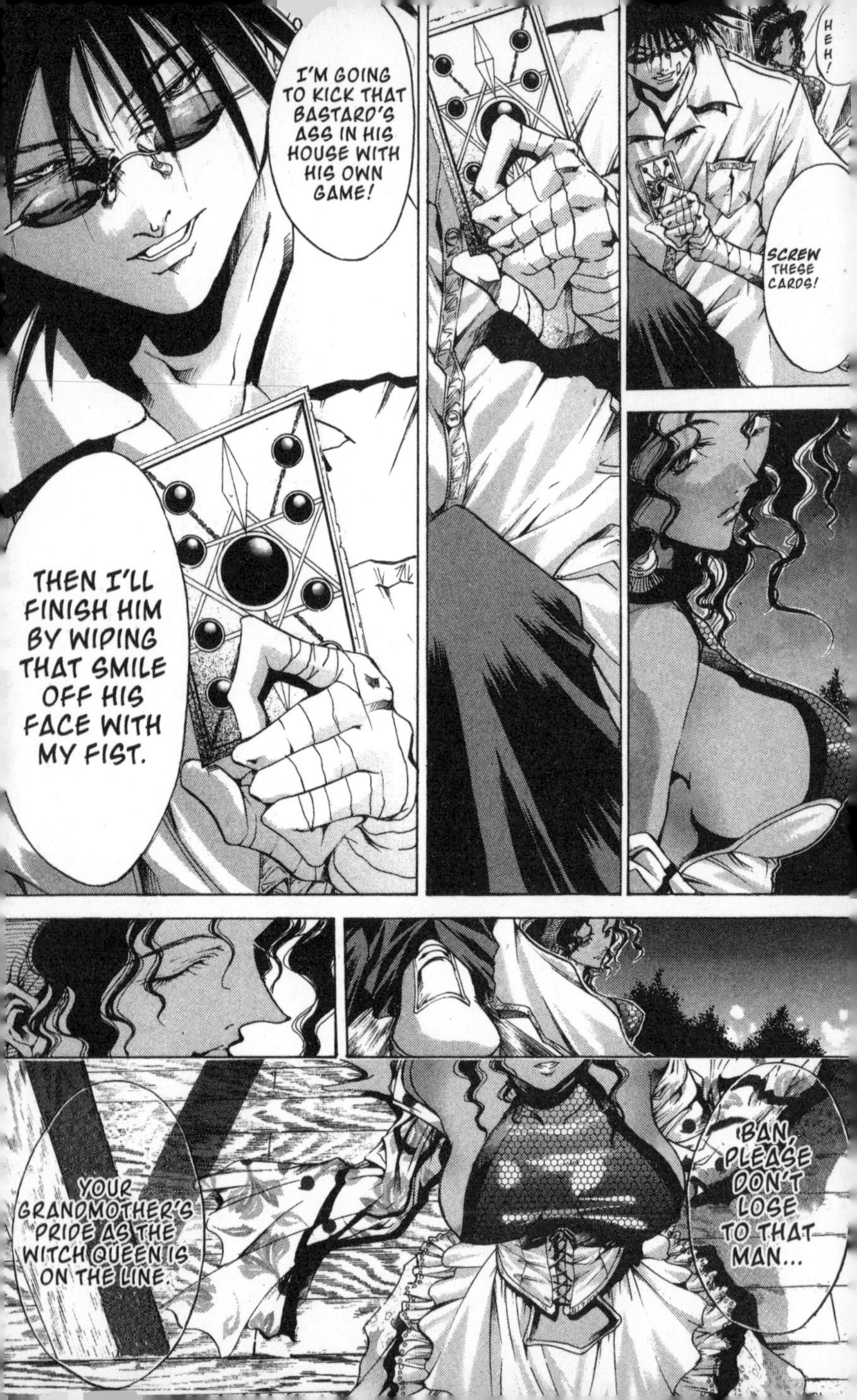
HEH!
SCREW THESE CARDS!
I'M GOING TO KICK THAT BASTARD'S ASS IN HIS HOUSE WITH HIS OWN GAME!
THEN I'LL FINISH HIM BY WIPING THAT SMILE OFF HIS FACE WITH MY FIST.
BAN, PLEASE DON'T LOSE TO THAT MAN...
YOUR GRANDMOTHER'S PRIDE AS THE WITCH QUEEN IS ON THE LINE.

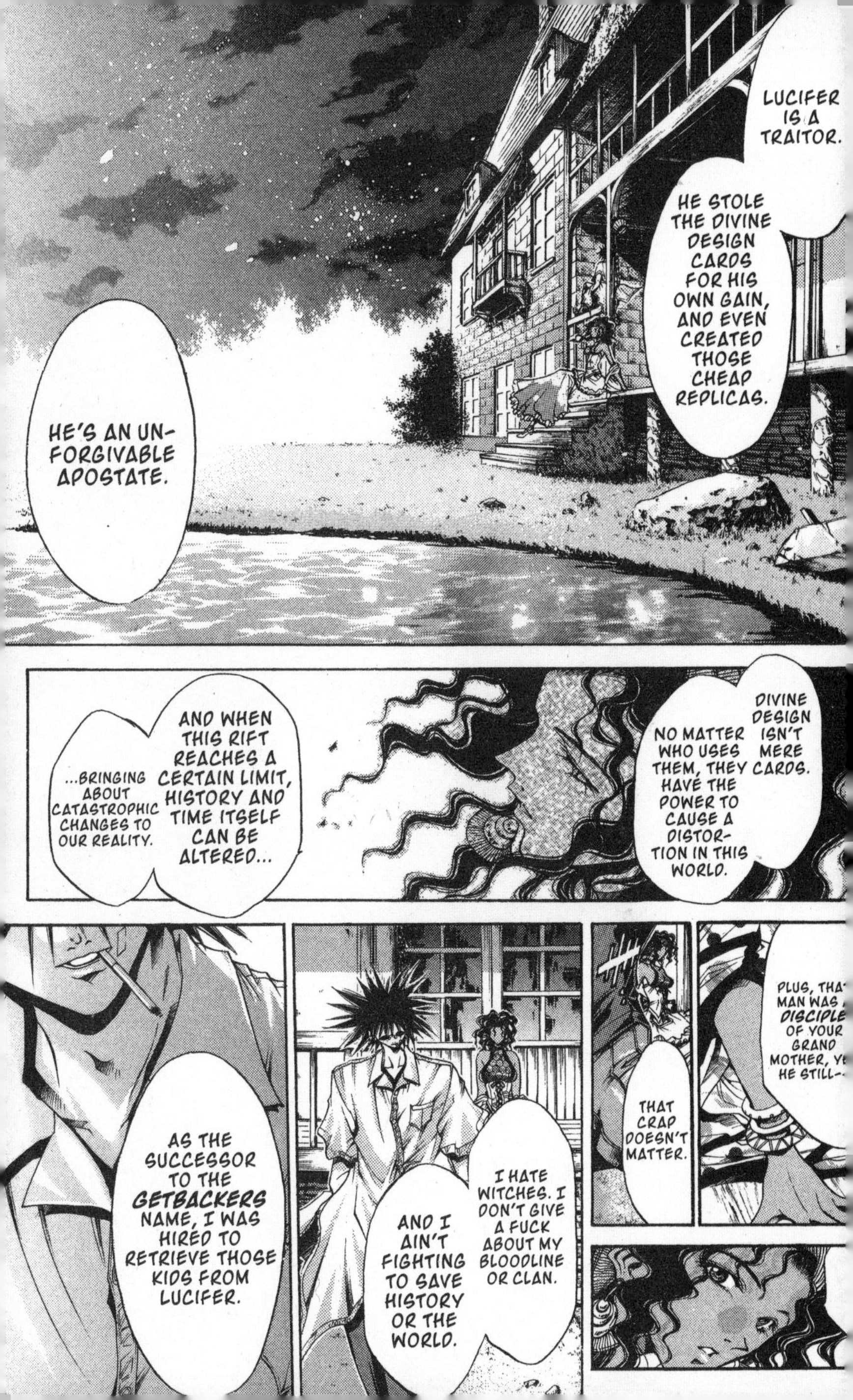

LUCIFER IS A TRAITOR.
HE STOLE THE DIVINE DESIGN CARDS FOR HIS OWN GAIN, AND EVEN CREATED THOSE CHEAP REPLICAS.
HE'S AN UN-FORGIVABLE APOSTATE.
DIVINE DESIGN ISN'T MERE CARDS.
NO MATTER WHO USES THEM, THEY HAVE THE POWER TO CAUSE A DISTOR-TION IN THIS WORLD.
AND WHEN THIS RIFT REACHES A CERTAIN LIMIT, HISTORY AND TIME ITSELF CAN BE ALTERED...
...BRINGING ABOUT CATASTROPHIC CHANGES TO OUR REALITY.
PLUS, THAT MAN WAS *DISCIPLE* OF YOUR GRAND MOTHER, YE HE STILL--
THAT CRAP DOESN'T MATTER.
I HATE WITCHES. I DON'T GIVE A FUCK ABOUT MY BLOODLINE OR CLAN.
AND I AIN'T FIGHTING TO SAVE HISTORY OR THE WORLD.
AS THE SUCCESSOR TO THE ***GETBACKERS*** NAME, I WAS HIRED TO RETRIEVE THOSE KIDS FROM LUCIFER.

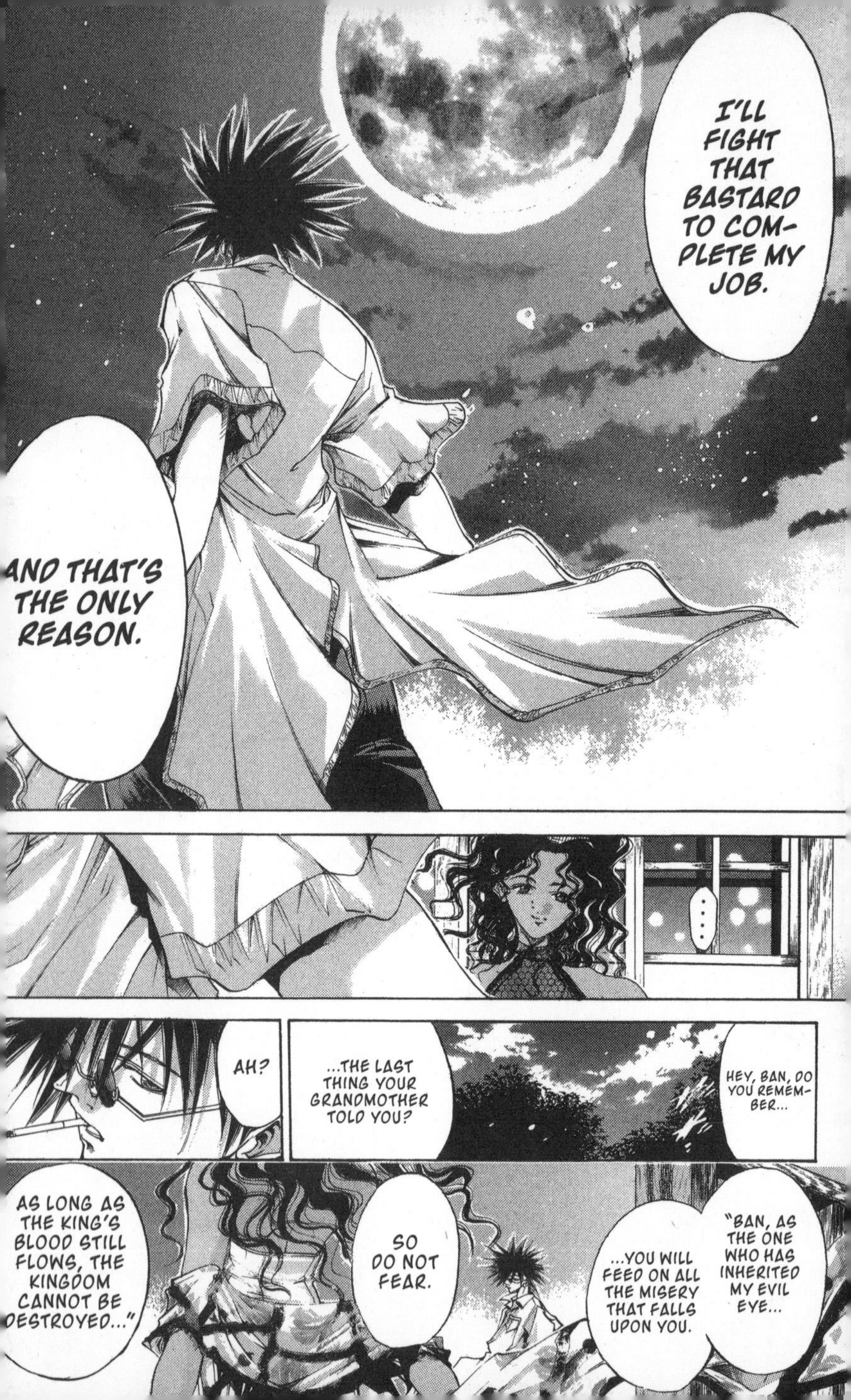
I'LL FIGHT THAT BASTARD TO COMPLETE MY JOB.
AND THAT'S THE ONLY REASON.
...
HEY, BAN, DO YOU REMEMBER...
...THE LAST THING YOUR GRANDMOTHER TOLD YOU?
AH?
"BAN, AS THE ONE WHO HAS INHERITED MY EVIL EYE...
...YOU WILL FEED ON ALL THE MISERY THAT FALLS UPON YOU.
SO DO NOT FEAR.
AS LONG AS THE KING'S BLOOD STILL FLOWS, THE KINGDOM CANNOT BE DESTROYED..."

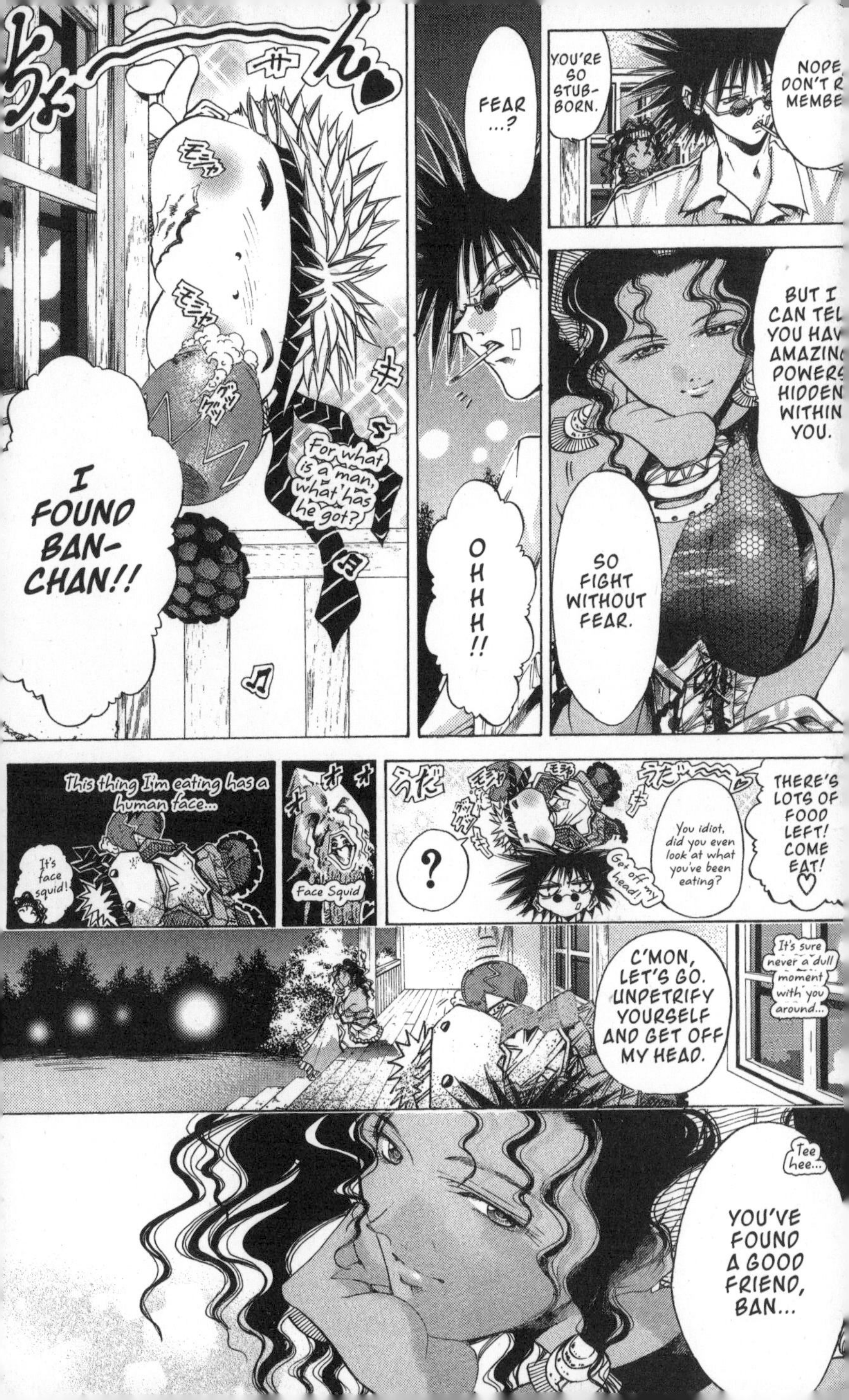
NOPE, DON'T R MEMBE
YOU'RE SO STUB-BORN.
BUT I CAN TEL YOU HAV AMAZING POWERS HIDDEN WITHIN YOU.
SO FIGHT WITHOUT FEAR.
FEAR ...?
OHHHH!!
For what is a man, what has he got?
I FOUND BAN-CHAN!!
THERE'S LOTS OF FOOD LEFT! COME EAT! ♡
You idiot, did you even look at what you've been eating?
Get off my head!
?
Face Squid
This thing I'm eating has a human face...
It's face squid!
It's sure never a dull moment with you around...
C'MON, LET'S GO. UNPETRIFY YOURSELF AND GET OFF MY HEAD.
Tee hee...
YOU'VE FOUND A GOOD FRIEND, BAN...

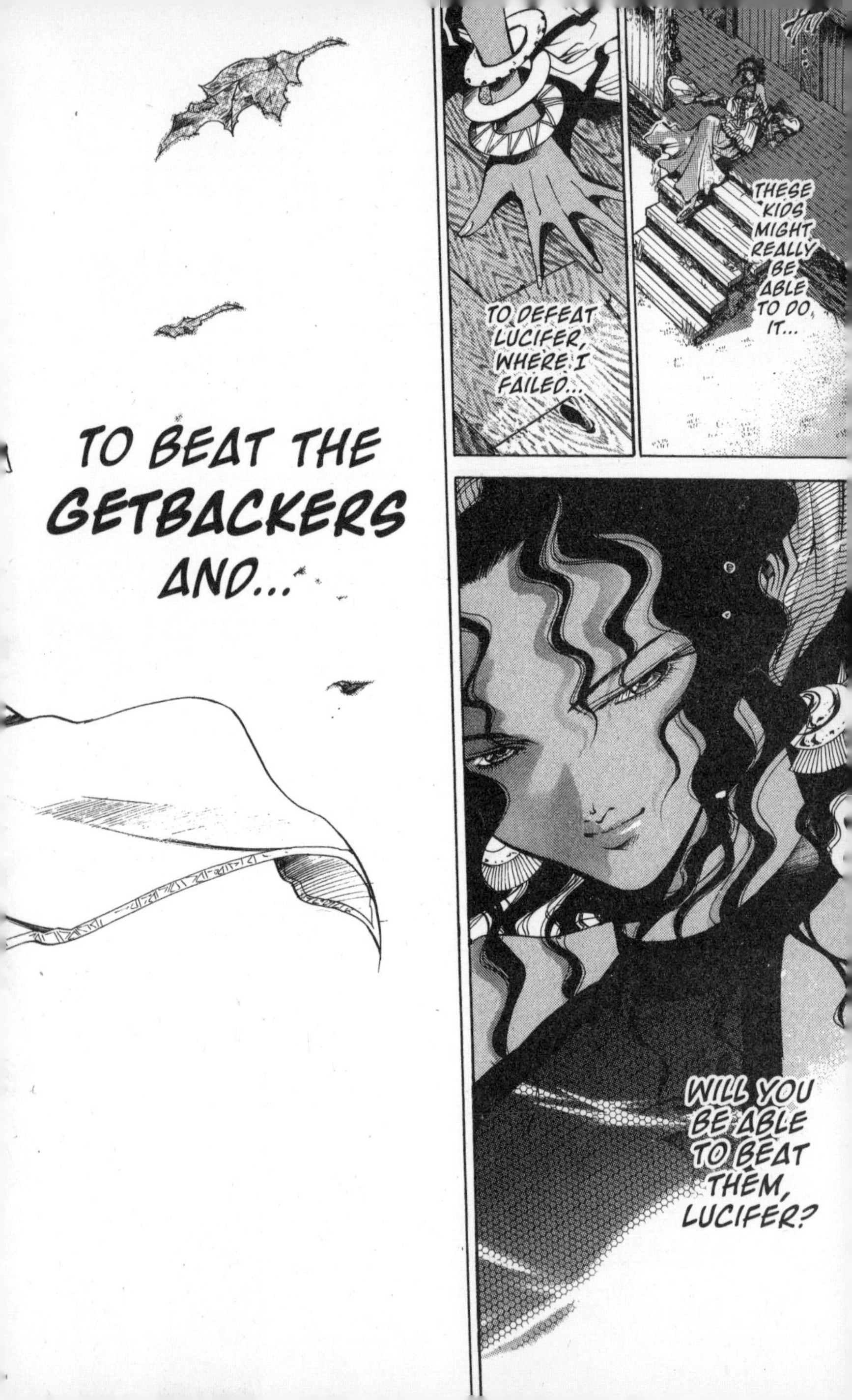
THESE KIDS MIGHT REALLY BE ABLE TO DO IT...
TO DEFEAT LUCIFER, WHERE I FAILED...
WILL YOU BE ABLE TO BEAT THEM, LUCIFER?
TO BEAT THE GETBACKERS AND...

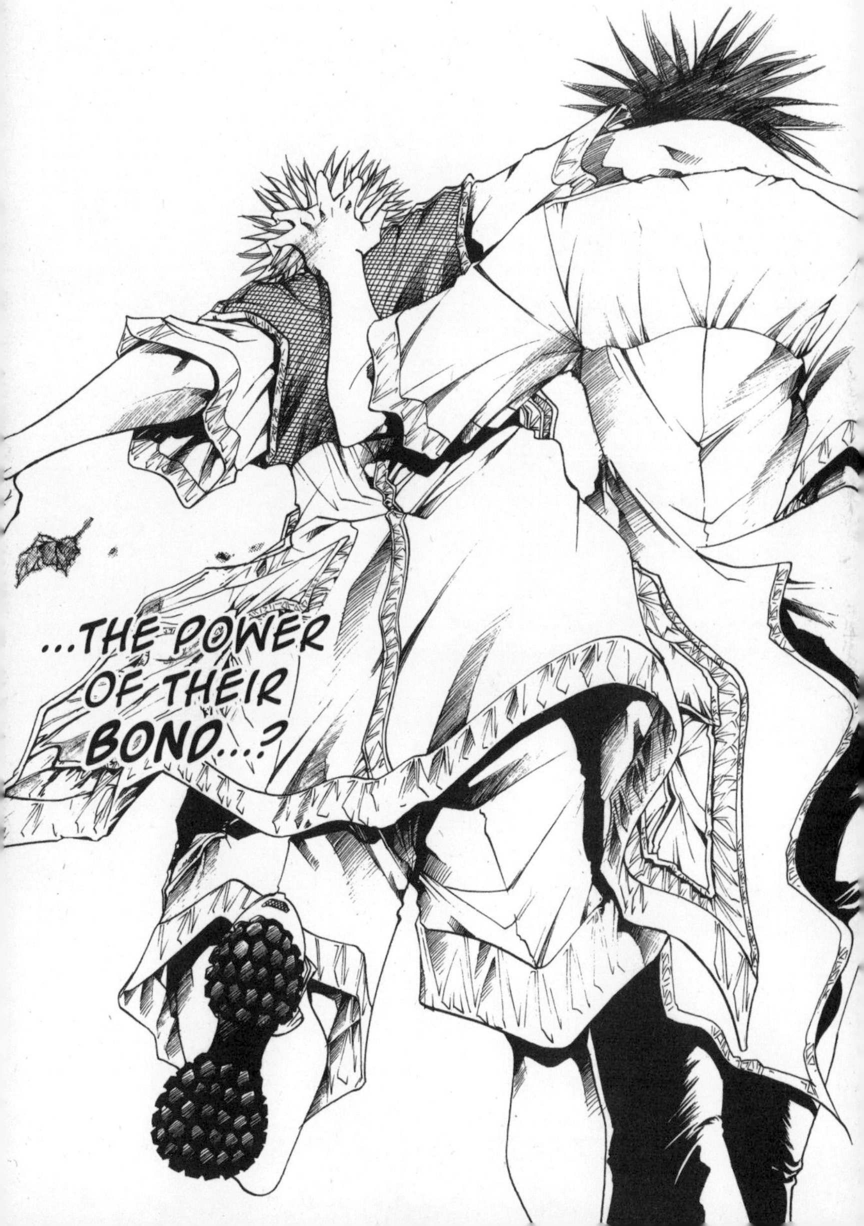
...THE POWER OF THEIR BOND...?

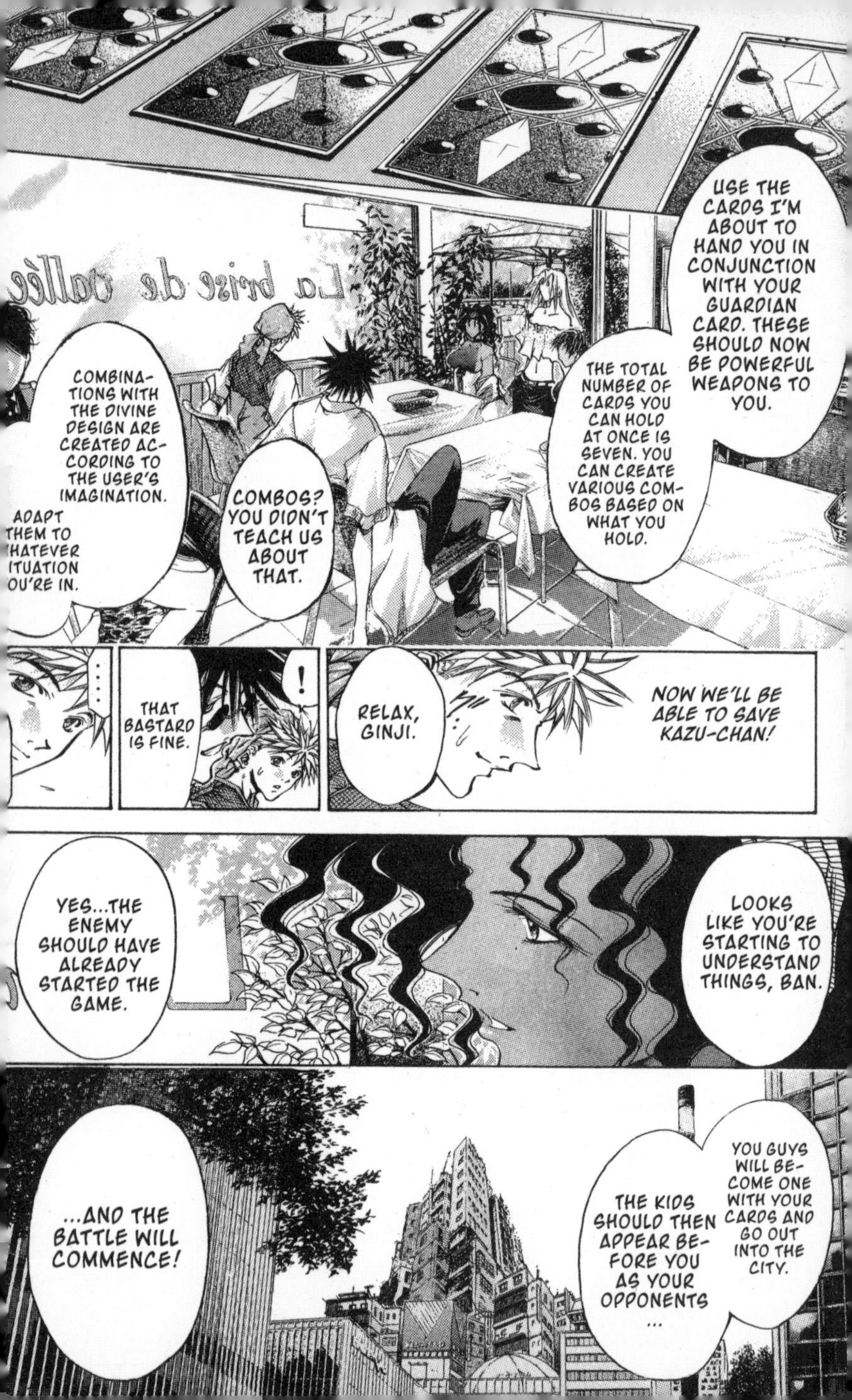
USE THE CARDS I'M ABOUT TO HAND YOU IN CONJUNCTION WITH YOUR GUARDIAN CARD. THESE SHOULD NOW BE POWERFUL WEAPONS TO YOU.
THE TOTAL NUMBER OF CARDS YOU CAN HOLD AT ONCE IS SEVEN. YOU CAN CREATE VARIOUS COMBOS BASED ON WHAT YOU HOLD.
COMBOS? YOU DIDN'T TEACH US ABOUT THAT.
COMBINATIONS WITH THE DIVINE DESIGN ARE CREATED ACCORDING TO THE USER'S IMAGINATION.
ADAPT THEM TO HATEVER ITUATION OU'RE IN.
NOW WE'LL BE ABLE TO SAVE KAZU-CHAN!
RELAX, GINJI.
!
THAT BASTARD IS FINE.
.....
LOOKS LIKE YOU'RE STARTING TO UNDERSTAND THINGS, BAN.
YES...THE ENEMY SHOULD HAVE ALREADY STARTED THE GAME.
YOU GUYS WILL BECOME ONE WITH YOUR CARDS AND GO OUT INTO THE CITY.
THE KIDS SHOULD THEN APPEAR BEFORE YOU AS YOUR OPPONENTS...
...AND THE BATTLE WILL COMMENCE!

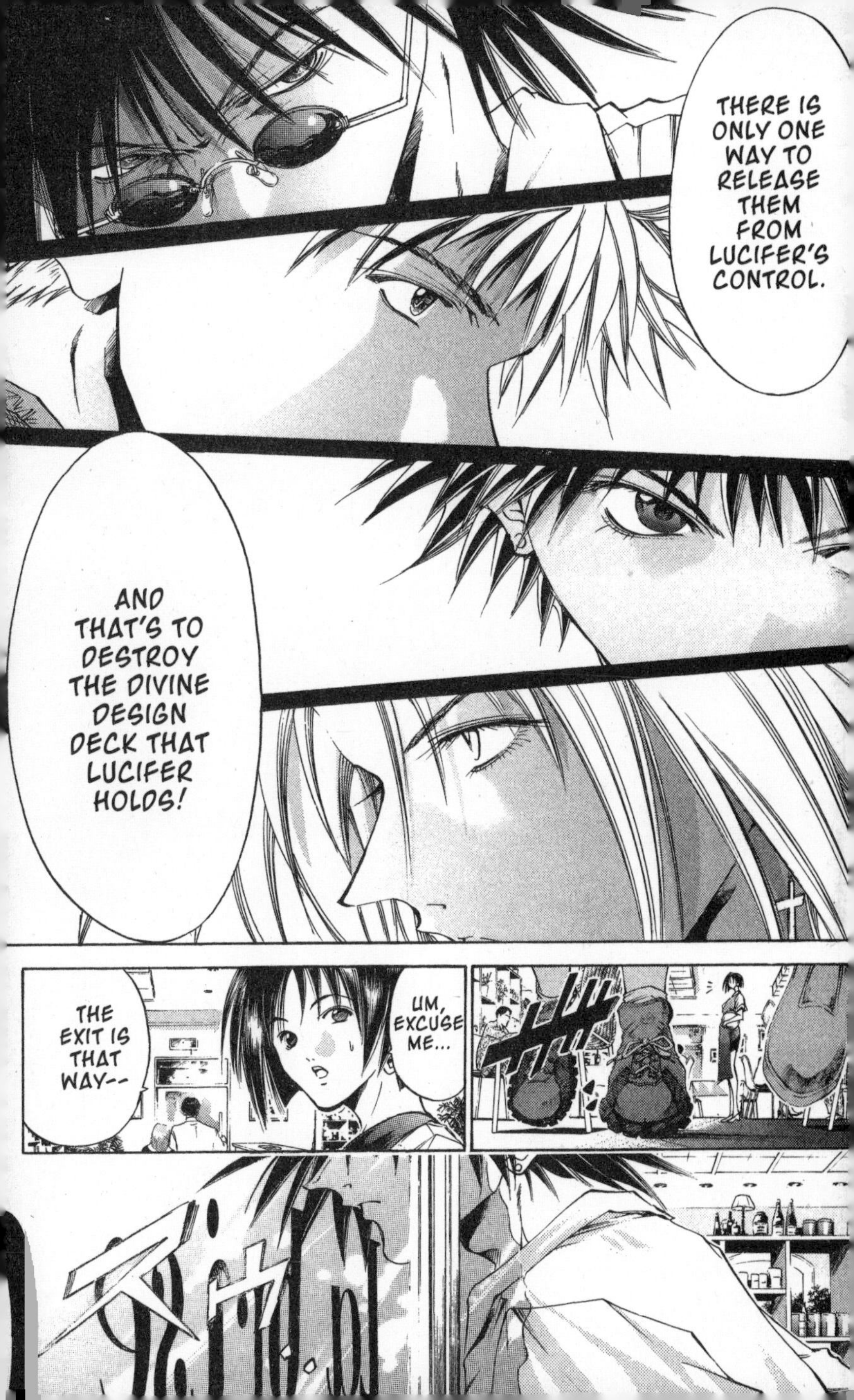
THERE IS ONLY ONE WAY TO RELEASE THEM FROM LUCIFER'S CONTROL.
AND THAT'S TO DESTROY THE DIVINE DESIGN DECK THAT LUCIFER HOLDS!
UM, EXCUSE ME...
THE EXIT IS THAT WAY--

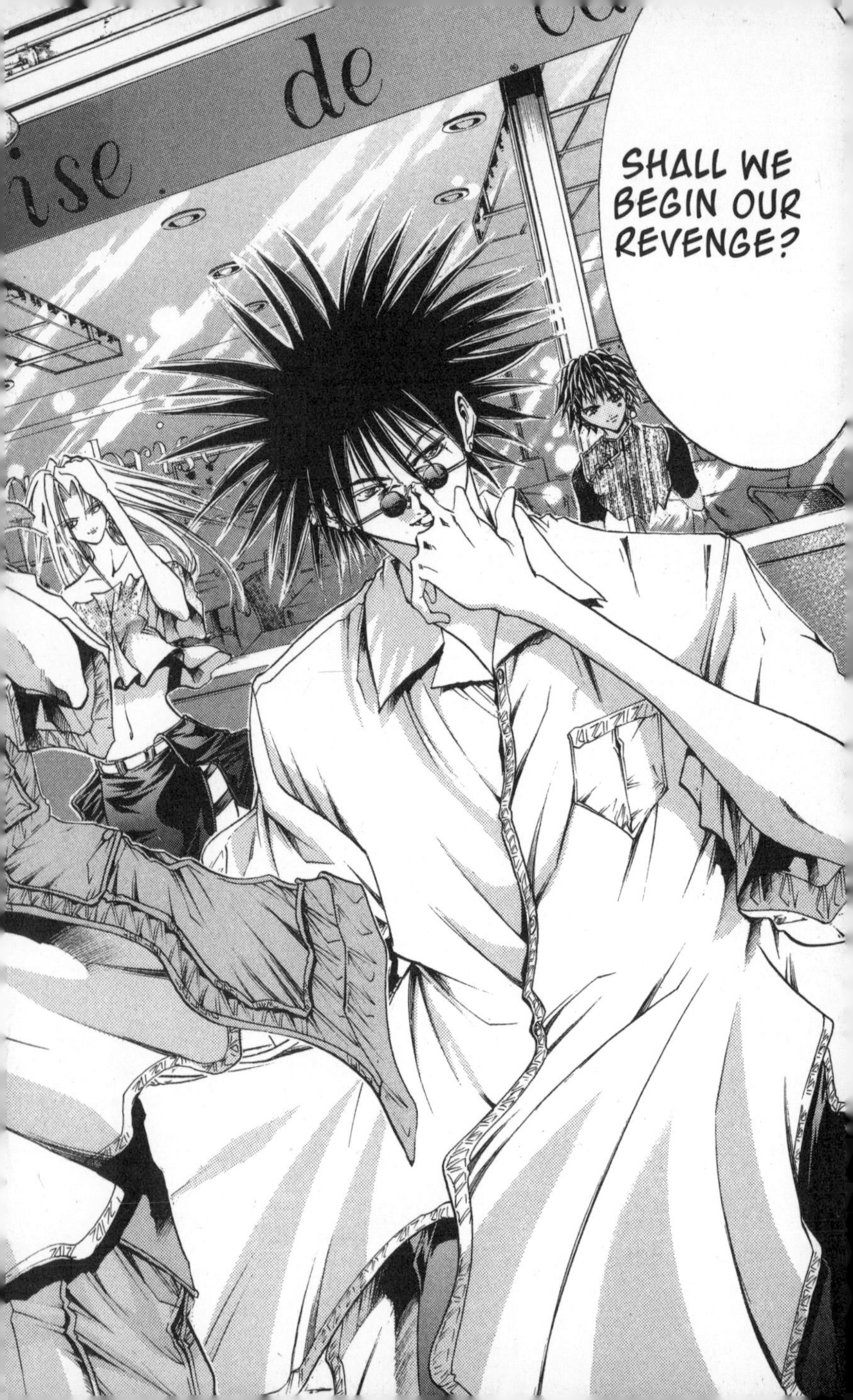
SHALL WE BEGIN OUR REVENGE?

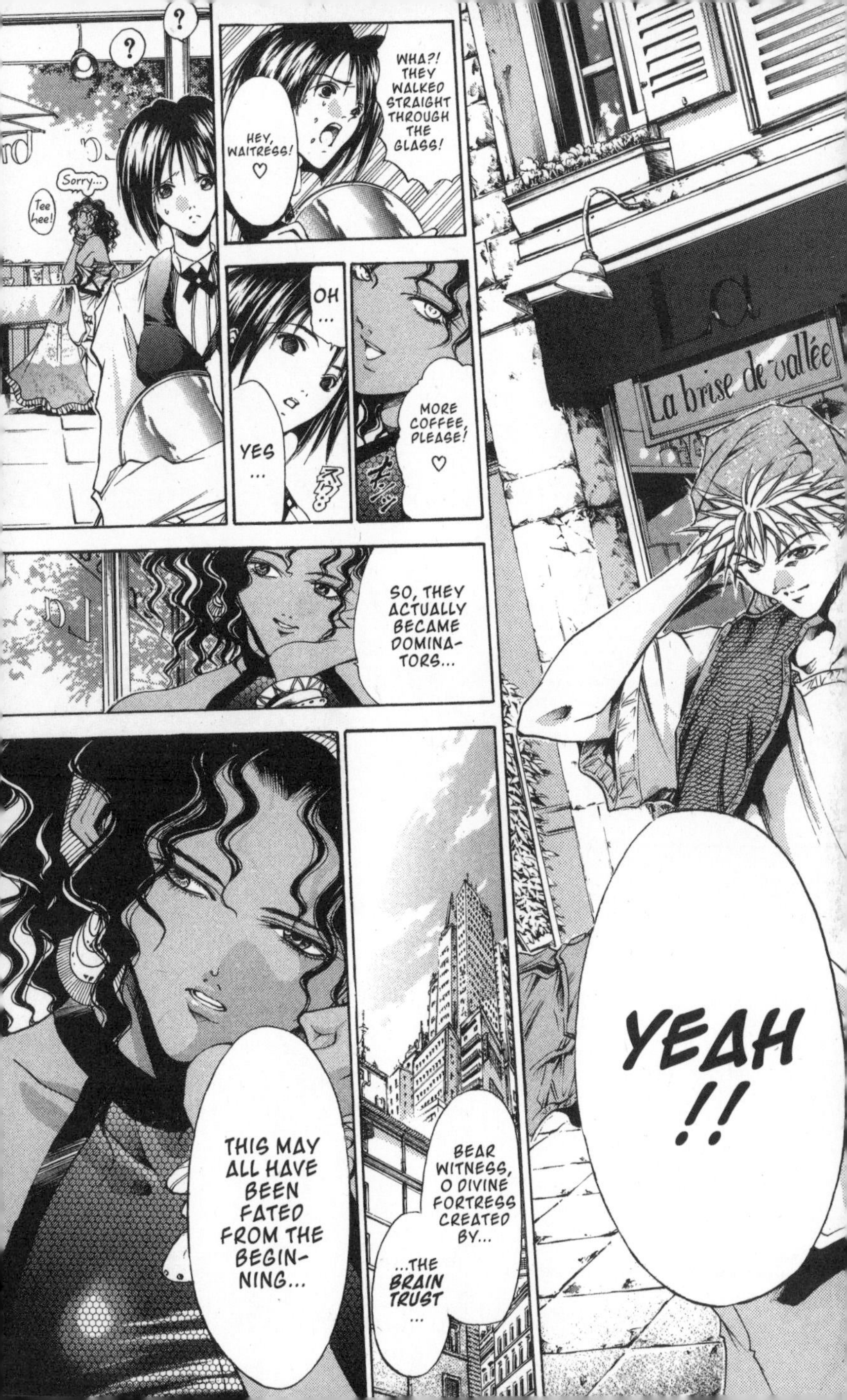

La
La brise de vallée
YEAH!!
WHA?! THEY WALKED STRAIGHT THROUGH THE GLASS!
HEY, WAITRESS! ♡
MORE COFFEE, PLEASE! ♡
OH...
YES...
?
?
Sorry...
Tee hee!
SO, THEY ACTUALLY BECAME DOMINA-TORS...
BEAR WITNESS, O DIVINE FORTRESS CREATED BY...
...THE BRAIN TRUST...
THIS MAY ALL HAVE BEEN FATED FROM THE BEGIN-NING...

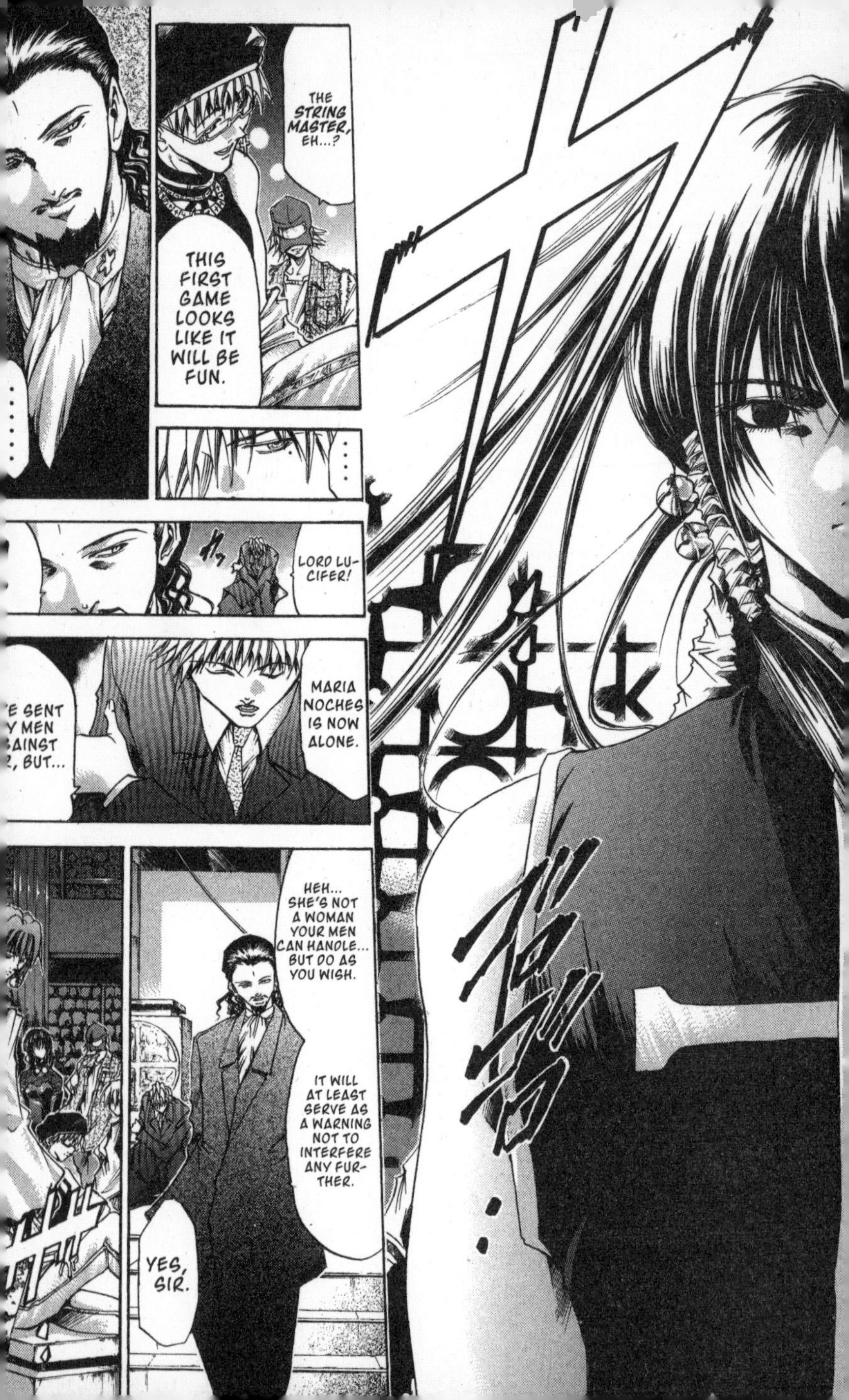
THE STRING MASTER, EH...?
THIS FIRST GAME LOOKS LIKE IT WILL BE FUN.
......
....
LORD LUCIFER!
MARIA NOCHES IS NOW ALONE.
E SENT Y MEN AINST R, BUT...
HEH... SHE'S NOT A WOMAN YOUR MEN CAN HANDLE... BUT DO AS YOU WISH.
IT WILL AT LEAST SERVE AS A WARNING NOT TO INTERFERE ANY FURTHER.
YES, SIR.

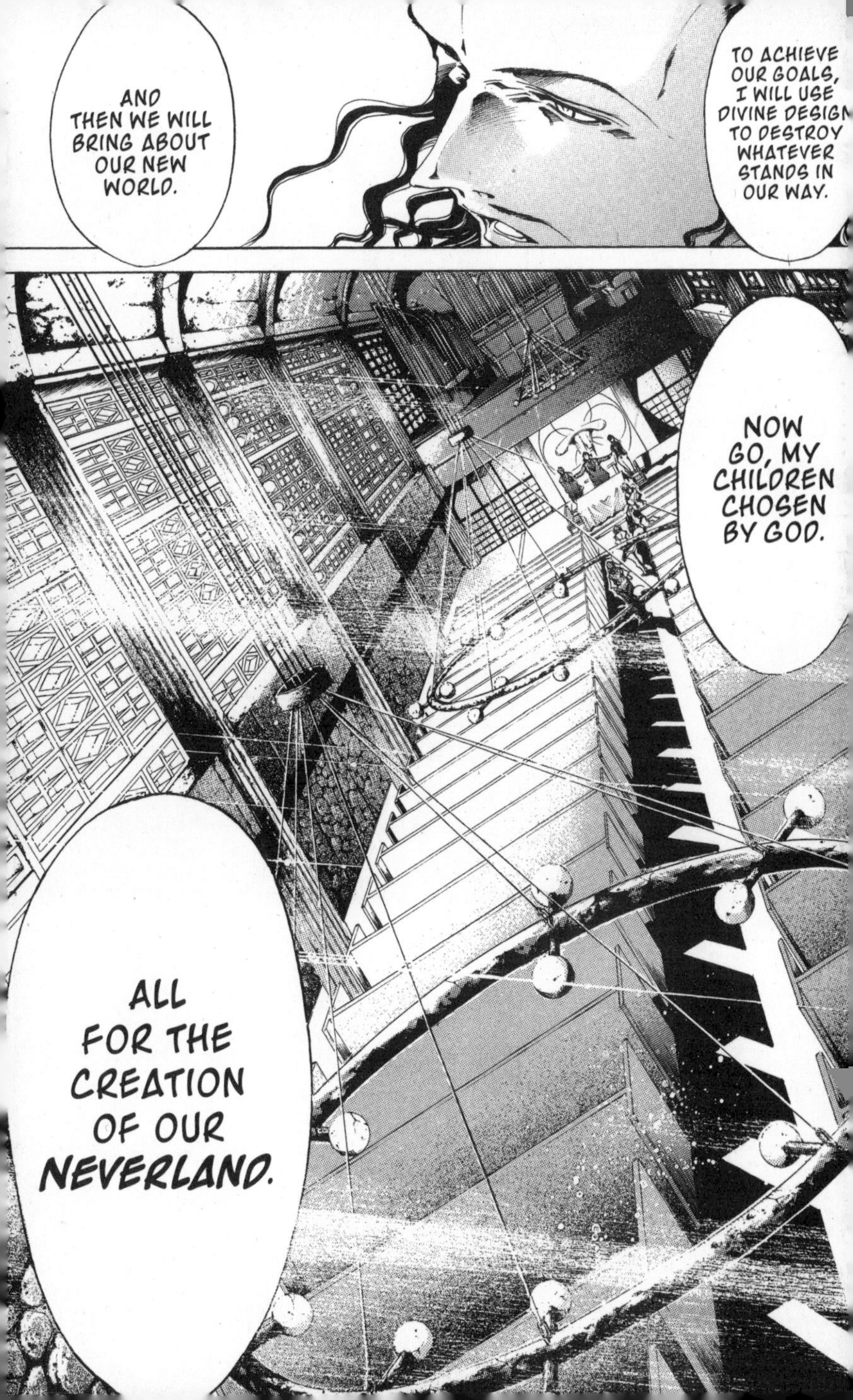
TO ACHIEVE OUR GOALS, I WILL USE DIVINE DESIGN TO DESTROY WHATEVER STANDS IN OUR WAY.
AND THEN WE WILL BRING ABOUT OUR NEW WORLD.
NOW GO, MY CHILDREN CHOSEN BY GOD.
ALL FOR THE CREATION OF OUR NEVERLAND.

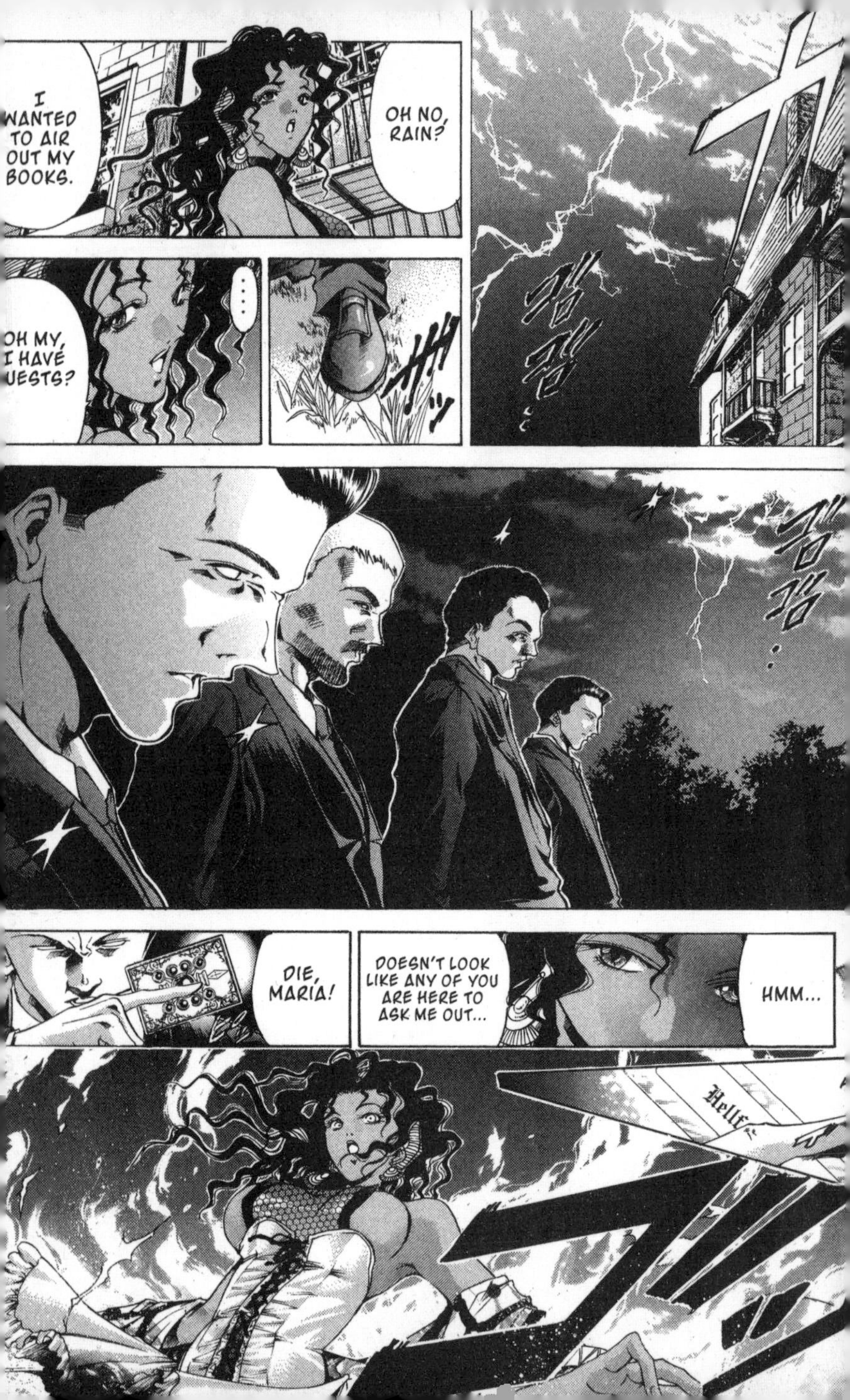
OH NO, RAIN?
I WANTED TO AIR OUT MY BOOKS.
...
OH MY, I HAVE UESTS?
HMM...
DOESN'T LOOK LIKE ANY OF YOU ARE HERE TO ASK ME OUT...
DIE, MARIA!

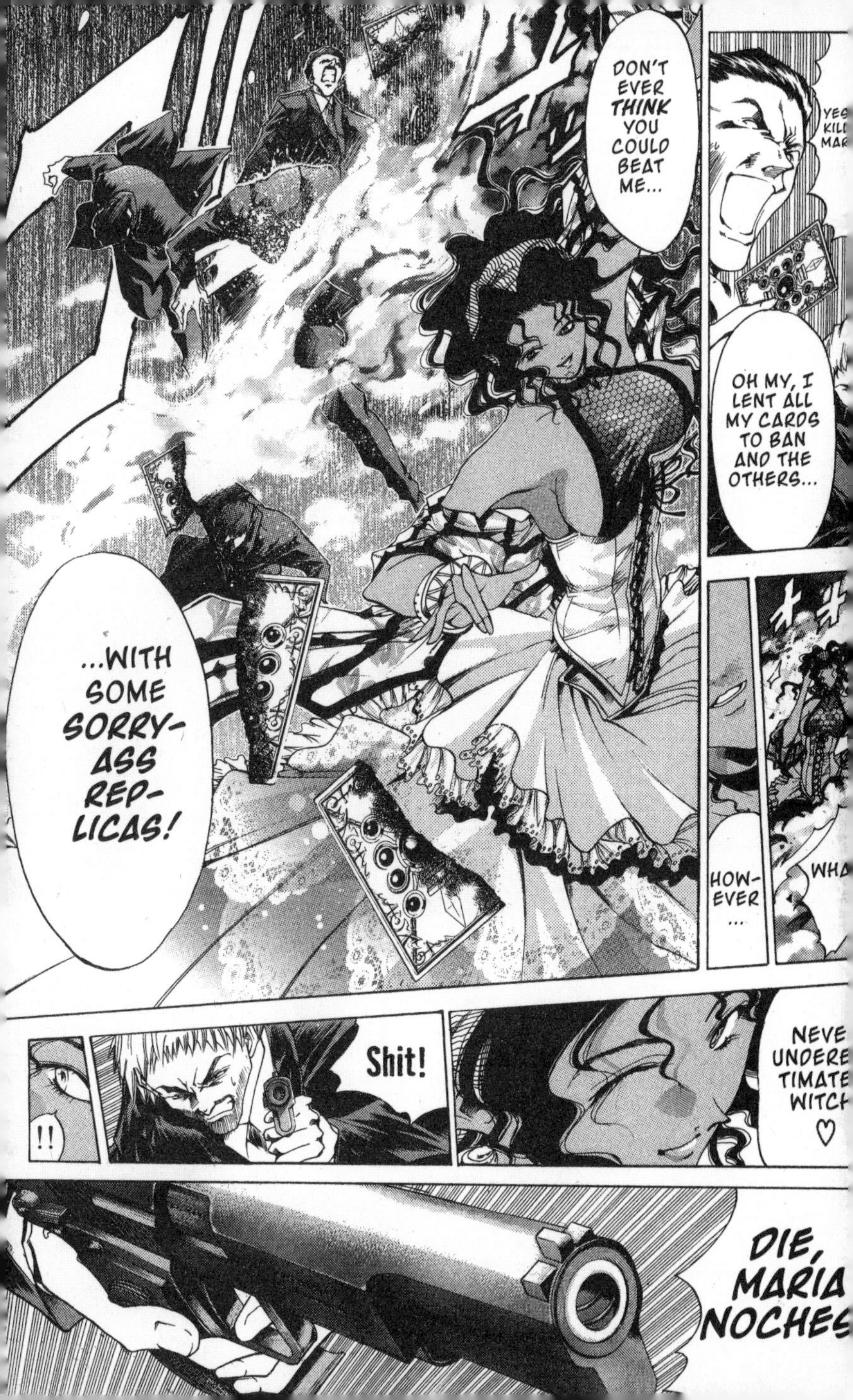
YES KILL MAR
OH MY, I LENT ALL MY CARDS TO BAN AND THE OTHERS...
HOW-EVER ...
WHA
DON'T EVER THINK YOU COULD BEAT ME...
...WITH SOME SORRY-ASS REP-LICAS!
NEVE UNDERE TIMATE WITCH ♡
Shit!
!!
DIE, MARIA NOCHES

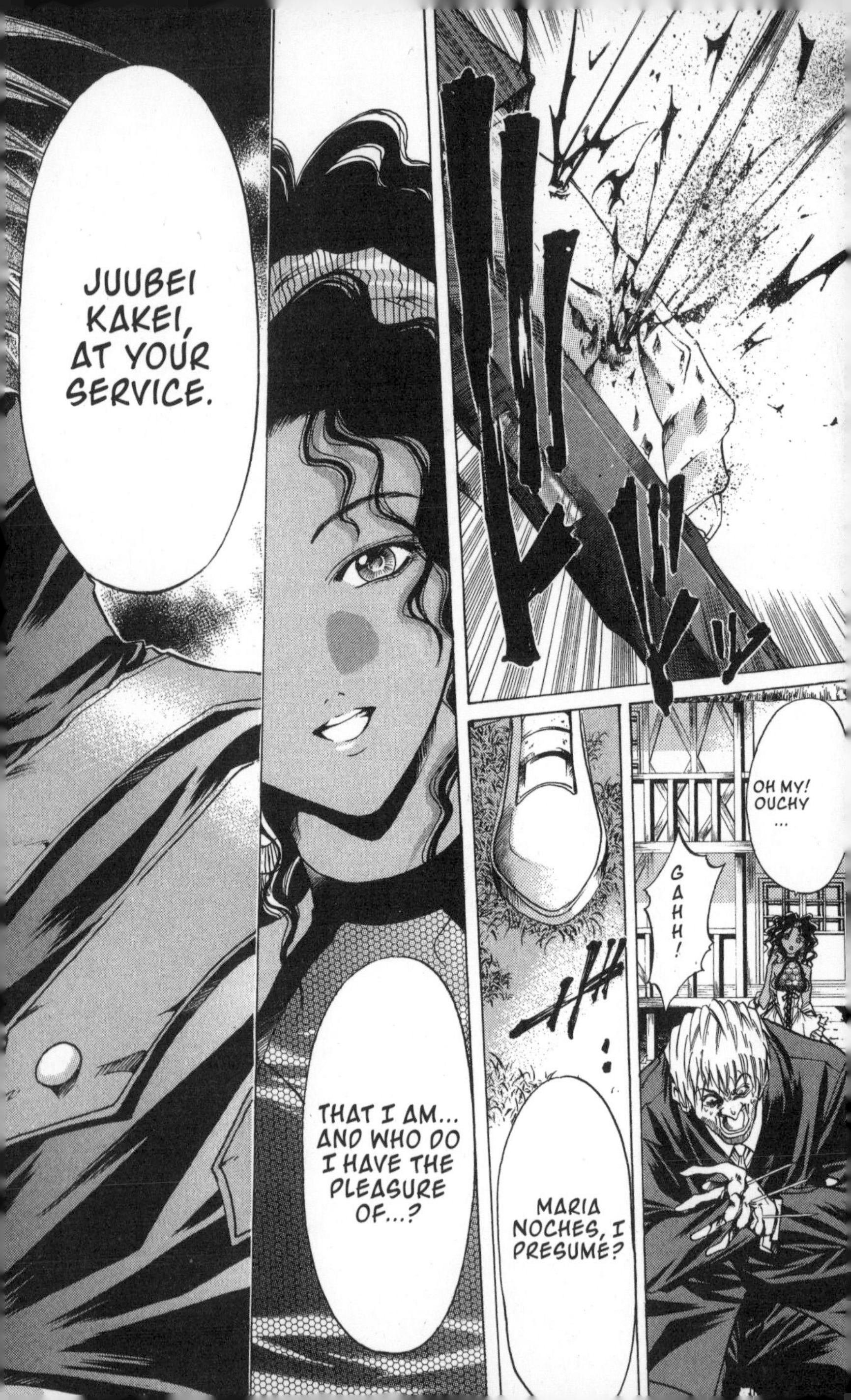
OH MY! OUCHY ...
GAHH!
MARIA NOCHES, I PRESUME?
THAT I AM... AND WHO DO I HAVE THE PLEASURE OF...?
JUUBEI KAKEI, AT YOUR SERVICE.

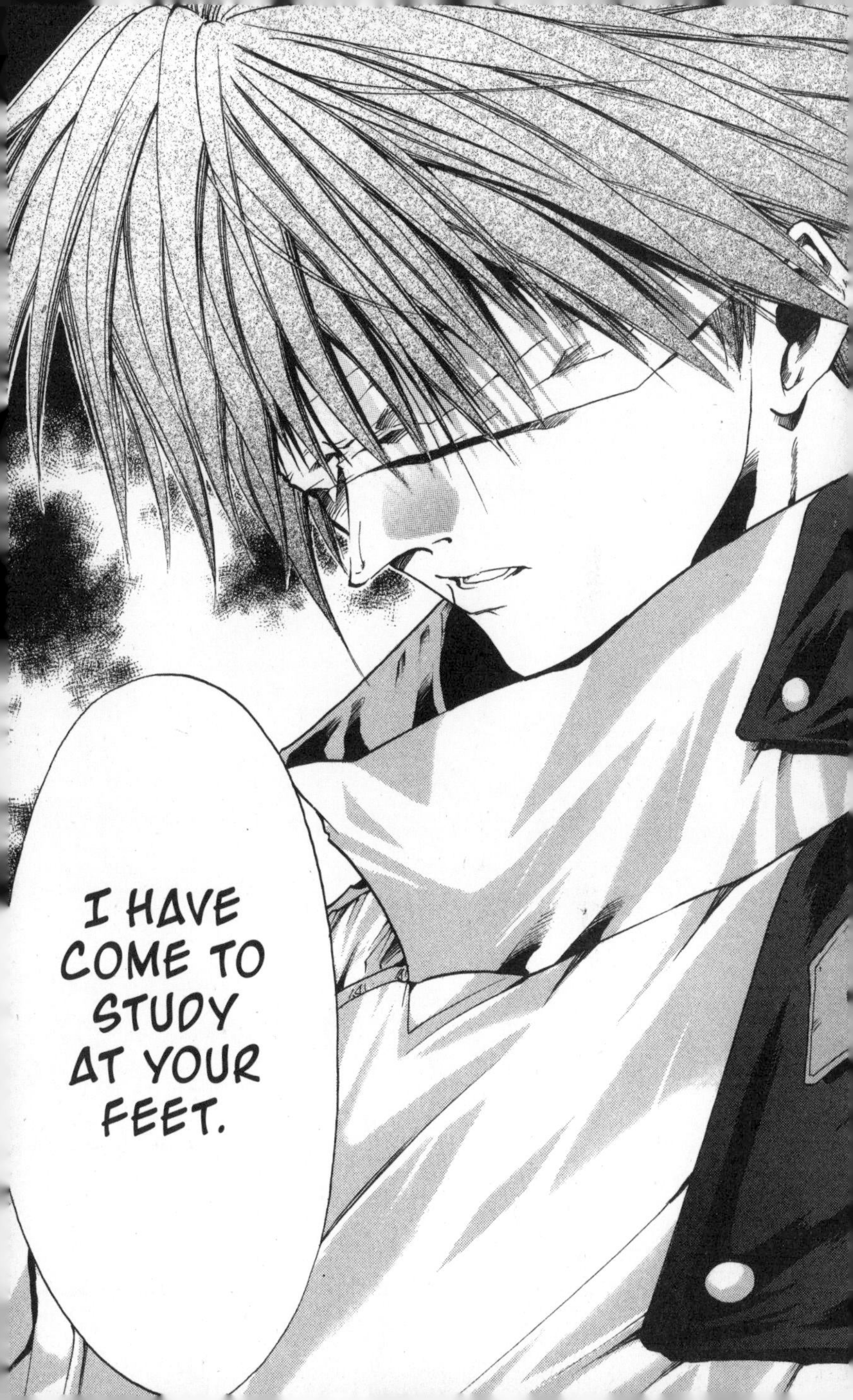
I HAVE COME TO STUDY AT YOUR FEET.

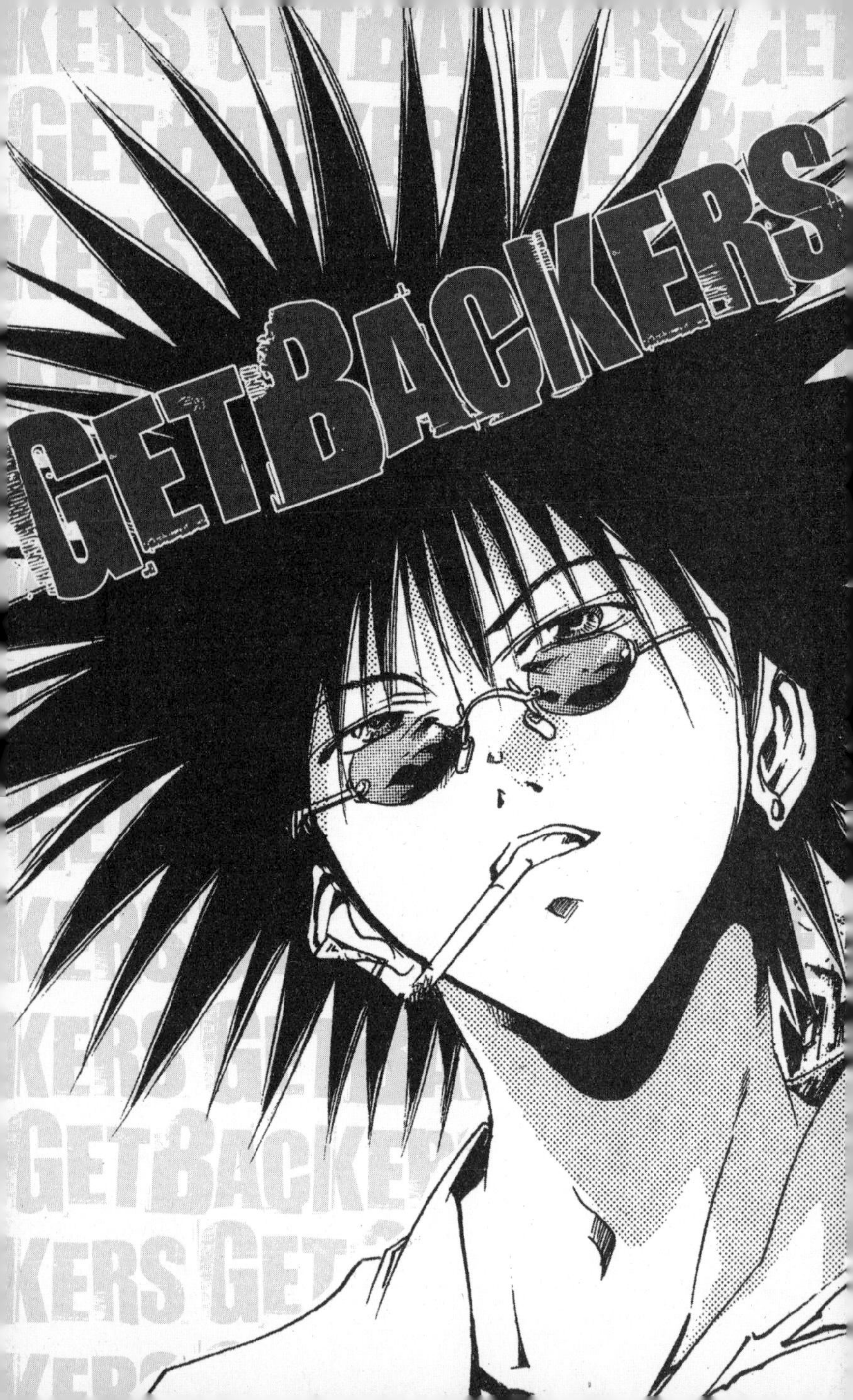
GETBACKERS

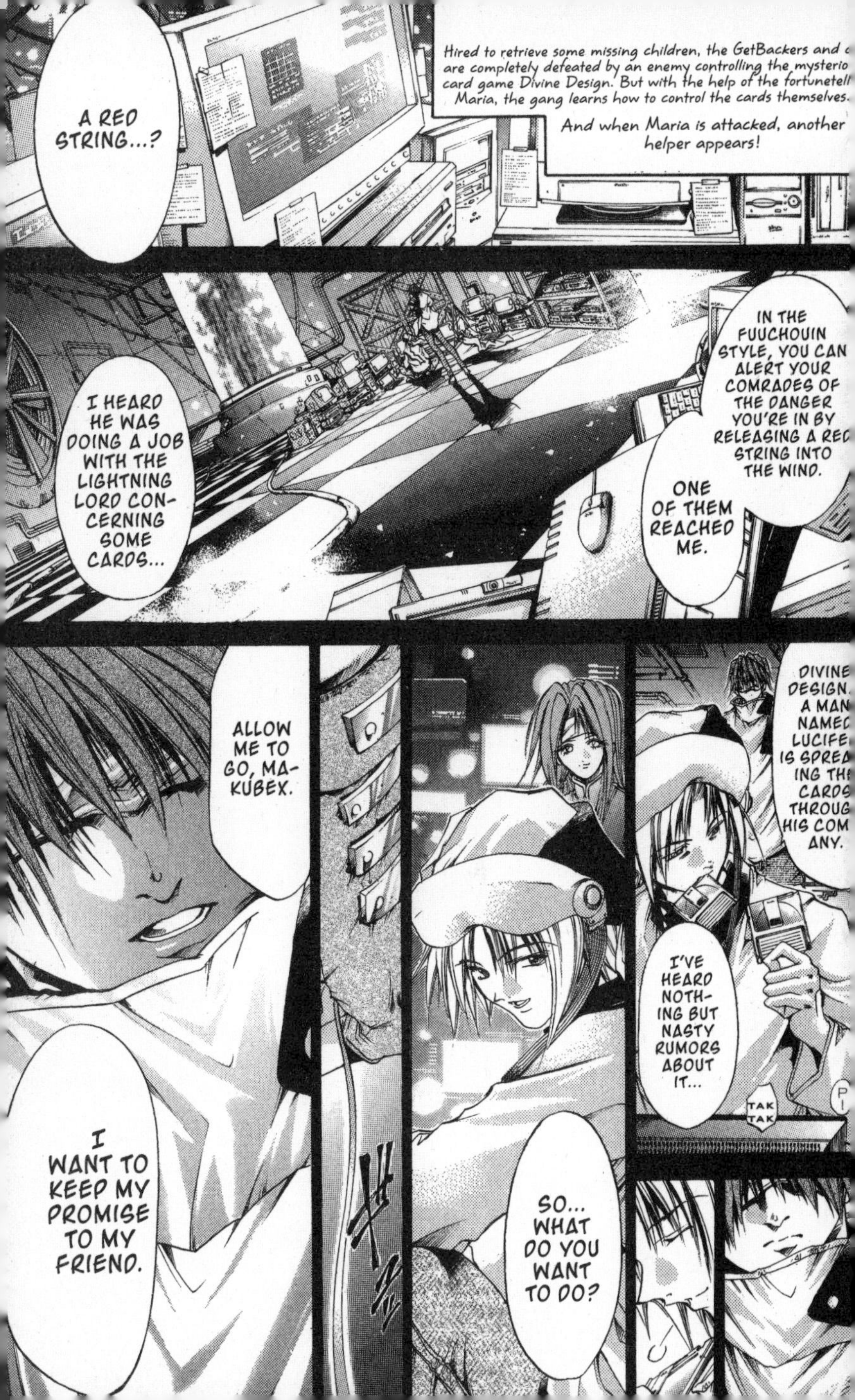
Hired to retrieve some missing children, the GetBackers and c are completely defeated by an enemy controlling the mysterio card game Divine Design. But with the help of the fortunetell Maria, the gang learns how to control the cards themselves.
And when Maria is attacked, another helper appears!
A RED STRING...?
IN THE FUUCHOUIN STYLE, YOU CAN ALERT YOUR COMRADES OF THE DANGER YOU'RE IN BY RELEASING A REC STRING INTO THE WIND.
ONE OF THEM REACHED ME.
I HEARD HE WAS DOING A JOB WITH THE LIGHTNING LORD CON-CERNING SOME CARDS...
DIVINE DESIGN. A MAN NAMED LUCIFE IS SPREA ING THE CARDS THROUG HIS COM ANY.
I'VE HEARD NOTH-ING BUT NASTY RUMORS ABOUT IT...
TAK TAK
SO... WHAT DO YOU WANT TO DO?
ALLOW ME TO GO, MA-KUBEX.
I WANT TO KEEP MY PROMISE TO MY FRIEND.

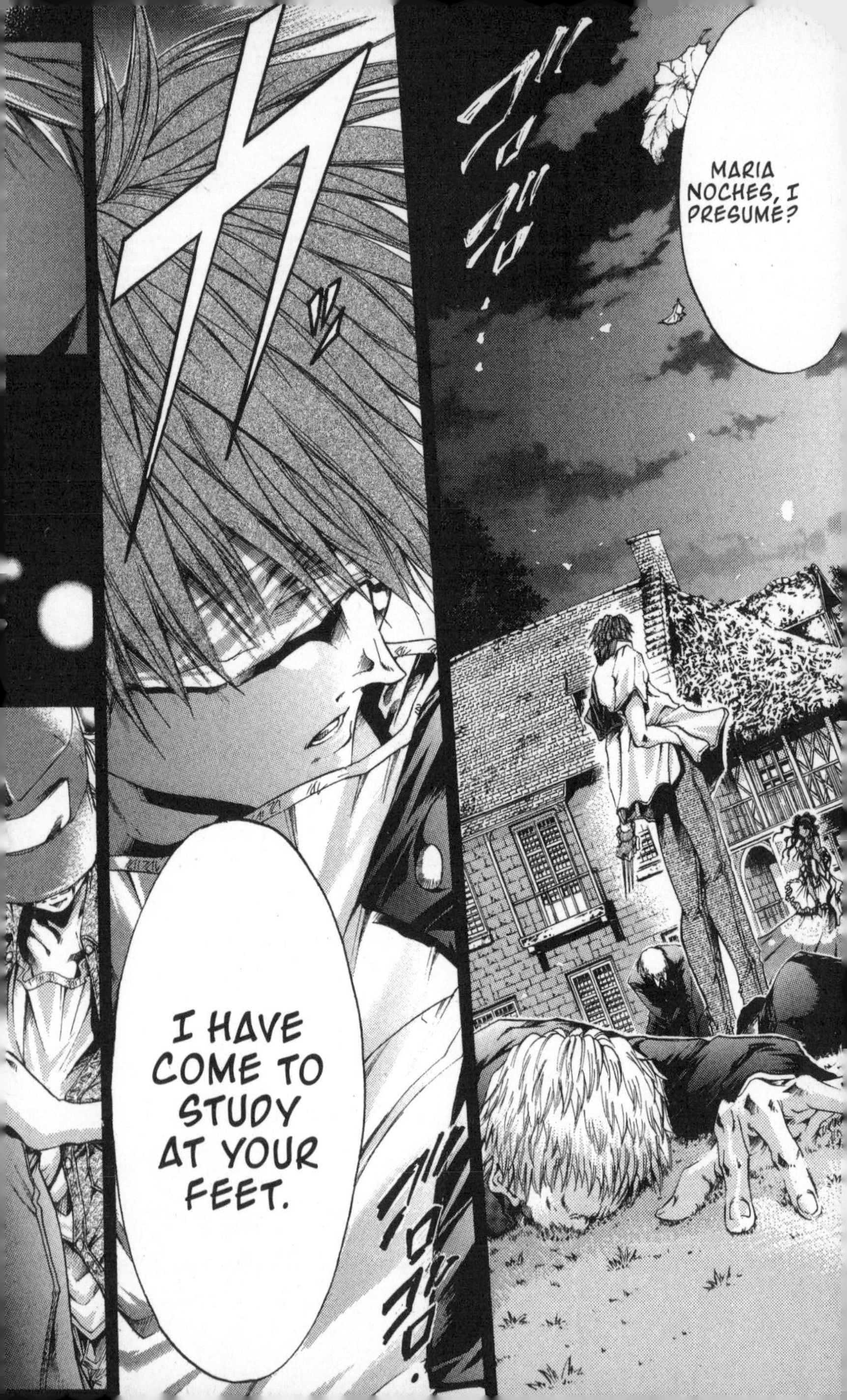
MARIA NOCHES, I PRESUME?
I HAVE COME TO STUDY AT YOUR FEET.

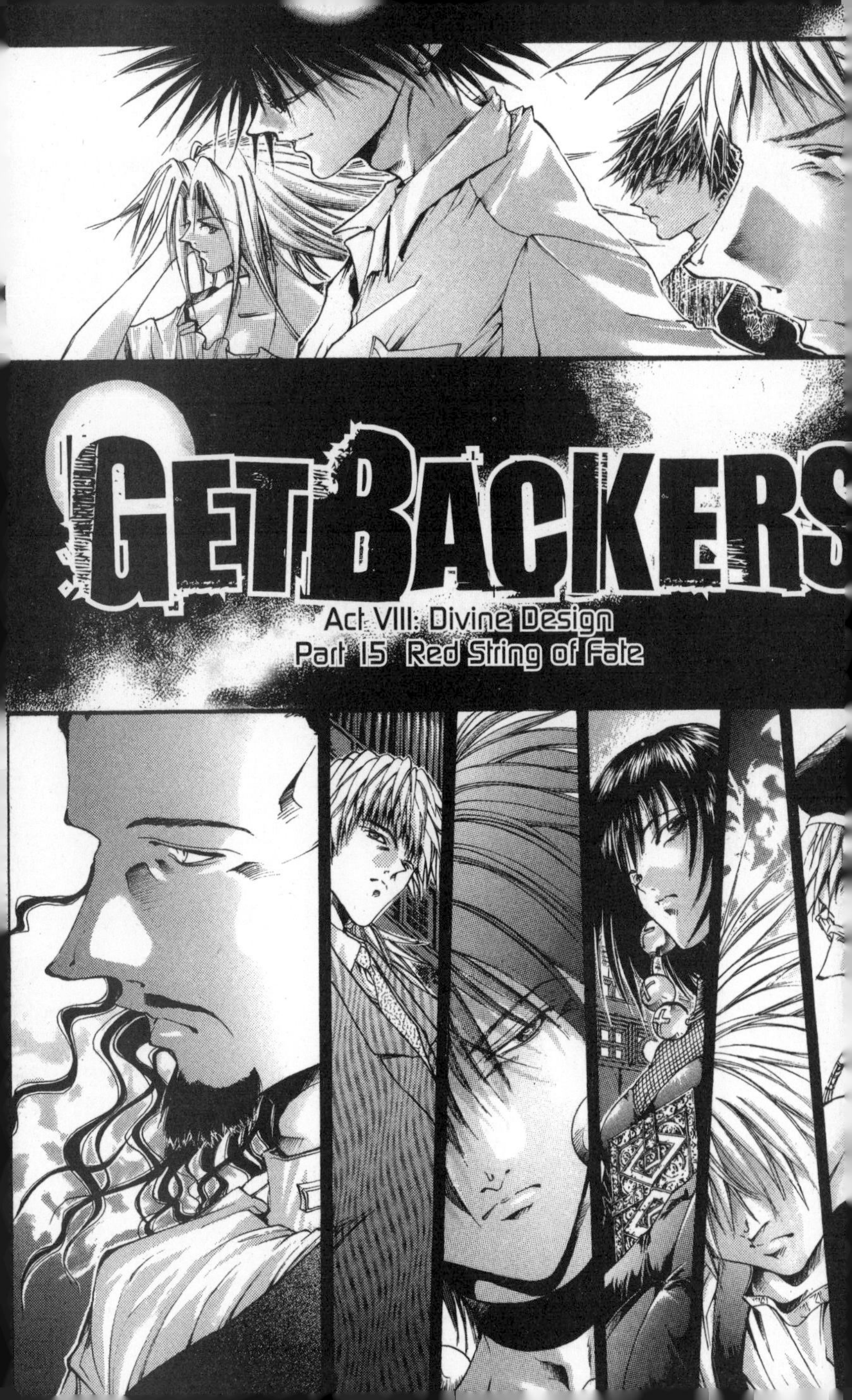
GET BACKERS
Act VIII: Divine Design
Part 15 Red String of Fate

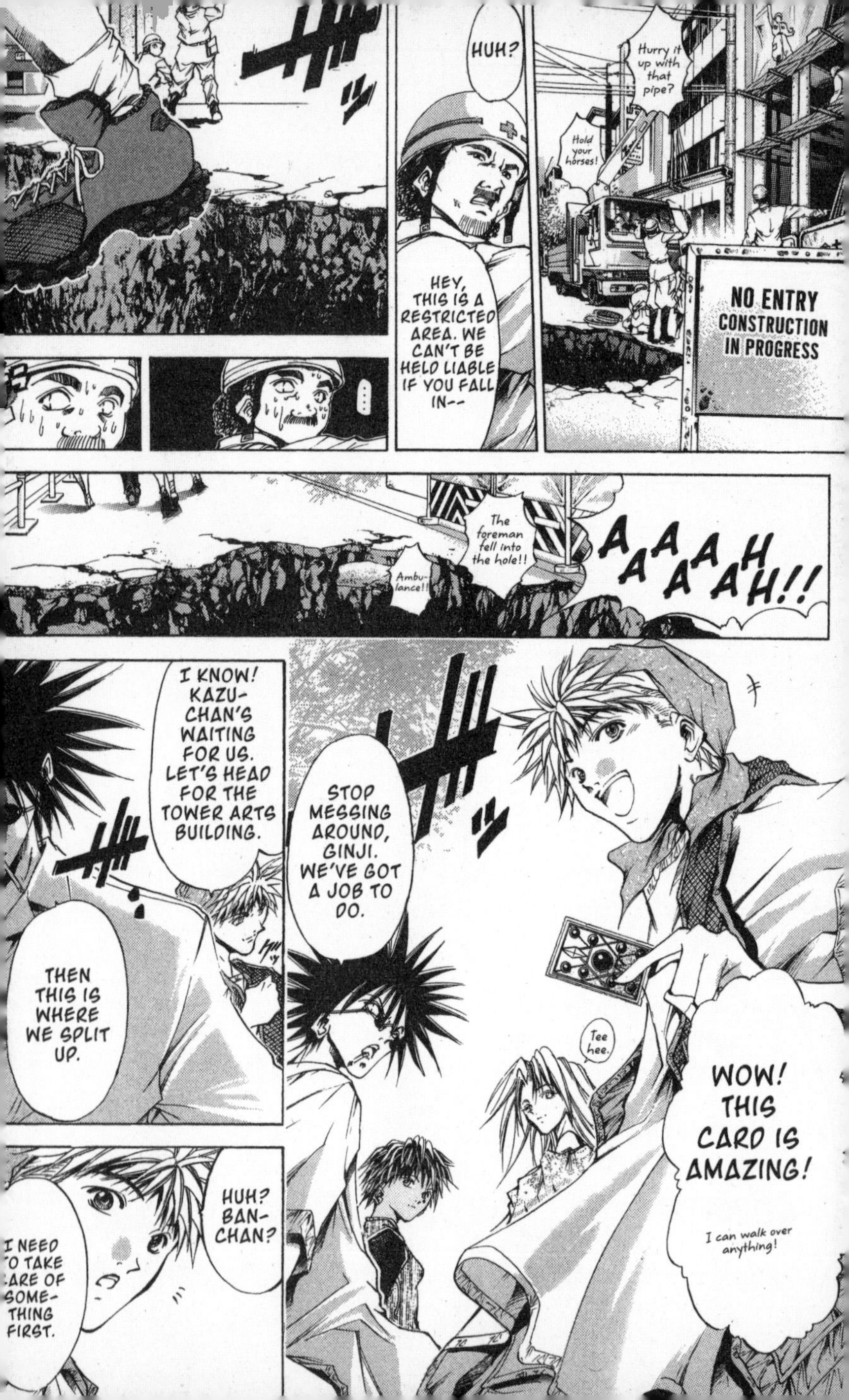
Hurry it up with that pipe?
Hold your horses!
NO ENTRY CONSTRUCTION IN PROGRESS
HUH?
HEY, THIS IS A RESTRICTED AREA. WE CAN'T BE HELD LIABLE IF YOU FALL IN--
...
AAAAAH!!
The foreman fell into the hole!!
Ambulance!!
WOW! THIS CARD IS AMAZING!
I can walk over anything!
Tee hee.
STOP MESSING AROUND, GINJI. WE'VE GOT A JOB TO DO.
I KNOW! KAZU-CHAN'S WAITING FOR US. LET'S HEAD FOR THE TOWER ARTS BUILDING.
THEN THIS IS WHERE WE SPLIT UP.
HUH? BAN-CHAN?
I NEED TO TAKE CARE OF SOMETHING FIRST.

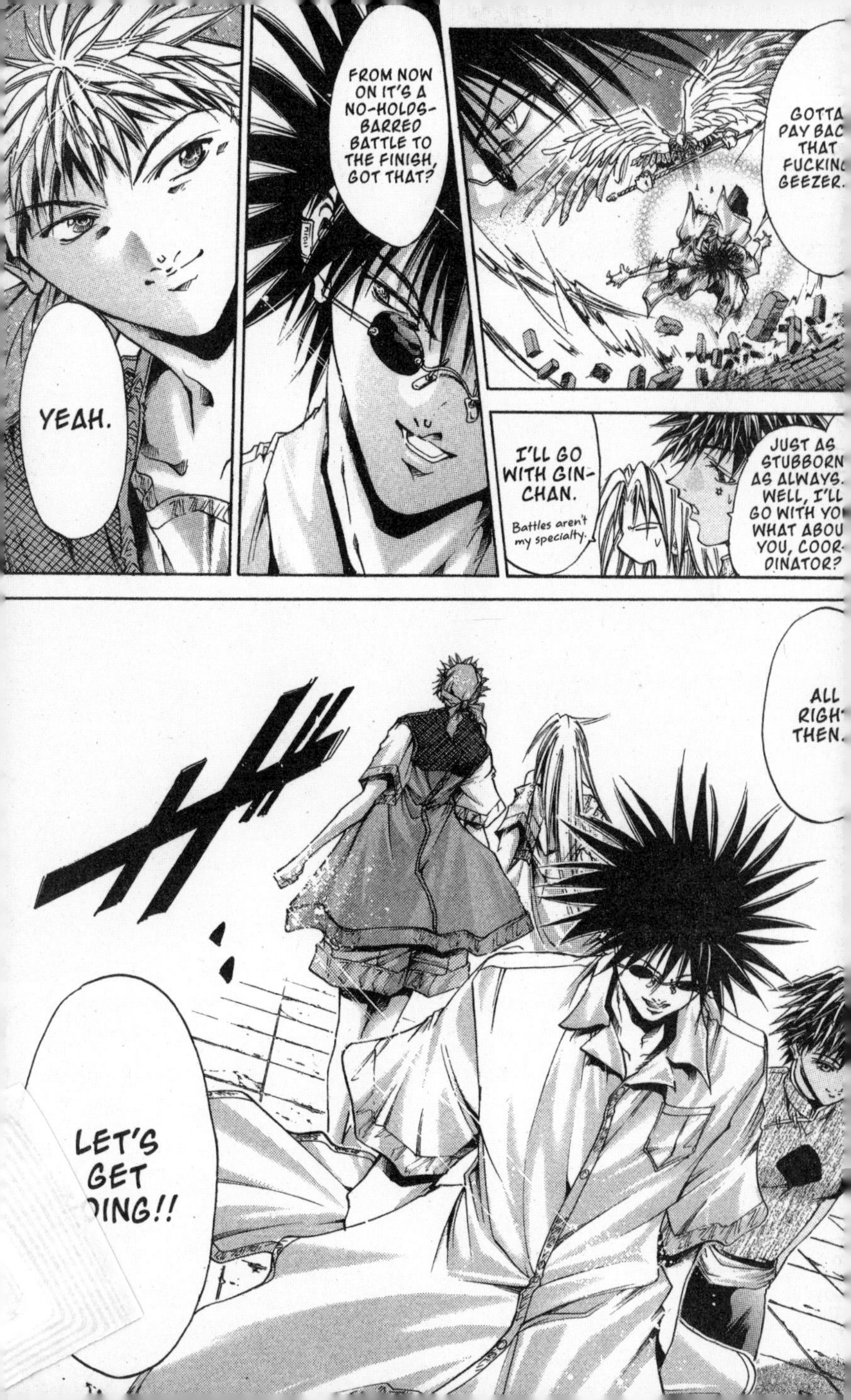
GOTTA PAY BAC THAT FUCKIN GEEZER.
JUST AS STUBBORN AS ALWAYS. WELL, I'LL GO WITH YOU WHAT ABOU YOU, COOR-DINATOR?
I'LL GO WITH GIN-CHAN.
Battles aren't my specialty.
FROM NOW ON IT'S A NO-HOLDS-BARRED BATTLE TO THE FINISH, GOT THAT?
YEAH.
ALL RIGH THEN.
LET'S GET OING!!

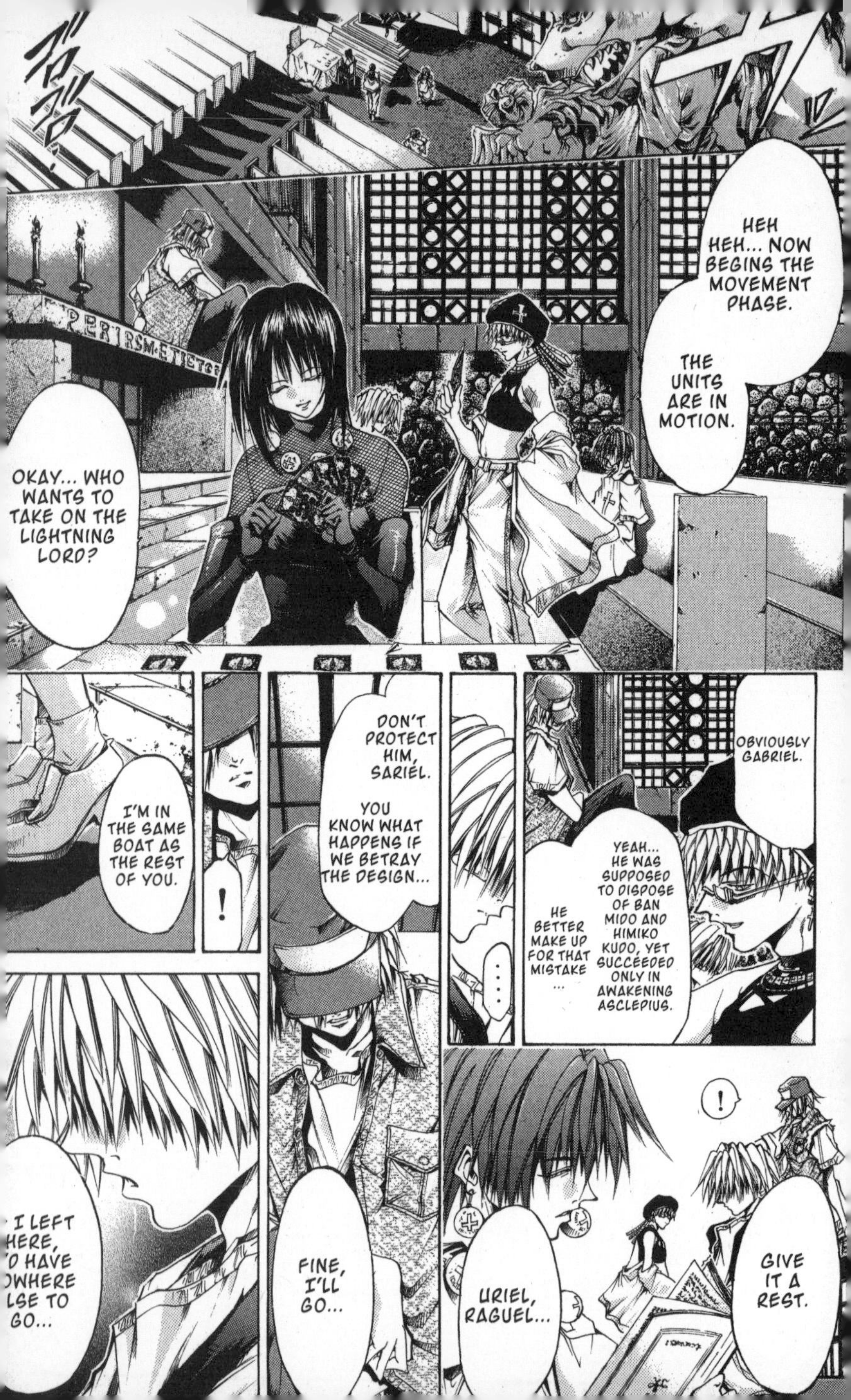
HEH HEH... NOW BEGINS THE MOVEMENT PHASE.
THE UNITS ARE IN MOTION.
OKAY... WHO WANTS TO TAKE ON THE LIGHTNING LORD?
OBVIOUSLY GABRIEL.
YEAH... HE WAS SUPPOSED TO DISPOSE OF BAN MIDO AND HIMIKO KUDO, YET SUCCEEDED ONLY IN AWAKENING ASCLEPIUS.
HE BETTER MAKE UP FOR THAT MISTAKE...
....
DON'T PROTECT HIM, SARIEL.
YOU KNOW WHAT HAPPENS IF WE BETRAY THE DESIGN...
!
I'M IN THE SAME BOAT AS THE REST OF YOU.
!
GIVE IT A REST.
URIEL, RAGUEL...
FINE, I'LL GO...
I LEFT HERE, D HAVE OWHERE LSE TO GO...

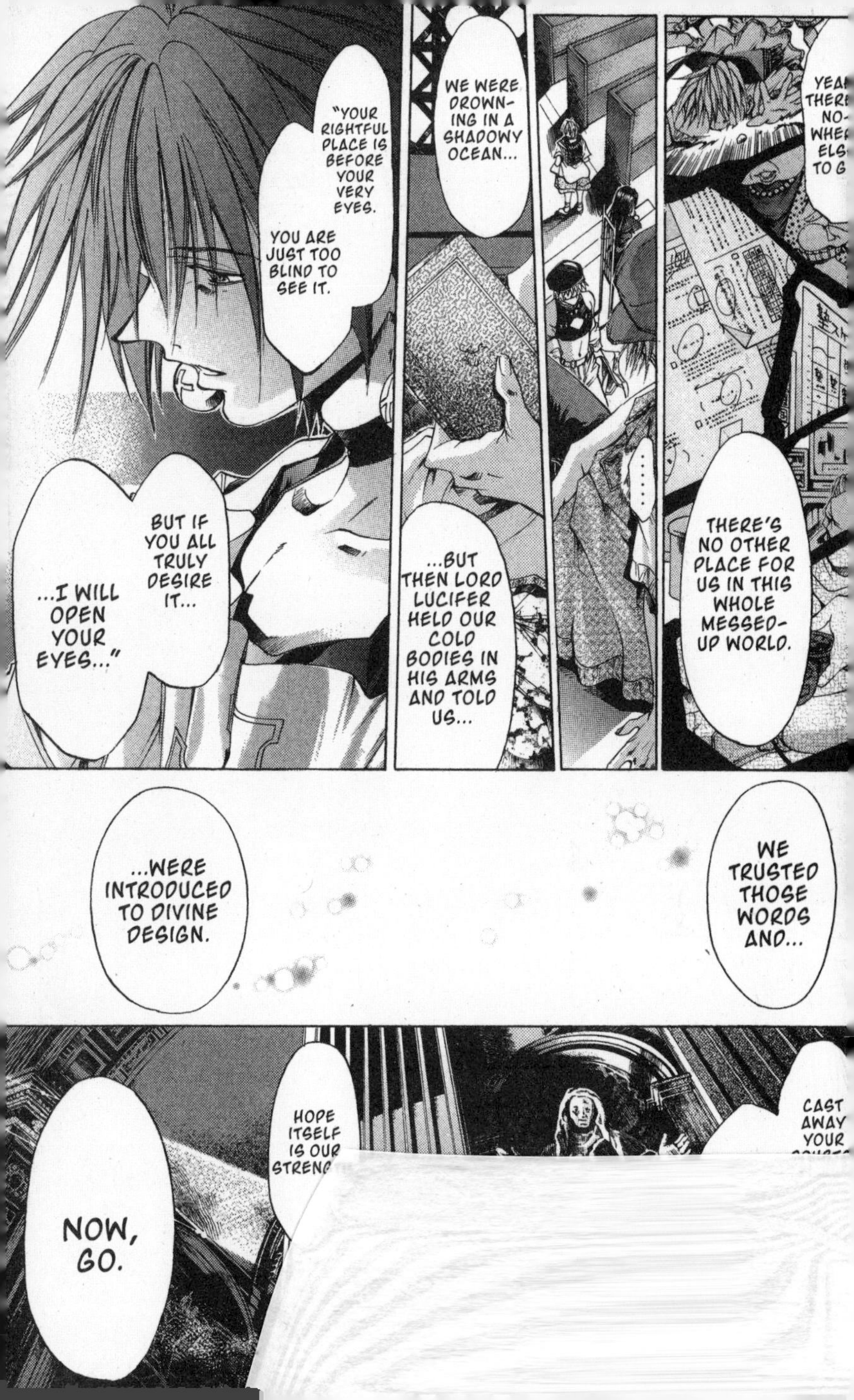
YEA THERE NO- WHER ELS TO G
......
THERE'S NO OTHER PLACE FOR US IN THIS WHOLE MESSED-UP WORLD.
WE WERE DROWN-ING IN A SHADOWY OCEAN...
...BUT THEN LORD LUCIFER HELD OUR COLD BODIES IN HIS ARMS AND TOLD US...
"YOUR RIGHTFUL PLACE IS BEFORE YOUR VERY EYES.
YOU ARE JUST TOO BLIND TO SEE IT.
BUT IF YOU ALL TRULY DESIRE IT...
...I WILL OPEN YOUR EYES..."
WE TRUSTED THOSE WORDS AND...
...WERE INTRODUCED TO DIVINE DESIGN.
CAST AWAY YOUR
HOPE ITSELF IS OUR
NOW, GO.

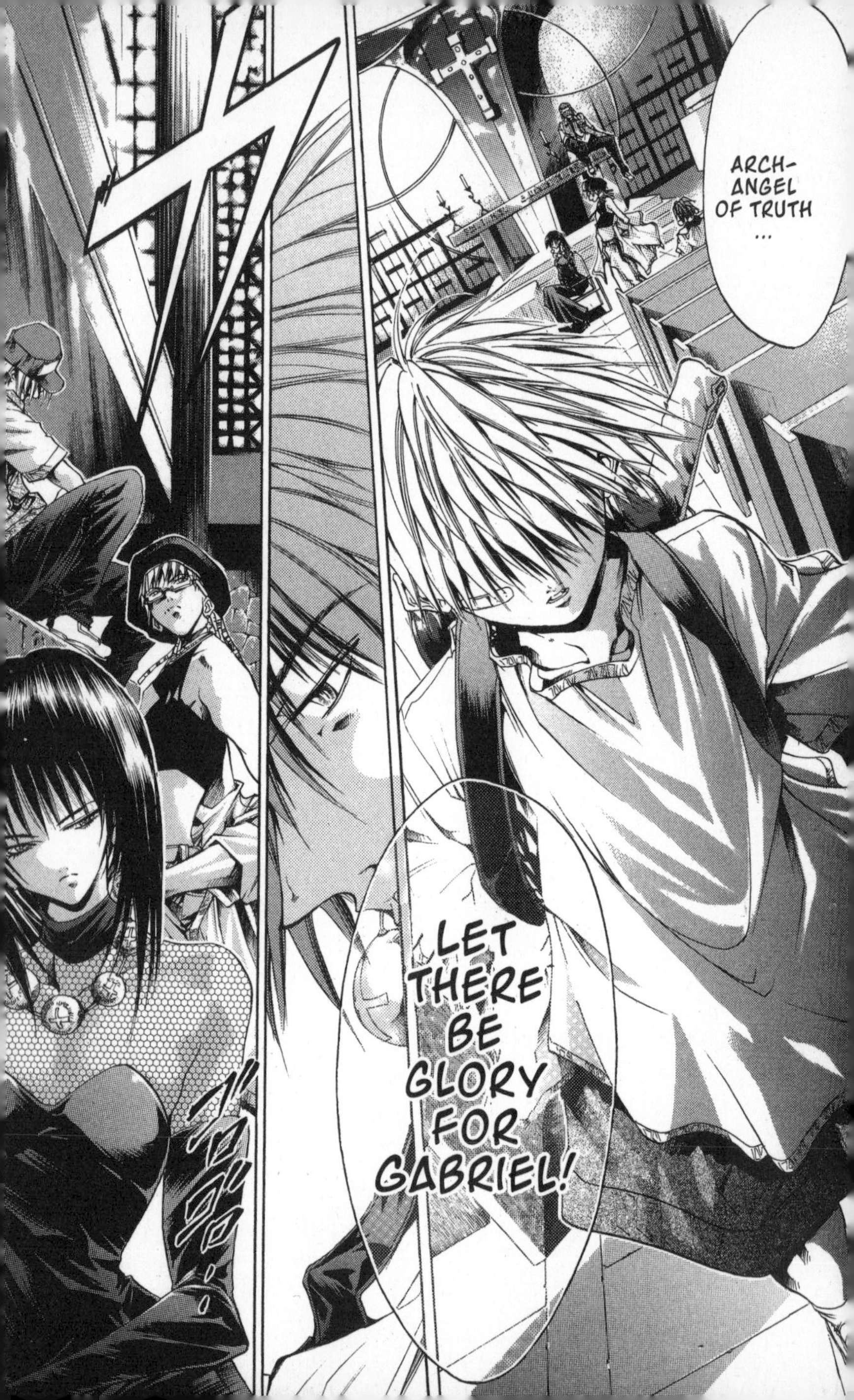
ARCH-ANGEL OF TRUTH ...
LET THERE BE GLORY FOR GABRIEL!

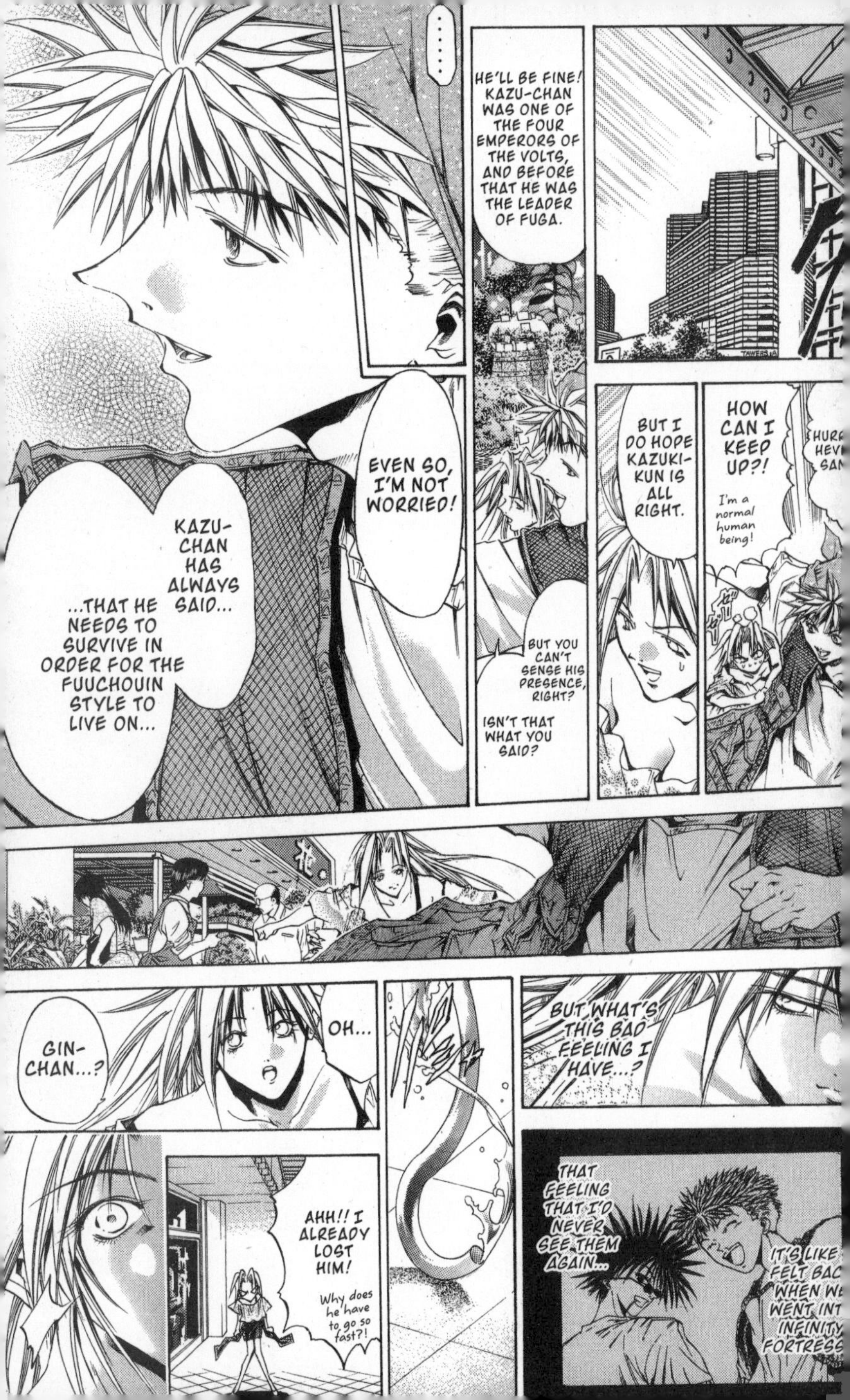
HOW CAN I KEEP UP?!
I'm a normal human being!
BUT I DO HOPE KAZUKI-KUN IS ALL RIGHT.
HE'LL BE FINE! KAZU-CHAN WAS ONE OF THE FOUR EMPERORS OF THE VOLTS, AND BEFORE THAT HE WAS THE LEADER OF FUGA.
BUT YOU CAN'T SENSE HIS PRESENCE, RIGHT?
ISN'T THAT WHAT YOU SAID?
......
EVEN SO, I'M NOT WORRIED!
KAZU-CHAN HAS ALWAYS SAID...
...THAT HE NEEDS TO SURVIVE IN ORDER FOR THE FUUCHOUIN STYLE TO LIVE ON...
BUT WHAT'S THIS BAD FEELING I HAVE...?
OH...
GIN-CHAN...?
IT'S LIKE FELT BAC WHEN WE WENT INT INFINITY FORTRESS
THAT FEELING THAT I'D NEVER SEE THEM AGAIN...
AHH!! I ALREADY LOST HIM!
Why does he have to go so fast?!

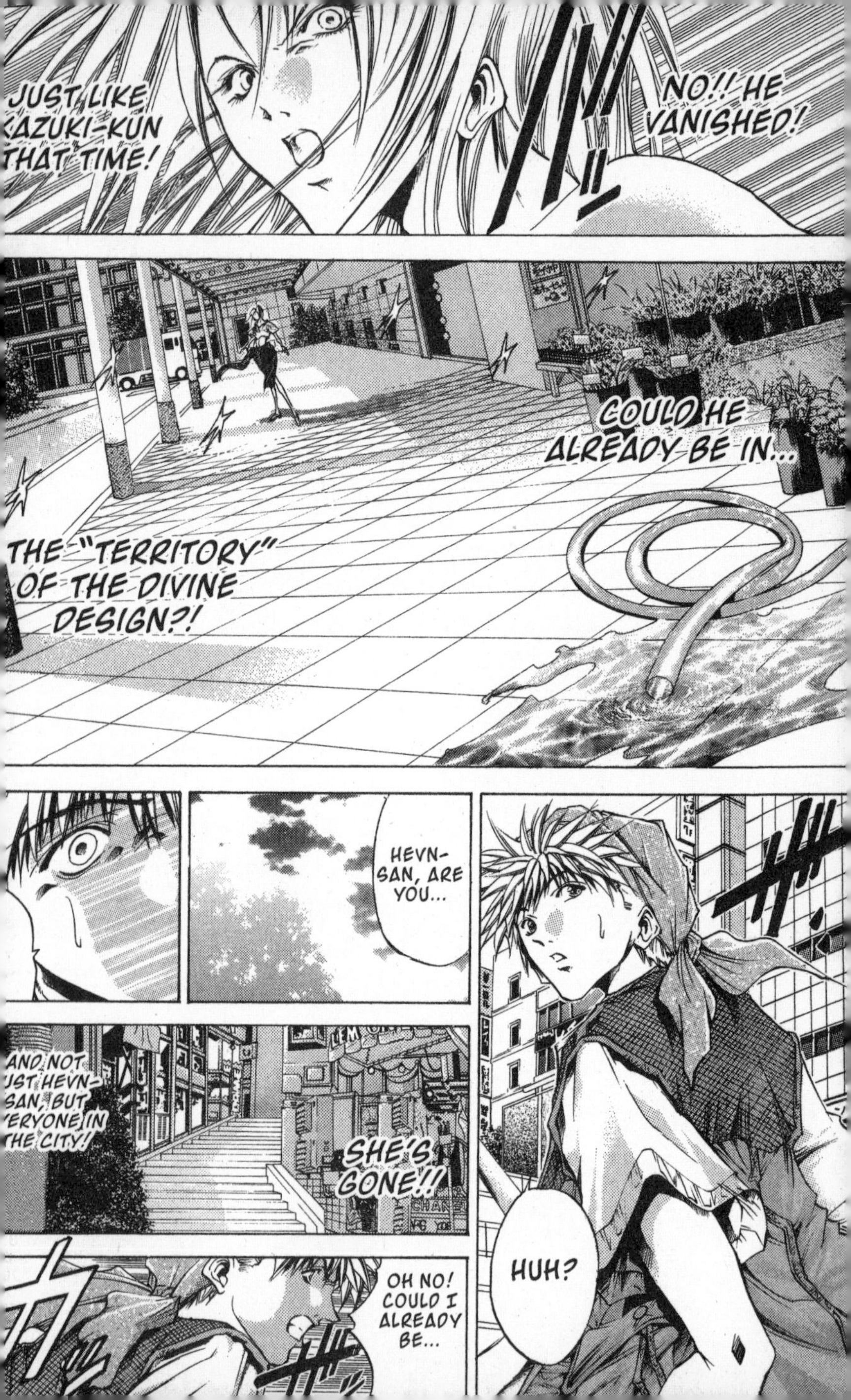
NO!! HE VANISHED!
JUST LIKE KAZUKI-KUN THAT TIME!
COULD HE ALREADY BE IN...
THE "TERRITORY" OF THE DIVINE DESIGN?!
HUH?
HEVN-SAN, ARE YOU...
SHE'S GONE!!
AND NOT UST HEVN-SAN, BUT ERYONE IN THE CITY!
OH NO! COULD I ALREADY BE...

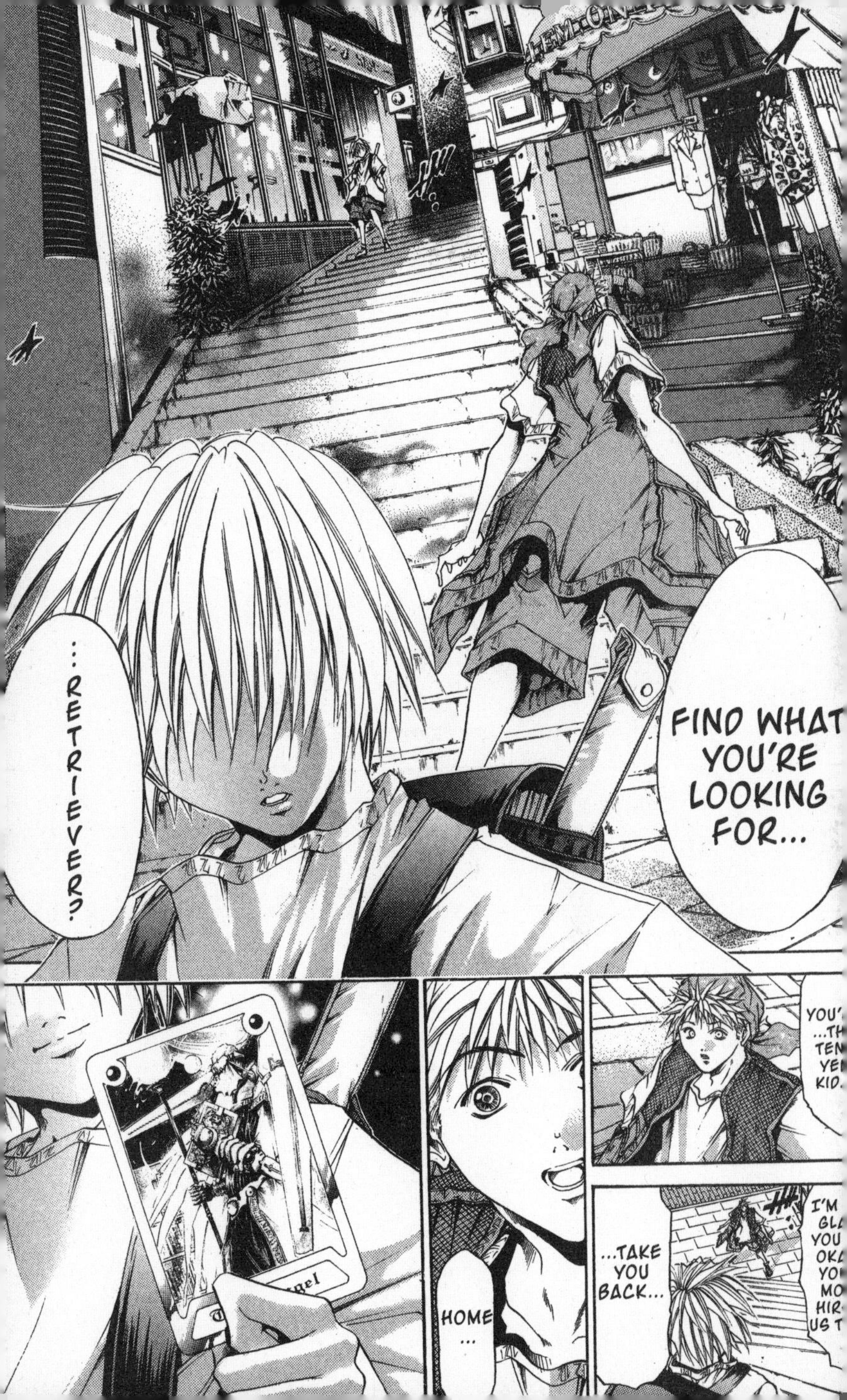
FIND WHAT YOU'RE LOOKING FOR...
...RETRIEVER?
YOU'. ...TH TEN YE KID.
I'M GL YOU OK YO MO HIR US T
...TAKE YOU BACK...
HOME ...

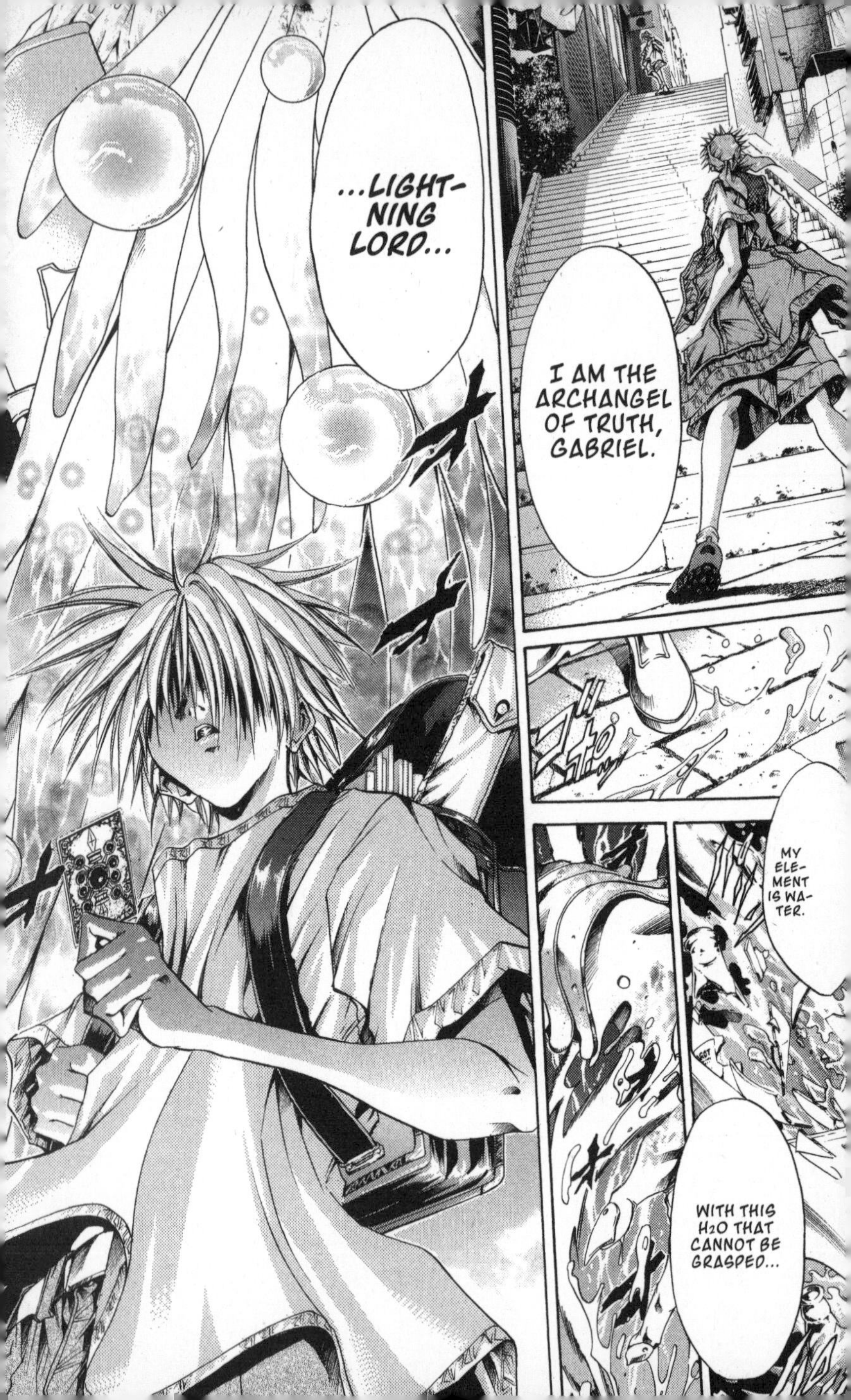
I AM THE ARCHANGEL OF TRUTH, GABRIEL.
MY ELEMENT IS WATER.
WITH THIS H_2O THAT CANNOT BE GRASPED...
...LIGHTNING LORD...

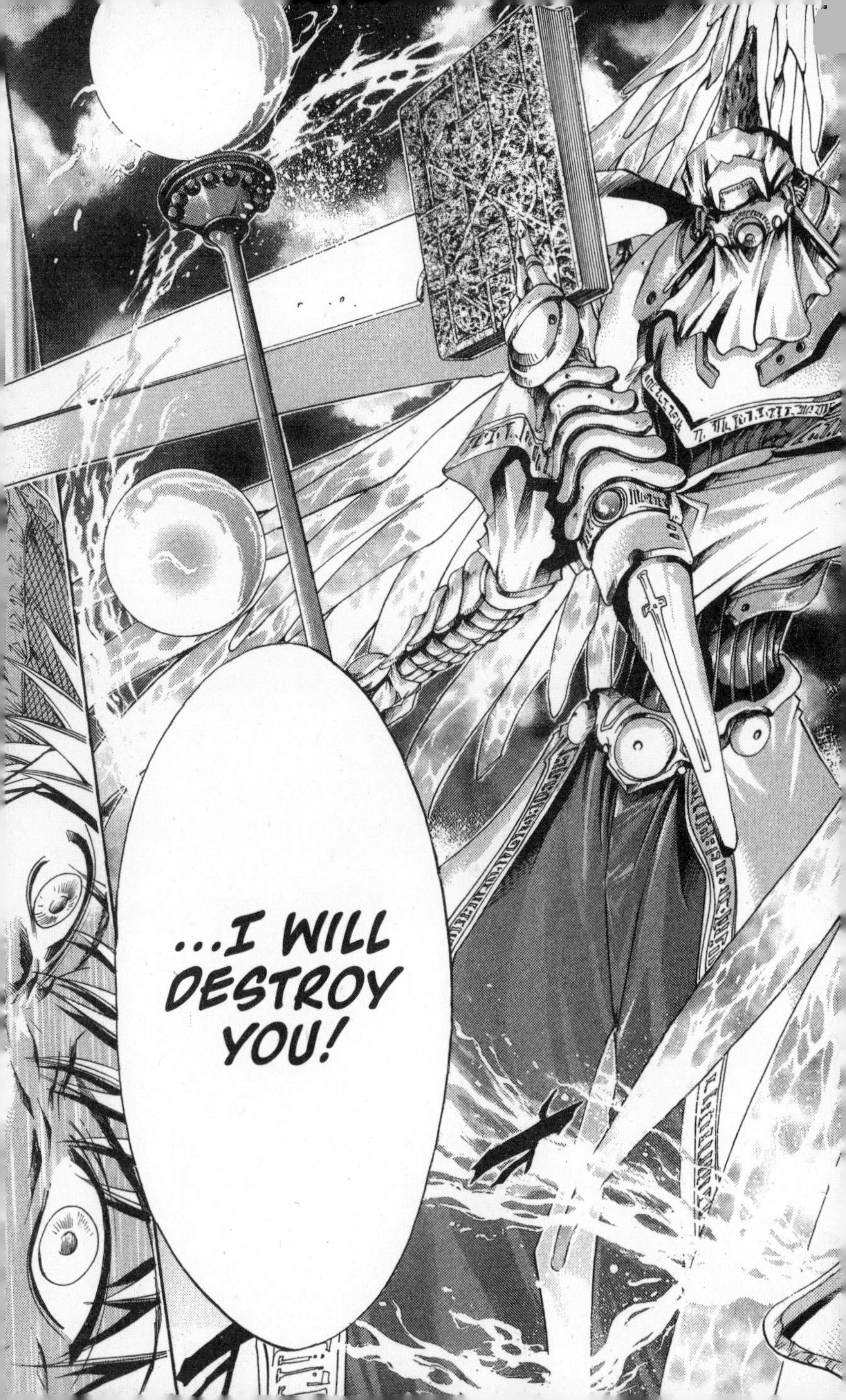
...I WILL DESTROY YOU!

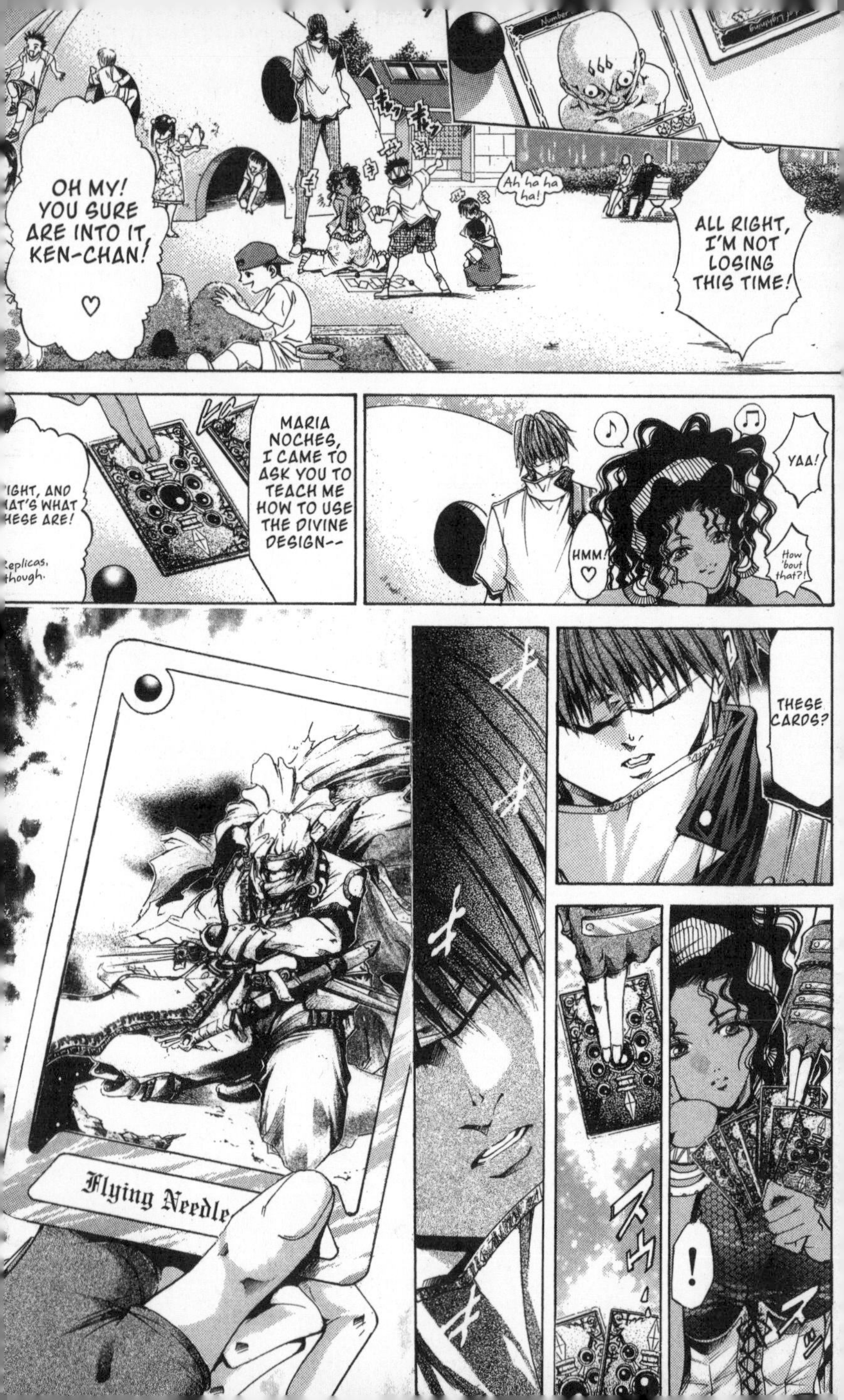

ALL RIGHT, I'M NOT LOSING THIS TIME!
Ah ha ha ha!
OH MY! YOU SURE ARE INTO IT KEN-CHAN! ♡
YAA!
How 'bout that?!
HMM! ♡
MARIA NOCHES, I CAME TO ASK YOU TO TEACH ME HOW TO USE THE DIVINE DESIGN--
IGHT, AND AT'S WHAT HESE ARE!
eplicas, though.
THESE CARDS?
!
Flying Needle

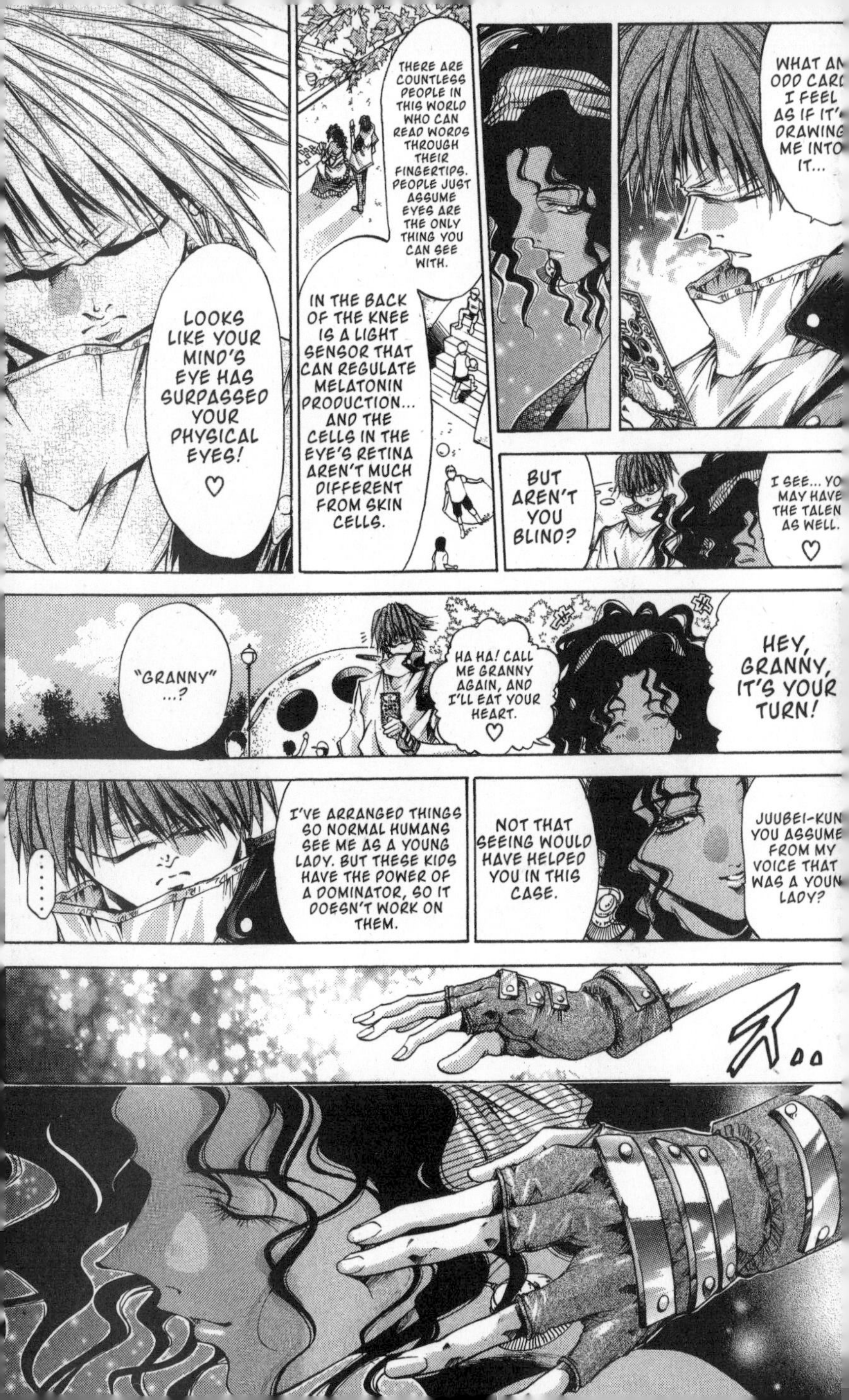
WHAT AN ODD CARD I FEEL AS IF IT' DRAWING ME INTO IT...
I SEE... YO MAY HAVE THE TALEN AS WELL. ♡
BUT AREN'T YOU BLIND?
THERE ARE COUNTLESS PEOPLE IN THIS WORLD WHO CAN READ WORDS THROUGH THEIR FINGERTIPS. PEOPLE JUST ASSUME EYES ARE THE ONLY THING YOU CAN SEE WITH.
IN THE BACK OF THE KNEE IS A LIGHT SENSOR THAT CAN REGULATE MELATONIN PRODUCTION... AND THE CELLS IN THE EYE'S RETINA AREN'T MUCH DIFFERENT FROM SKIN CELLS.
LOOKS LIKE YOUR MIND'S EYE HAS SURPASSED YOUR PHYSICAL EYES! ♡
HEY, GRANNY, IT'S YOUR TURN!
HA HA! CALL ME GRANNY AGAIN, AND I'LL EAT YOUR HEART. ♡
"GRANNY" ...?
JUUBEI-KUN YOU ASSUME FROM MY VOICE THAT WAS A YOUN LADY?
NOT THAT SEEING WOULD HAVE HELPED YOU IN THIS CASE.
I'VE ARRANGED THINGS SO NORMAL HUMANS SEE ME AS A YOUNG LADY. BUT THESE KIDS HAVE THE POWER OF A DOMINATOR, SO IT DOESN'T WORK ON THEM.
......

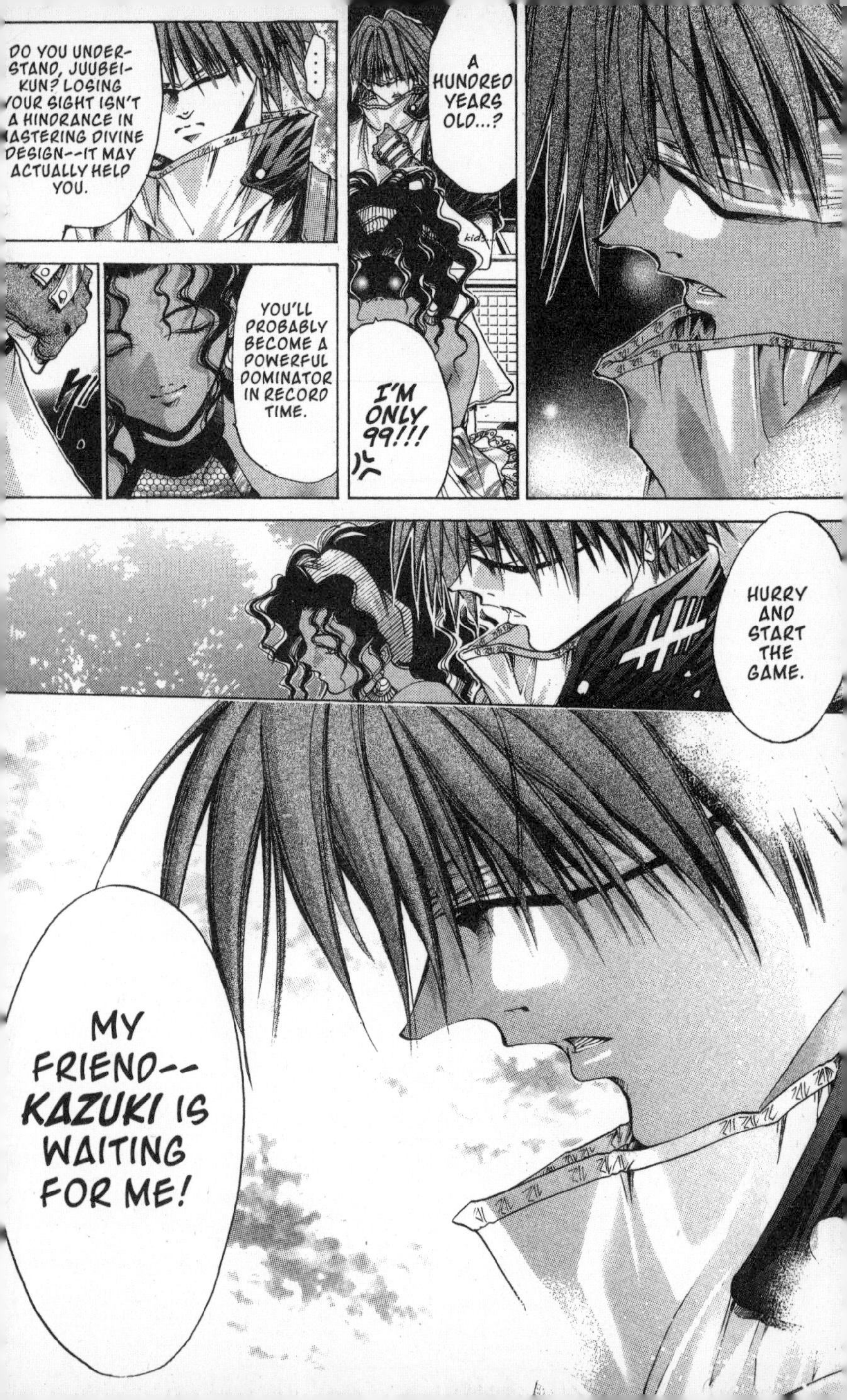
A HUNDRED YEARS OLD...?
kids...
I'M ONLY 99!!!
....
DO YOU UNDERSTAND, JUUBEI-KUN? LOSING YOUR SIGHT ISN'T A HINDRANCE IN MASTERING DIVINE DESIGN--IT MAY ACTUALLY HELP YOU.
YOU'LL PROBABLY BECOME A POWERFUL DOMINATOR IN RECORD TIME.
HURRY AND START THE GAME.
MY FRIEND--**KAZUKI** IS WAITING FOR ME!

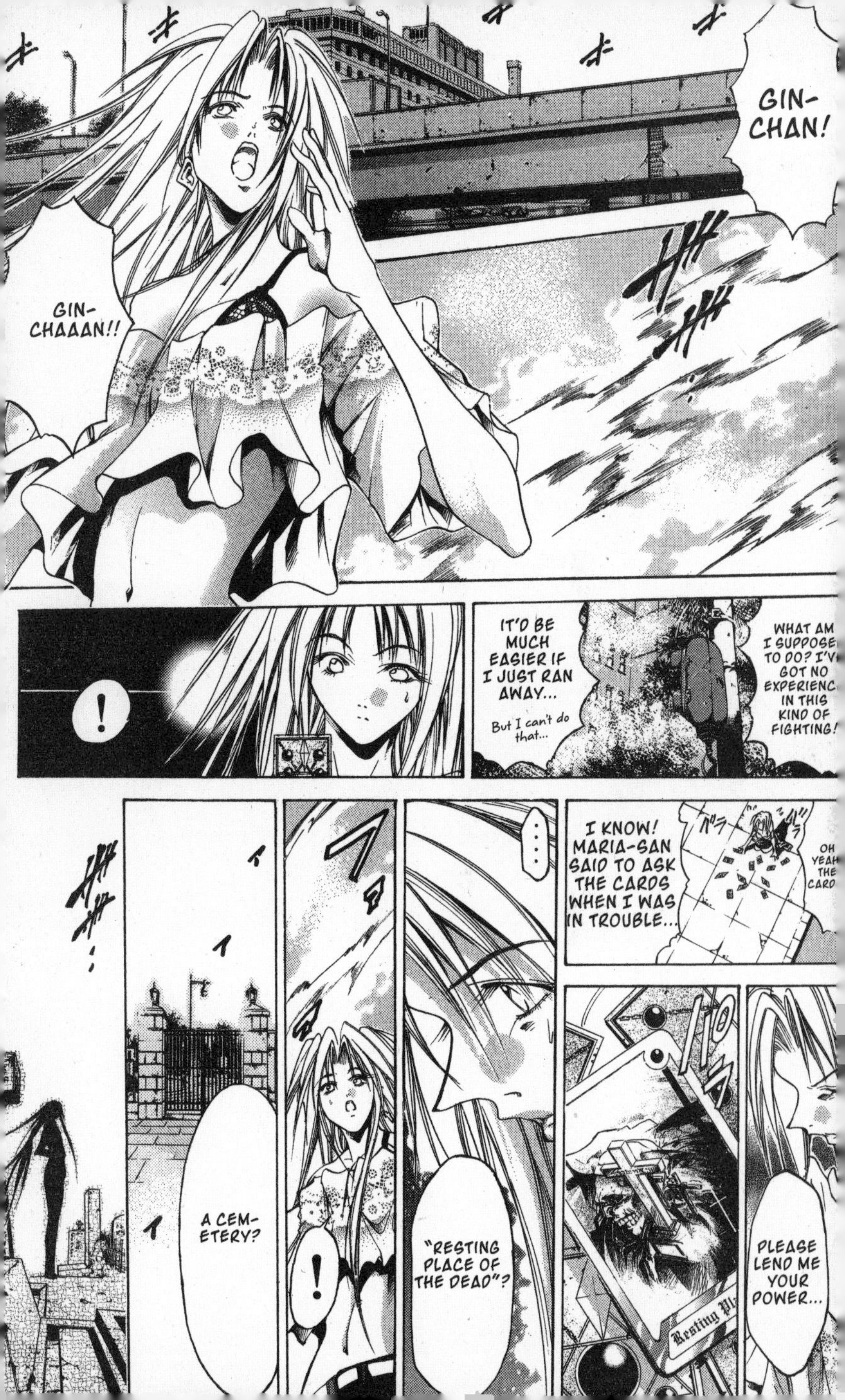
GIN-CHAN!
GIN-CHAAAN!!
WHAT AM I SUPPOSE TO DO? I'VE GOT NO EXPERIENC IN THIS KIND OF FIGHTING!
IT'D BE MUCH EASIER IF I JUST RAN AWAY...
But I can't do that...
!
OH YEAH THE CARD
I KNOW! MARIA-SAN SAID TO ASK THE CARDS WHEN I WAS IN TROUBLE...
PLEASE LEND ME YOUR POWER...
Resting Pl
...
"RESTING PLACE OF THE DEAD"?
!
A CEM-ETERY?

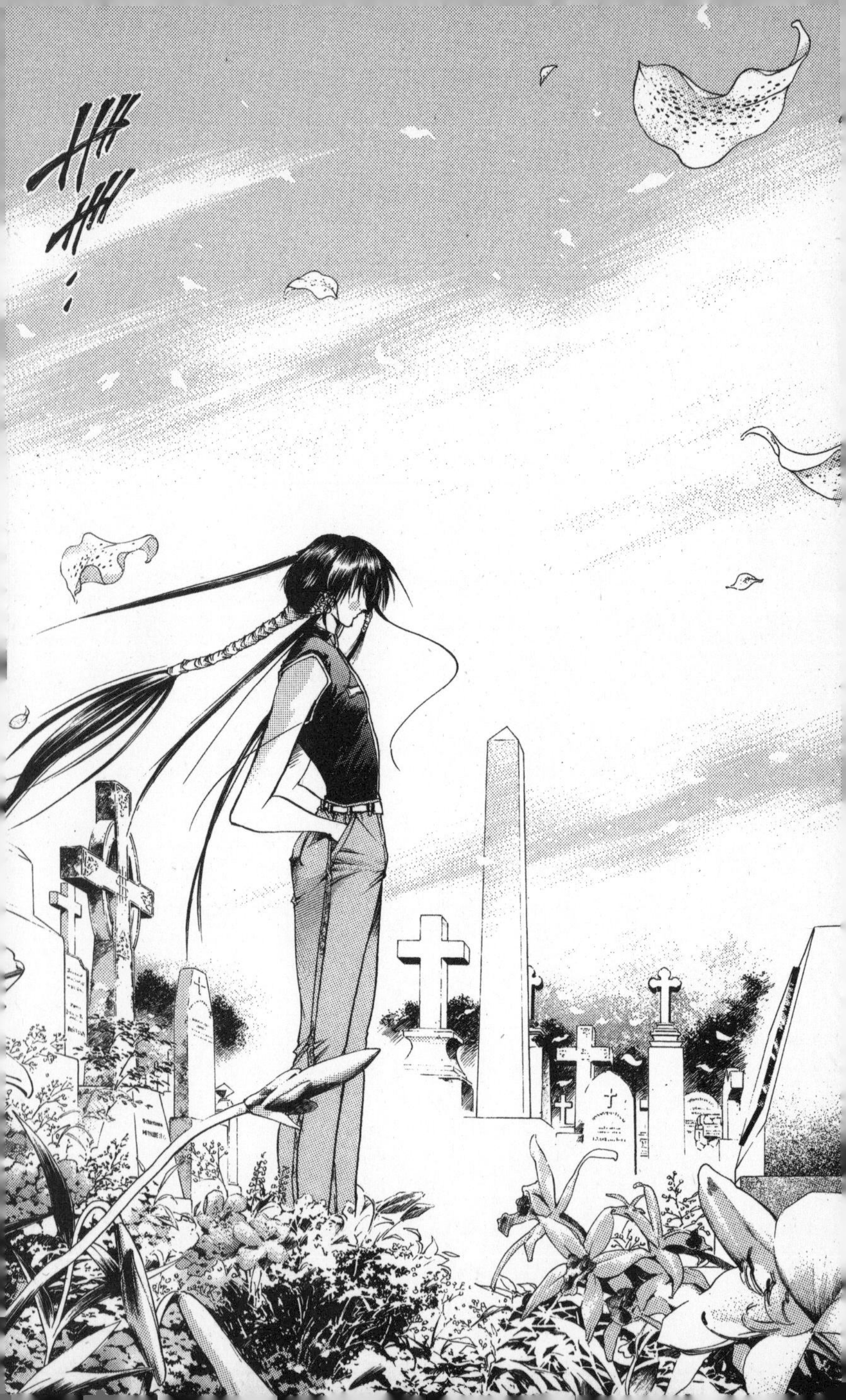

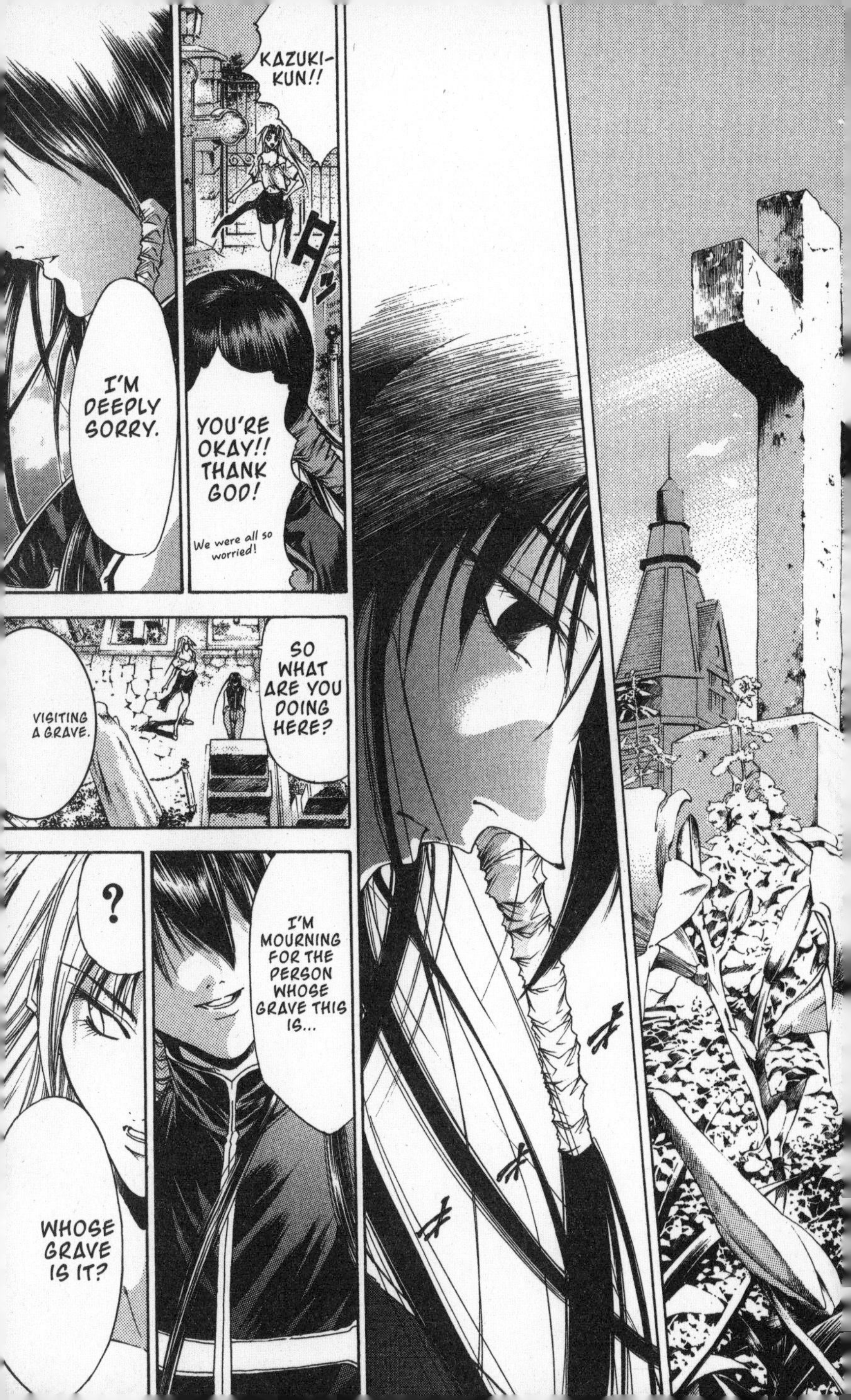
KAZUKI-KUN!!
YOU'RE OKAY!! THANK GOD!
We were all so worried!
I'M DEEPLY SORRY.
SO WHAT ARE YOU DOING HERE?
VISITING A GRAVE.
I'M MOURNING FOR THE PERSON WHOSE GRAVE THIS IS...
?
WHOSE GRAVE IS IT?

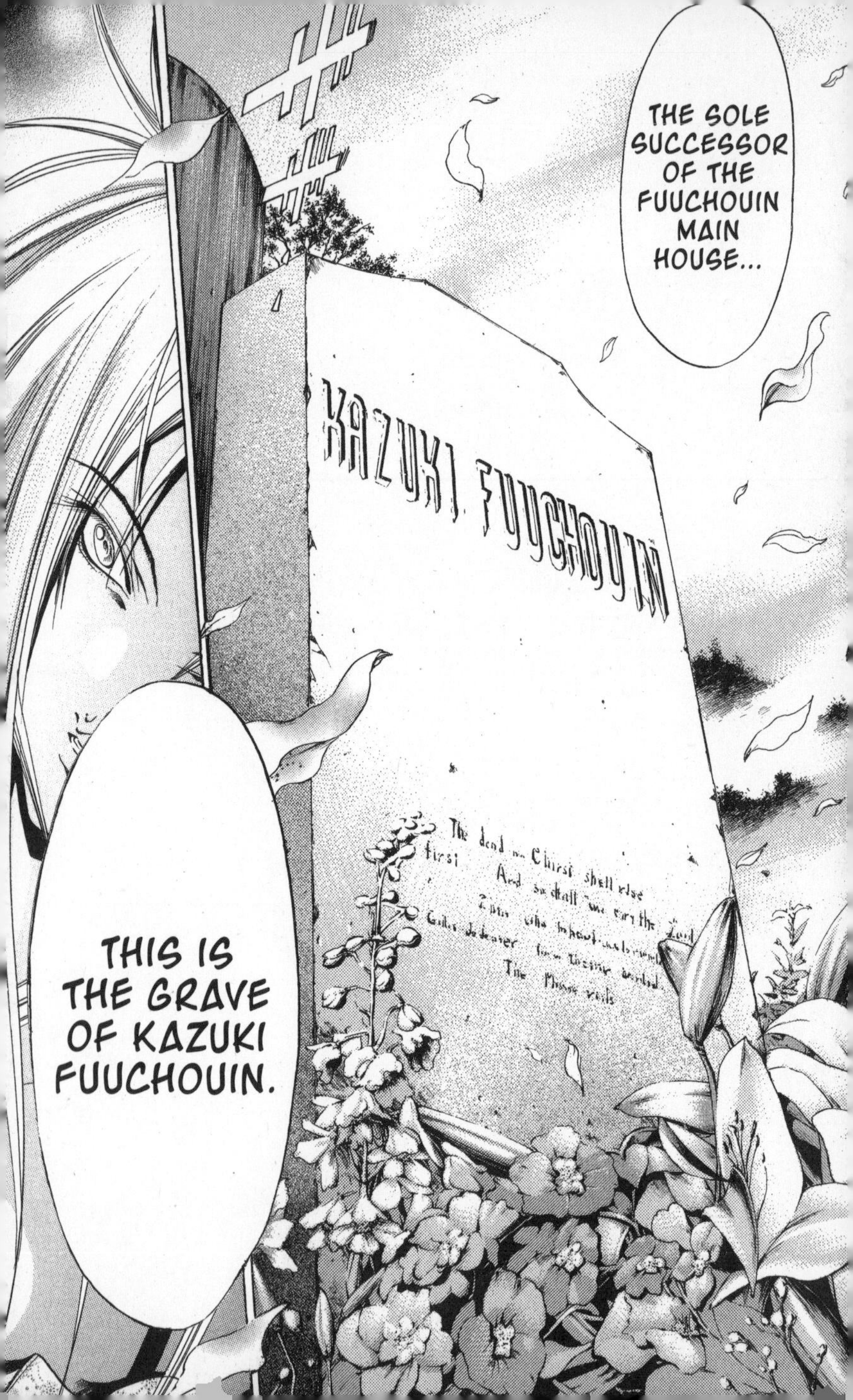
THE SOLE SUCCESSOR OF THE FUUCHOUIN MAIN HOUSE...
KAZUKI FUUCHOUIN
THIS IS THE GRAVE OF KAZUKI FUUCHOUIN.

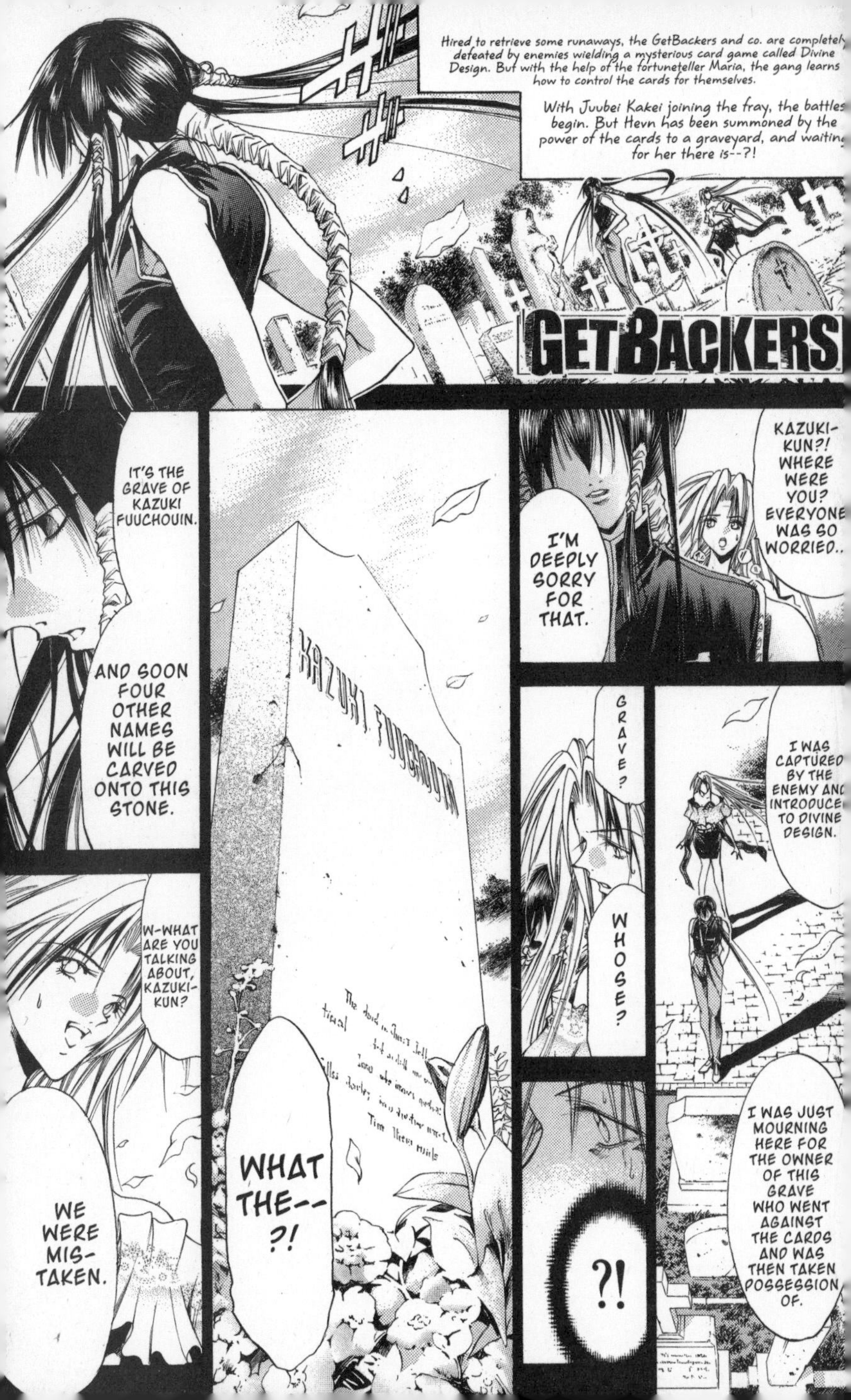

Hired to retrieve some runaways, the GetBackers and co. are completely defeated by enemies wielding a mysterious card game called Divine Design. But with the help of the fortuneteller Maria, the gang learns how to control the cards for themselves.
With Juubei Kakei joining the fray, the battles begin. But Hevn has been summoned by the power of the cards to a graveyard, and waiting for her there is--?!
GETBACKERS
KAZUKI-KUN?! WHERE WERE YOU? EVERYONE WAS SO WORRIED..
I'M DEEPLY SORRY FOR THAT.
I WAS CAPTURED BY THE ENEMY AND INTRODUCED TO DIVINE DESIGN.
GRAVE?
WHOSE?
I WAS JUST MOURNING HERE FOR THE OWNER OF THIS GRAVE WHO WENT AGAINST THE CARDS AND WAS THEN TAKEN POSSESSION OF.
?!
KAZUKI FUUCHOUIN
WHAT THE--?!
IT'S THE GRAVE OF KAZUKI FUUCHOUIN.
AND SOON FOUR OTHER NAMES WILL BE CARVED ONTO THIS STONE.
W-WHAT ARE YOU TALKING ABOUT, KAZUKI-KUN?
WE WERE MIS-TAKEN.

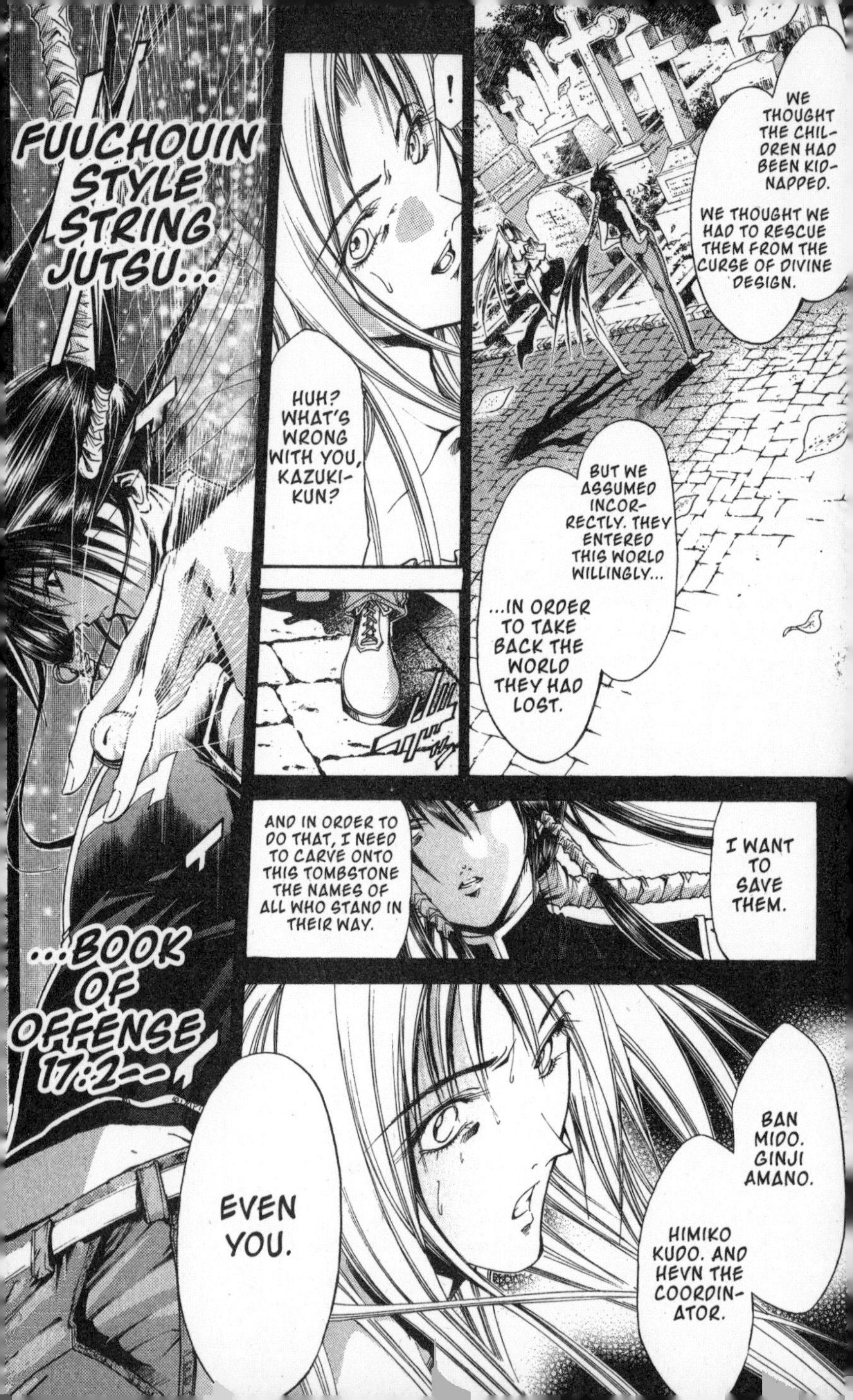
WE THOUGHT THE CHILDREN HAD BEEN KIDNAPPED.
WE THOUGHT WE HAD TO RESCUE THEM FROM THE CURSE OF DIVINE DESIGN.
BUT WE ASSUMED INCORRECTLY. THEY ENTERED THIS WORLD WILLINGLY...
...IN ORDER TO TAKE BACK THE WORLD THEY HAD LOST.
!
HUH? WHAT'S WRONG WITH YOU, KAZUKI-KUN?
I WANT TO SAVE THEM.
AND IN ORDER TO DO THAT, I NEED TO CARVE ONTO THIS TOMBSTONE THE NAMES OF ALL WHO STAND IN THEIR WAY.
BAN MIDO. GINJI AMANO.
HIMIKO KUDO. AND HEVN THE COORDINATOR.
EVEN YOU.
FUUCHOUIN STYLE STRING JUTSU...
...BOOK OF OFFENSE 17:2--

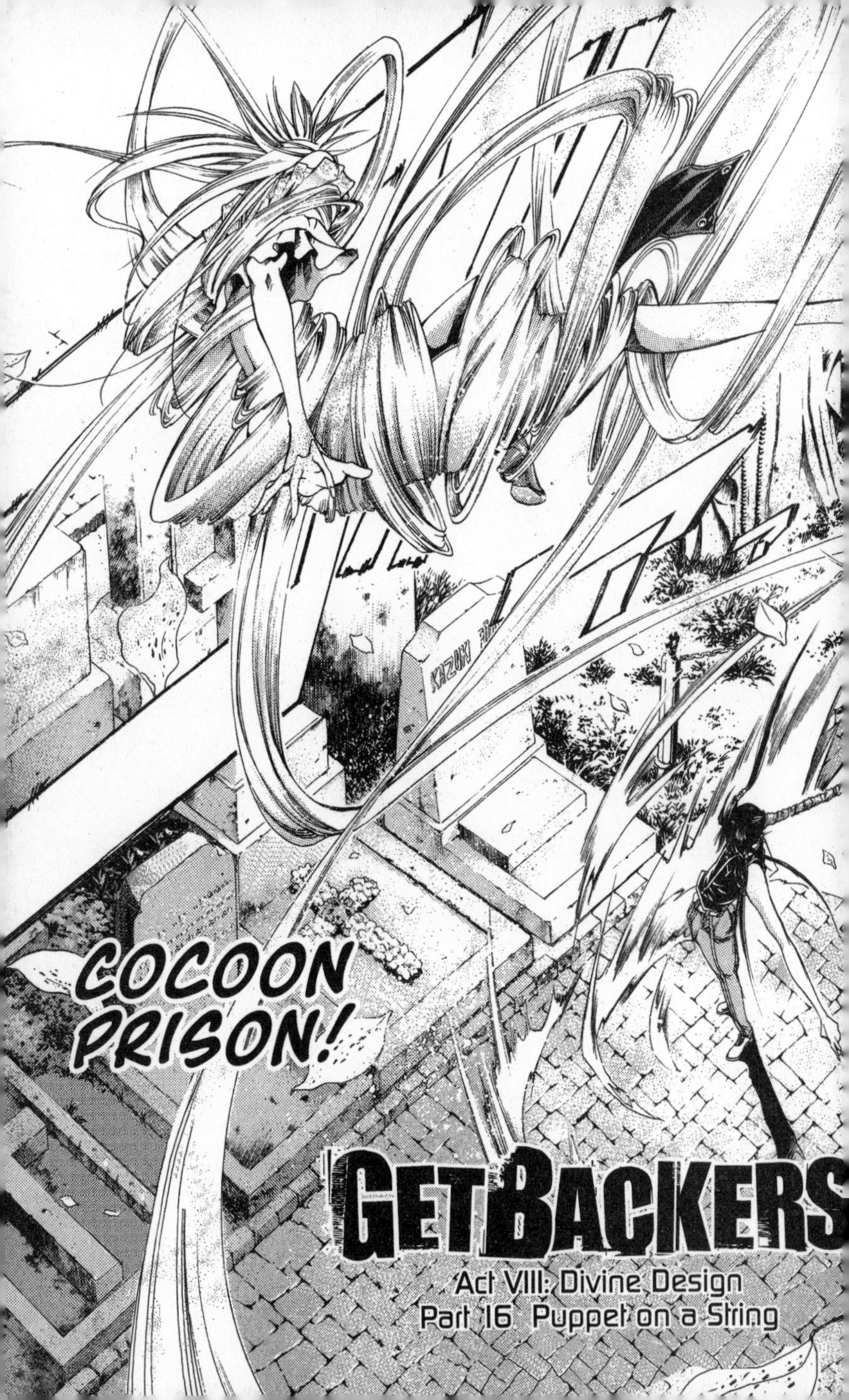
COCOON PRISON!
GETBACKERS
Act VIII: Divine Design
Part 16 Puppet on a String

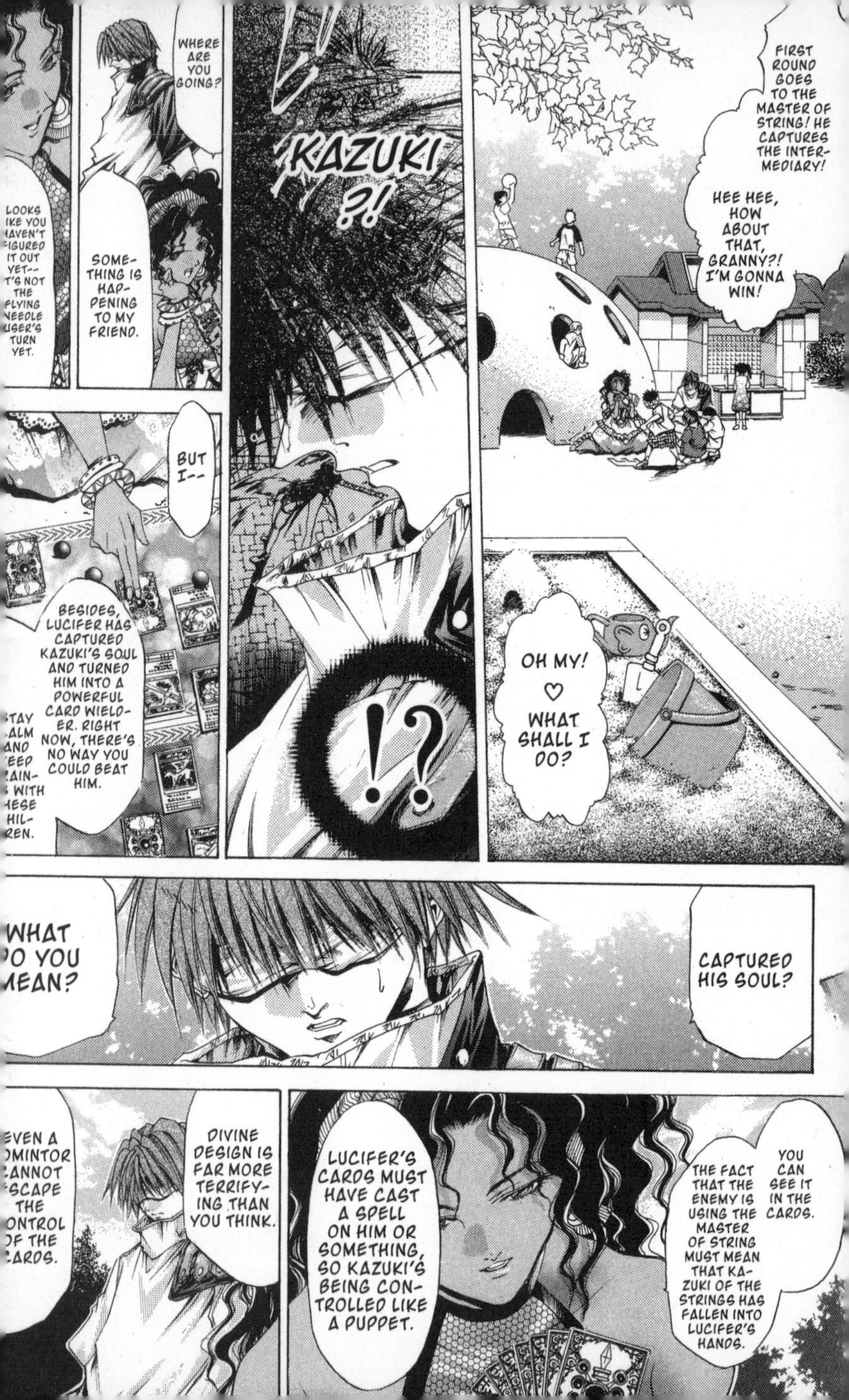
FIRST ROUND GOES TO THE MASTER OF STRING! HE CAPTURES THE INTER-MEDIARY!
HEE HEE, HOW ABOUT THAT, GRANNY?! I'M GONNA WIN!
OH MY! ♡ WHAT SHALL I DO?
KAZUKI ?!
!?
WHERE ARE YOU GOING?
SOME-THING IS HAP-PENING TO MY FRIEND.
LOOKS LIKE YOU HAVEN'T FIGURED IT OUT YET-- IT'S NOT THE FLYING NEEDLE USER'S TURN YET.
BUT I--
BESIDES, LUCIFER HAS CAPTURED KAZUKI'S SOUL AND TURNED HIM INTO A POWERFUL CARD WIELD-ER. RIGHT NOW, THERE'S NO WAY YOU COULD BEAT HIM.
STAY CALM AND KEEP PLAYIN-G WITH THESE CHIL-DREN.
CAPTURED HIS SOUL?
WHAT DO YOU MEAN?
YOU CAN SEE IT IN THE CARDS.
THE FACT THAT THE ENEMY IS USING THE MASTER OF STRING MUST MEAN THAT KA-ZUKI OF THE STRINGS HAS FALLEN INTO LUCIFER'S HANDS.
LUCIFER'S CARDS MUST HAVE CAST A SPELL ON HIM OR SOMETHING, SO KAZUKI'S BEING CON-TROLLED LIKE A PUPPET.
DIVINE DESIGN IS FAR MORE TERRIFY-ING THAN YOU THINK.
EVEN A DOMINTOR CANNOT ESCAPE THE CONTROL OF THE CARDS.

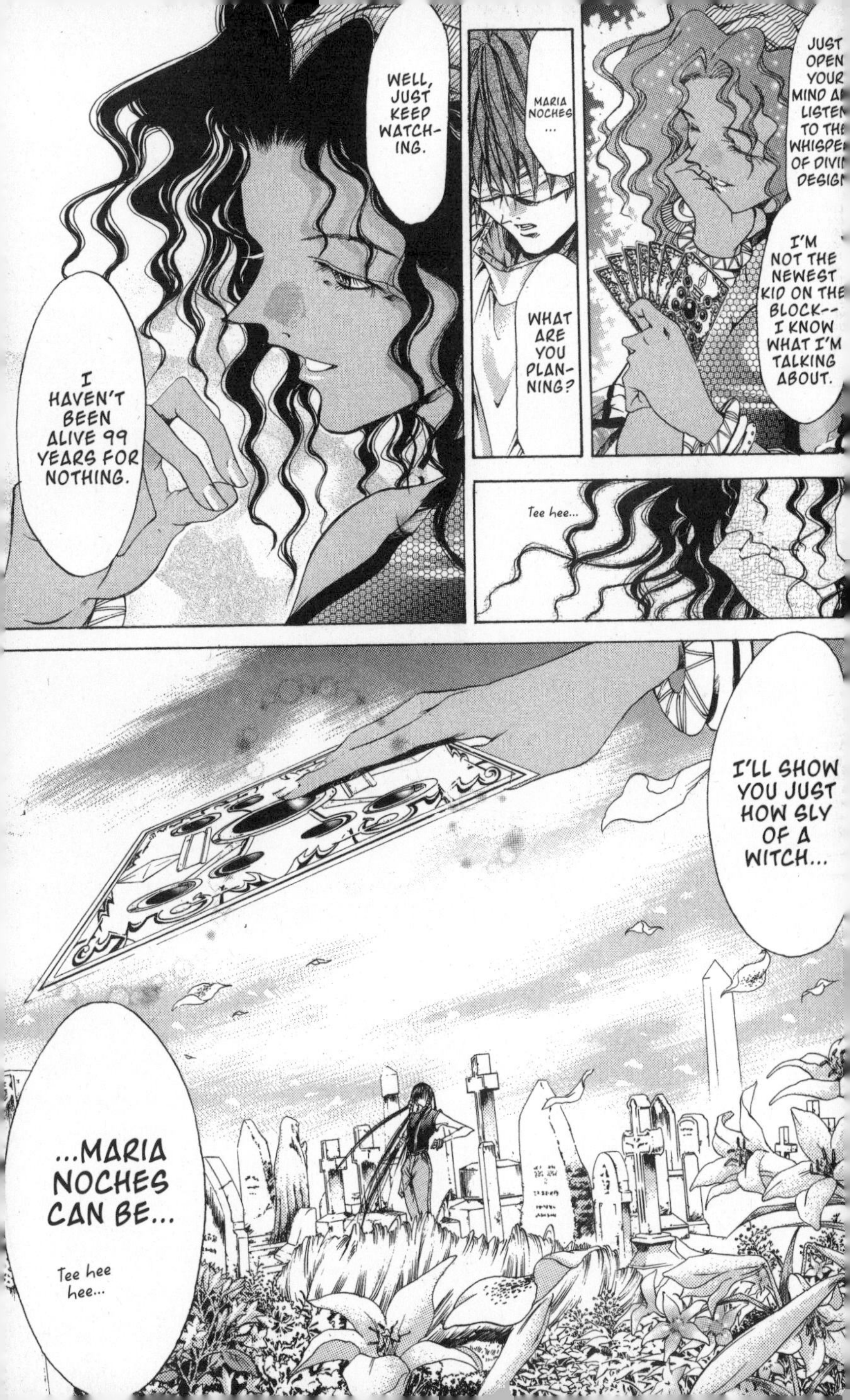
JUST OPEN YOUR MIND A LISTEN TO THE WHISPE OF DIVI DESIG
I'M NOT THE NEWEST KID ON THE BLOCK-- I KNOW WHAT I'M TALKING ABOUT.
MARIA NOCHES ...
WHAT ARE YOU PLANNING?
Tee hee...
WELL, JUST KEEP WATCHING.
I HAVEN'T BEEN ALIVE 99 YEARS FOR NOTHING.
I'LL SHOW YOU JUST HOW SLY OF A WITCH...
...MARIA NOCHES CAN BE...
Tee hee hee...

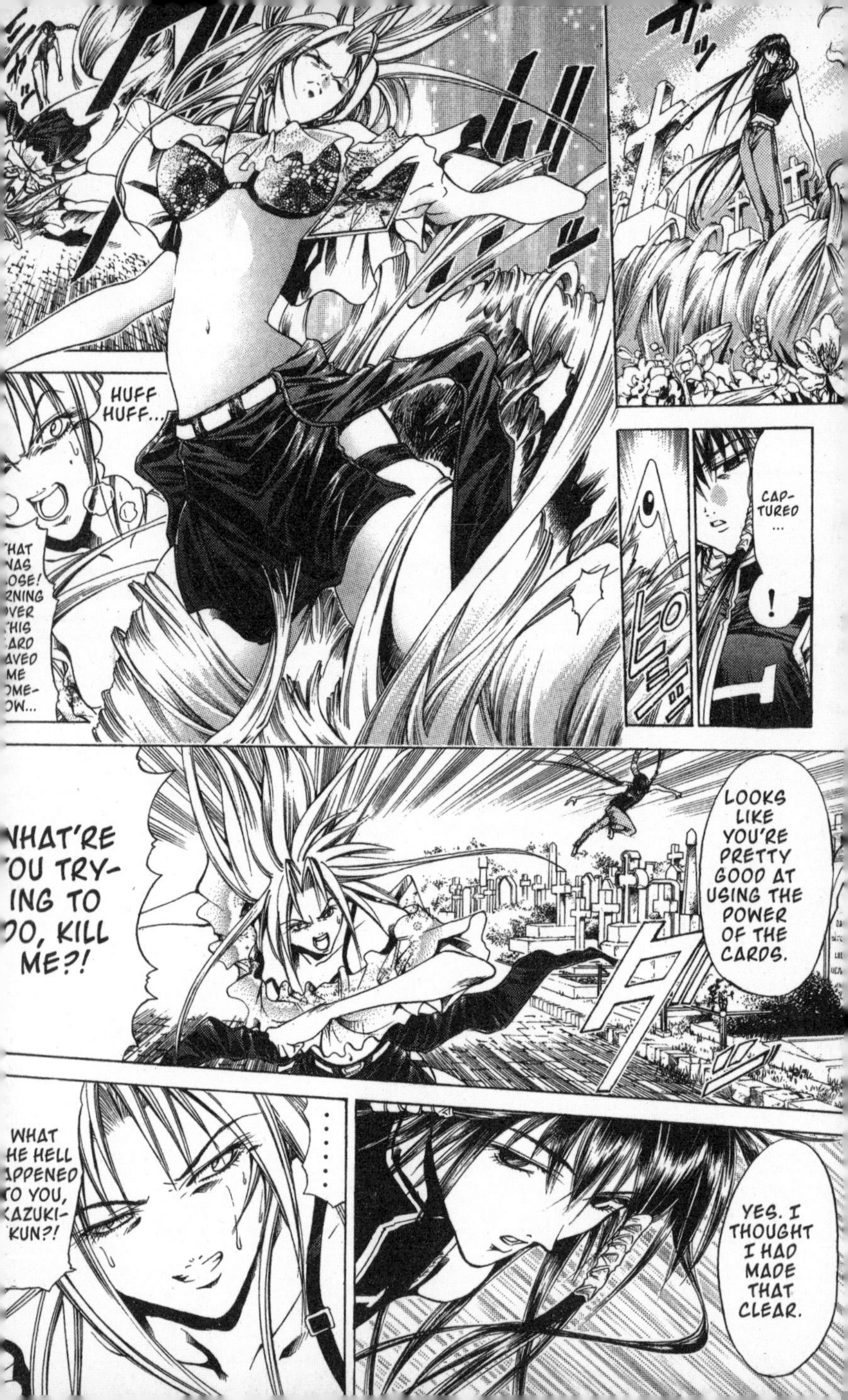
CAPTURED...
!
HUFF HUFF...
THAT WAS CLOSE! TURNING OVER THIS CARD SAVED ME SOMEHOW...
LOOKS LIKE YOU'RE PRETTY GOOD AT USING THE POWER OF THE CARDS.
WHAT'RE YOU TRYING TO DO, KILL ME?!
YES. I THOUGHT I HAD MADE THAT CLEAR.
.....
WHAT THE HELL HAPPENED TO YOU, KAZUKI-KUN?!

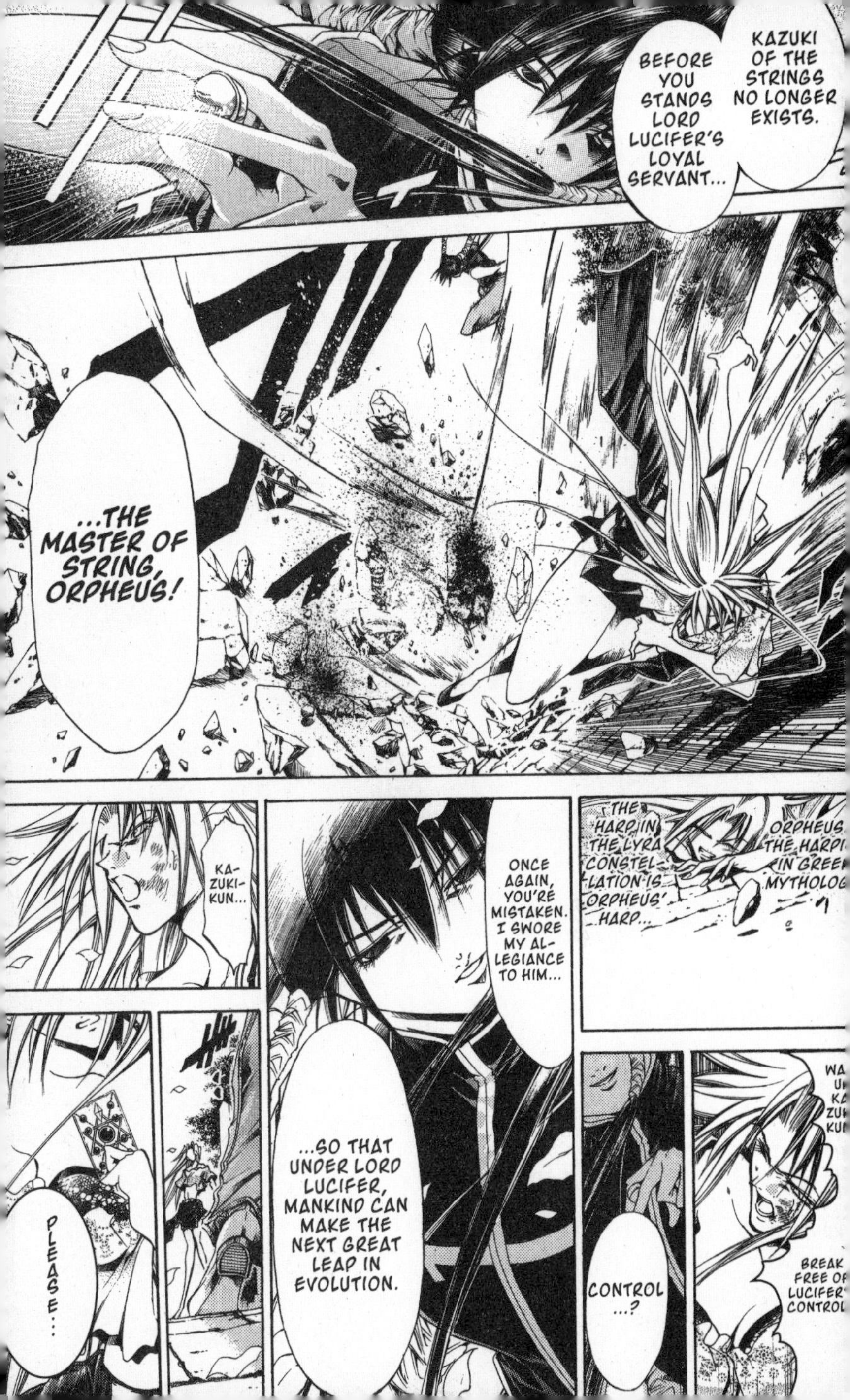
KAZUKI OF THE STRINGS NO LONGER EXISTS.
BEFORE YOU STANDS LORD LUCIFER'S LOYAL SERVANT...
...THE MASTER OF STRING, ORPHEUS!
ORPHEUS, THE HARPI IN GREE MYTHOLOG
THE HARP IN THE LYRA CONSTEL-LATION IS ORPHEUS' HARP...
WA U KA ZU KUN
BREAK FREE OF LUCIFER' CONTROL
CONTROL ...?
ONCE AGAIN, YOU'RE MISTAKEN. I SWORE MY AL-LEGIANCE TO HIM...
...SO THAT UNDER LORD LUCIFER, MANKIND CAN MAKE THE NEXT GREAT LEAP IN EVOLUTION.
KA-ZUKI-KUN...
PLEASE...

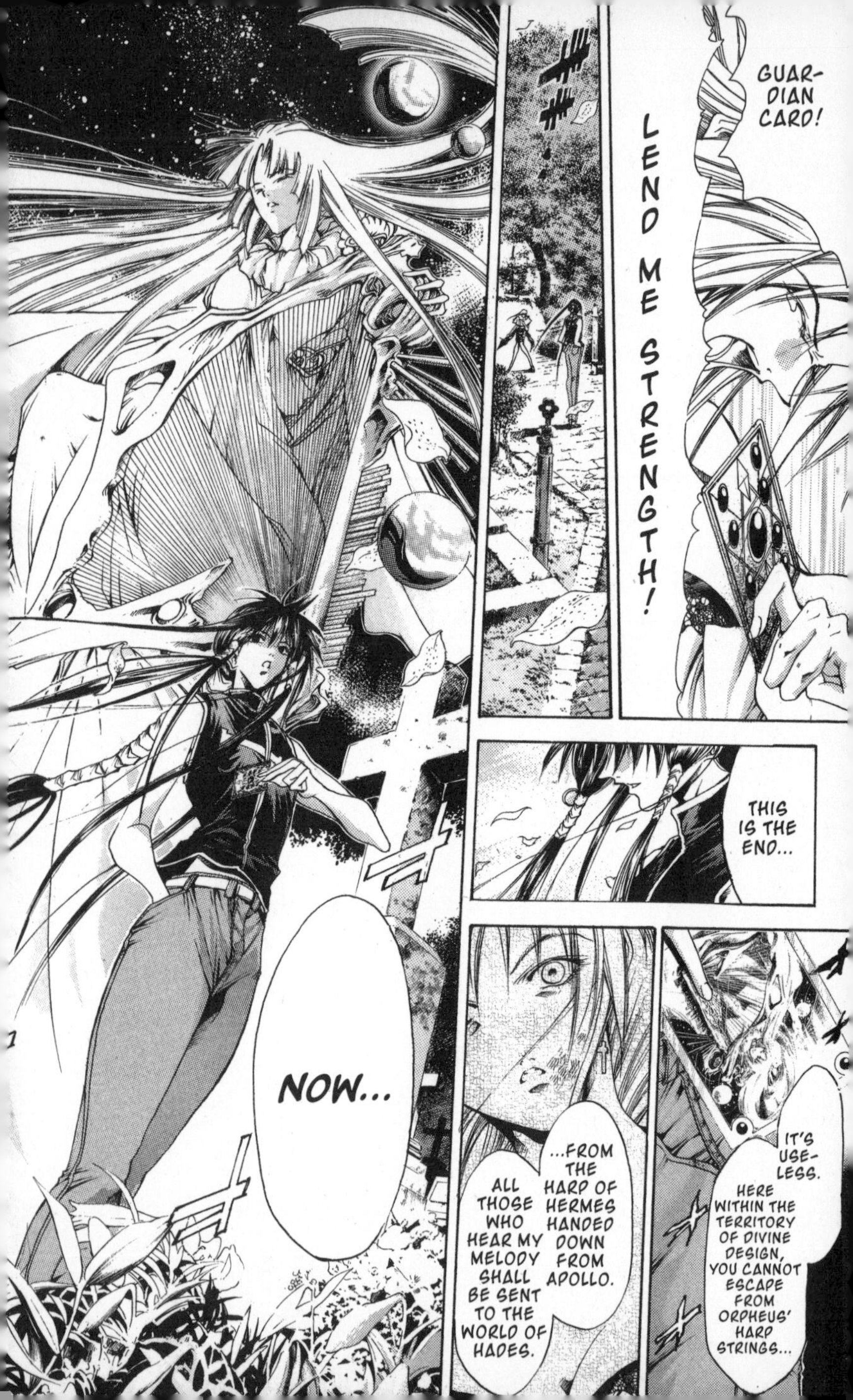
GUARDIAN CARD!
LEND ME STRENGTH!
THIS IS THE END...
IT'S USELESS.
HERE WITHIN THE TERRITORY OF DIVINE DESIGN, YOU CANNOT ESCAPE FROM ORPHEUS' HARP STRINGS...
...FROM THE HARP OF HERMES HANDED DOWN FROM APOLLO.
ALL THOSE WHO HEAR MY MELODY SHALL BE SENT TO THE WORLD OF HADES.
NOW...

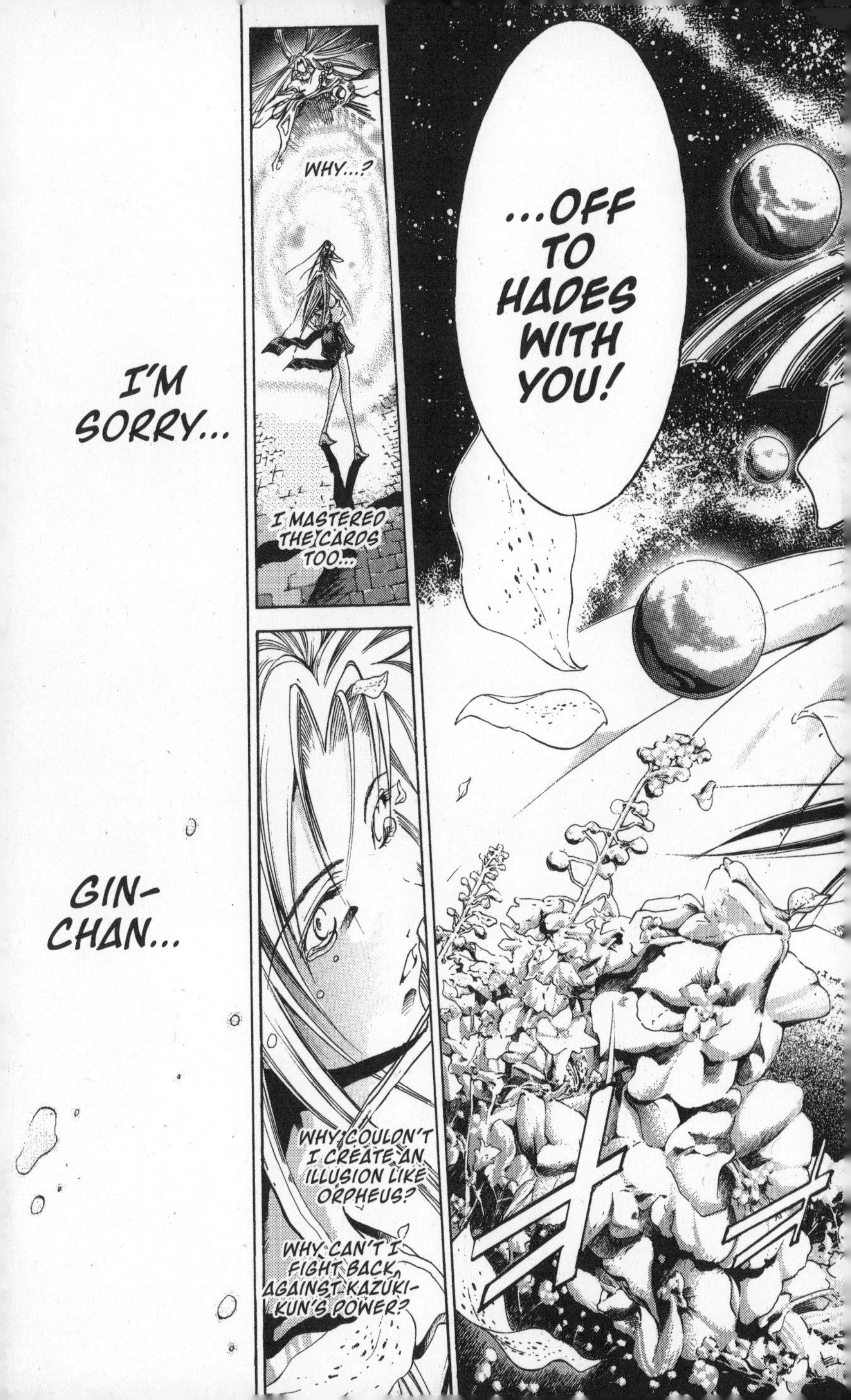
...OFF TO HADES WITH YOU!
WHY...?
I MASTERED THE CARDS TOO...
WHY COULDN'T I CREATE AN ILLUSION LIKE ORPHEUS?
WHY CAN'T I FIGHT BACK AGAINST KAZUKI-KUN'S POWER?
I'M SORRY...
GIN-CHAN...

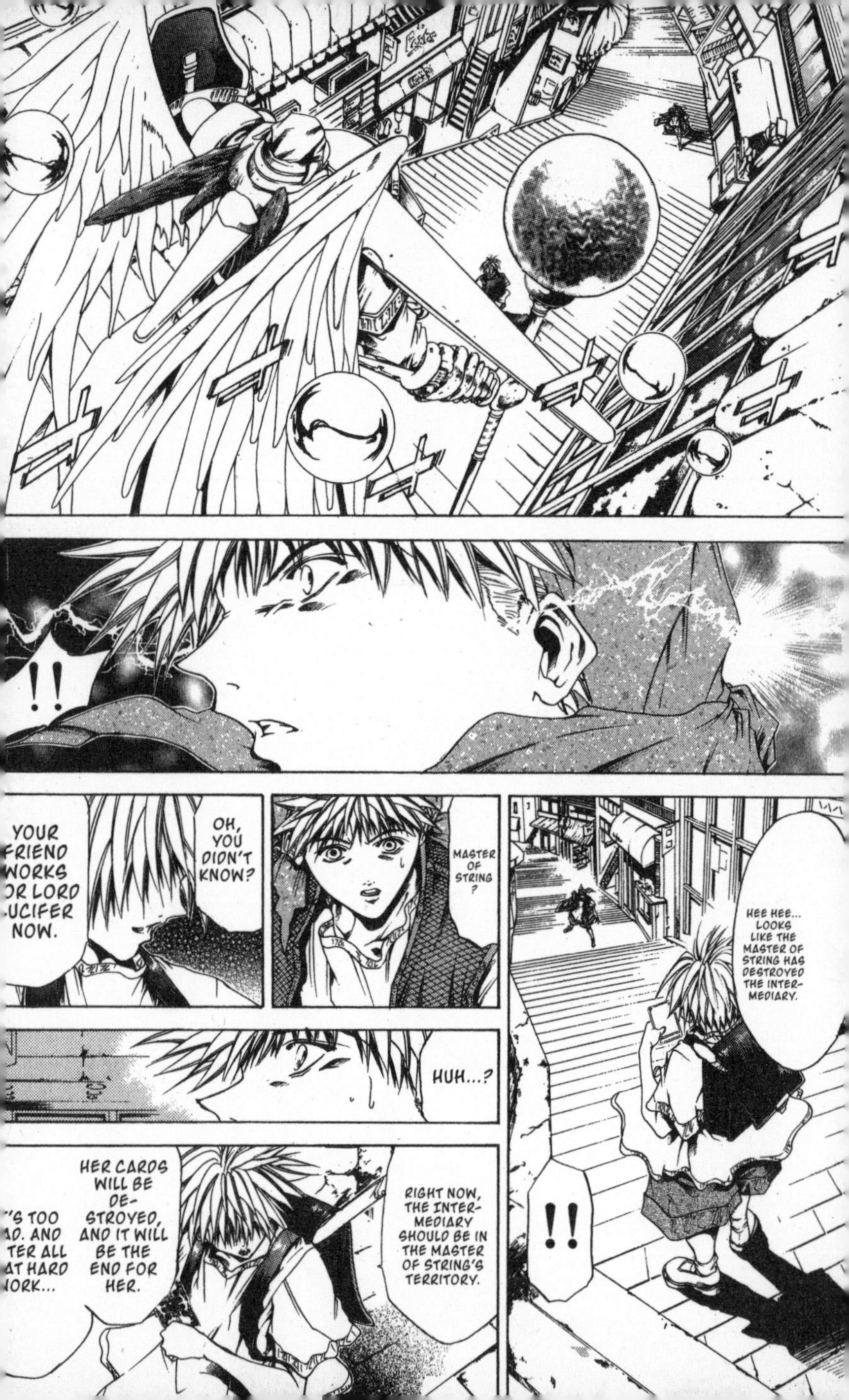
!!
HEE HEE... LOOKS LIKE THE MASTER OF STRING HAS DESTROYED THE INTER-MEDIARY.
!!
MASTER OF STRING?
OH, YOU DIDN'T KNOW?
YOUR FRIEND WORKS FOR LORD LUCIFER NOW.
HUH...?
RIGHT NOW, THE INTER-MEDIARY SHOULD BE IN THE MASTER OF STRING'S TERRITORY.
HER CARDS WILL BE DE-STROYED, AND IT WILL BE THE END FOR HER.
'S TOO AD. AND TER ALL AT HARD ORK...

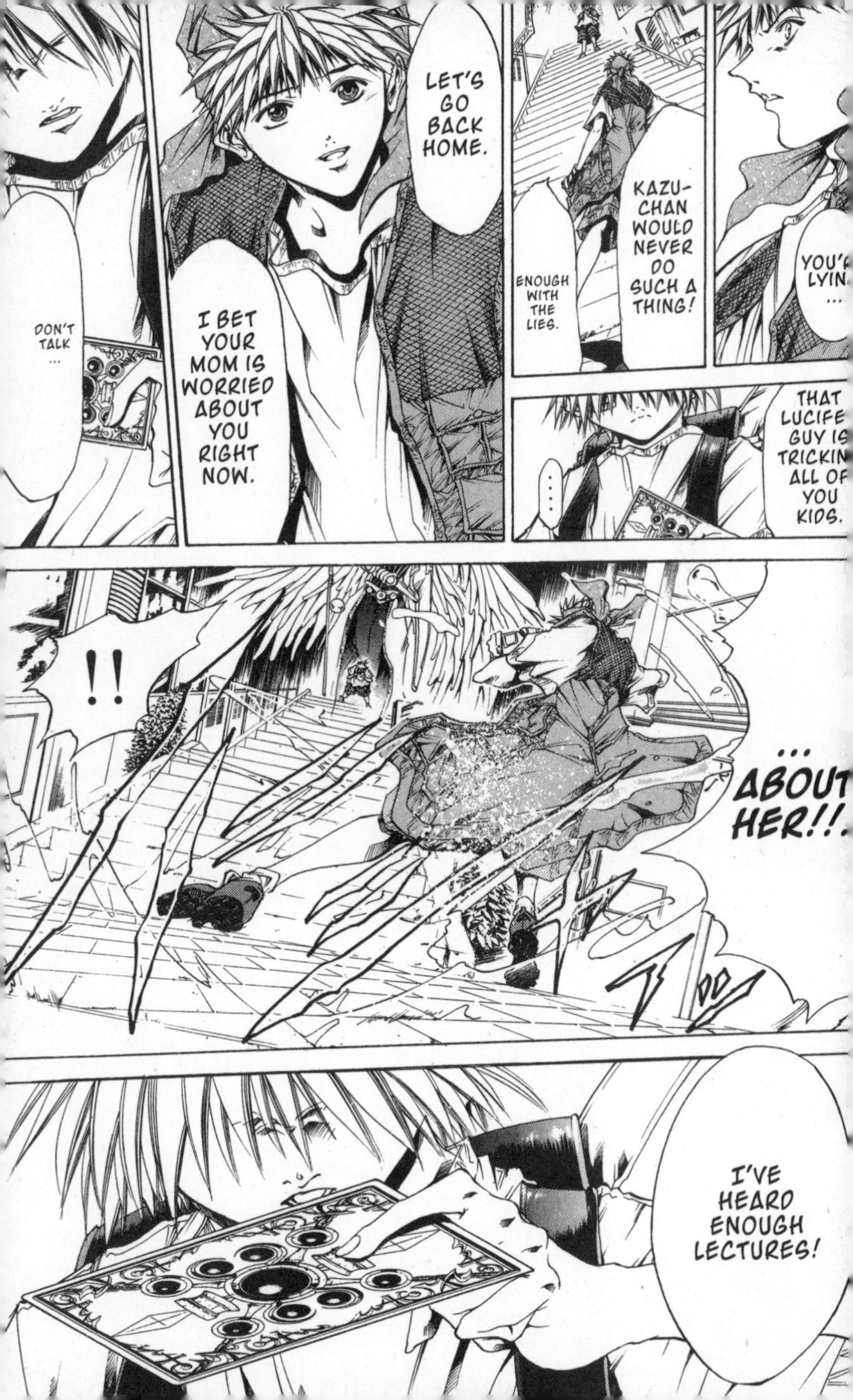
YOU'R LYIN ...
KAZU-CHAN WOULD NEVER DO SUCH A THING!
ENOUGH WITH THE LIES.
THAT LUCIFE GUY IS TRICKIN ALL OF YOU KIDS.
...
LET'S GO BACK HOME.
I BET YOUR MOM IS WORRIED ABOUT YOU RIGHT NOW.
DON'T TALK ...
... ABOUT HER!!
!!
I'VE HEARD ENOUGH LECTURES!

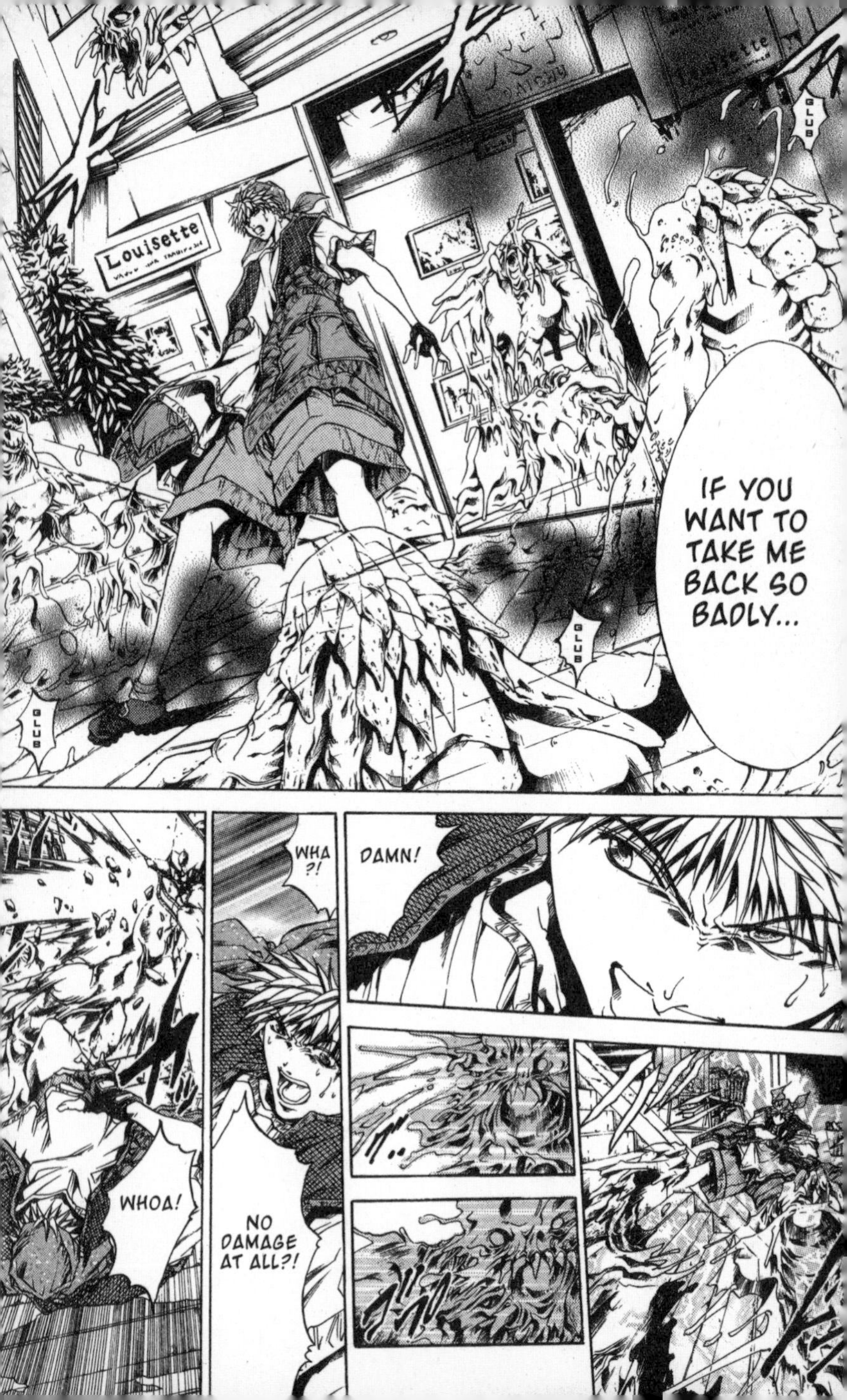
GLUB
IF YOU WANT TO TAKE ME BACK SO BADLY...
GLUB
Louisette
GLUB
DAMN!
WHA ?!
NO DAMAGE AT ALL?!
WHOA!

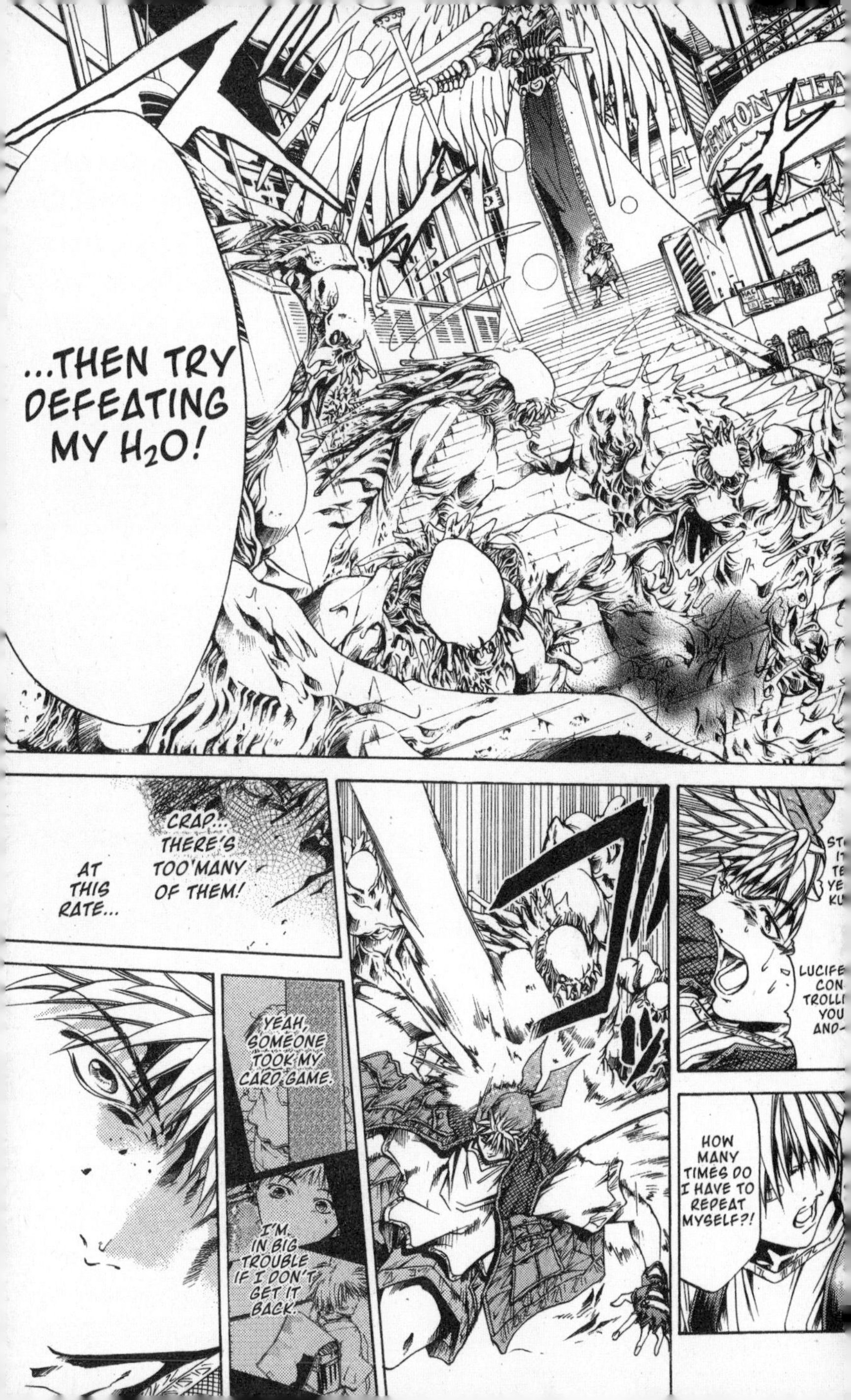
...THEN TRY DEFEATING MY H_2O!
LUCIFE CON TROLLI YOU AND–
CRAP... THERE'S TOO MANY OF THEM!
AT THIS RATE...
HOW MANY TIMES DO I HAVE TO REPEAT MYSELF?!
YEAH, SOMEONE TOOK MY CARD GAME.
I'M IN BIG TROUBLE IF I DON'T GET IT BACK.

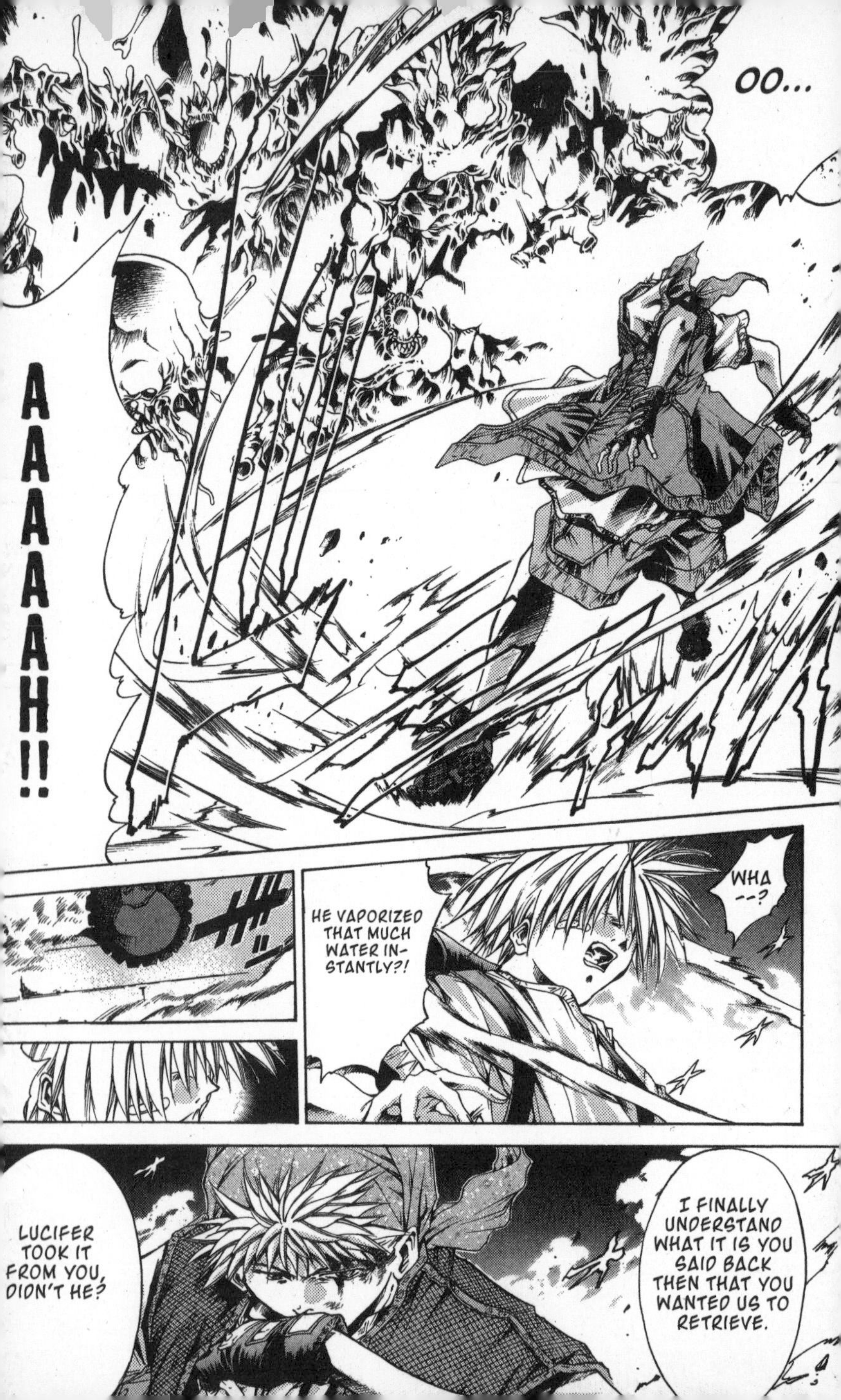
OO...
AAAAAAAH!!
WHA --?
HE VAPORIZED THAT MUCH WATER IN-STANTLY?!
I FINALLY UNDERSTAND WHAT IT IS YOU SAID BACK THEN THAT YOU WANTED US TO RETRIEVE.
LUCIFER TOOK IT FROM YOU, DIDN'T HE?

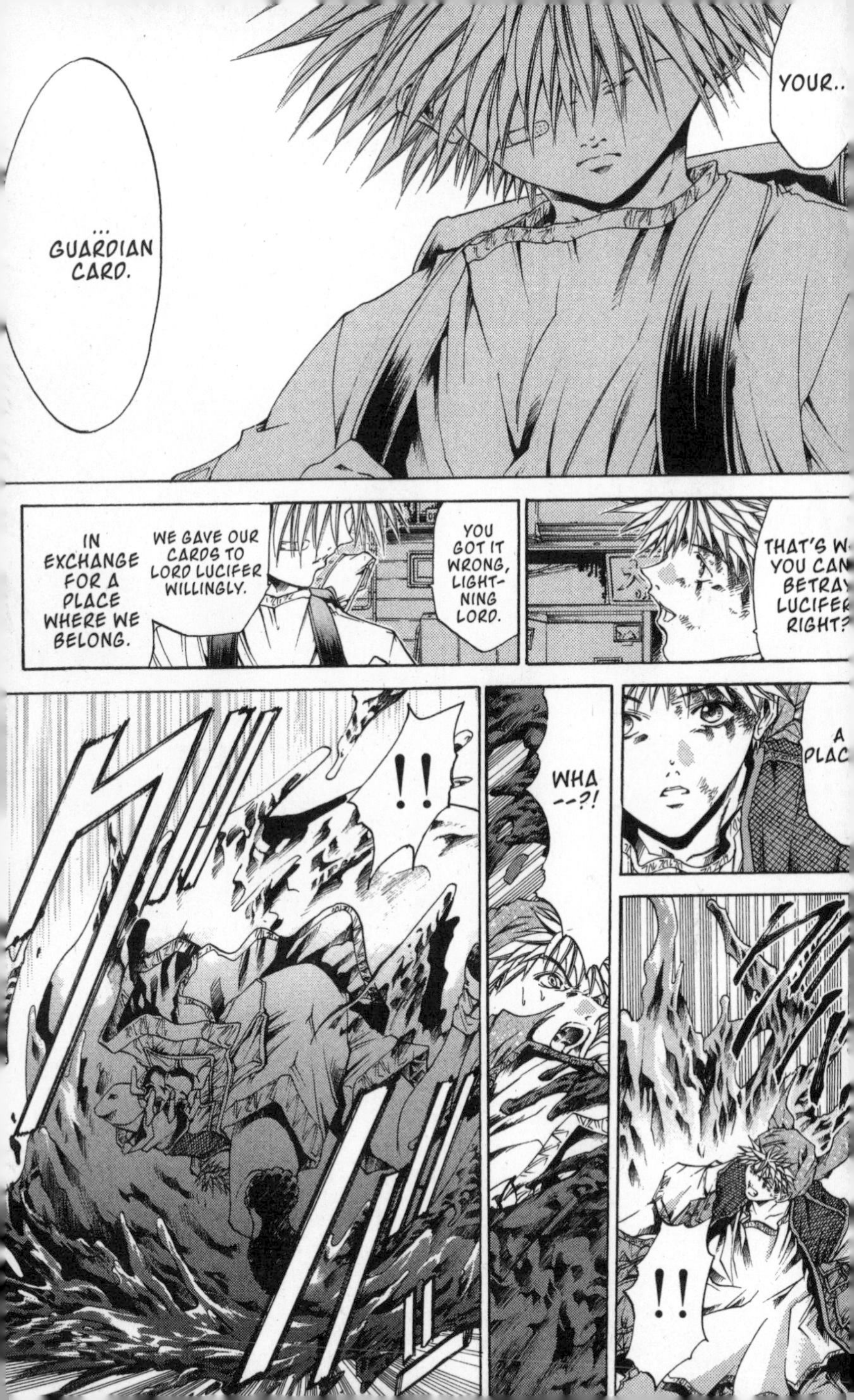
YOUR..
...GUARDIAN CARD.
THAT'S W
YOU CAN
BETRA
LUCIFER
RIGHT?
YOU GOT IT WRONG, LIGHT-NING LORD.
WE GAVE OUR CARDS TO LORD LUCIFER WILLINGLY.
IN EXCHANGE FOR A PLACE WHERE WE BELONG.
A PLAC
!!
WHA--?!
!!

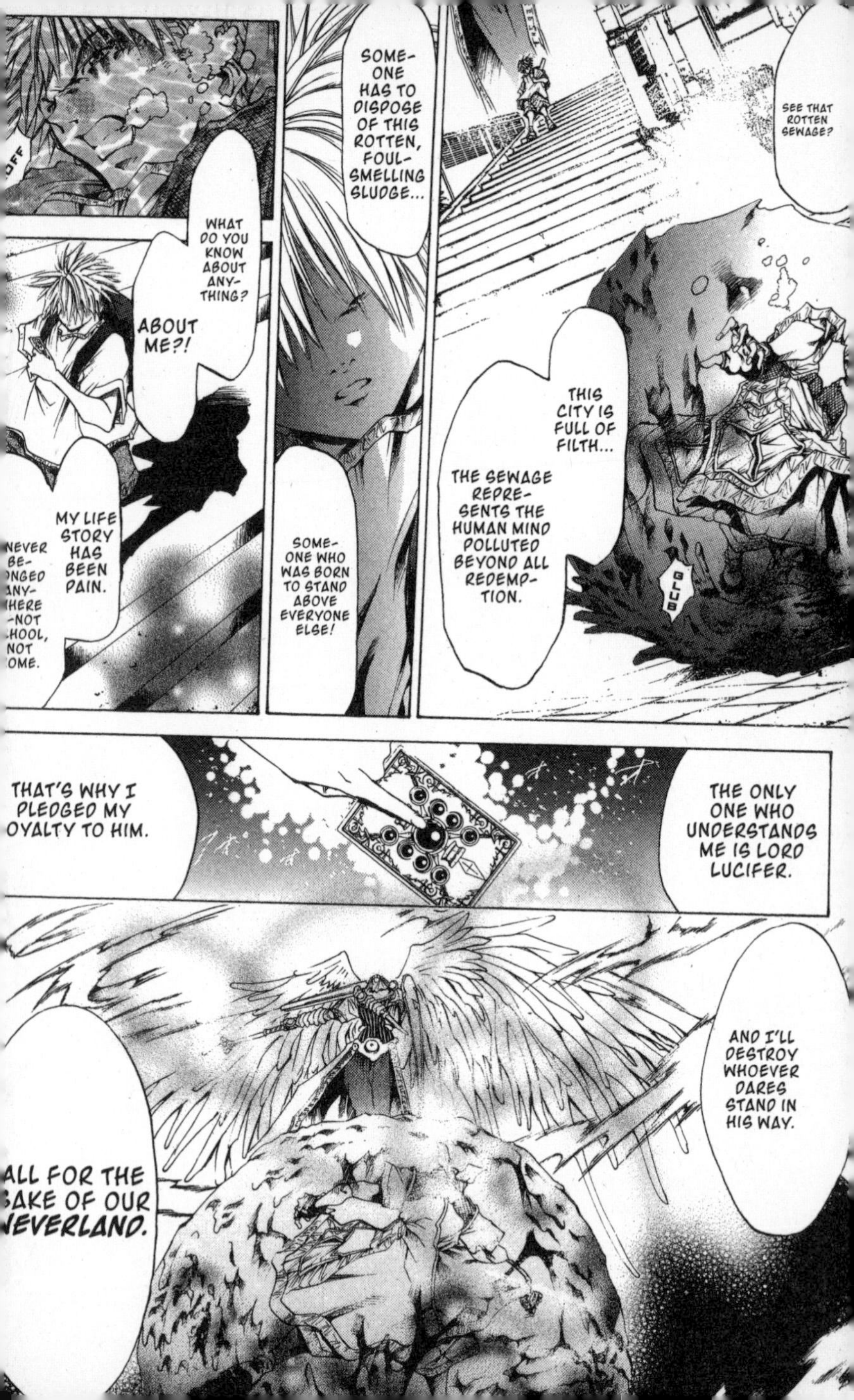
SEE THAT ROTTEN SEWAGE?
THIS CITY IS FULL OF FILTH...
THE SEWAGE REPRE-SENTS THE HUMAN MIND POLLUTED BEYOND ALL REDEMP-TION.
GLUB
SOME-ONE HAS TO DISPOSE OF THIS ROTTEN, FOUL-SMELLING SLUDGE...
SOME-ONE WHO WAS BORN TO STAND ABOVE EVERYONE ELSE!
OFF
WHAT DO YOU KNOW ABOUT ANY-THING?
ABOUT ME?!
MY LIFE STORY HAS BEEN PAIN.
NEVER BE-ONGED ANY-HERE -NOT CHOOL, NOT OME.
THE ONLY ONE WHO UNDERSTANDS ME IS LORD LUCIFER.
THAT'S WHY I PLEDGED MY OYALTY TO HIM.
AND I'LL DESTROY WHOEVER DARES STAND IN HIS WAY.
ALL FOR THE AKE OF OUR EVERLAND.

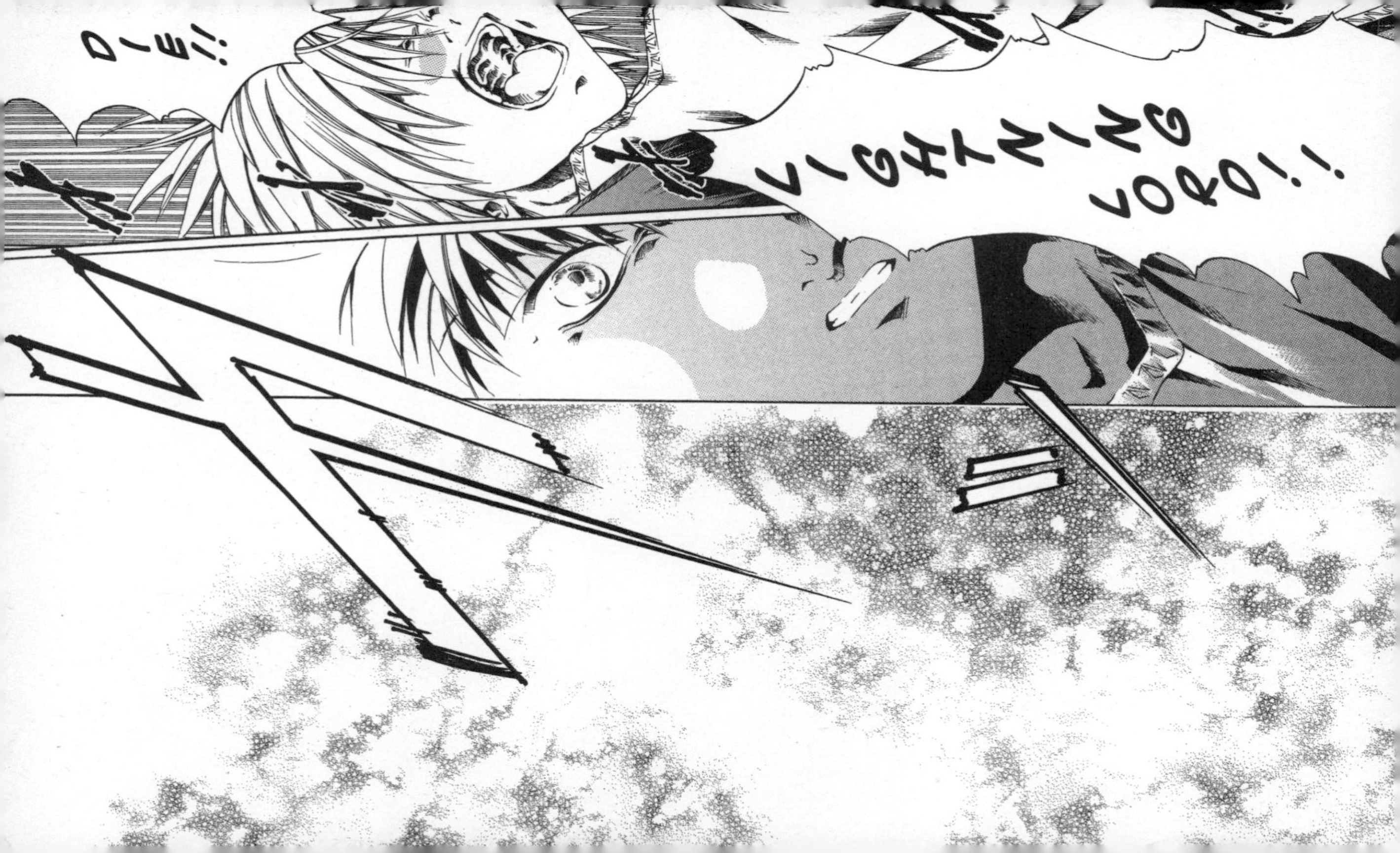
DIE!!
LIGHTNING LORD!!

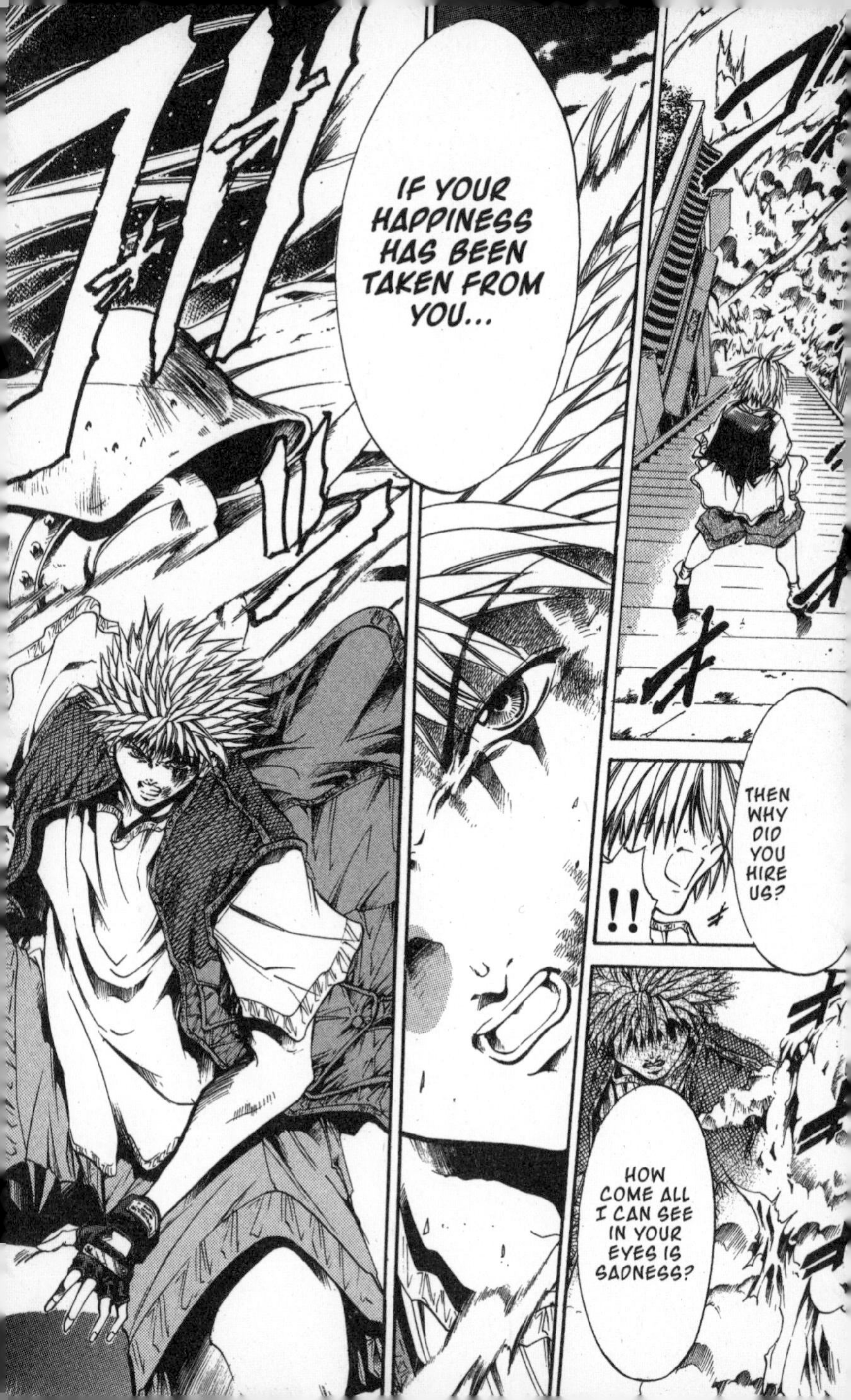
THEN WHY DID YOU HIRE US?
!!
HOW COME ALL I CAN SEE IN YOUR EYES IS SADNESS?
IF YOUR HAPPINESS HAS BEEN TAKEN FROM YOU...

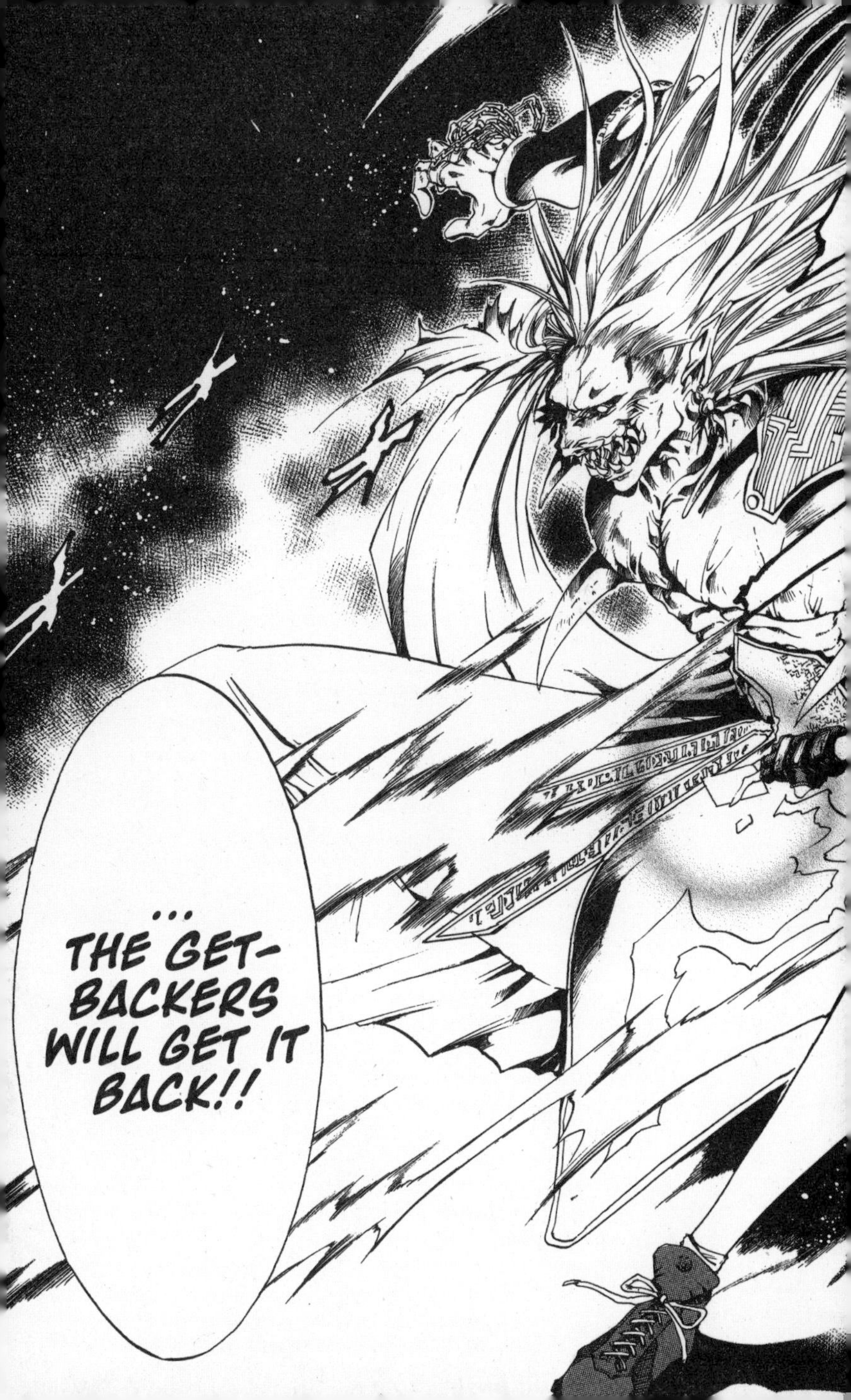
...THE GET-BACKERS WILL GET IT BACK!!

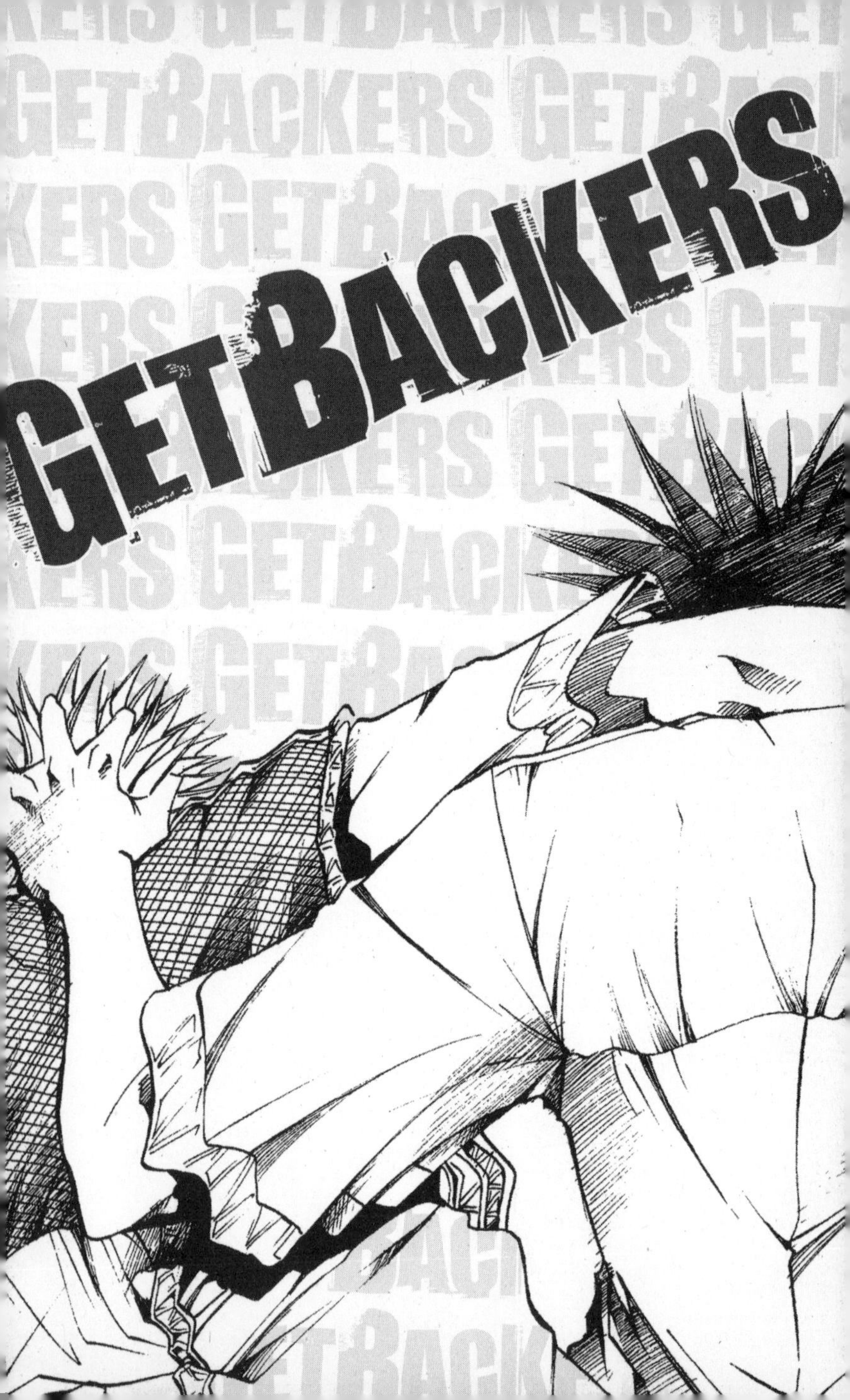
GETBACKERS

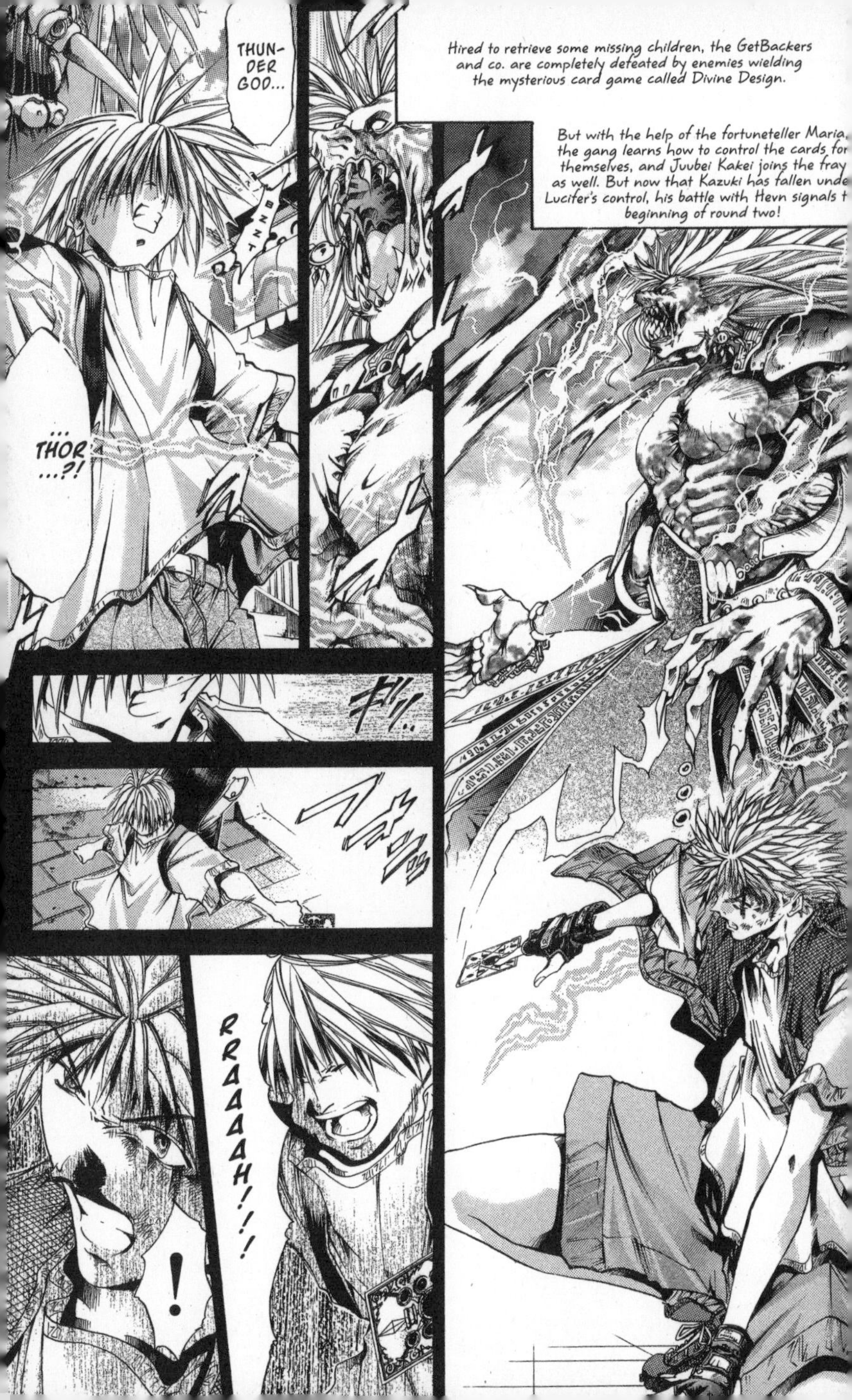
Hired to retrieve some missing children, the GetBackers and co. are completely defeated by enemies wielding the mysterious card game called Divine Design.
But with the help of the fortuneteller Maria, the gang learns how to control the cards for themselves, and Juubei Kakei joins the fray as well. But now that Kazuki has fallen unde Lucifer's control, his battle with Hevn signals t beginning of round two!
THUNDER GOD...
BZZT
...THOR...?!
RRAAAAAH!!!
!

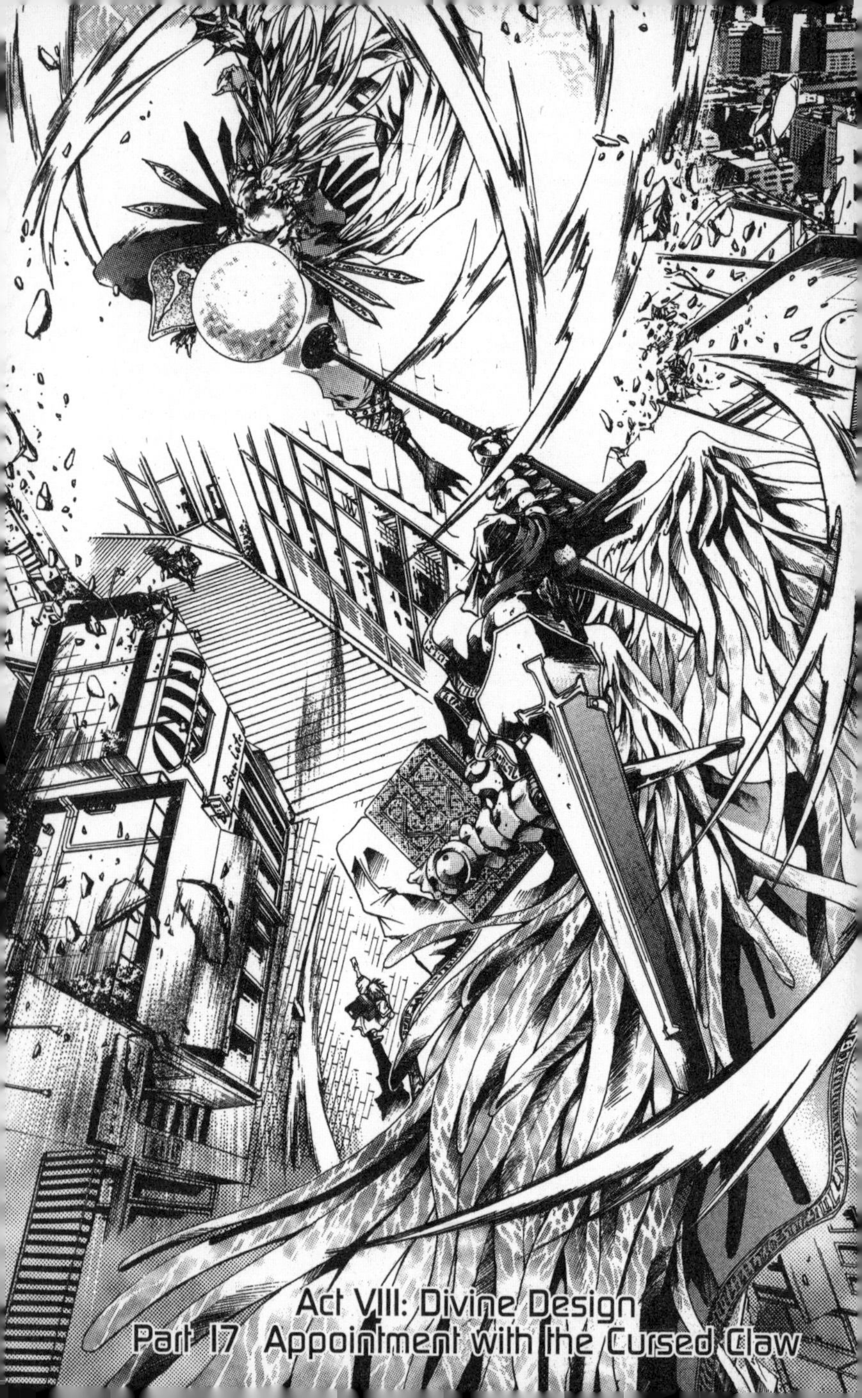

Act VIII: Divine Design
Part 17 Appointment with the Cursed Claw

GetBackers

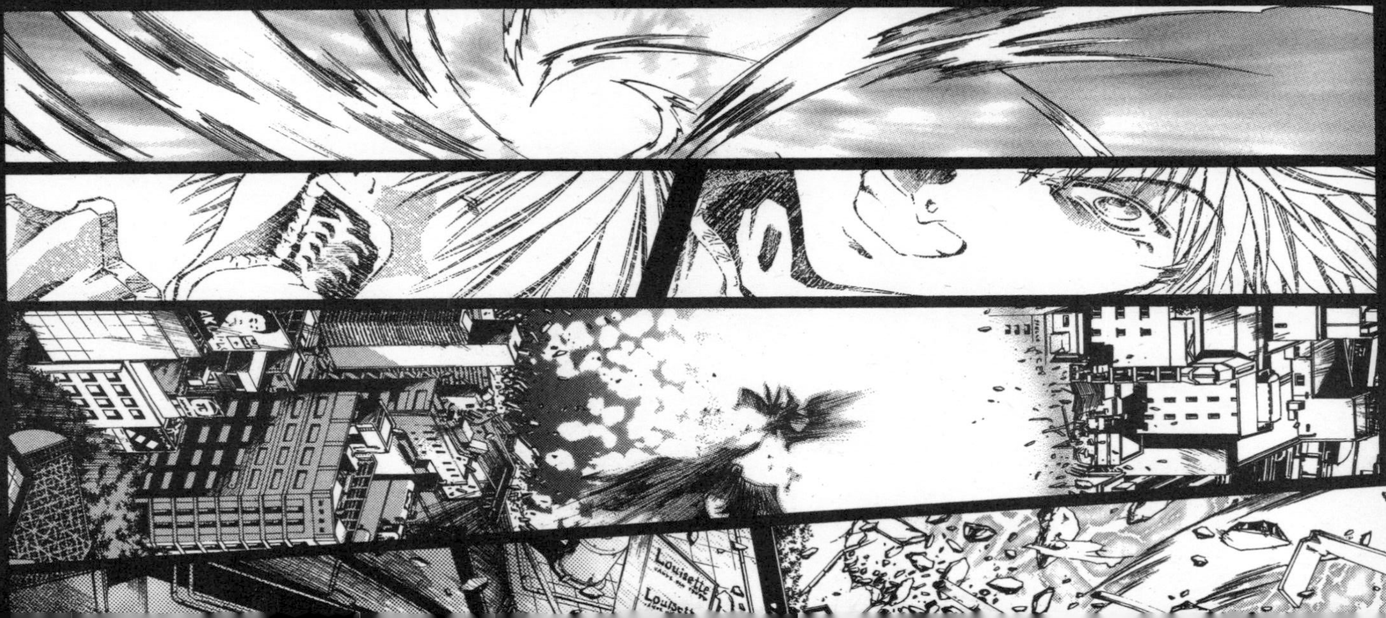
Louisette
Louisette

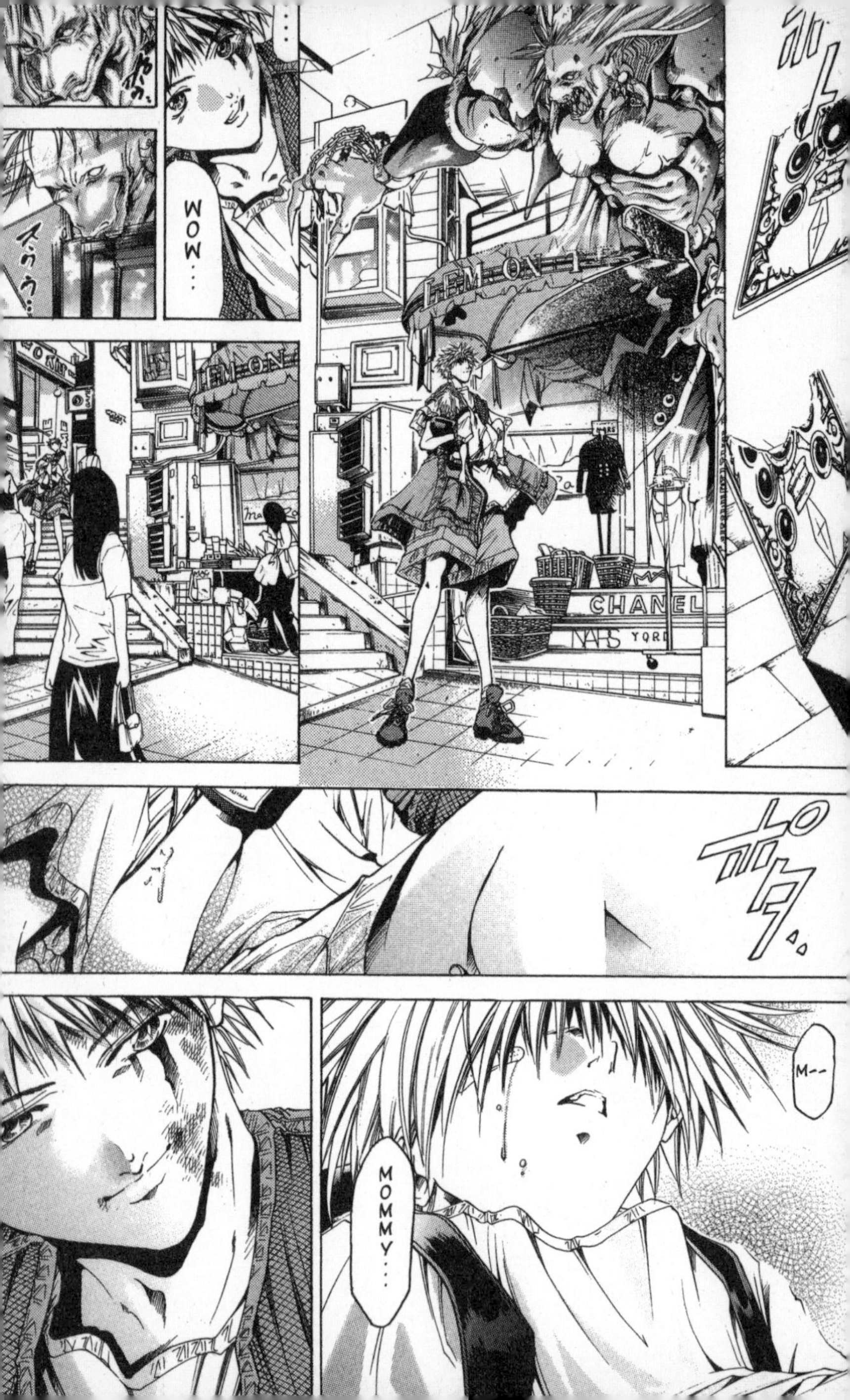
WOW...
M--
MOMMY...

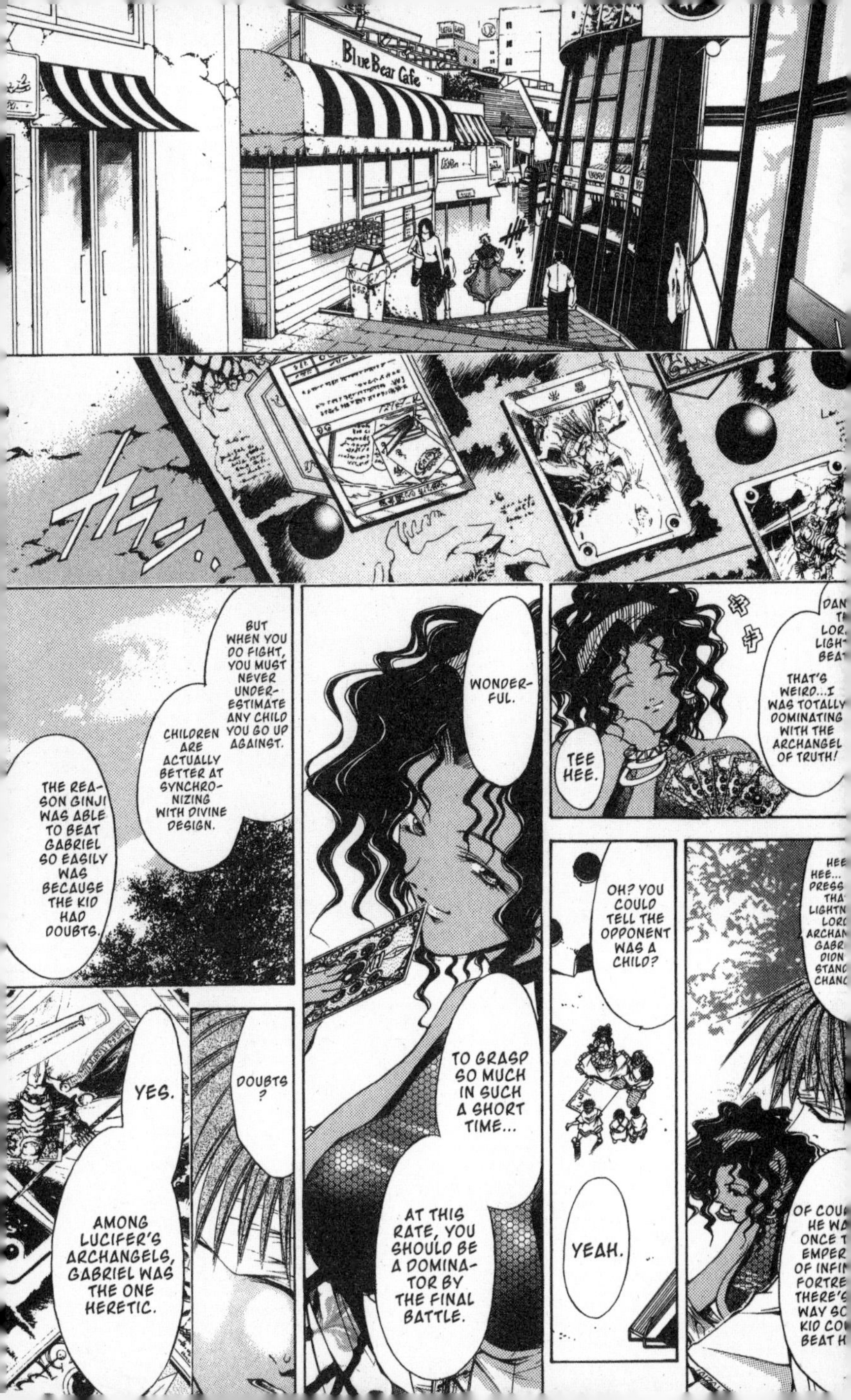

Blue Bear Cafe
カラン..
DAN TH LORD LIGHT BEAT
THAT'S WEIRD...I WAS TOTALLY DOMINATING WITH THE ARCHANGEL OF TRUTH!
TEE HEE.
HEE HEE... PRESS THA LIGHTN LORD ARCHAN GABR DION STAND CHANC
OH? YOU COULD TELL THE OPPONENT WAS A CHILD?
OF COU HE WA ONCE T EMPER OF INFIN FORTRE THERE'S WAY SO KID CO BEAT H
YEAH.
WONDERFUL.
TO GRASP SO MUCH IN SUCH A SHORT TIME...
AT THIS RATE, YOU SHOULD BE A DOMINATOR BY THE FINAL BATTLE.
BUT WHEN YOU DO FIGHT, YOU MUST NEVER UNDERESTIMATE ANY CHILD YOU GO UP AGAINST.
CHILDREN ARE ACTUALLY BETTER AT SYNCHRONIZING WITH DIVINE DESIGN.
THE REASON GINJI WAS ABLE TO BEAT GABRIEL SO EASILY WAS BECAUSE THE KID HAD DOUBTS.
DOUBTS?
YES.
AMONG LUCIFER'S ARCHANGELS, GABRIEL WAS THE ONE HERETIC.

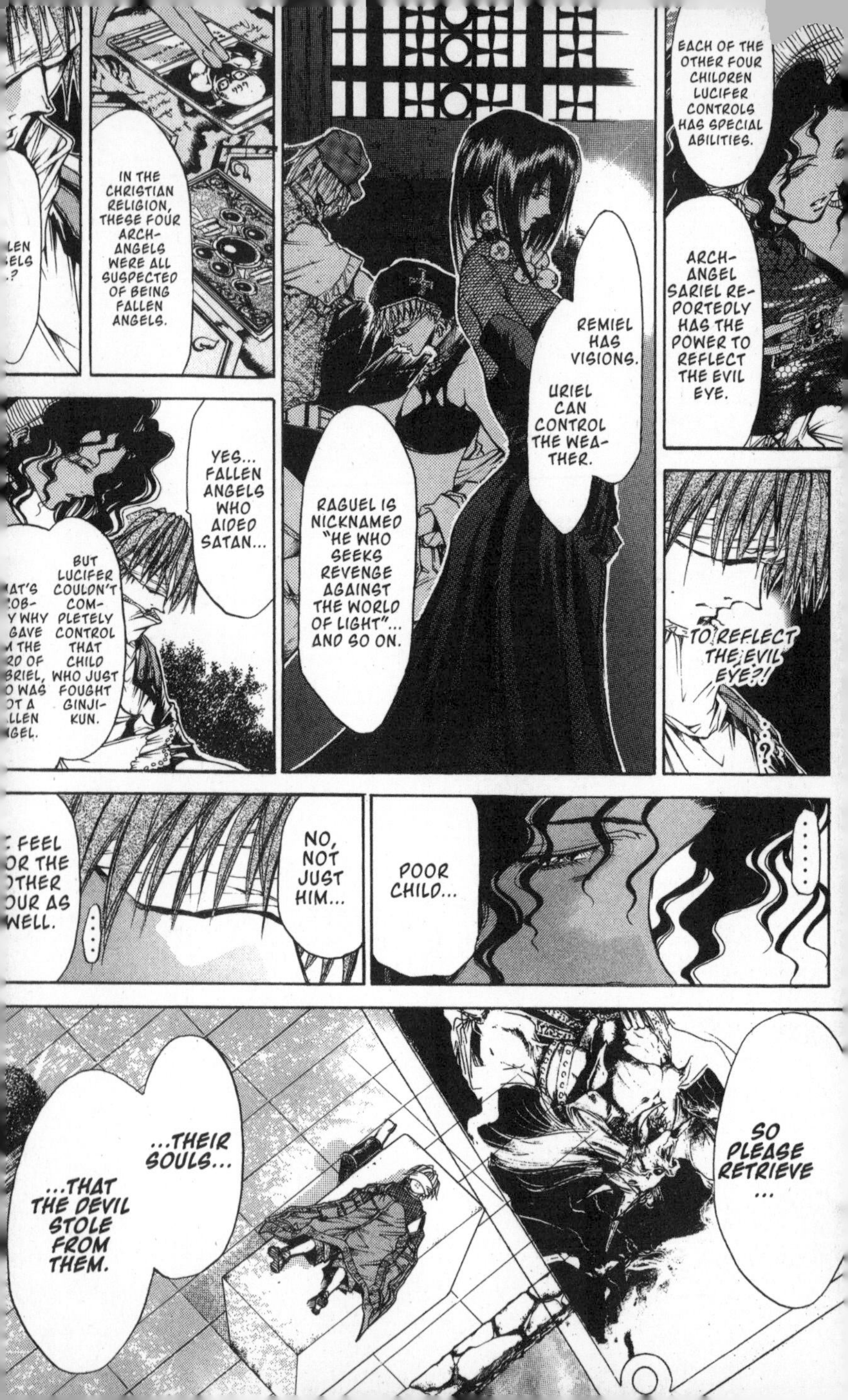
EACH OF THE OTHER FOUR CHILDREN LUCIFER CONTROLS HAS SPECIAL ABILITIES.
ARCH-ANGEL SARIEL RE-PORTEDLY HAS THE POWER TO REFLECT THE EVIL EYE.
TO REFLECT THE EVIL EYE?!
REMIEL HAS VISIONS.
URIEL CAN CONTROL THE WEA-THER.
RAGUEL IS NICKNAMED "HE WHO SEEKS REVENGE AGAINST THE WORLD OF LIGHT"... AND SO ON.
IN THE CHRISTIAN RELIGION, THESE FOUR ARCH-ANGELS WERE ALL SUSPECTED OF BEING FALLEN ANGELS.
LEN ELS .?
YES... FALLEN ANGELS WHO AIDED SATAN...
BUT LUCIFER COULDN'T COM-PLETELY CONTROL THAT CHILD WHO JUST FOUGHT GINJI-KUN.
AT'S ROB-Y WHY GAVE M THE RD OF BRIEL, O WAS T A LLEN GEL.
......
POOR CHILD...
NO, NOT JUST HIM...
E FEEL OR THE OTHER OUR AS WELL.
...
SO PLEASE RETRIEVE...
...THEIR SOULS...
...THAT THE DEVIL STOLE FROM THEM.

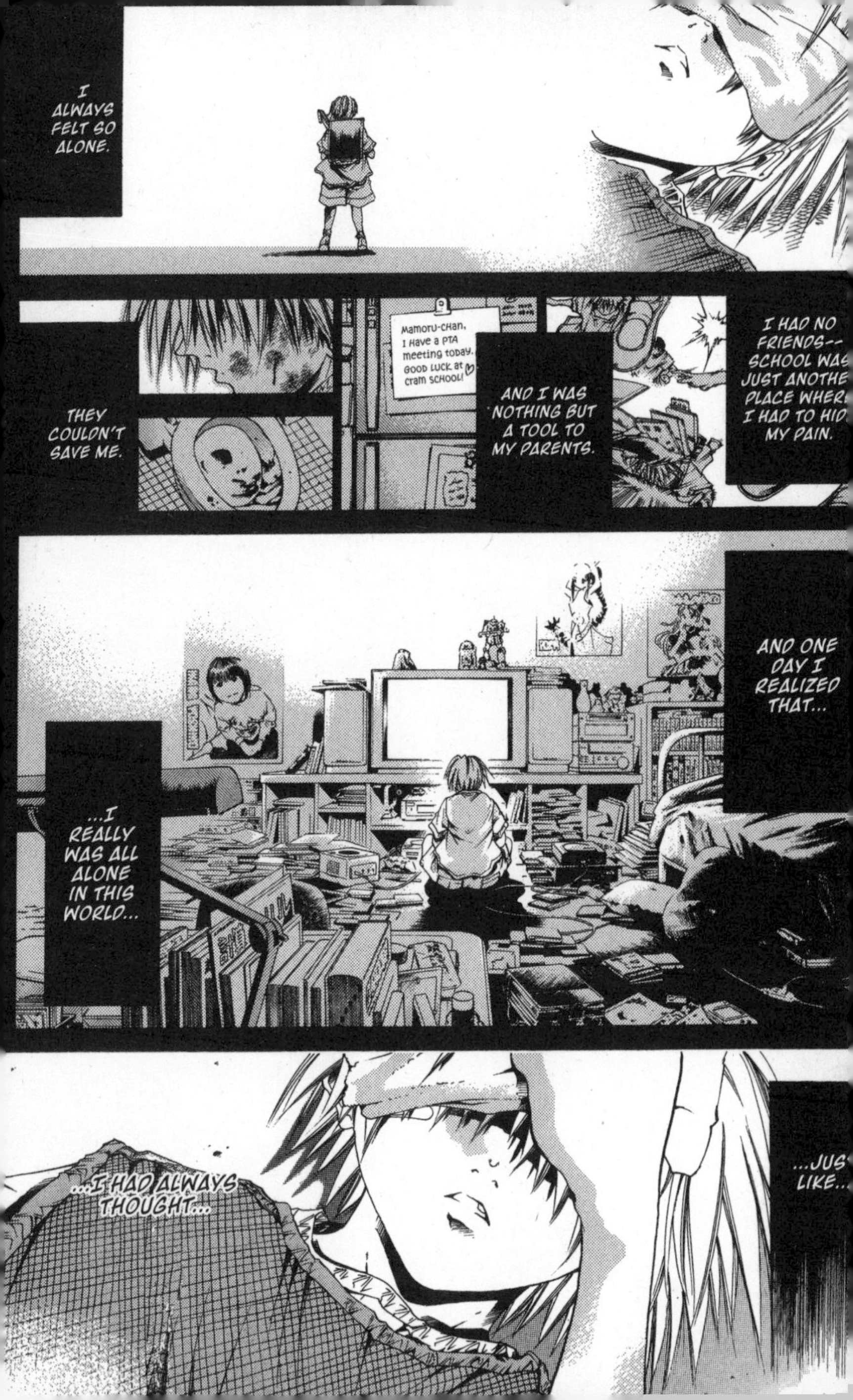
I ALWAYS FELT SO ALONE.
I HAD NO FRIENDS-- SCHOOL WAS JUST ANOTHE PLACE WHER I HAD TO HID MY PAIN.
Mamoru-chan, I have a PTA meeting today. Good luck at cram school!
AND I WAS NOTHING BUT A TOOL TO MY PARENTS.
THEY COULDN'T SAVE ME.
AND ONE DAY I REALIZED THAT...
...I REALLY WAS ALL ALONE IN THIS WORLD...
...JUS LIKE...
...I HAD ALWAYS THOUGHT...

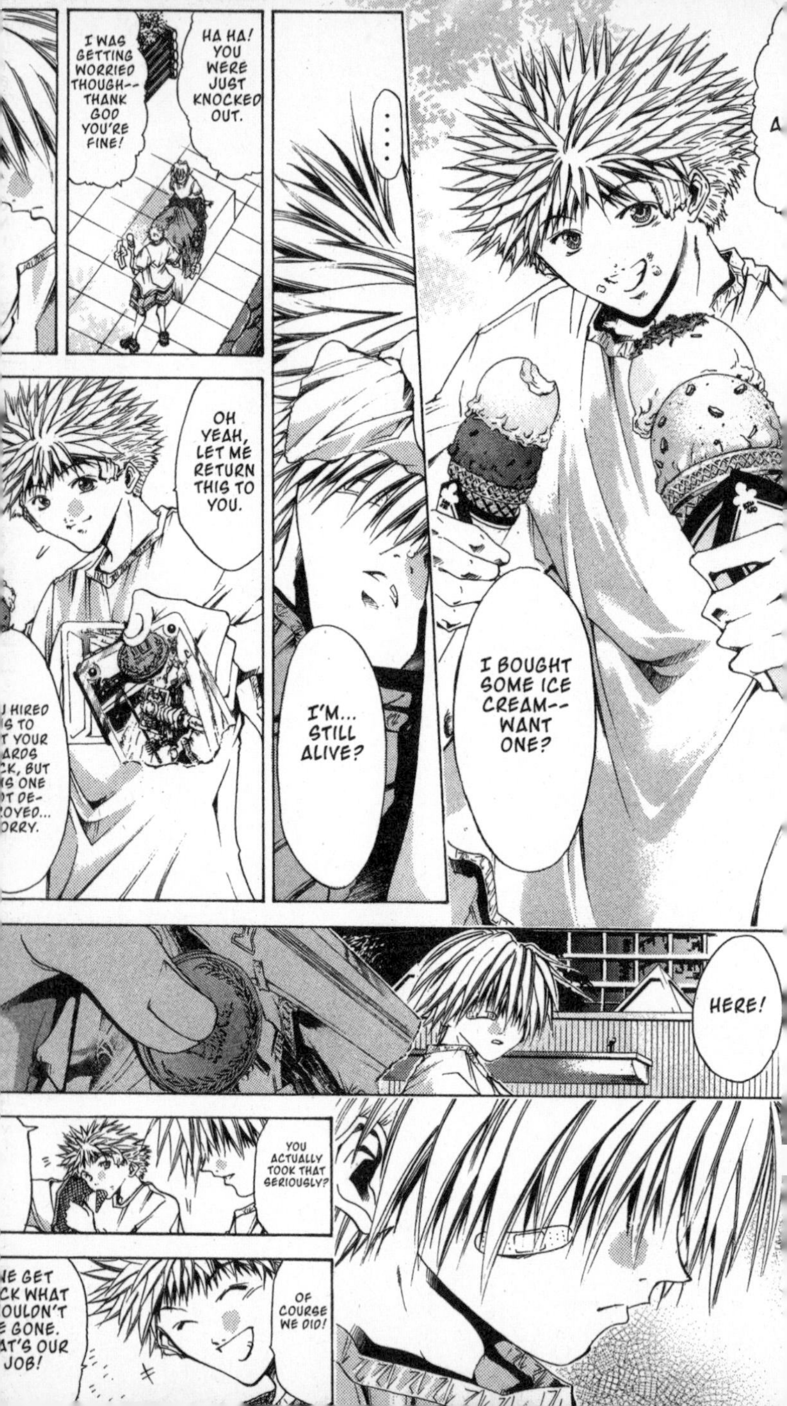
I BOUGHT SOME ICE CREAM--WANT ONE?
......
I'M... STILL ALIVE?
HA HA! YOU WERE JUST KNOCKED OUT.
I WAS GETTING WORRIED THOUGH--THANK GOD YOU'RE FINE!
OH YEAH, LET ME RETURN THIS TO YOU.
U HIRED S TO T YOUR ARDS CK, BUT S ONE OT DE- ROYED... ORRY.
HERE!
YOU ACTUALLY TOOK THAT SERIOUSLY?
OF COURSE WE DID!
E GET CK WHAT OULDN'T E GONE. AT'S OUR JOB!

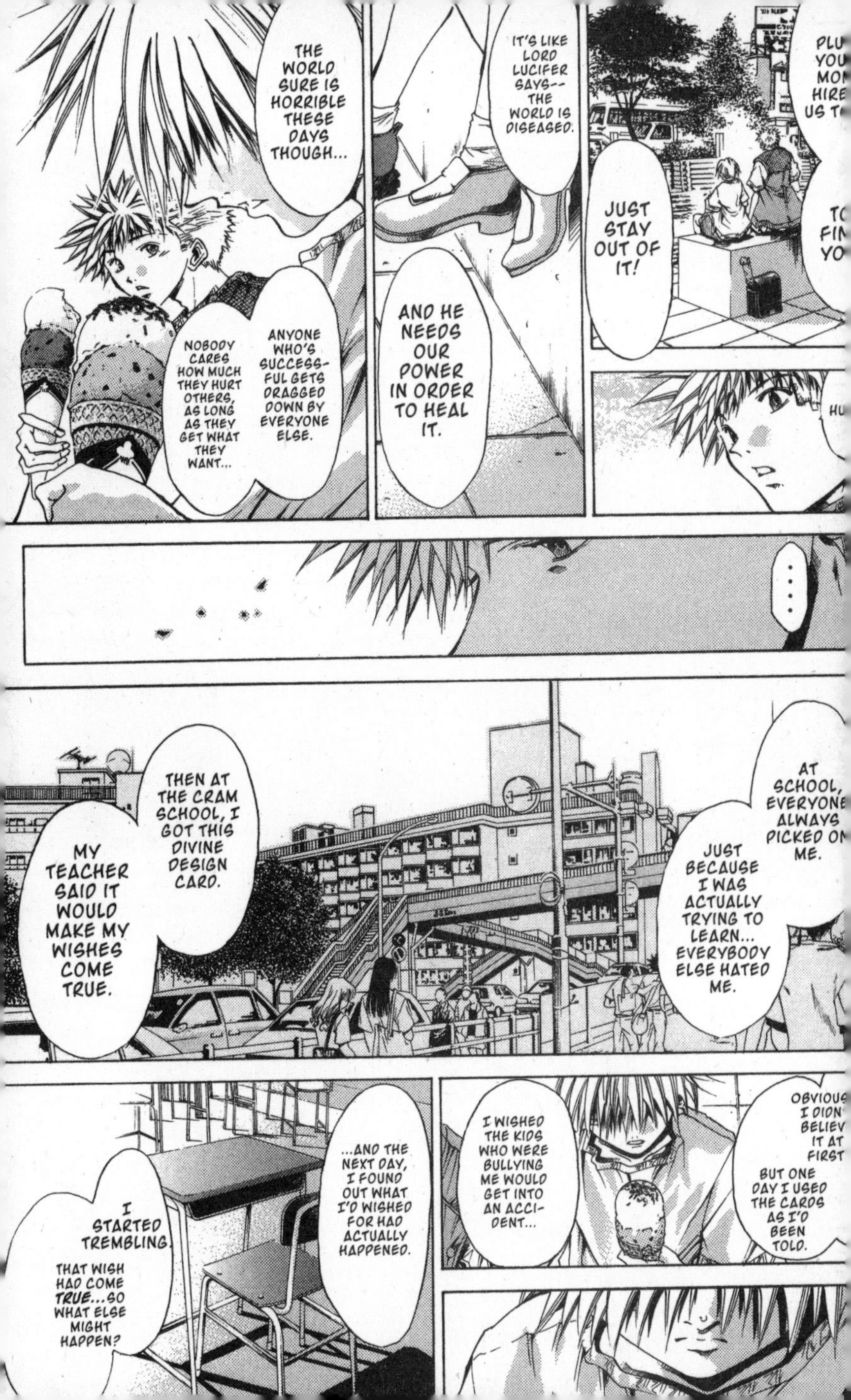
PLU YOU MON HIRE US T
TO FIN YO
JUST STAY OUT OF IT!
HU
IT'S LIKE LORD LUCIFER SAYS-- THE WORLD IS DISEASED.
AND HE NEEDS OUR POWER IN ORDER TO HEAL IT.
THE WORLD SURE IS HORRIBLE THESE DAYS THOUGH...
ANYONE WHO'S SUCCESS-FUL GETS DRAGGED DOWN BY EVERYONE ELSE.
NOBODY CARES HOW MUCH THEY HURT OTHERS, AS LONG AS THEY GET WHAT THEY WANT...
....
AT SCHOOL, EVERYONE ALWAYS PICKED ON ME.
JUST BECAUSE I WAS ACTUALLY TRYING TO LEARN... EVERYBODY ELSE HATED ME.
THEN AT THE CRAM SCHOOL, I GOT THIS DIVINE DESIGN CARD.
MY TEACHER SAID IT WOULD MAKE MY WISHES COME TRUE.
OBVIOUS I DIDN' BELIEVE IT AT FIRST
BUT ONE DAY I USED THE CARDS AS I'D BEEN TOLD.
I WISHED THE KIDS WHO WERE BULLYING ME WOULD GET INTO AN ACCI-DENT...
...AND THE NEXT DAY, I FOUND OUT WHAT I'D WISHED FOR HAD ACTUALLY HAPPENED.
I STARTED TREMBLING.
THAT WISH HAD COME *TRUE*... SO WHAT ELSE MIGHT HAPPEN?

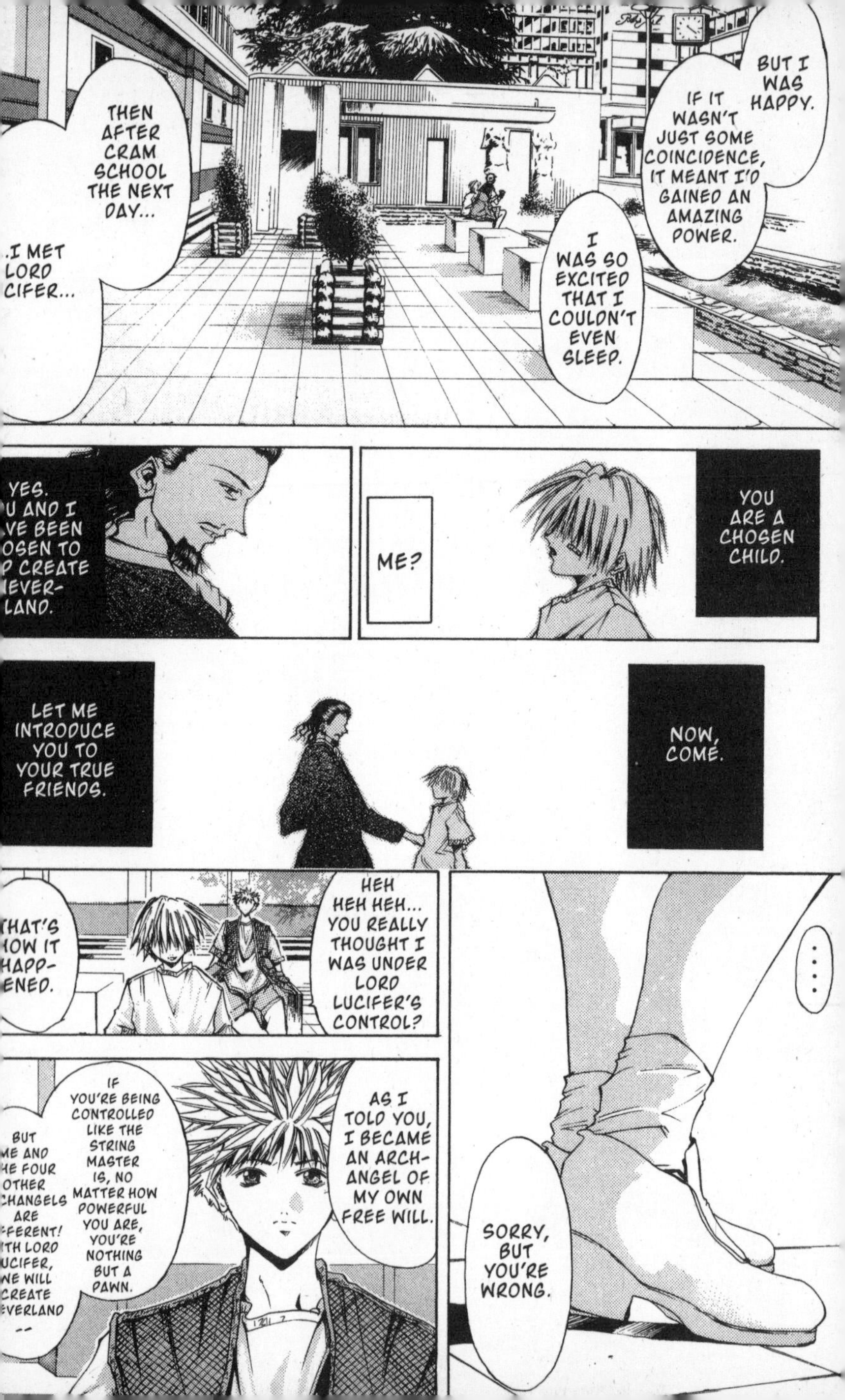
BUT I WAS HAPPY.
IF IT WASN'T JUST SOME COINCIDENCE, IT MEANT I'D GAINED AN AMAZING POWER.
I WAS SO EXCITED THAT I COULDN'T EVEN SLEEP.
THEN AFTER CRAM SCHOOL THE NEXT DAY...
.I MET LORD CIFER...
YOU ARE A CHOSEN CHILD.
ME?
YES. U AND I VE BEEN OSEN TO P CREATE NEVER-LAND.
NOW, COME.
LET ME INTRODUCE YOU TO YOUR TRUE FRIENDS.
...
SORRY, BUT YOU'RE WRONG.
HEH HEH HEH... YOU REALLY THOUGHT I WAS UNDER LORD LUCIFER'S CONTROL?
HAT'S HOW IT HAPP-ENED.
AS I TOLD YOU, I BECAME AN ARCH-ANGEL OF MY OWN FREE WILL.
IF YOU'RE BEING CONTROLLED LIKE THE STRING MASTER IS, NO MATTER HOW POWERFUL YOU ARE, YOU'RE NOTHING BUT A PAWN.
BUT ME AND HE FOUR OTHER CHANGELS ARE FFERENT! TH LORD UCIFER, WE WILL CREATE EVERLAND --

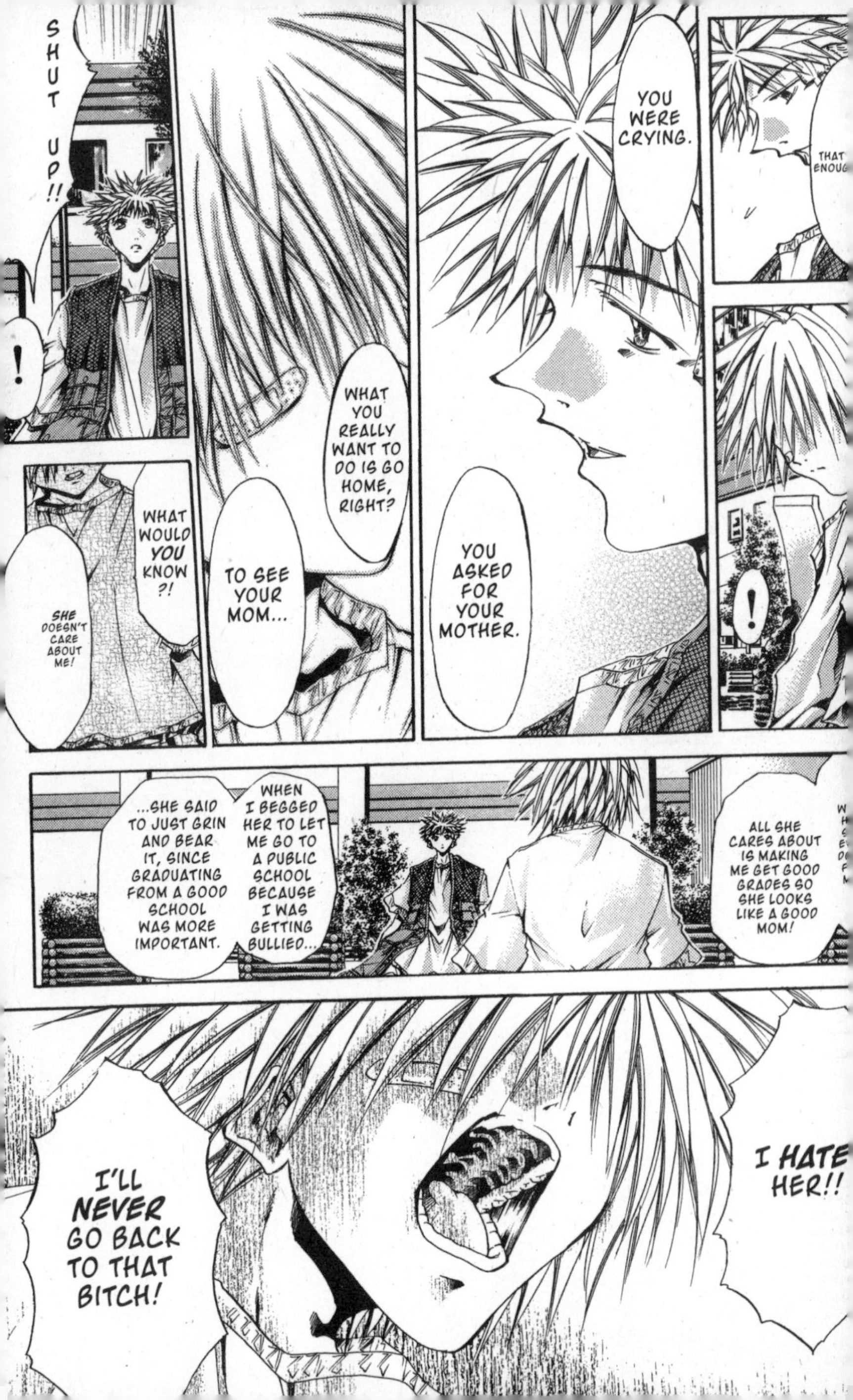

THAT
!
YOU WERE CRYING.
YOU ASKED FOR YOUR MOTHER.
WHAT YOU REALLY WANT TO DO IS GO HOME, RIGHT?
TO SEE YOUR MOM...
SHUT UP!!
!
WHAT WOULD YOU KNOW?!
SHE DOESN'T CARE ABOUT ME!
ALL SHE CARES ABOUT IS MAKING ME GET GOOD GRADES SO SHE LOOKS LIKE A GOOD MOM!
WHEN I BEGGED HER TO LET ME GO TO A PUBLIC SCHOOL BECAUSE I WAS GETTING BULLIED...
...SHE SAID TO JUST GRIN AND BEAR IT, SINCE GRADUATING FROM A GOOD SCHOOL WAS MORE IMPORTANT.
I HATE HER!!
I'LL NEVER GO BACK TO THAT BITCH!

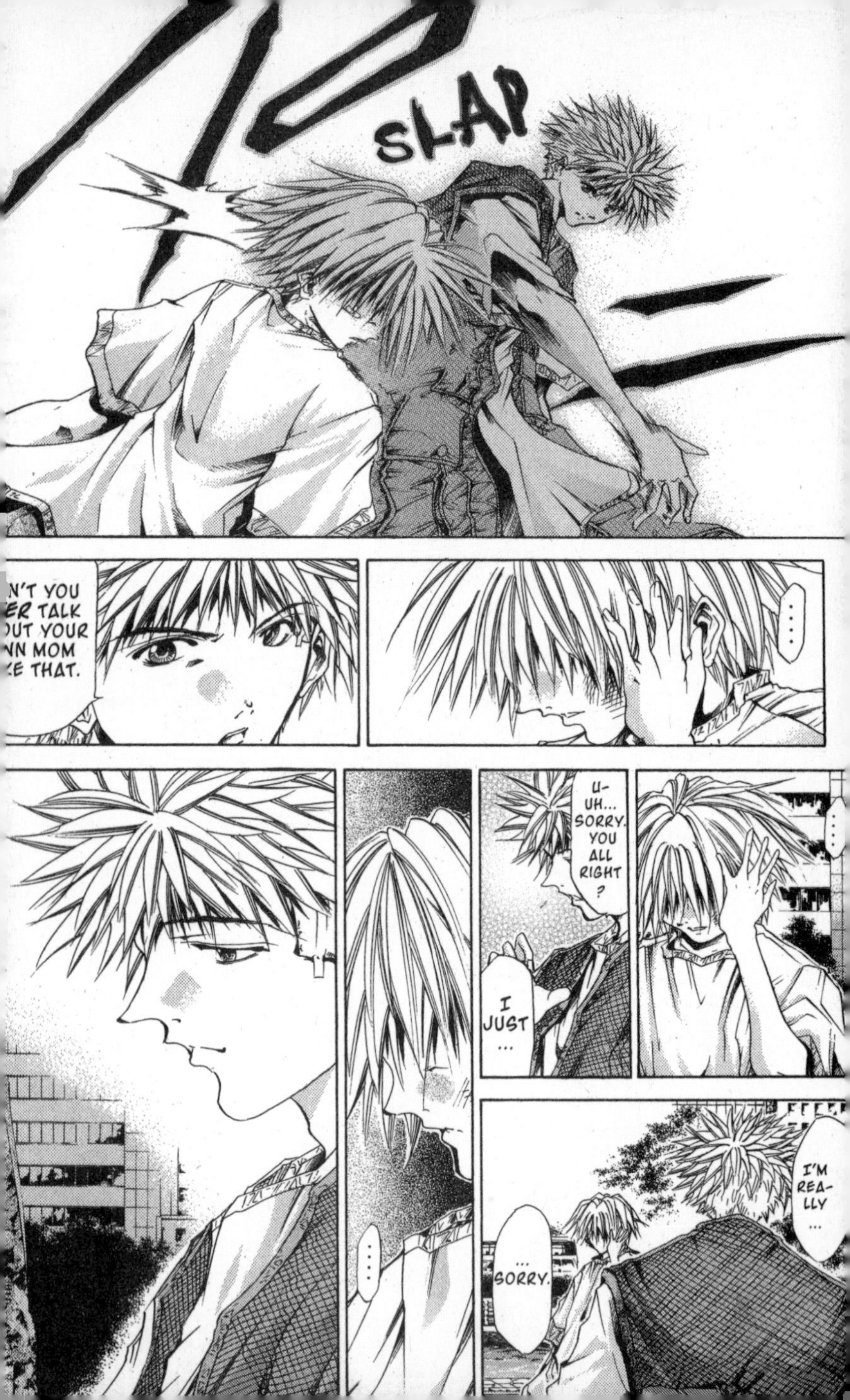
SLAP
....
N'T YOU ER TALK UT YOUR WN MOM E THAT.
....
U-UH... SORRY. YOU ALL RIGHT?
I JUST...
I'M REALLY...
...SORRY.
....

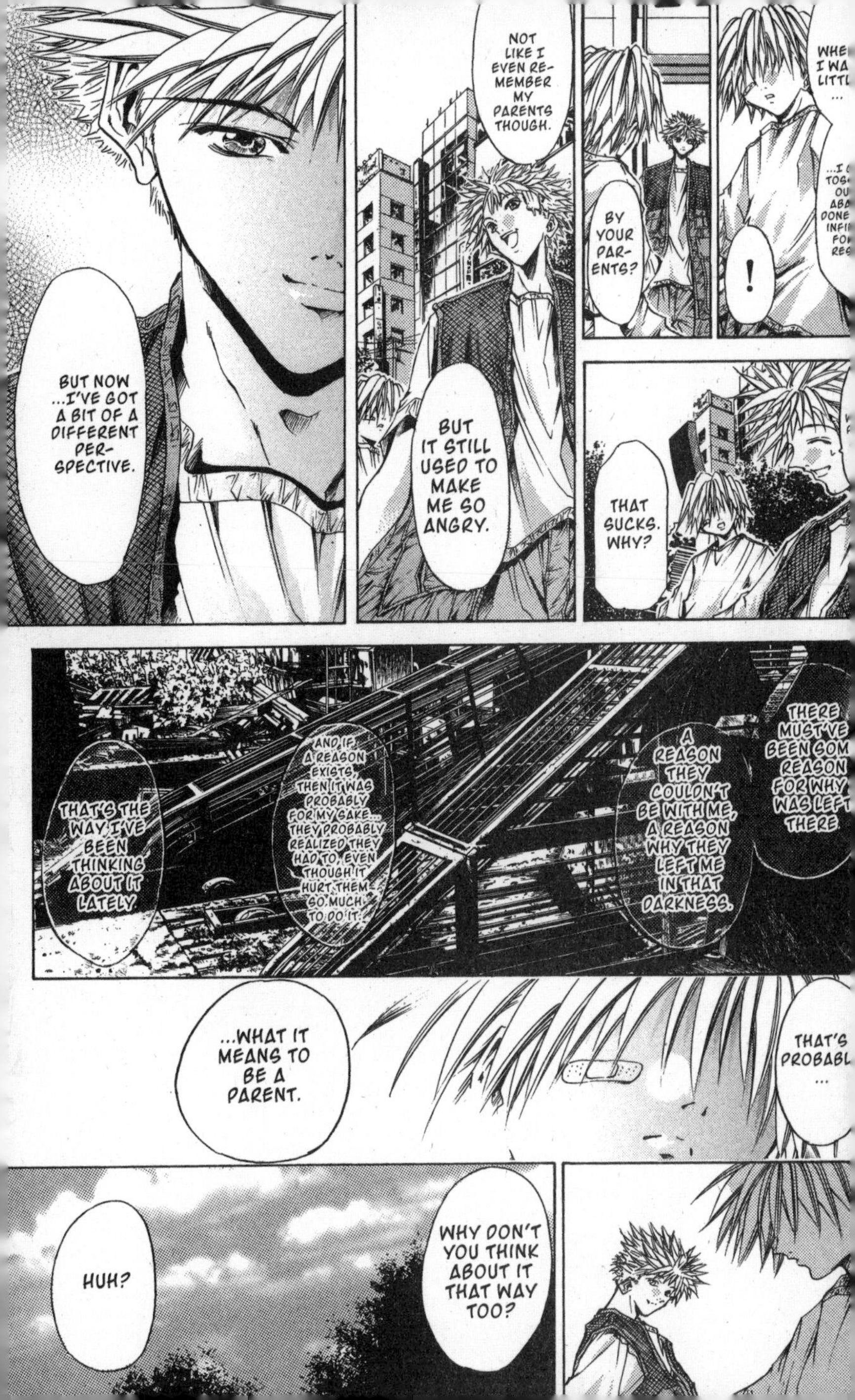
WHE I WA LITTL ...
!
BY YOUR PAR-ENTS?
THAT SUCKS. WHY?
NOT LIKE I EVEN RE-MEMBER MY PARENTS THOUGH.
BUT IT STILL USED TO MAKE ME SO ANGRY.
BUT NOW ...I'VE GOT A BIT OF A DIFFERENT PER-SPECTIVE.
THERE MUST'VE BEEN SOM REASON FOR WHY WAS LEFT THERE.
A REASON THEY COULDN'T BE WITH ME, A REASON WHY THEY LEFT ME IN THAT DARKNESS.
AND IF A REASON EXISTS, THEN IT WAS PROBABLY FOR MY SAKE... THEY PROBABLY REALIZED THEY HAD TO, EVEN THOUGH IT HURT THEM SO MUCH TO DO IT.
THAT'S THE WAY I'VE BEEN THINKING ABOUT IT LATELY.
THAT'S PROBABL ...
...WHAT IT MEANS TO BE A PARENT.
WHY DON'T YOU THINK ABOUT IT THAT WAY TOO?
HUH?

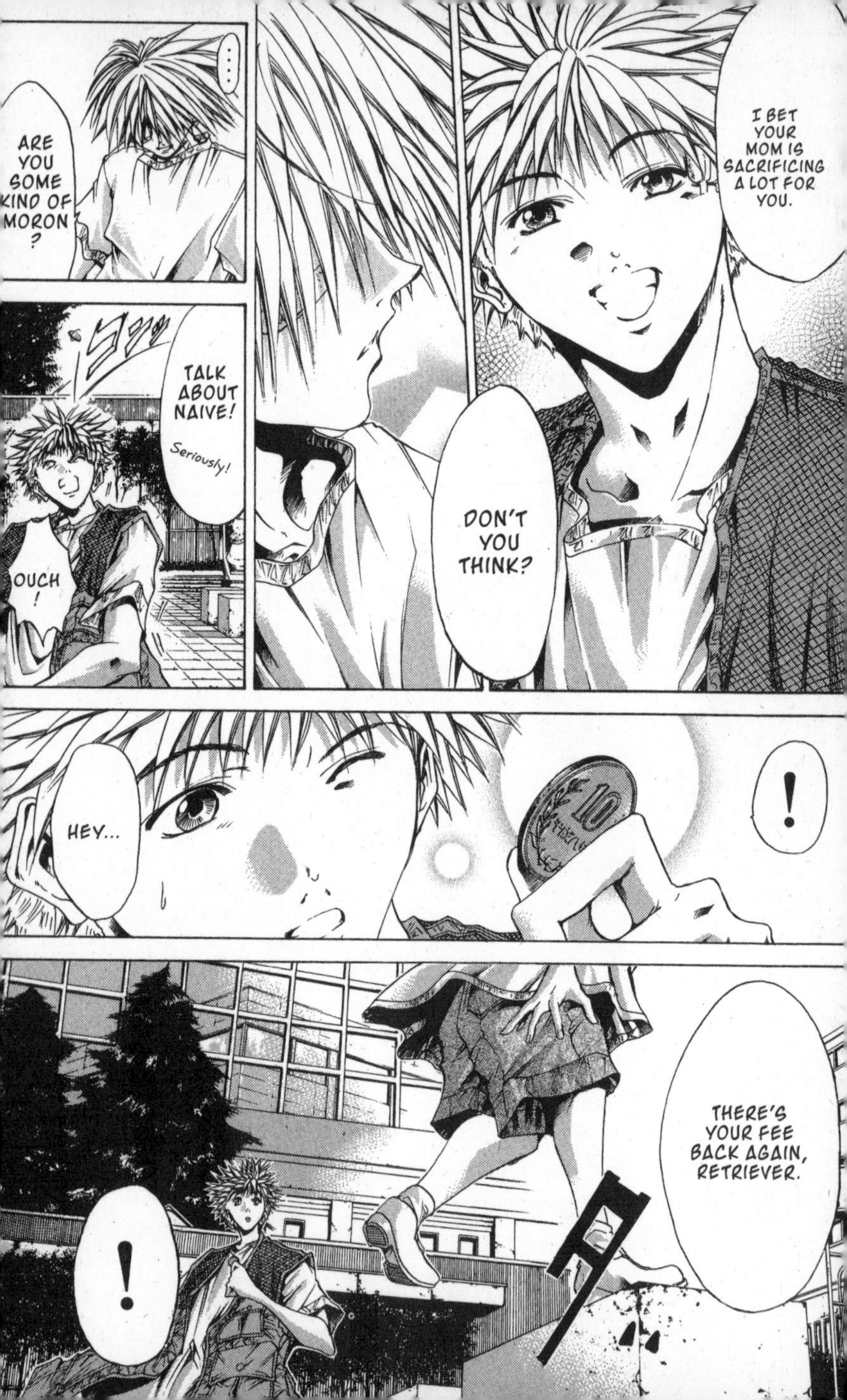
I BET YOUR MOM IS SACRIFICING A LOT FOR YOU.
DON'T YOU THINK?
...
ARE YOU SOME KIND OF MORON?
TALK ABOUT NAIVE!
Seriously!
OUCH!
!
HEY...
THERE'S YOUR FEE BACK AGAIN, RETRIEVER.
!

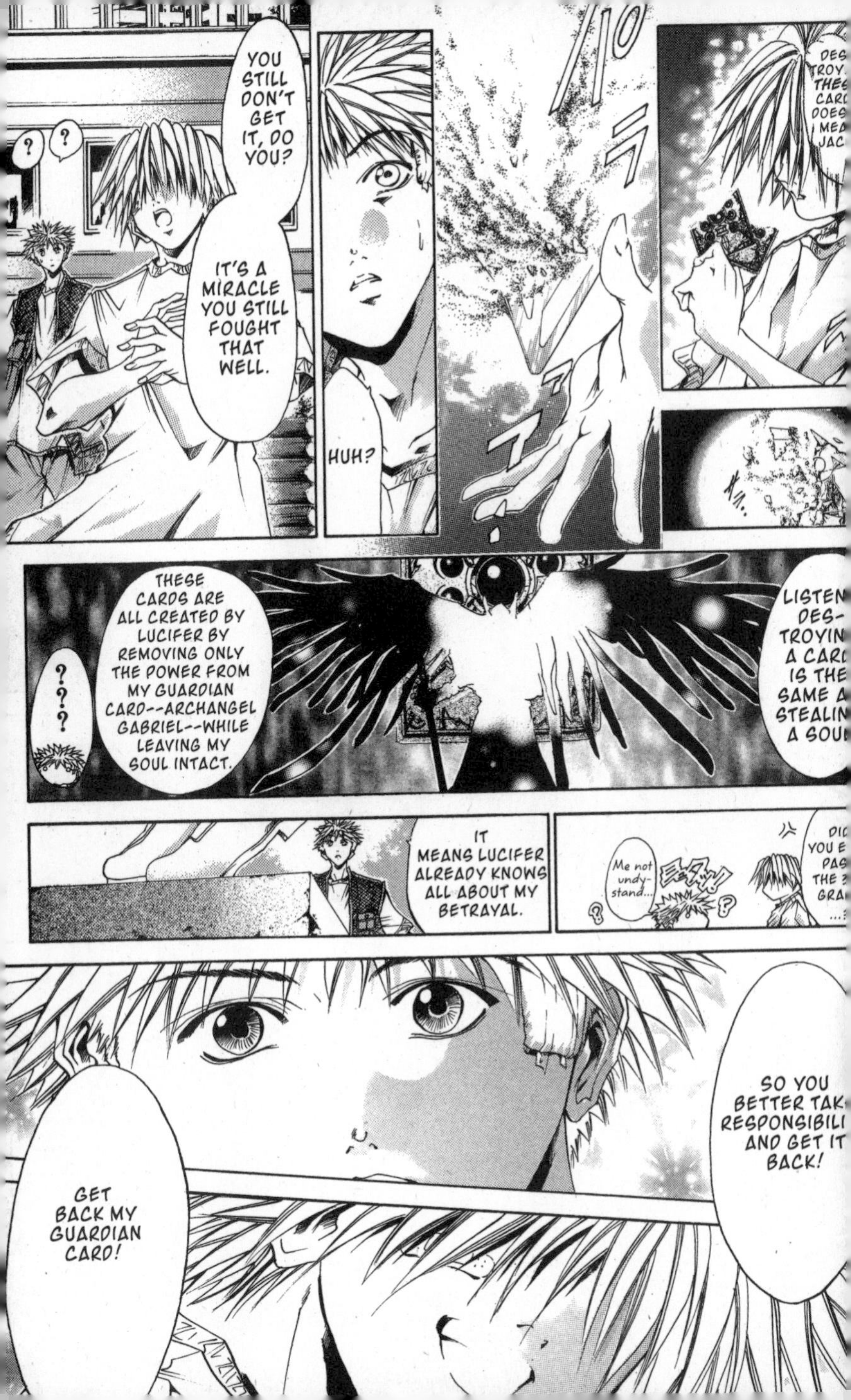
DES- TROYI THES CARD DOES MEA JAC
HUH?
YOU STILL DON'T GET IT, DO YOU?
IT'S A MIRACLE YOU STILL FOUGHT THAT WELL.
? ?
LISTEN DES- TROYIN A CARD IS THE SAME A STEALIN A SOU
THESE CARDS ARE ALL CREATED BY LUCIFER BY REMOVING ONLY THE POWER FROM MY GUARDIAN CARD--ARCHANGEL GABRIEL--WHILE LEAVING MY SOUL INTACT.
? ? ?
DID YOU E PAS THE 3 GRA ...?
Me not undy-stand...
? ?
IT MEANS LUCIFER ALREADY KNOWS ALL ABOUT MY BETRAYAL.
SO YOU BETTER TAK RESPONSIBILI AND GET IT BACK!
GET BACK MY GUARDIAN CARD!

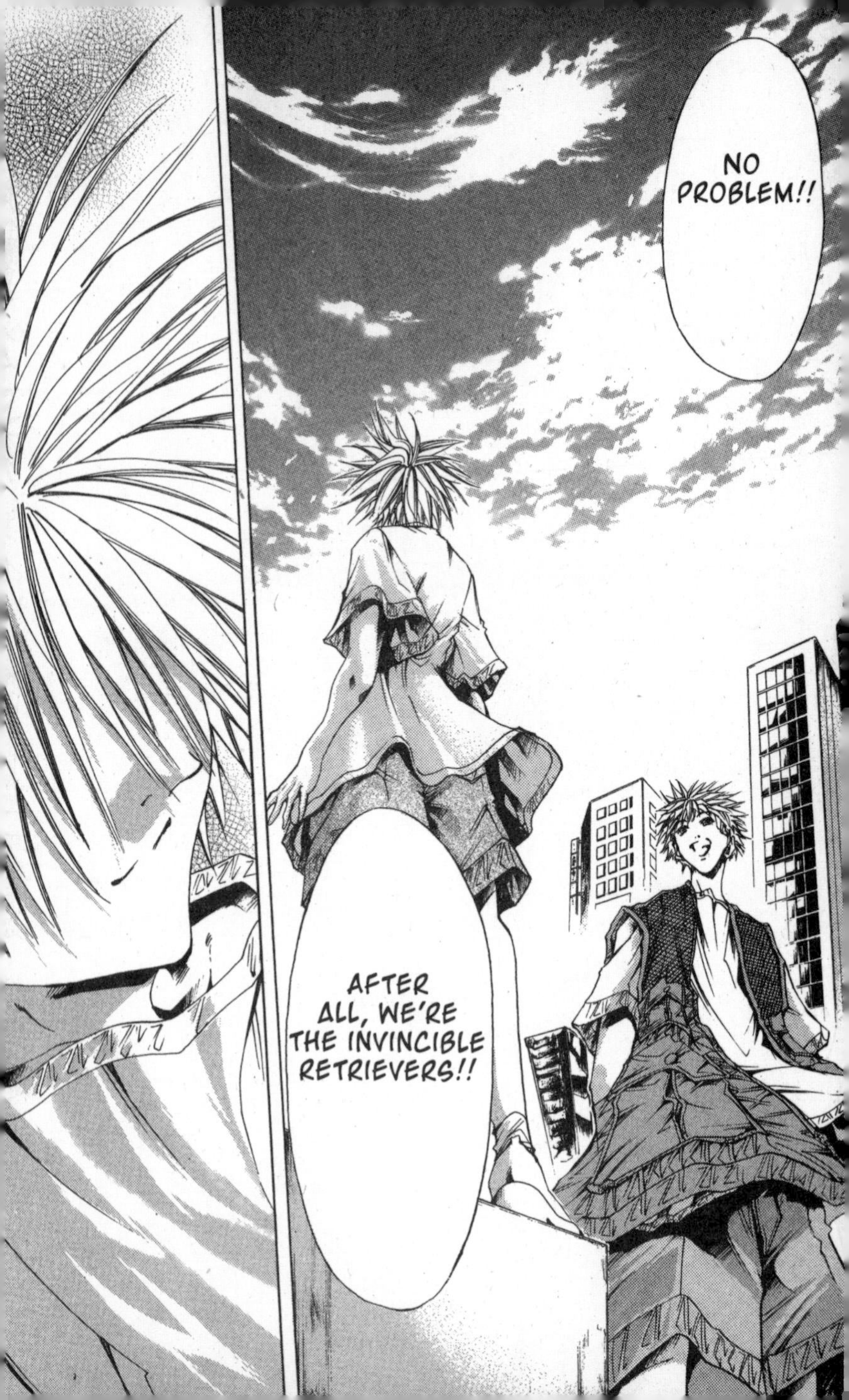
NO PROBLEM!!
AFTER ALL, WE'RE THE INVINCIBLE RETRIEVERS!!

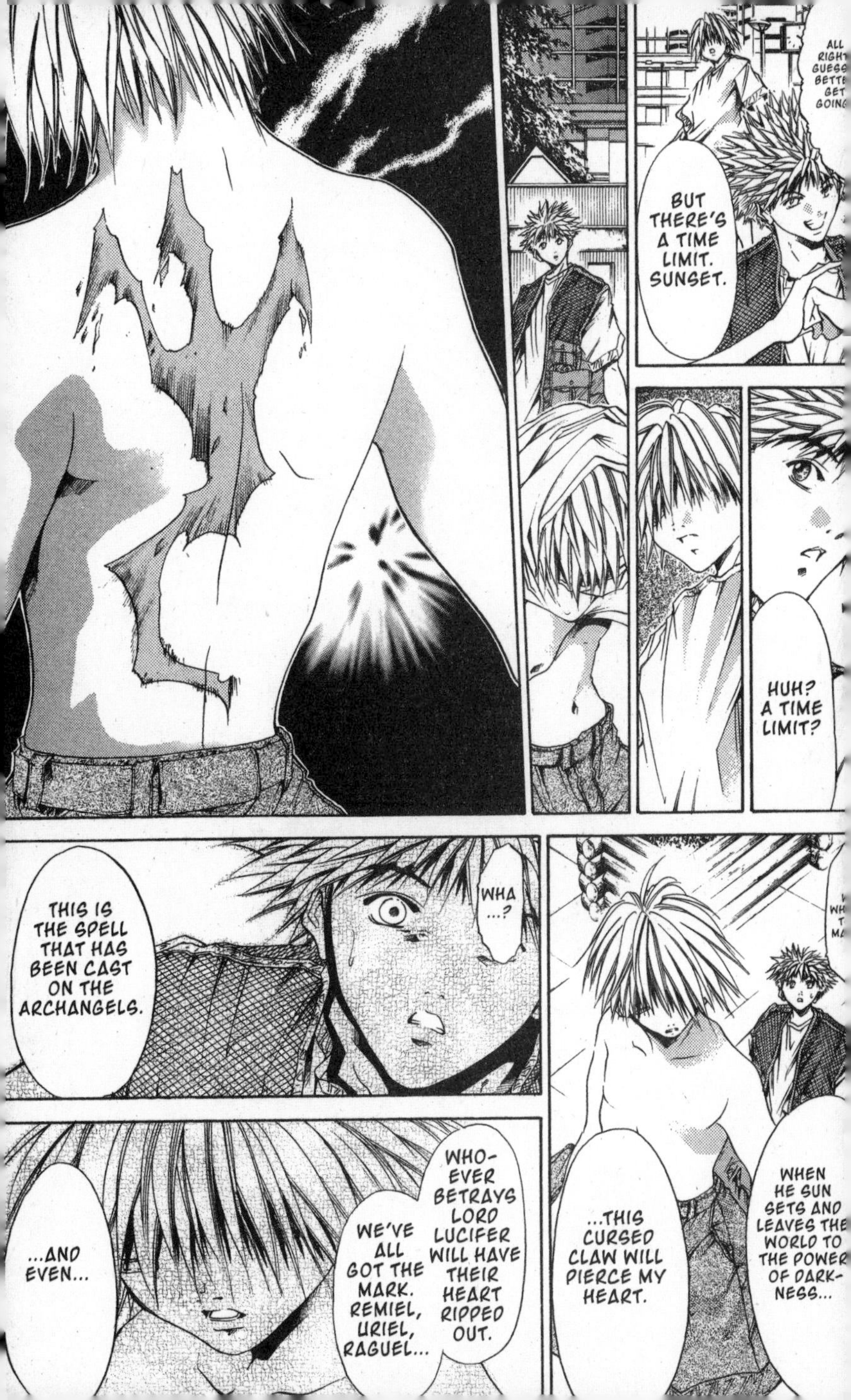
ALL RIGHT GUESS BETTE GET GOING
BUT THERE'S A TIME LIMIT. SUNSET.
HUH? A TIME LIMIT?
WHEN HE SUN SETS AND LEAVES THE WORLD TO THE POWER OF DARK-NESS...
...THIS CURSED CLAW WILL PIERCE MY HEART.
WHA ...?
THIS IS THE SPELL THAT HAS BEEN CAST ON THE ARCHANGELS.
WHO-EVER BETRAYS LORD LUCIFER WILL HAVE THEIR HEART RIPPED OUT.
WE'VE ALL GOT THE MARK. REMIEL, URIEL, RAGUEL...
...AND EVEN...

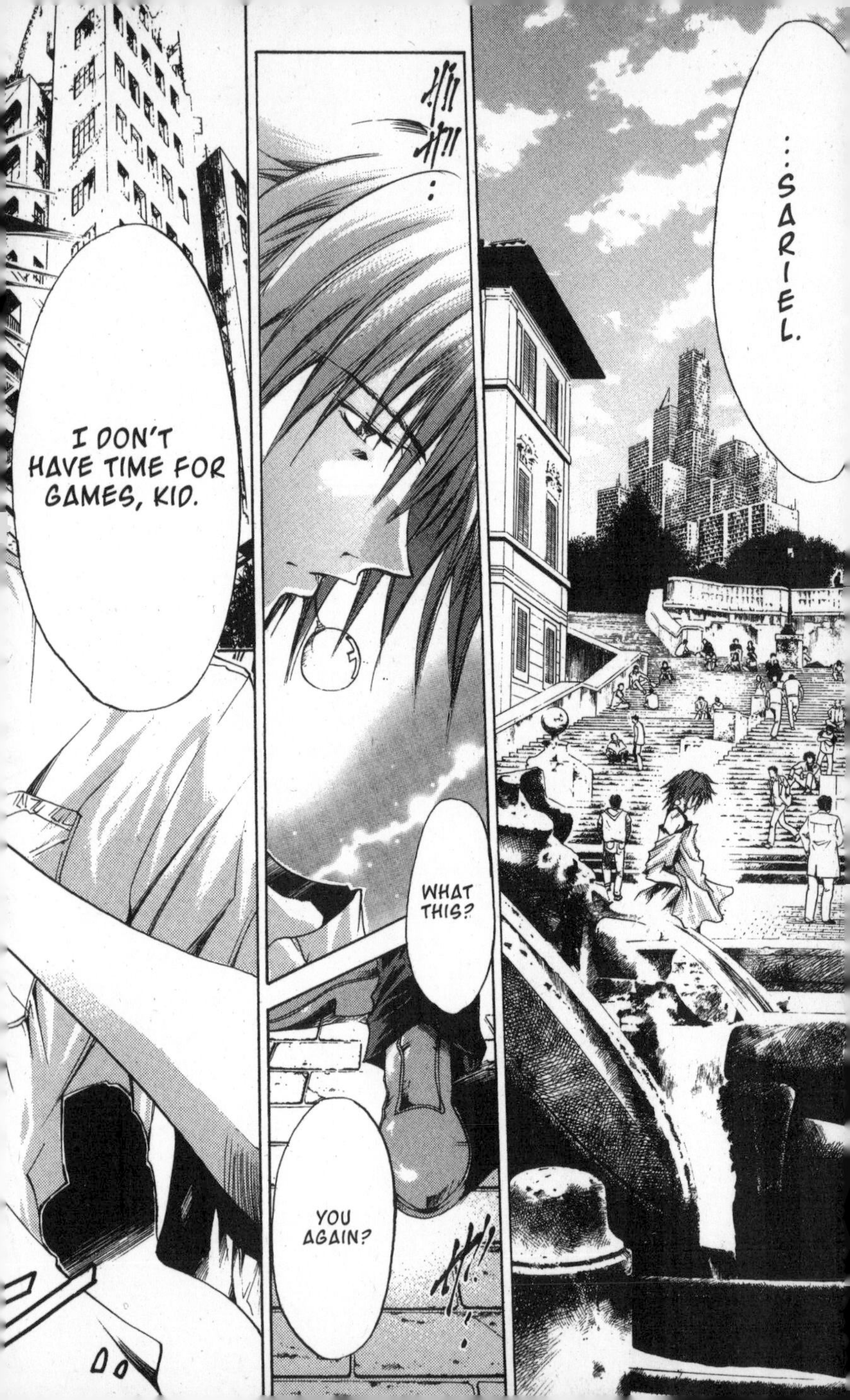
...SARIEL.
WHAT THIS?
YOU AGAIN?
I DON'T HAVE TIME FOR GAMES, KID.

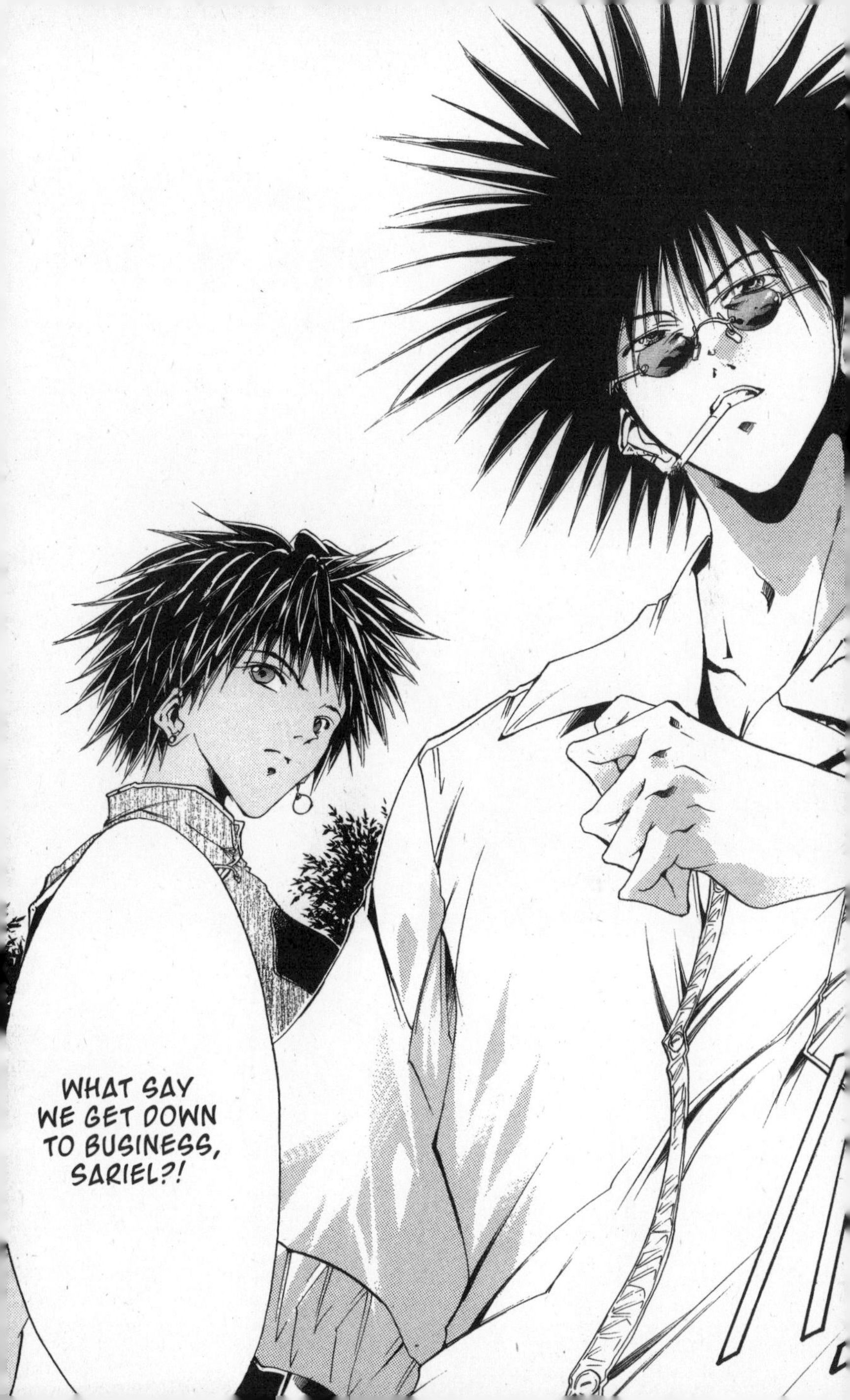
WHAT SAY WE GET DOWN TO BUSINESS, SARIEL?!

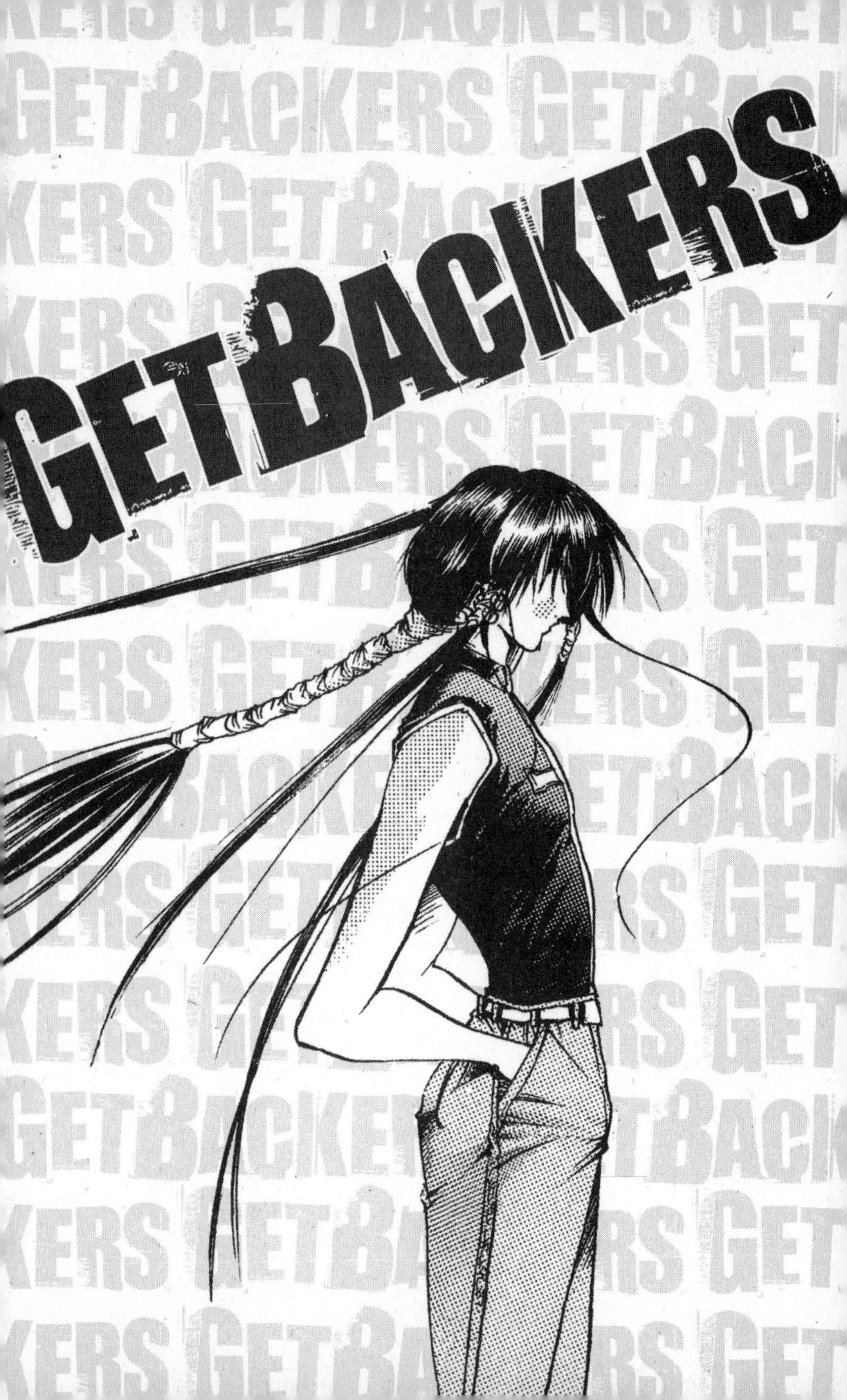
GETBACKERS

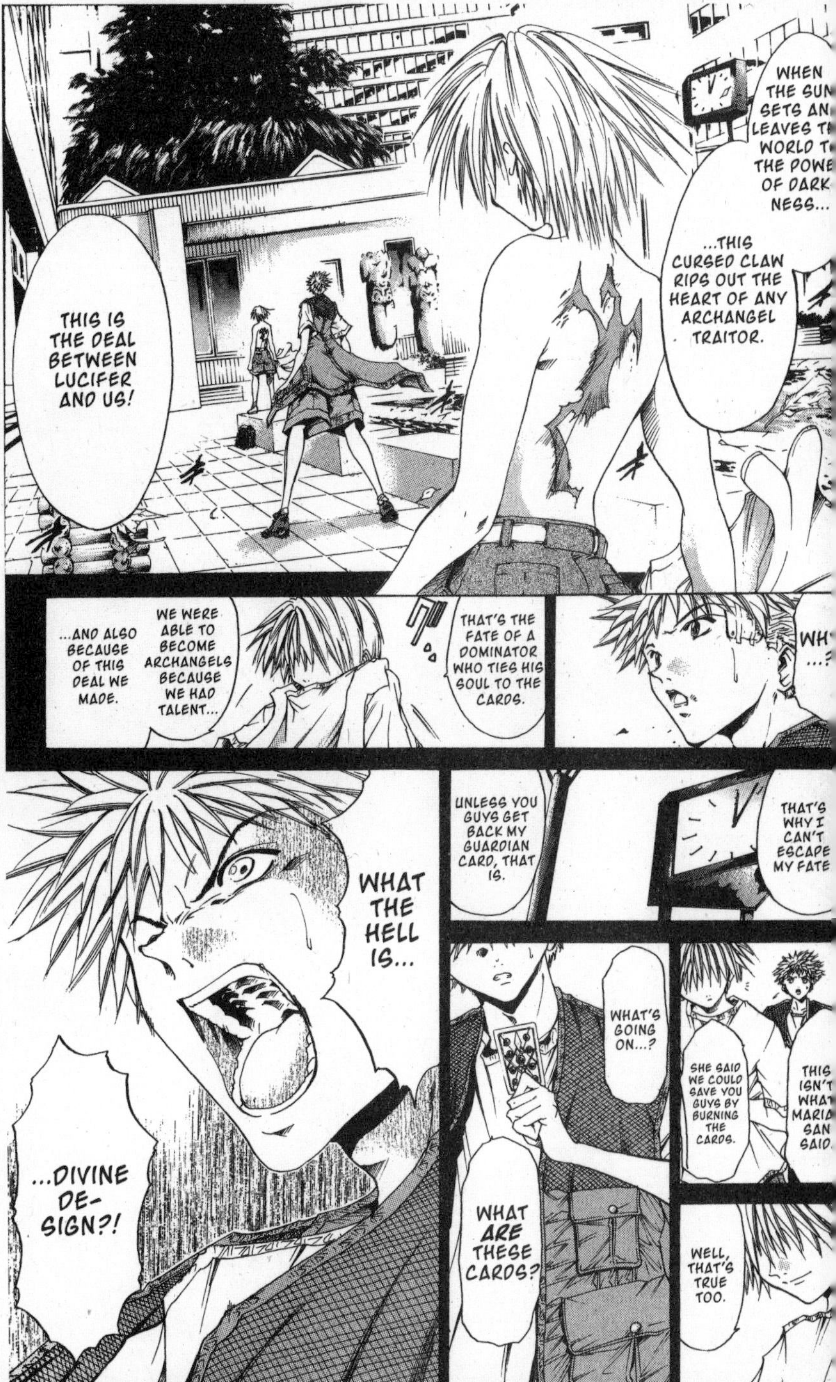
WHEN THE SUN SETS AN LEAVES T WORLD T THE POWE OF DARK-NESS...
...THIS CURSED CLAW RIPS OUT THE HEART OF ANY ARCHANGEL TRAITOR.
THIS IS THE DEAL BETWEEN LUCIFER AND US!
WH ...?
THAT'S THE FATE OF A DOMINATOR WHO TIES HIS SOUL TO THE CARDS.
WE WERE ABLE TO BECOME ARCHANGELS BECAUSE WE HAD TALENT...
...AND ALSO BECAUSE OF THIS DEAL WE MADE.
THAT'S WHY I CAN'T ESCAPE MY FATE
UNLESS YOU GUYS GET BACK MY GUARDIAN CARD, THAT IS.
THIS ISN'T WHA MARIA SAN SAID.
SHE SAID WE COULD SAVE YOU GUYS BY BURNING THE CARDS.
WELL, THAT'S TRUE TOO.
WHAT'S GOING ON...?
WHAT ARE THESE CARDS?
WHAT THE HELL IS...
...DIVINE DE-SIGN?!

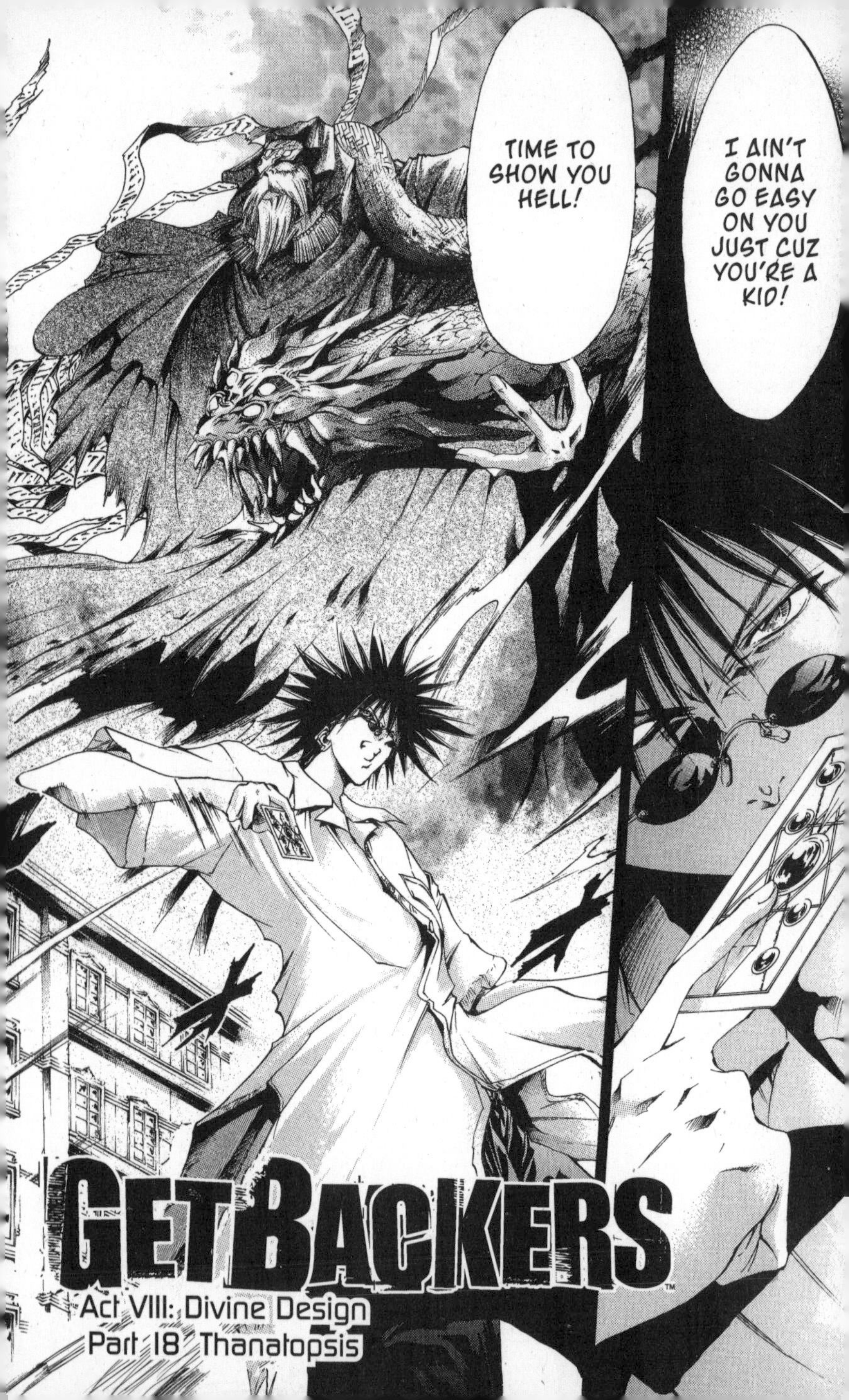
I AIN'T GONNA GO EASY ON YOU JUST CUZ YOU'RE A KID!
TIME TO SHOW YOU HELL!
GETBACKERS™
Act VIII: Divine Design
Part 18 Thanatopsis

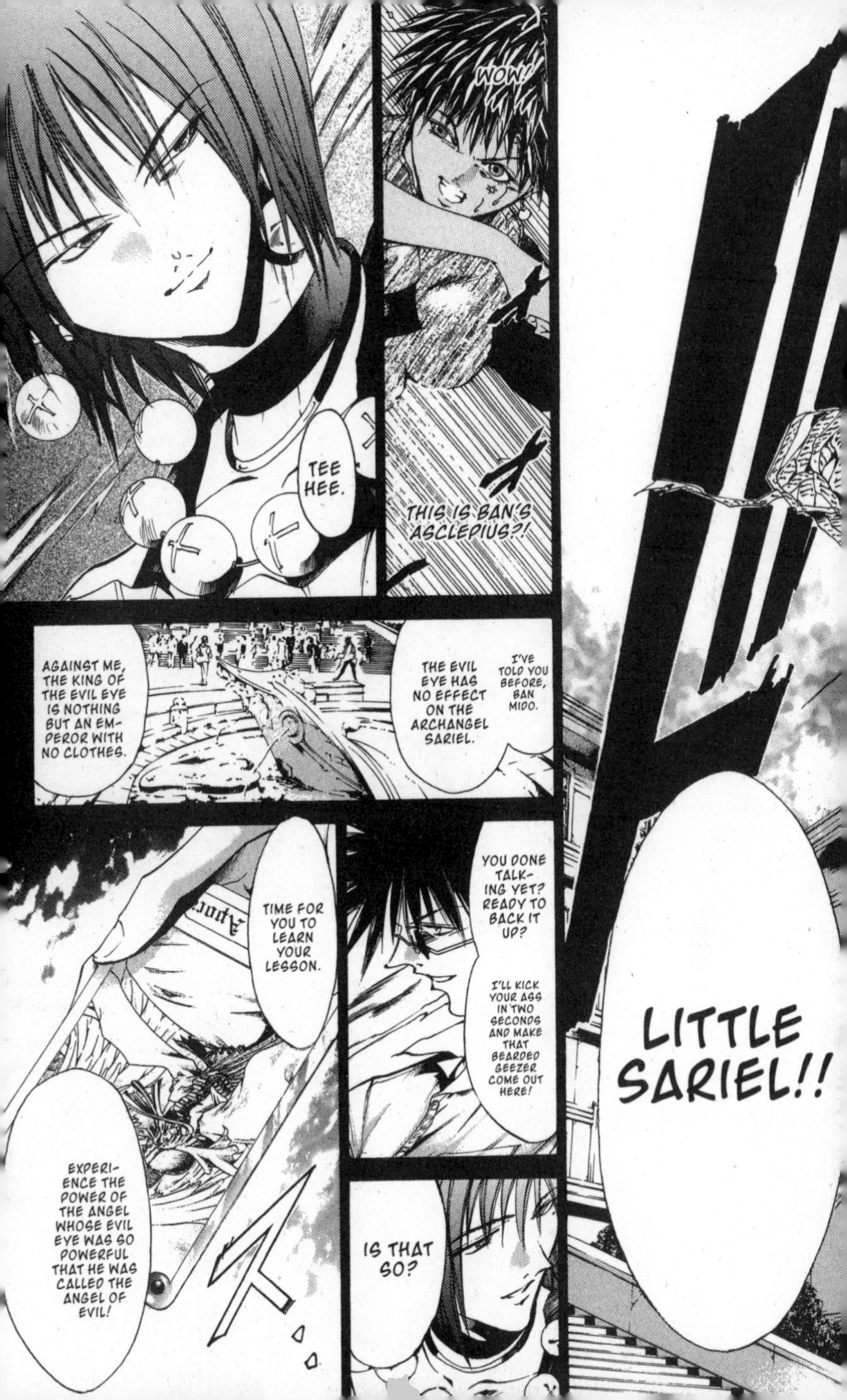
LITTLE SARIEL!!
WOW!
THIS IS BAN'S ASCLEPIUS?!
TEE HEE.
I'VE TOLD YOU BEFORE, BAN MIDO.
THE EVIL EYE HAS NO EFFECT ON THE ARCHANGEL SARIEL.
AGAINST ME, THE KING OF THE EVIL EYE IS NOTHING BUT AN EMPEROR WITH NO CLOTHES.
YOU DONE TALKING YET? READY TO BACK IT UP?
I'LL KICK YOUR ASS IN TWO SECONDS AND MAKE THAT BEARDED GEEZER COME OUT HERE!
IS THAT SO?
TIME FOR YOU TO LEARN YOUR LESSON.
EXPERIENCE THE POWER OF THE ANGEL WHOSE EVIL EYE WAS SO POWERFUL THAT HE WAS CALLED THE ANGEL OF EVIL!

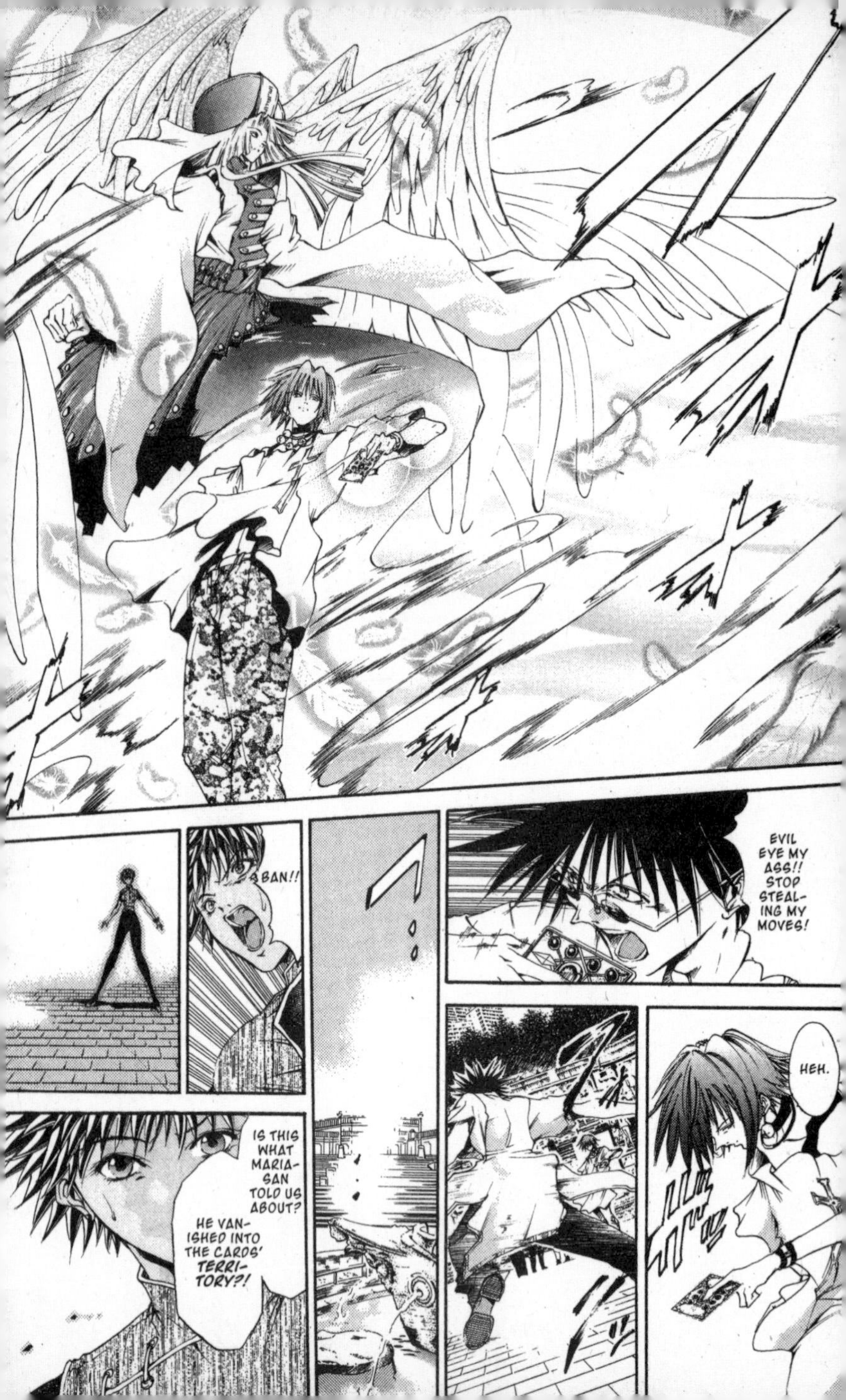
EVIL EYE MY ASS!! STOP STEAL-ING MY MOVES!
HEH.
BAN!!
IS THIS WHAT MARIA-SAN TOLD US ABOUT?
HE VAN-ISHED INTO THE CARDS' TERRI-TORY?!

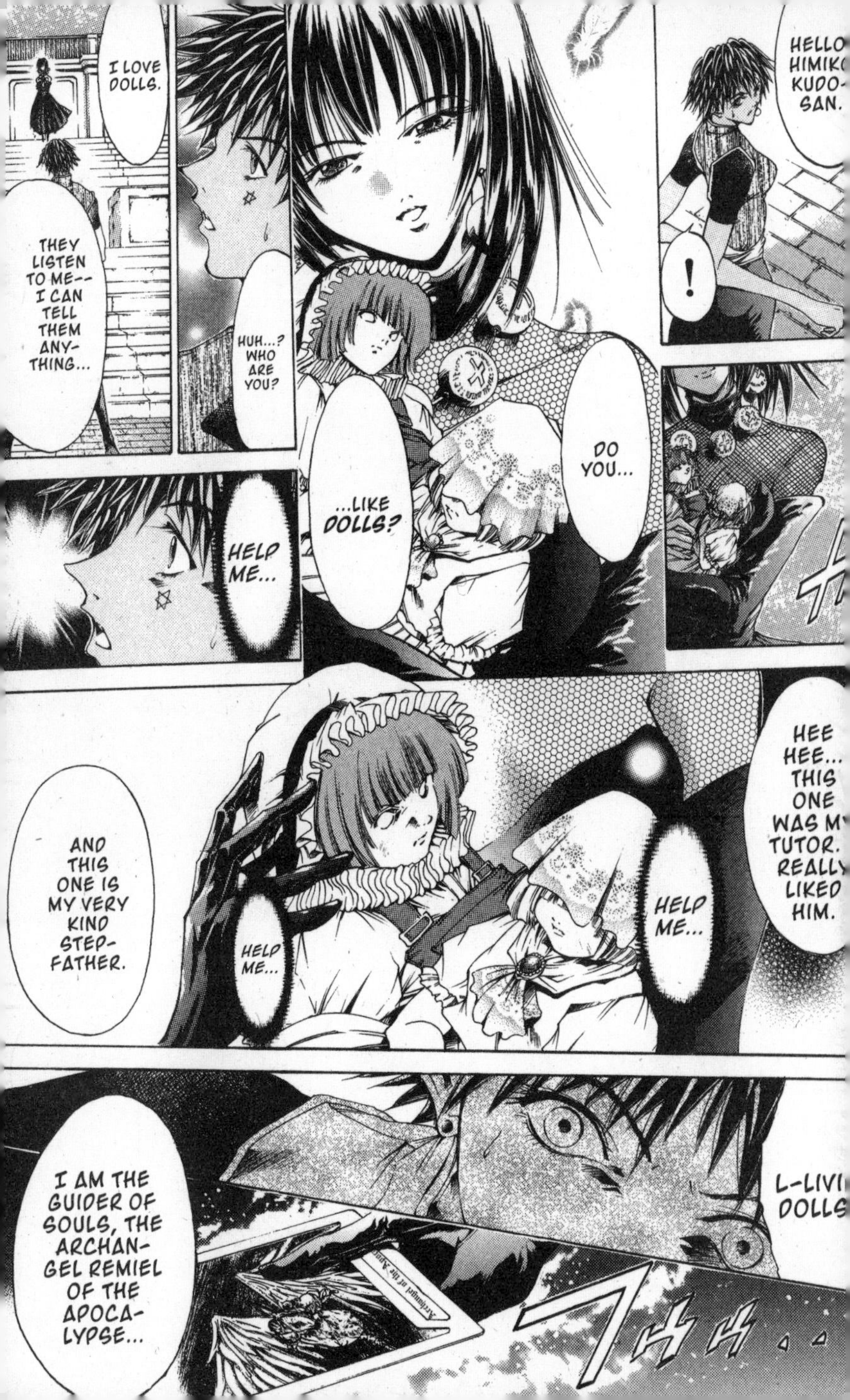
HELLO HIMIKO KUDO-SAN.
!
HUH...? WHO ARE YOU?
DO YOU...
...LIKE DOLLS?
I LOVE DOLLS.
THEY LISTEN TO ME-- I CAN TELL THEM ANYTHING...
HELP ME...
HEE HEE... THIS ONE WAS MY TUTOR. REALLY LIKED HIM.
HELP ME...
AND THIS ONE IS MY VERY KIND STEP-FATHER.
HELP ME...
L-LIVI DOLLS
I AM THE GUIDER OF SOULS, THE ARCHANGEL REMIEL OF THE APOCALYPSE...

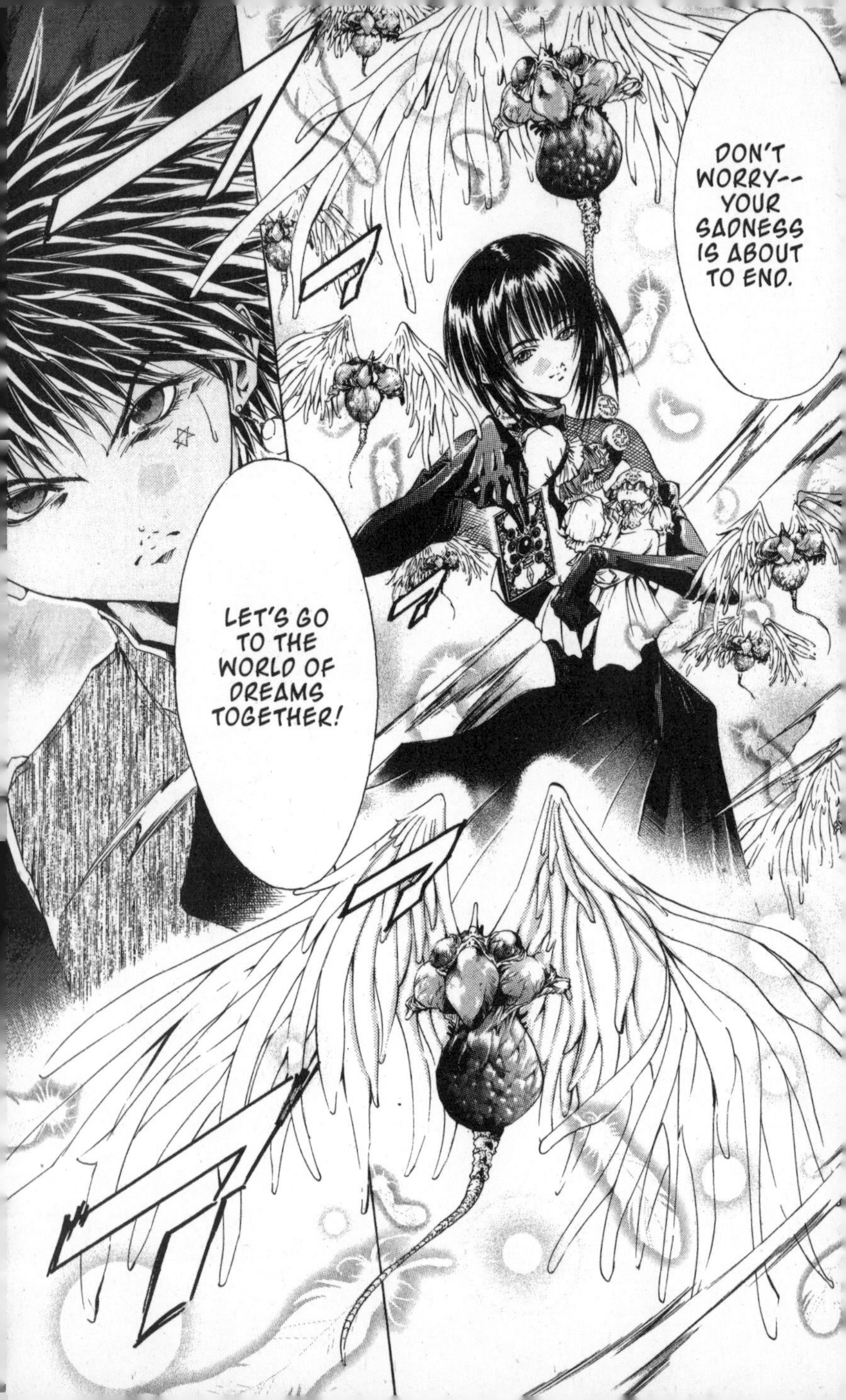
DON'T WORRY--YOUR SADNESS IS ABOUT TO END.
LET'S GO TO THE WORLD OF DREAMS TOGETHER!

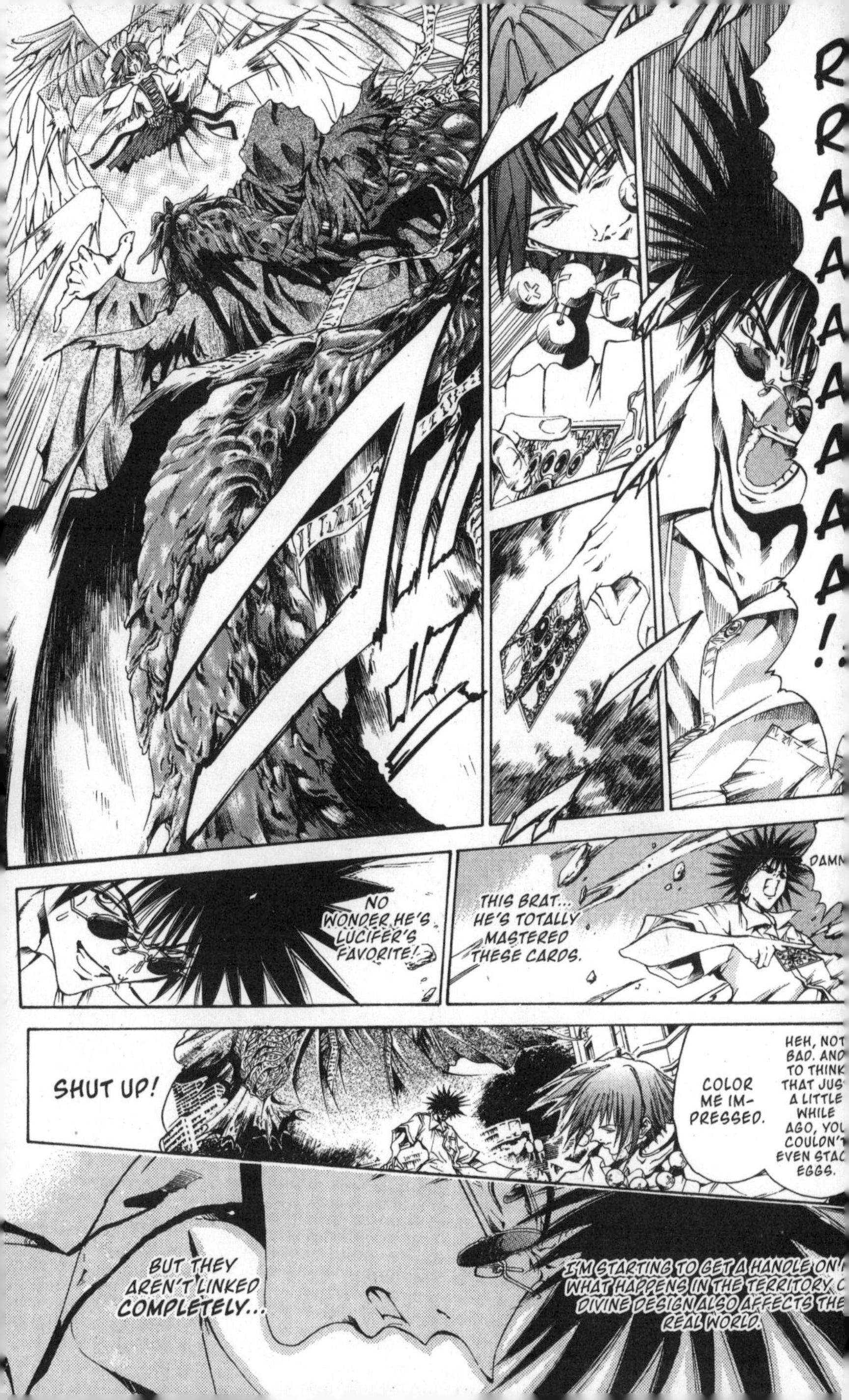
RRAAAAAAA!!
DAMN
THIS BRAT... HE'S TOTALLY MASTERED THESE CARDS.
NO WONDER HE'S LUCIFER'S FAVORITE!
HEH, NOT BAD. AND TO THINK THAT JUST A LITTLE WHILE AGO, YOU COULDN'T EVEN STAC EGGS.
COLOR ME IM-PRESSED.
SHUT UP!
I'M STARTING TO GET A HANDLE ON WHAT HAPPENS IN THE TERRITORY O DIVINE DESIGN ALSO AFFECTS THE REAL WORLD.
BUT THEY AREN'T LINKED COMPLETELY...

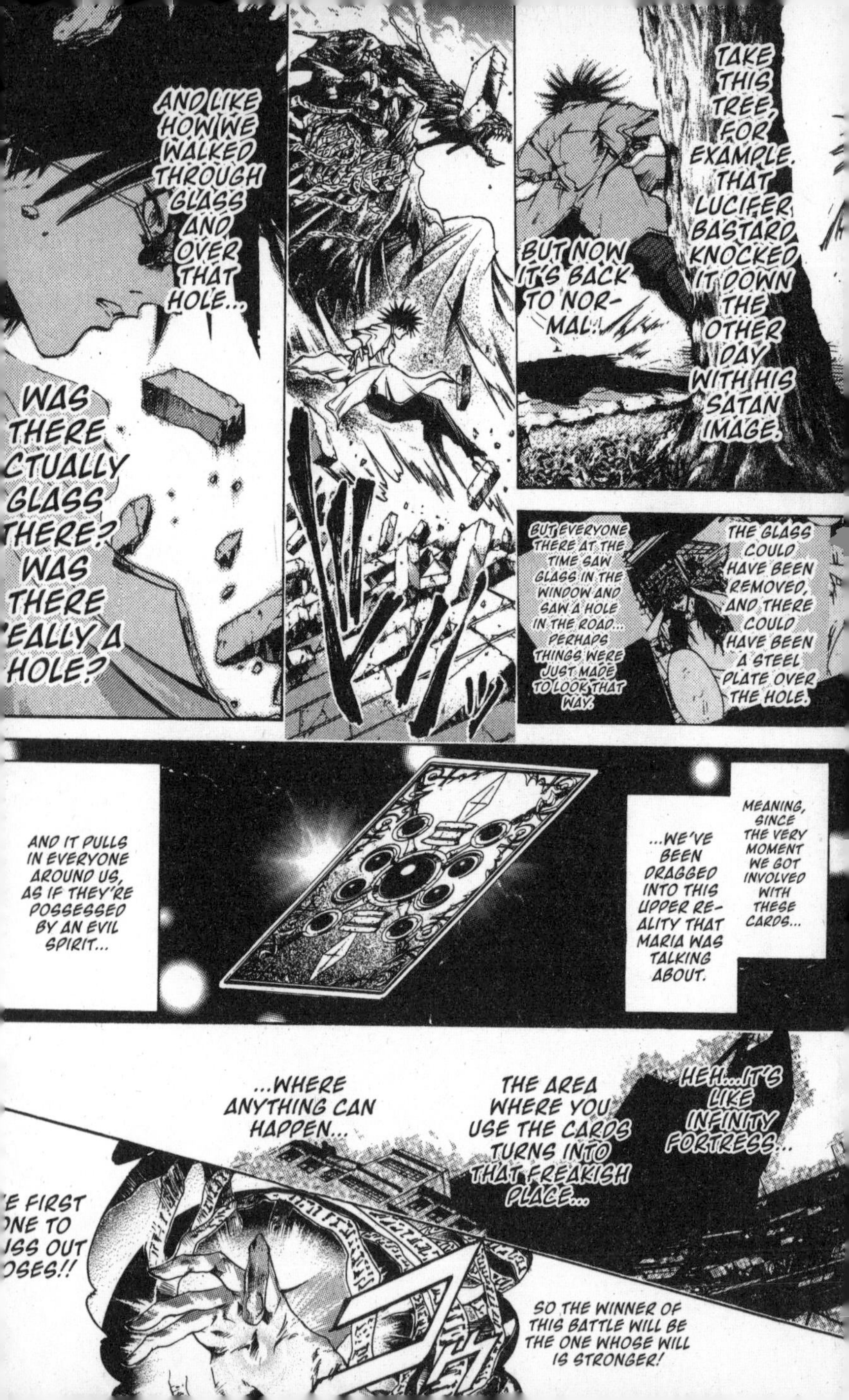
TAKE THIS TREE, FOR EXAMPLE. THAT LUCIFER BASTARD KNOCKED IT DOWN THE OTHER DAY WITH HIS SATAN IMAGE.
BUT NOW IT'S BACK TO NOR-MAL.
THE GLASS COULD HAVE BEEN REMOVED, AND THERE COULD HAVE BEEN A STEEL PLATE OVER THE HOLE.
BUT EVERYONE THERE AT THE TIME SAW GLASS IN THE WINDOW AND SAW A HOLE IN THE ROAD... PERHAPS THINGS WERE JUST MADE TO LOOK THAT WAY.
AND LIKE HOW WE WALKED THROUGH GLASS AND OVER THAT HOLE...
WAS THERE CTUALLY GLASS THERE? WAS THERE EALLY A HOLE?
MEANING, SINCE THE VERY MOMENT WE GOT INVOLVED WITH THESE CARDS...
...WE'VE BEEN DRAGGED INTO THIS UPPER RE-ALITY THAT MARIA WAS TALKING ABOUT.
AND IT PULLS IN EVERYONE AROUND US, AS IF THEY'RE POSSESSED BY AN EVIL SPIRIT...
HEH...IT'S LIKE INFINITY FORTRESS...
THE AREA WHERE YOU USE THE CARDS TURNS INTO THAT FREAKISH PLACE...
...WHERE ANYTHING CAN HAPPEN...
SO THE WINNER OF THIS BATTLE WILL BE THE ONE WHOSE WILL IS STRONGER!
E FIRST ONE TO ISS OUT OSES!!

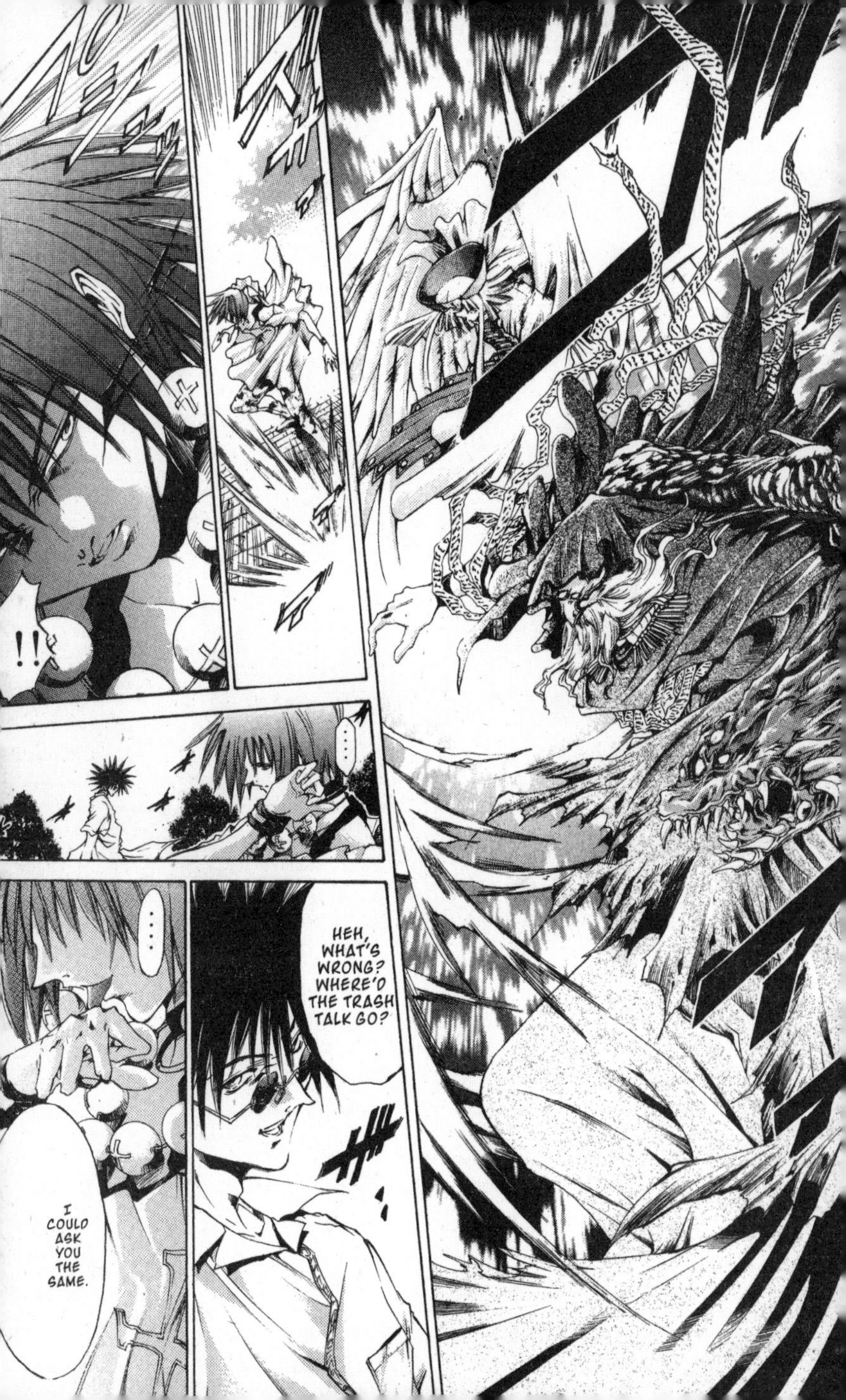
!!
....
HEH, WHAT'S WRONG? WHERE'D THE TRASH TALK GO?
....
I COULD ASK YOU THE SAME.

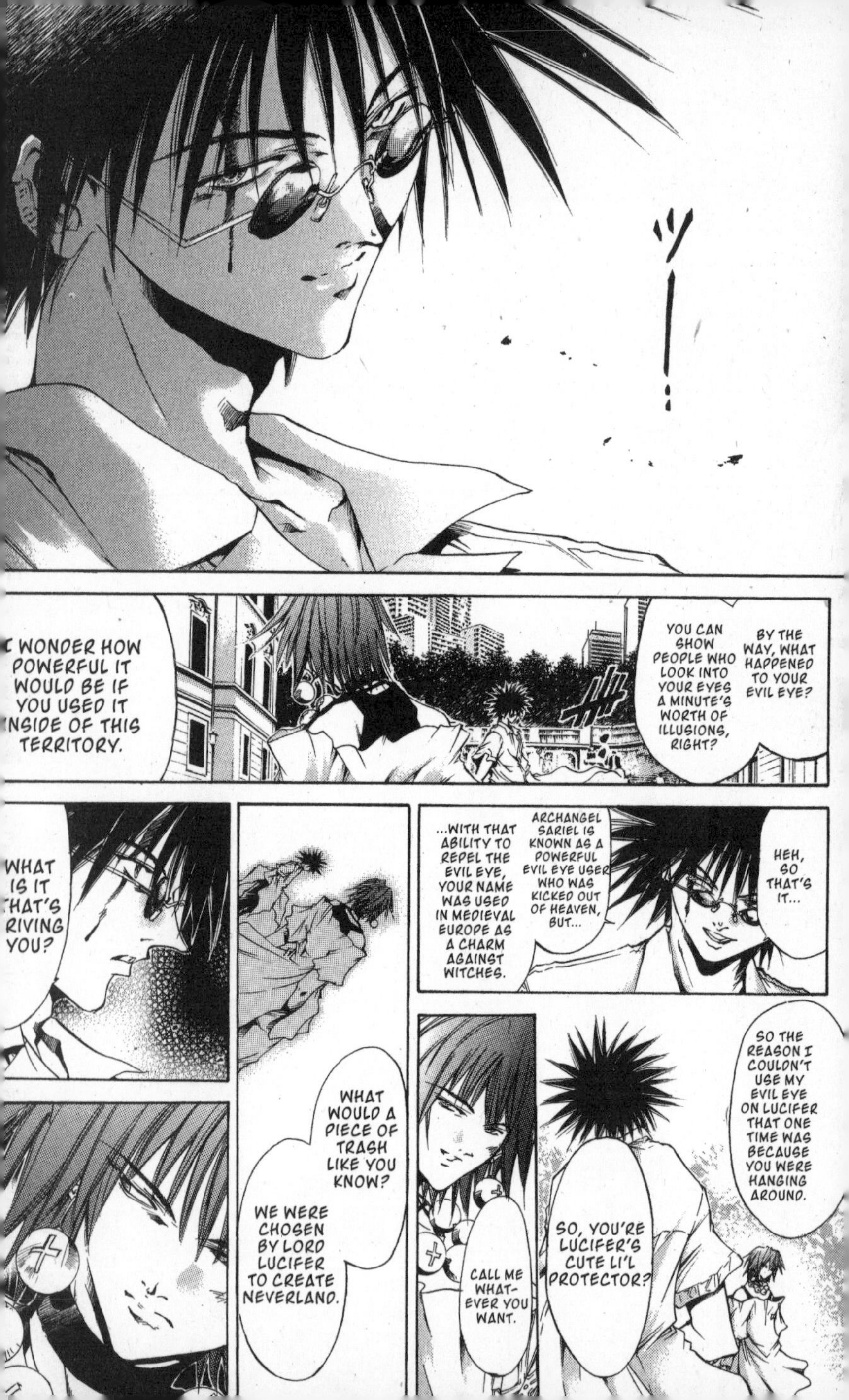

ツー!
BY THE WAY, WHAT HAPPENED TO YOUR EVIL EYE?
YOU CAN SHOW PEOPLE WHO LOOK INTO YOUR EYES A MINUTE'S WORTH OF ILLUSIONS, RIGHT?
I WONDER HOW POWERFUL IT WOULD BE IF YOU USED IT INSIDE OF THIS TERRITORY.
HEH, SO THAT'S IT...
ARCHANGEL SARIEL IS KNOWN AS A POWERFUL EVIL EYE USER WHO WAS KICKED OUT OF HEAVEN, BUT...
...WITH THAT ABILITY TO REPEL THE EVIL EYE, YOUR NAME WAS USED IN MEDIEVAL EUROPE AS A CHARM AGAINST WITCHES.
SO THE REASON I COULDN'T USE MY EVIL EYE ON LUCIFER THAT ONE TIME WAS BECAUSE YOU WERE HANGING AROUND.
SO, YOU'RE LUCIFER'S CUTE LI'L PROTECTOR?
CALL ME WHATEVER YOU WANT.
WHAT WOULD A PIECE OF TRASH LIKE YOU KNOW?
WE WERE CHOSEN BY LORD LUCIFER TO CREATE NEVERLAND.
WHAT IS IT THAT'S DRIVING YOU?

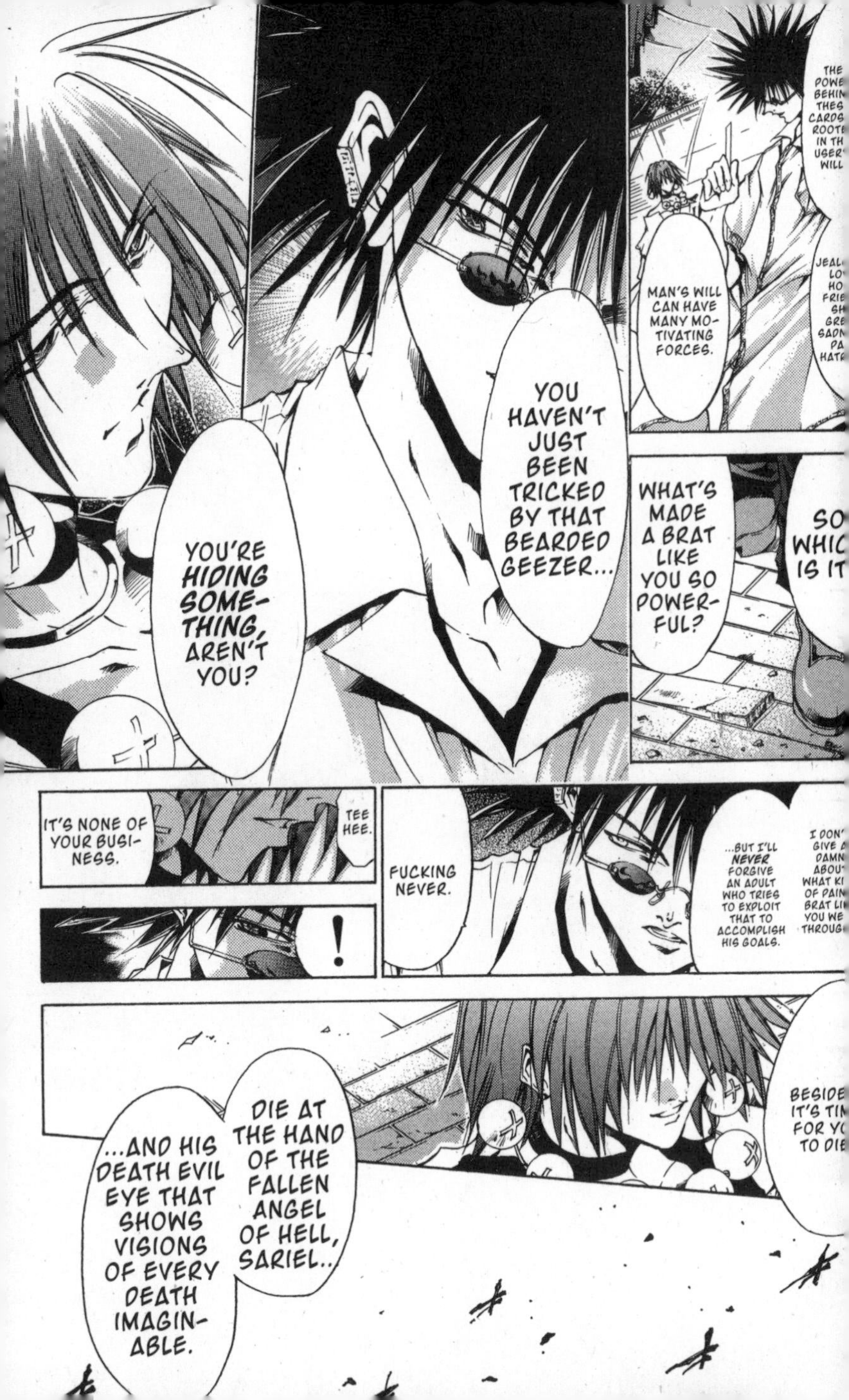
THE POWE BEHIN THES CARDS ROOTE IN TH USER' WILL
JEAL LO HO FRIE SH GRE SADN PA HATR
MAN'S WILL CAN HAVE MANY MOTIVATING FORCES.
SO WHIC IS IT
WHAT'S MADE A BRAT LIKE YOU SO POWERFUL?
YOU HAVEN'T JUST BEEN TRICKED BY THAT BEARDED GEEZER...
YOU'RE *HIDING SOMETHING,* AREN'T YOU?
I DON' GIVE A DAMN ABOUT WHAT KI OF PAIN BRAT LI YOU WE THROUG
...BUT I'LL *NEVER* FORGIVE AN ADULT WHO TRIES TO EXPLOIT THAT TO ACCOMPLISH HIS GOALS.
FUCKING NEVER.
TEE HEE.
IT'S NONE OF YOUR BUSINESS.
!
BESIDE IT'S TI FOR YO TO DIE
DIE AT THE HAND OF THE FALLEN ANGEL OF HELL, SARIEL..
...AND HIS DEATH EVIL EYE THAT SHOWS VISIONS OF EVERY DEATH IMAGINABLE.

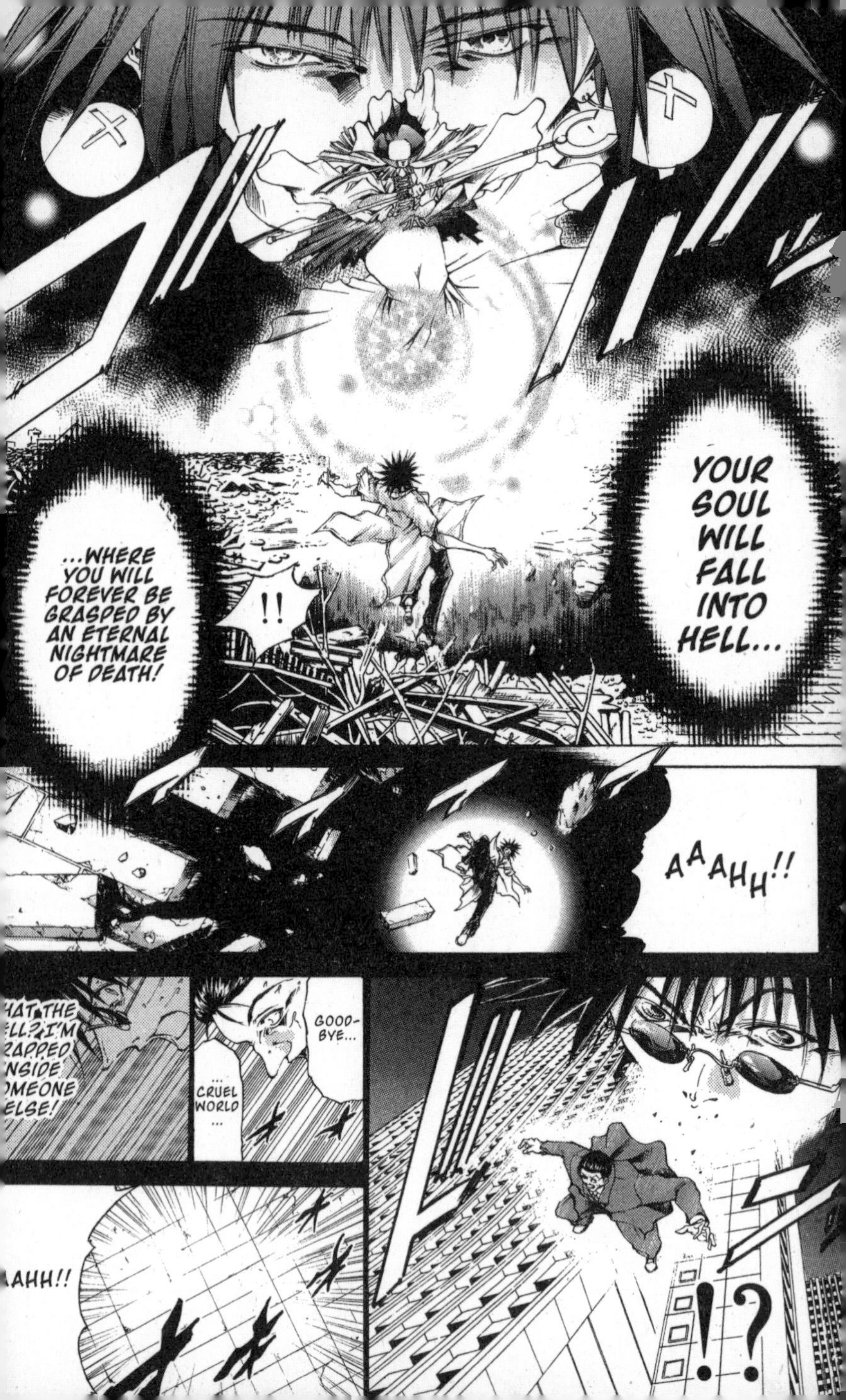
YOUR SOUL WILL FALL INTO HELL...
!!
...WHERE YOU WILL FOREVER BE GRASPED BY AN ETERNAL NIGHTMARE OF DEATH!
AAAHH!!
!
!?
GOOD-BYE...
...CRUEL WORLD...
HAT THE ELL?! I'M RAPPED INSIDE OMEONE ELSE!
AHH!!

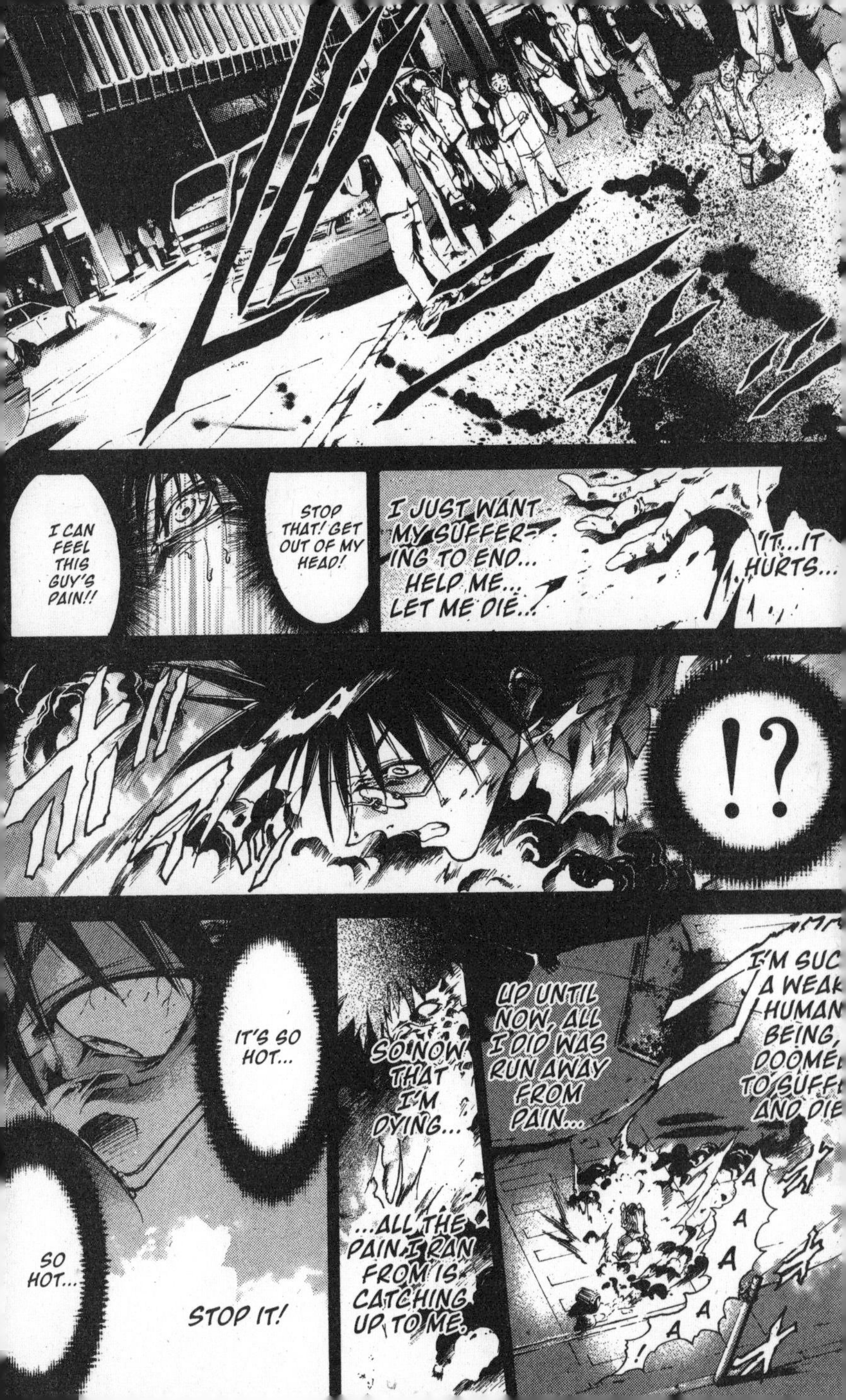
IT...IT HURTS...
I JUST WANT MY SUFFERING TO END... HELP ME... LET ME DIE...
STOP THAT! GET OUT OF MY HEAD!
I CAN FEEL THIS GUY'S PAIN!!
!?
I'M SUC A WEAK HUMAN BEING, DOOMED TO SUFF AND DIE
UP UNTIL NOW, ALL I DID WAS RUN AWAY FROM PAIN...
SO NOW THAT I'M DYING...
...ALL THE PAIN I RAN FROM IS CATCHING UP TO ME.
A A A A A A
IT'S SO HOT...
SO HOT...
STOP IT!

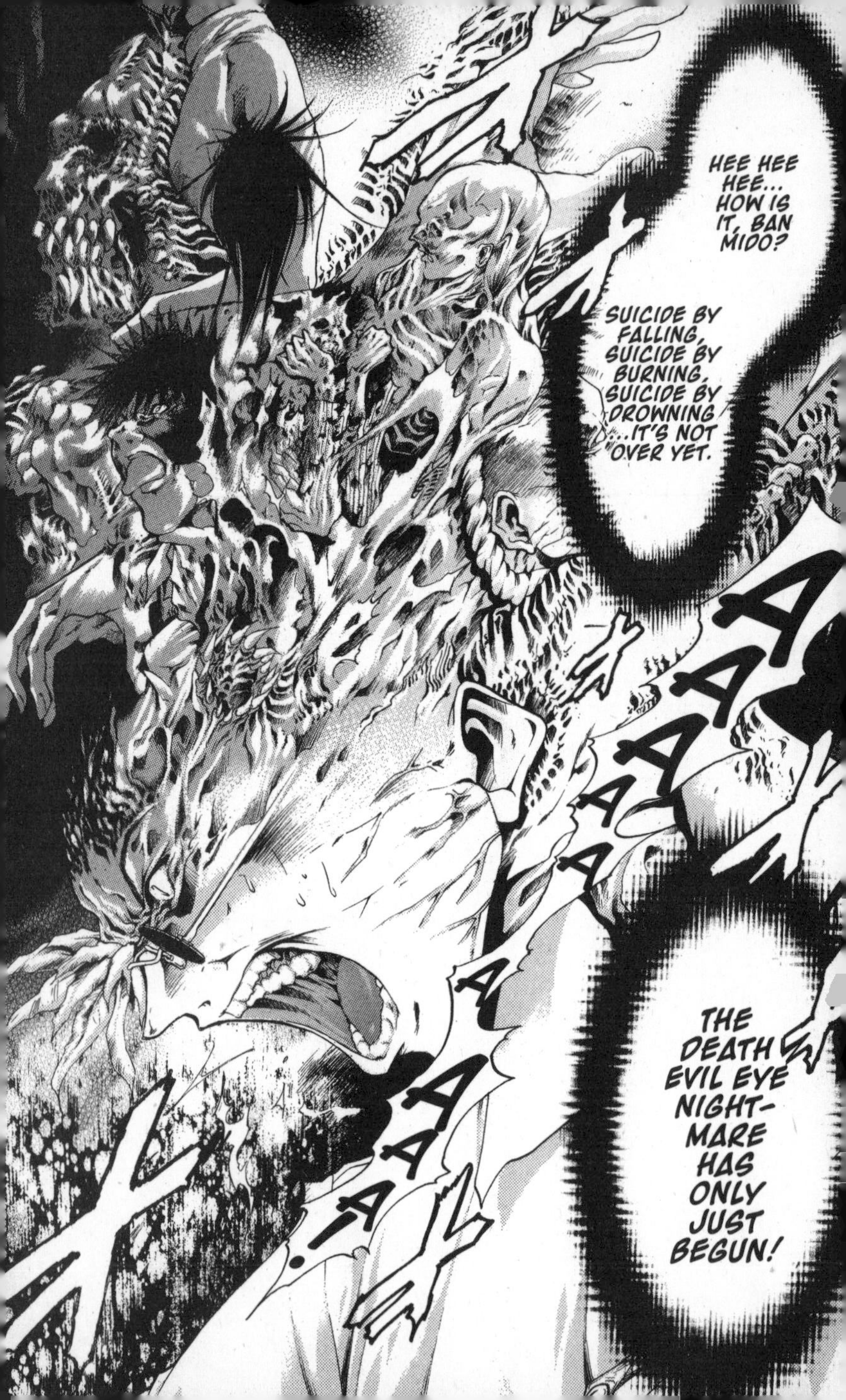
HEE HEE HEE... HOW IS IT, BAN MIDO?
SUICIDE BY FALLING, SUICIDE BY BURNING, SUICIDE BY DROWNING ...IT'S NOT OVER YET.
AAAAAAAAAAAAA!
THE DEATH EVIL EYE NIGHTMARE HAS ONLY JUST BEGUN!

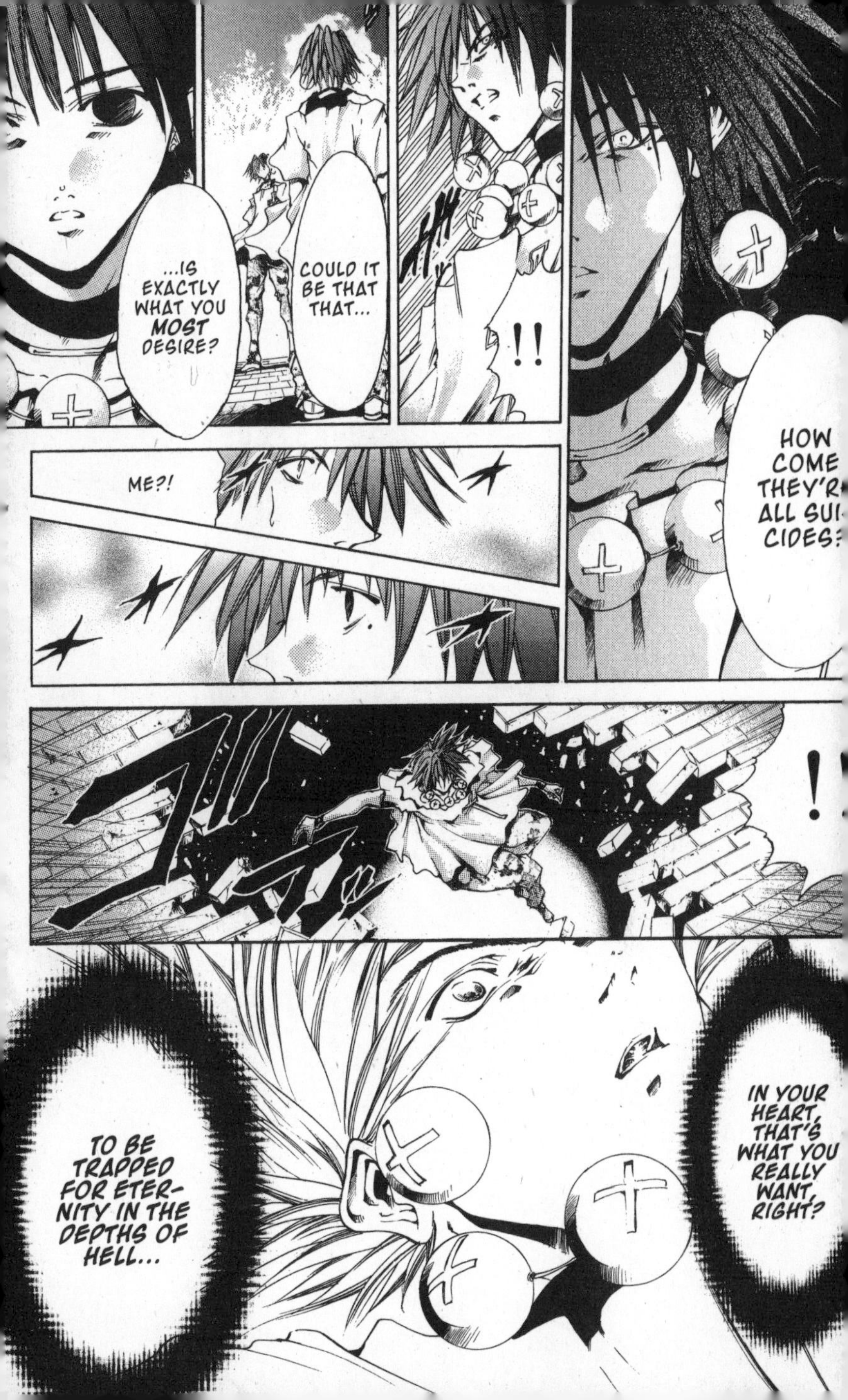
HOW COME THEY'R ALL SUI-CIDES?
!!
COULD IT BE THAT THAT...
...IS EXACTLY WHAT YOU MOST DESIRE?
ME?!
!
IN YOUR HEART, THAT'S WHAT YOU REALLY WANT, RIGHT?
TO BE TRAPPED FOR ETER-NITY IN THE DEPTHS OF HELL...

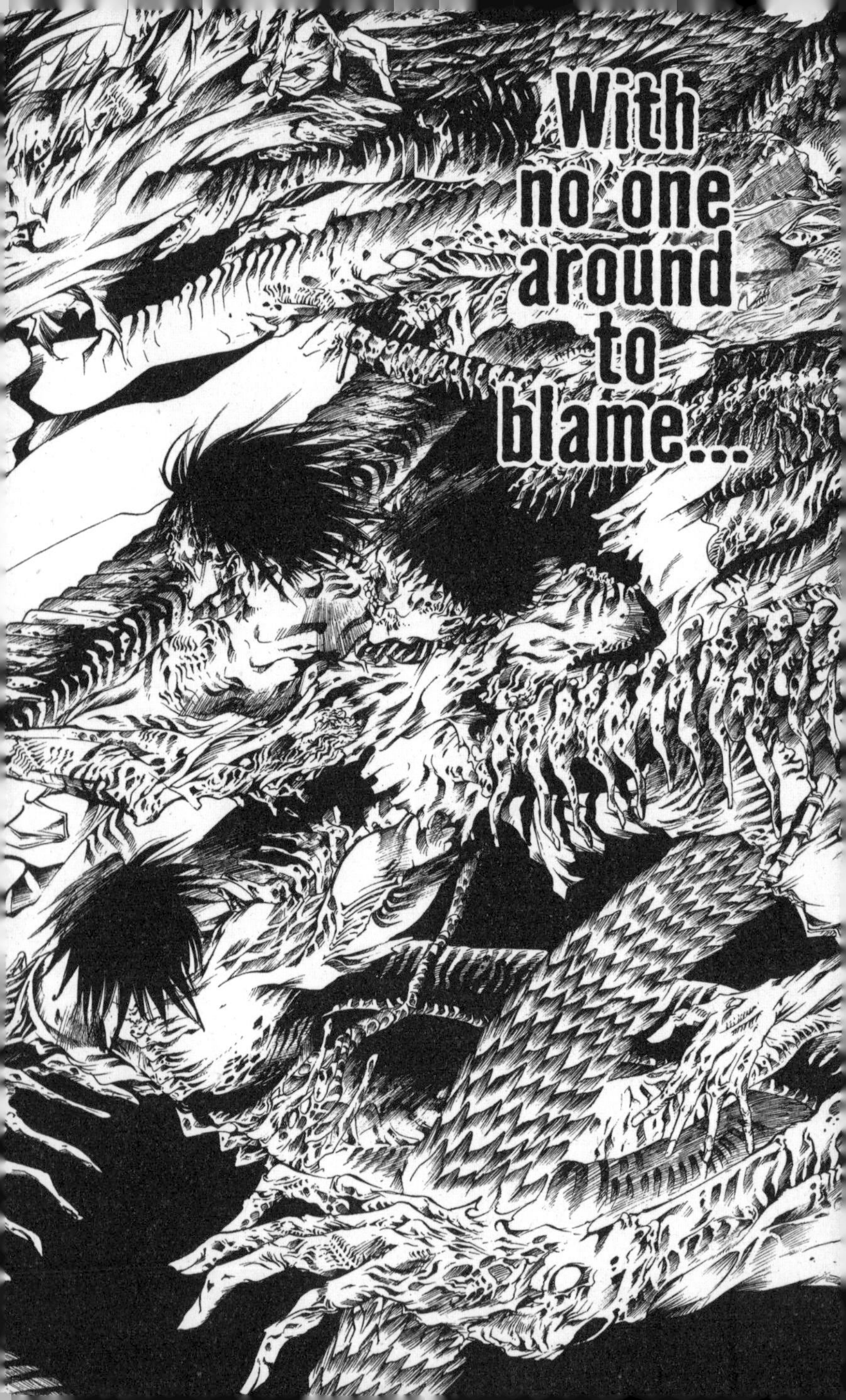
With no one around to blame....

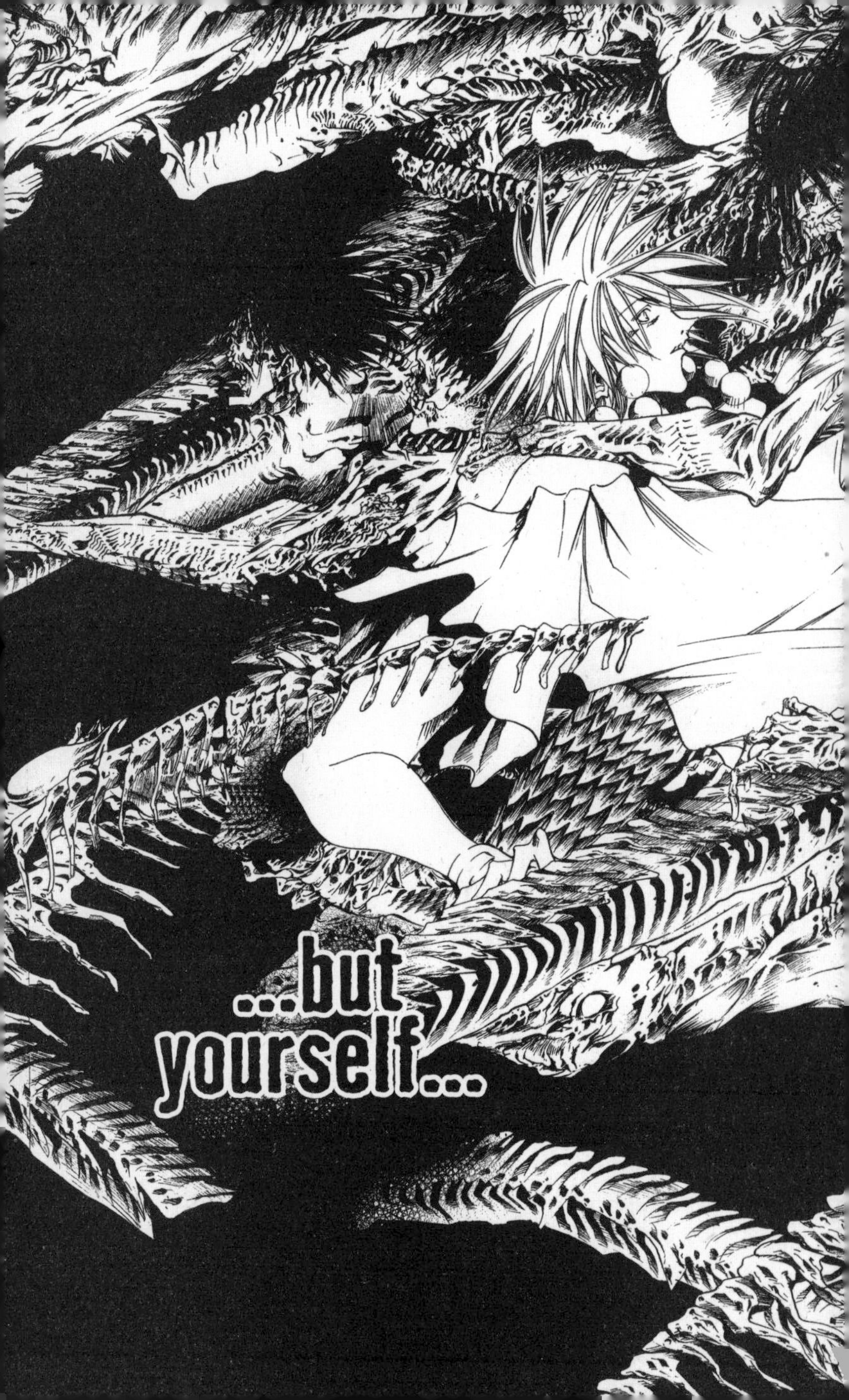
...but yourself...

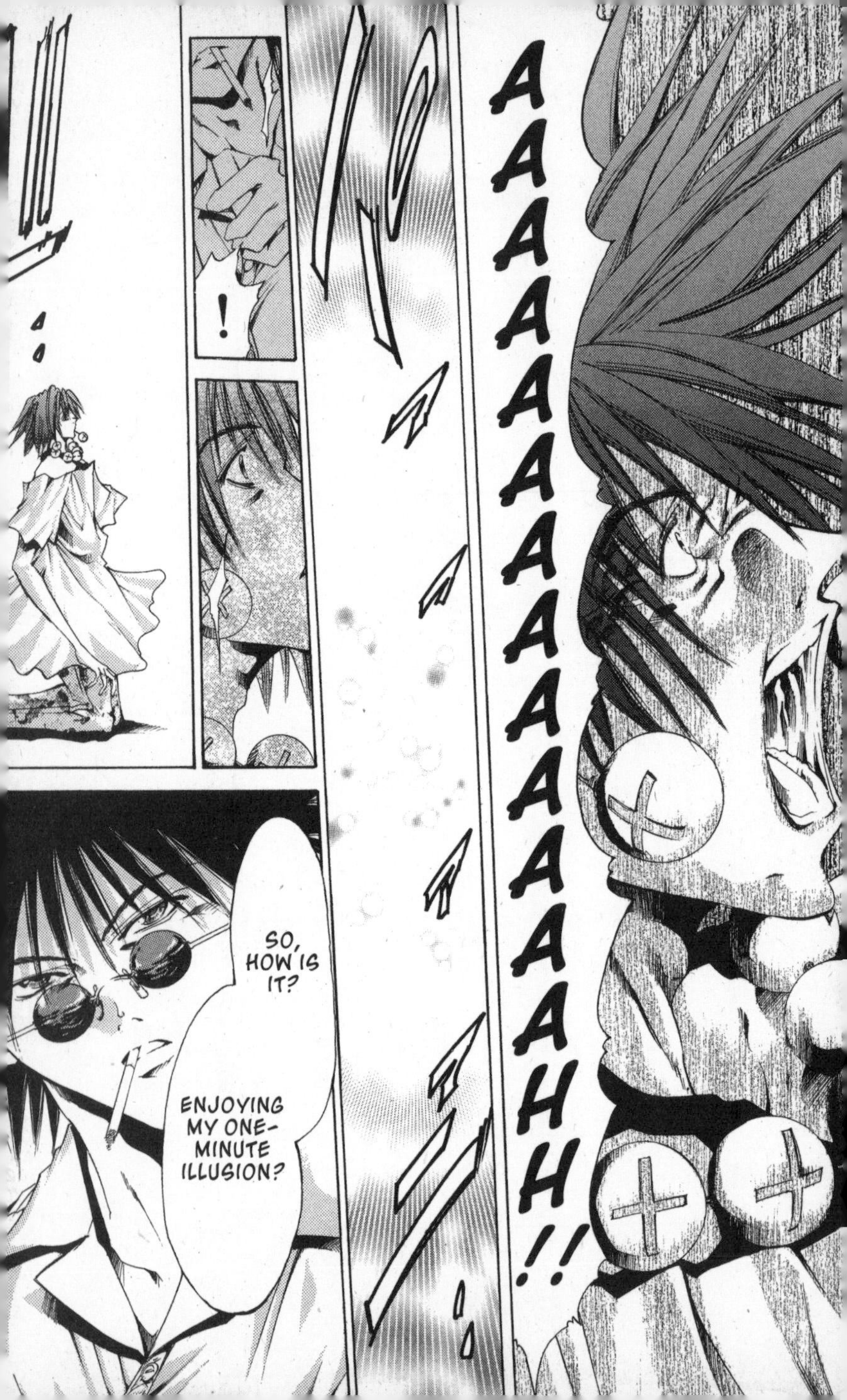
AAAAAAAAAAAAAAAAAAAAH!!
!
SO, HOW IS IT?
ENJOYING MY ONE-MINUTE ILLUSION?

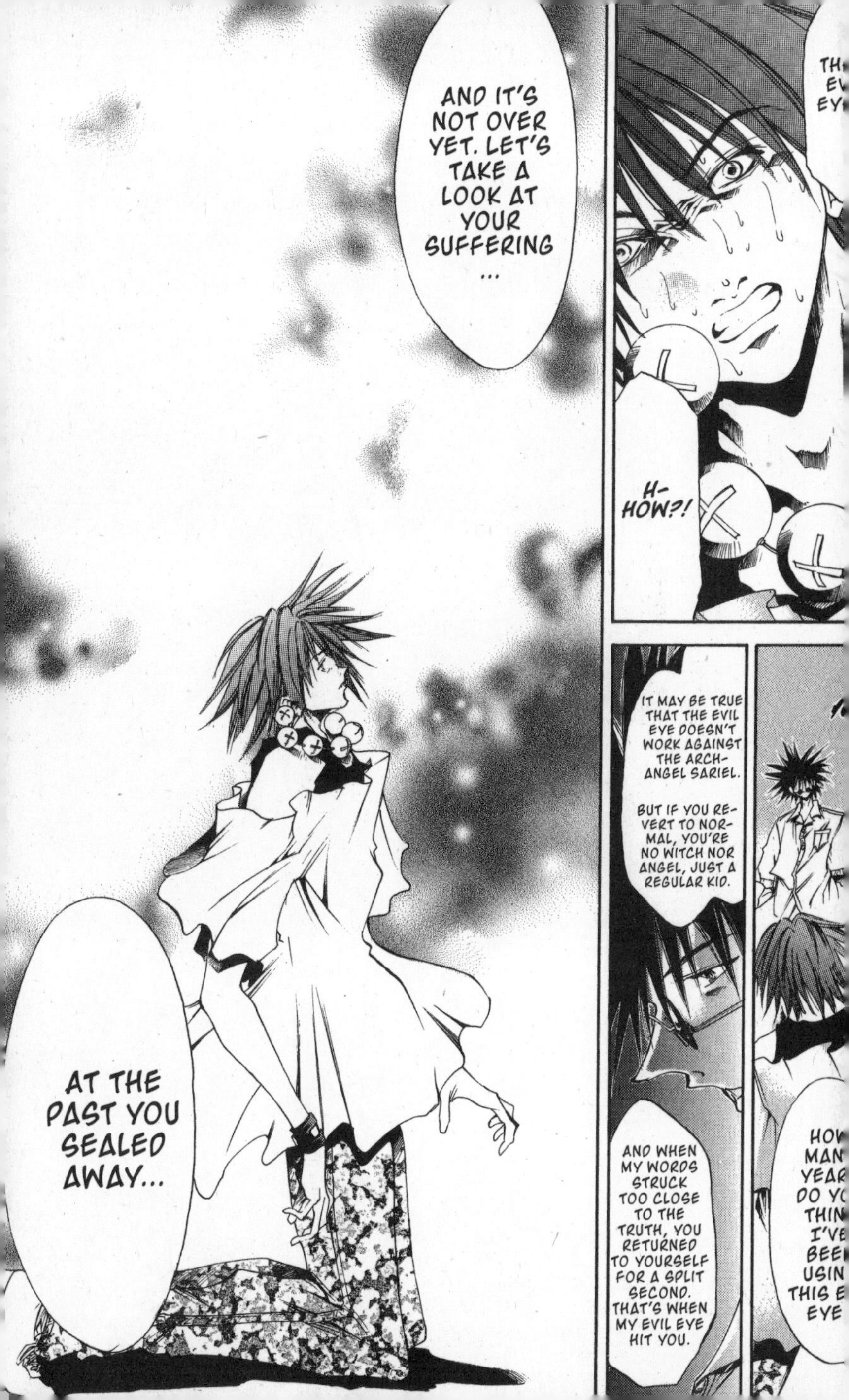
TH EV EY
H-HOW?!
HOW MAN YEAR DO YO THIN I'VE BEE USIN THIS E EYE
IT MAY BE TRUE THAT THE EVIL EYE DOESN'T WORK AGAINST THE ARCH-ANGEL SARIEL.
BUT IF YOU RE-VERT TO NOR-MAL, YOU'RE NO WITCH NOR ANGEL, JUST A REGULAR KID.
AND WHEN MY WORDS STRUCK TOO CLOSE TO THE TRUTH, YOU RETURNED TO YOURSELF FOR A SPLIT SECOND. THAT'S WHEN MY EVIL EYE HIT YOU.
AND IT'S NOT OVER YET. LET'S TAKE A LOOK AT YOUR SUFFERING...
AT THE PAST YOU SEALED AWAY...

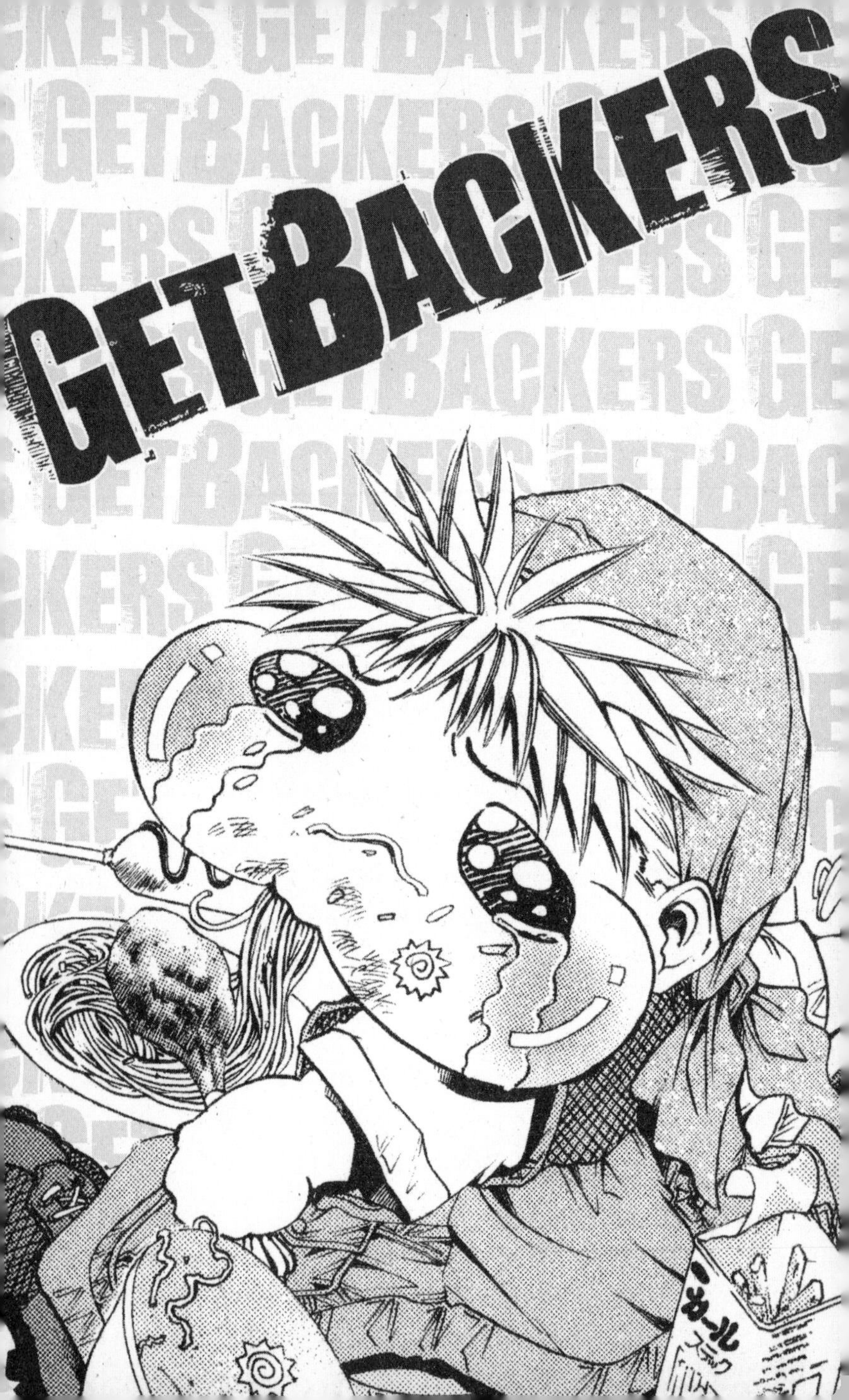
GETBACKERS
カール
スナック

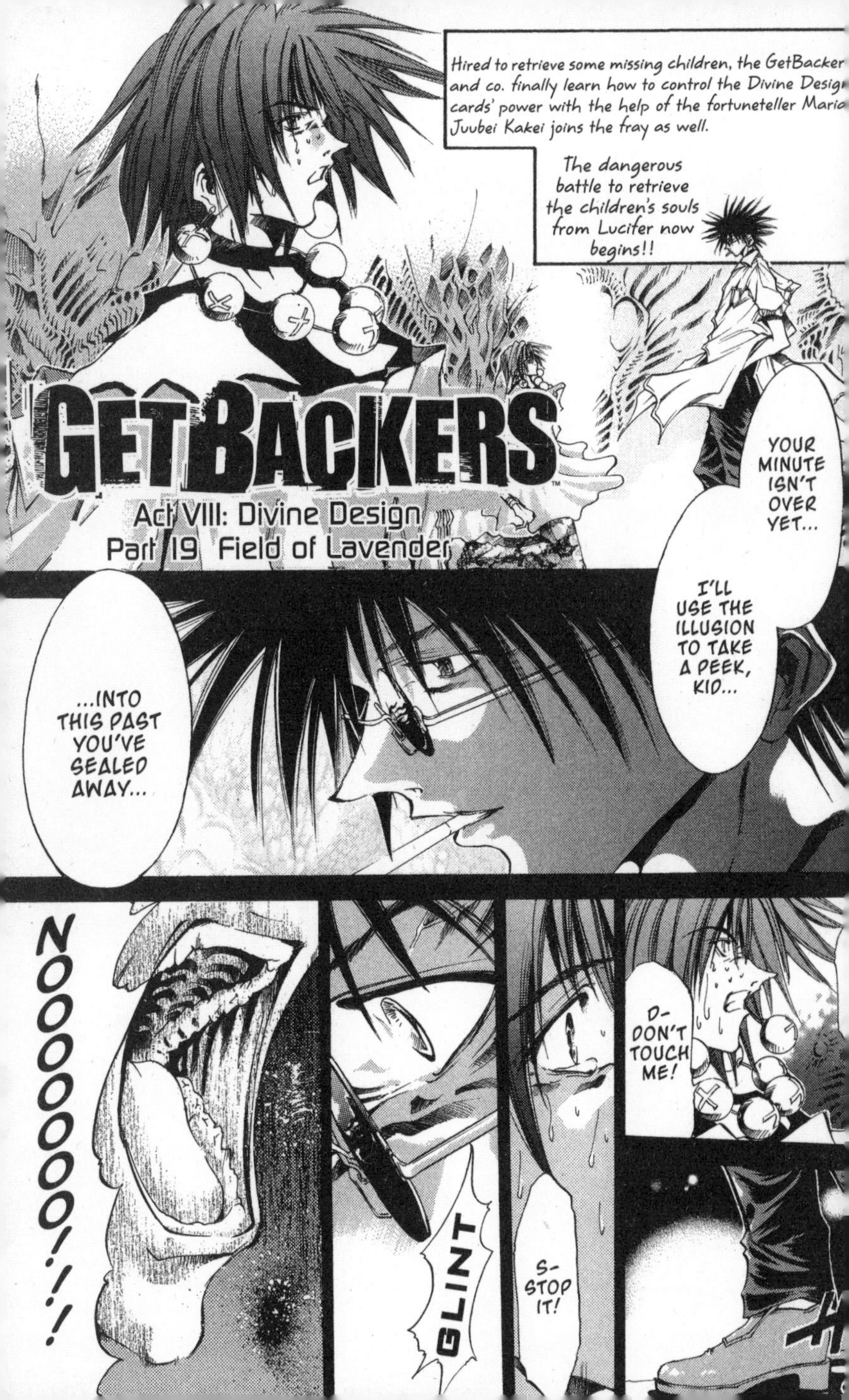
Hired to retrieve some missing children, the GetBacker and co. finally learn how to control the Divine Desig cards' power with the help of the fortuneteller Maria Juubei Kakei joins the fray as well.
The dangerous battle to retrieve the children's souls from Lucifer now begins!!
GETBACKERS™
Act VIII: Divine Design
Part 19 Field of Lavender
YOUR MINUTE ISN'T OVER YET...
I'LL USE THE ILLUSION TO TAKE A PEEK, KID...
...INTO THIS PAST YOU'VE SEALED AWAY...
D-DON'T TOUCH ME!
S-STOP IT!
GLINT
NOOOOOOOO!!!!

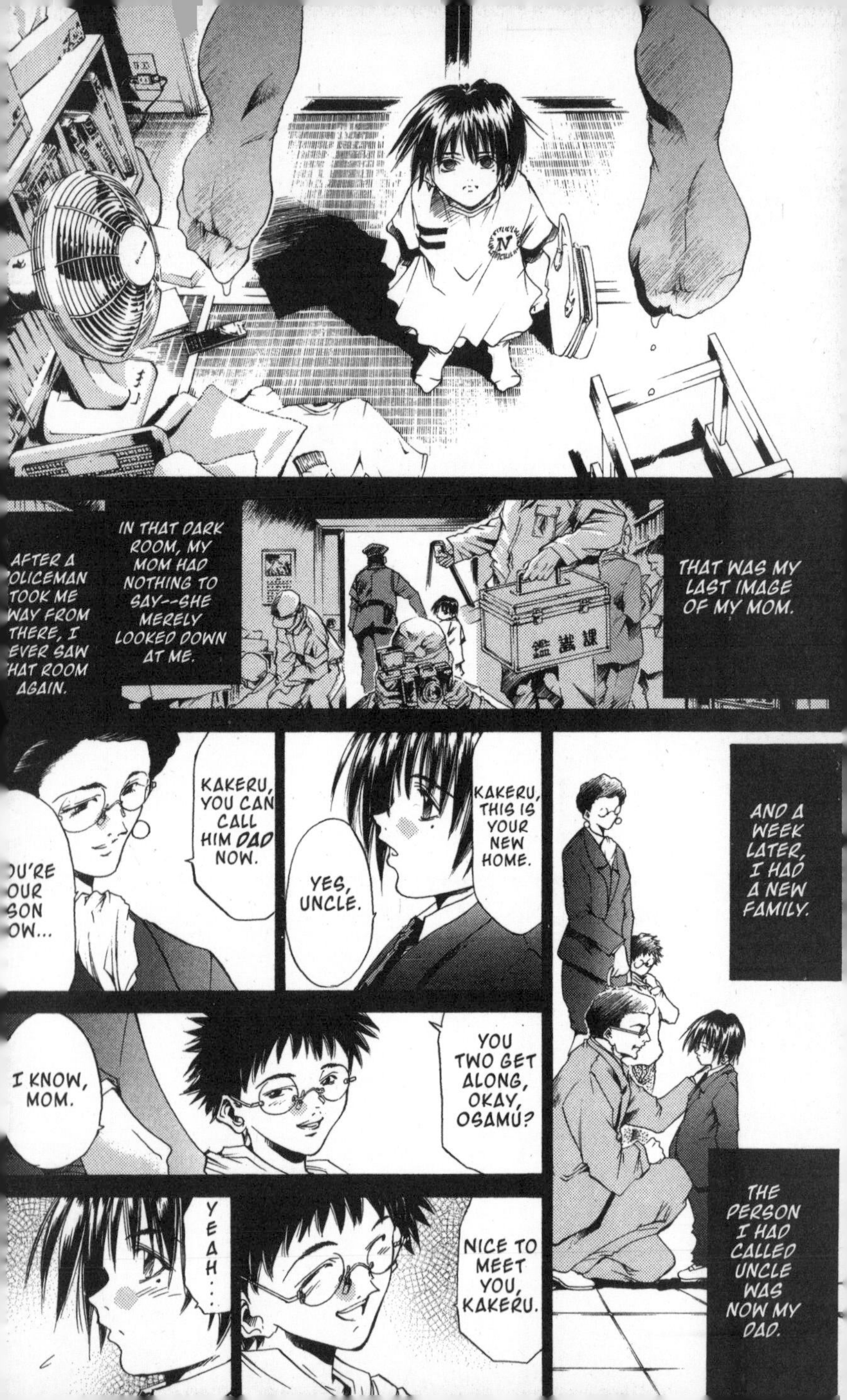
THAT WAS MY LAST IMAGE OF MY MOM.
監識課
IN THAT DARK ROOM, MY MOM HAD NOTHING TO SAY--SHE MERELY LOOKED DOWN AT ME.
AFTER A OLICEMAN TOOK ME WAY FROM THERE, I EVER SAW HAT ROOM AGAIN.
AND A WEEK LATER, I HAD A NEW FAMILY.
THE PERSON I HAD CALLED UNCLE WAS NOW MY DAD.
KAKERU, THIS IS YOUR NEW HOME.
YES, UNCLE.
KAKERU, YOU CAN CALL HIM DAD NOW.
OU'RE OUR SON OW...
YOU TWO GET ALONG, OKAY, OSAMU?
I KNOW, MOM.
NICE TO MEET YOU, KAKERU.
YEAH...

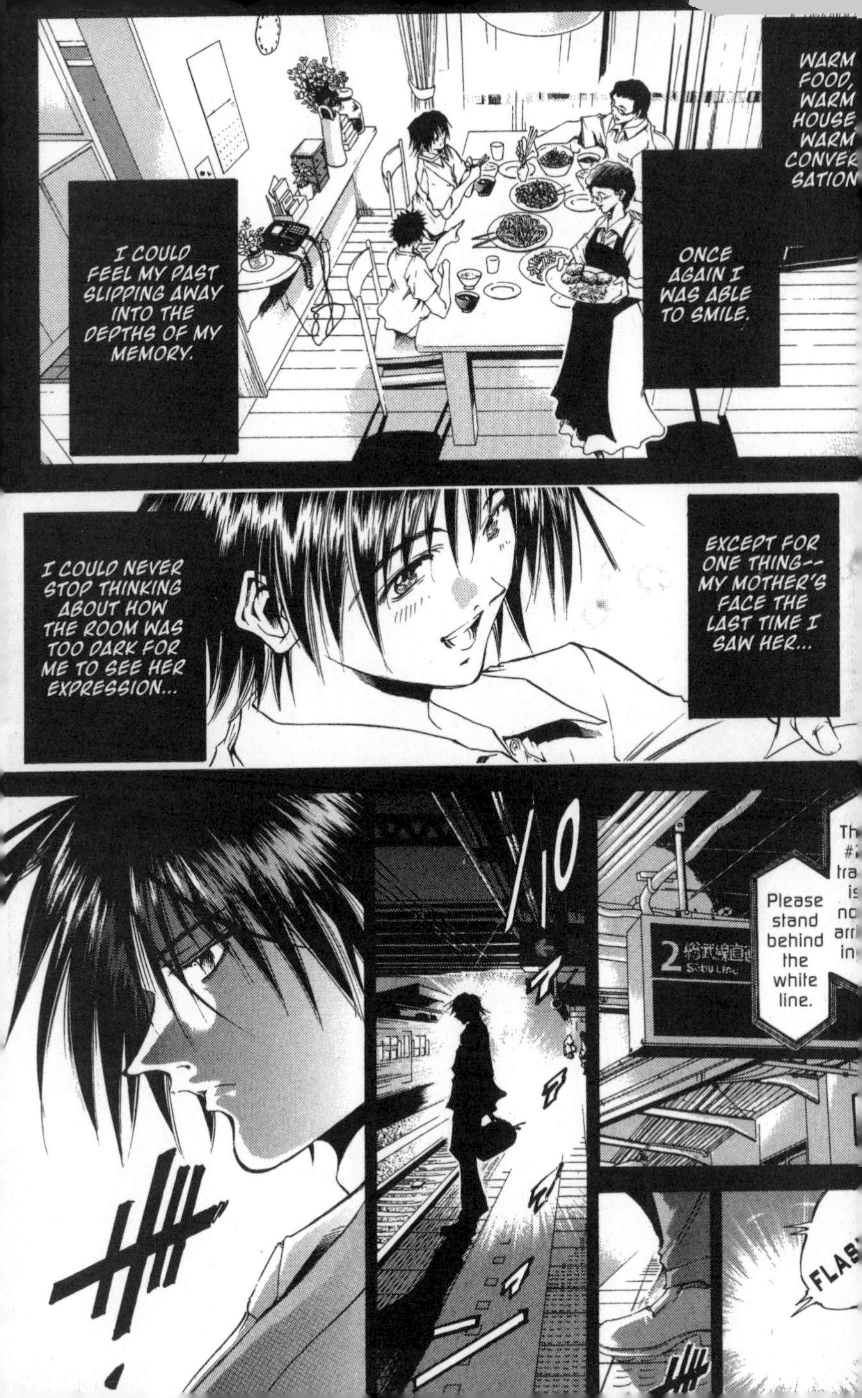
WARM FOOD, WARM HOUSE, WARM CONVERSATION
ONCE AGAIN I WAS ABLE TO SMILE.
I COULD FEEL MY PAST SLIPPING AWAY INTO THE DEPTHS OF MY MEMORY.
EXCEPT FOR ONE THING-- MY MOTHER'S FACE THE LAST TIME I SAW HER...
I COULD NEVER STOP THINKING ABOUT HOW THE ROOM WAS TOO DARK FOR ME TO SEE HER EXPRESSION...
Please stand behind the white line.
2 Sobu Line
FLAS

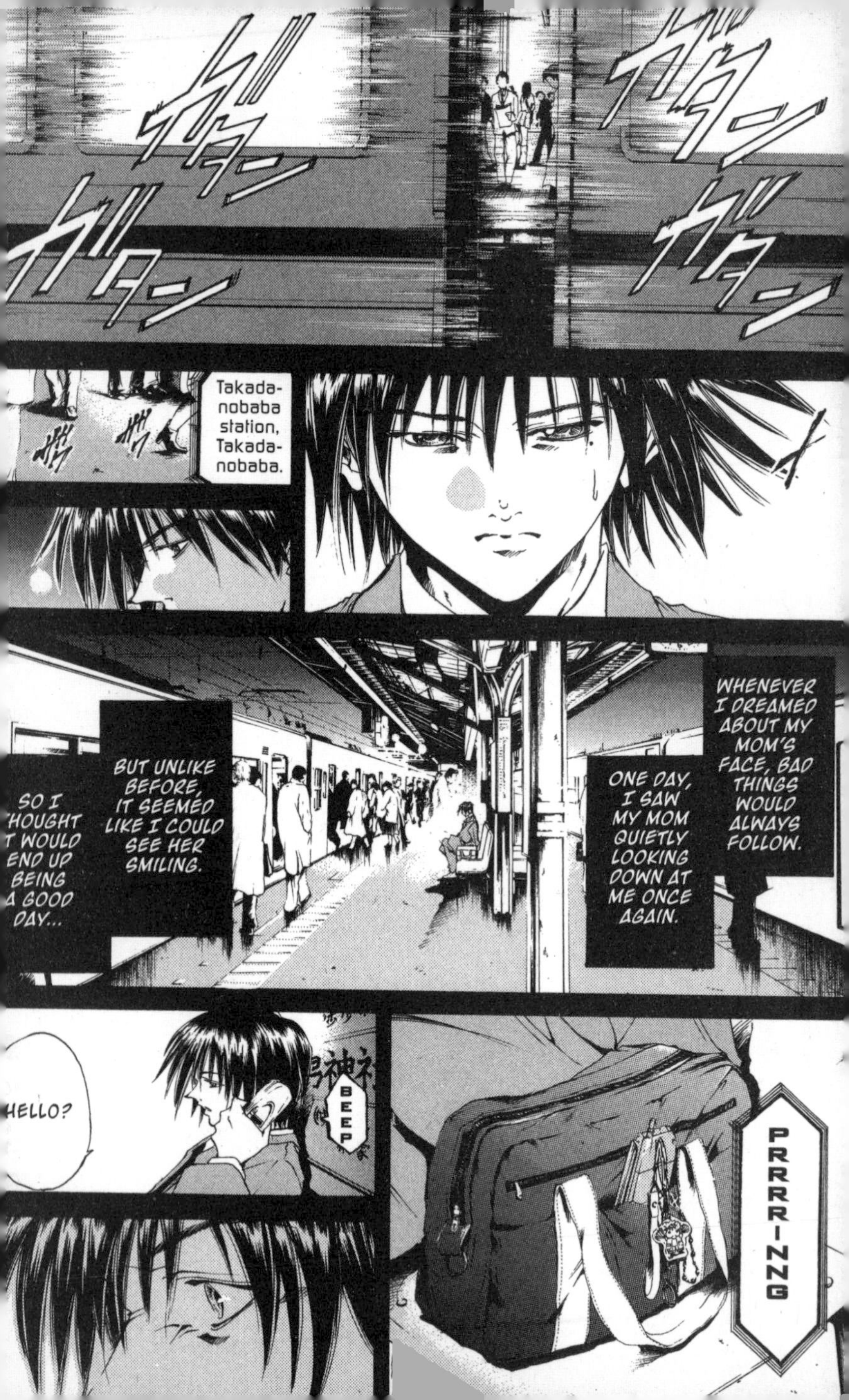
ガタン
ガタン
ガタン
ガタン
Takada-nobaba station, Takada-nobaba.
WHENEVER I DREAMED ABOUT MY MOM'S FACE, BAD THINGS WOULD ALWAYS FOLLOW.
ONE DAY, I SAW MY MOM QUIETLY LOOKING DOWN AT ME ONCE AGAIN.
BUT UNLIKE BEFORE, IT SEEMED LIKE I COULD SEE HER SMILING.
SO I HOUGHT T WOULD END UP BEING A GOOD DAY...
PRRRING
BEEP
HELLO?

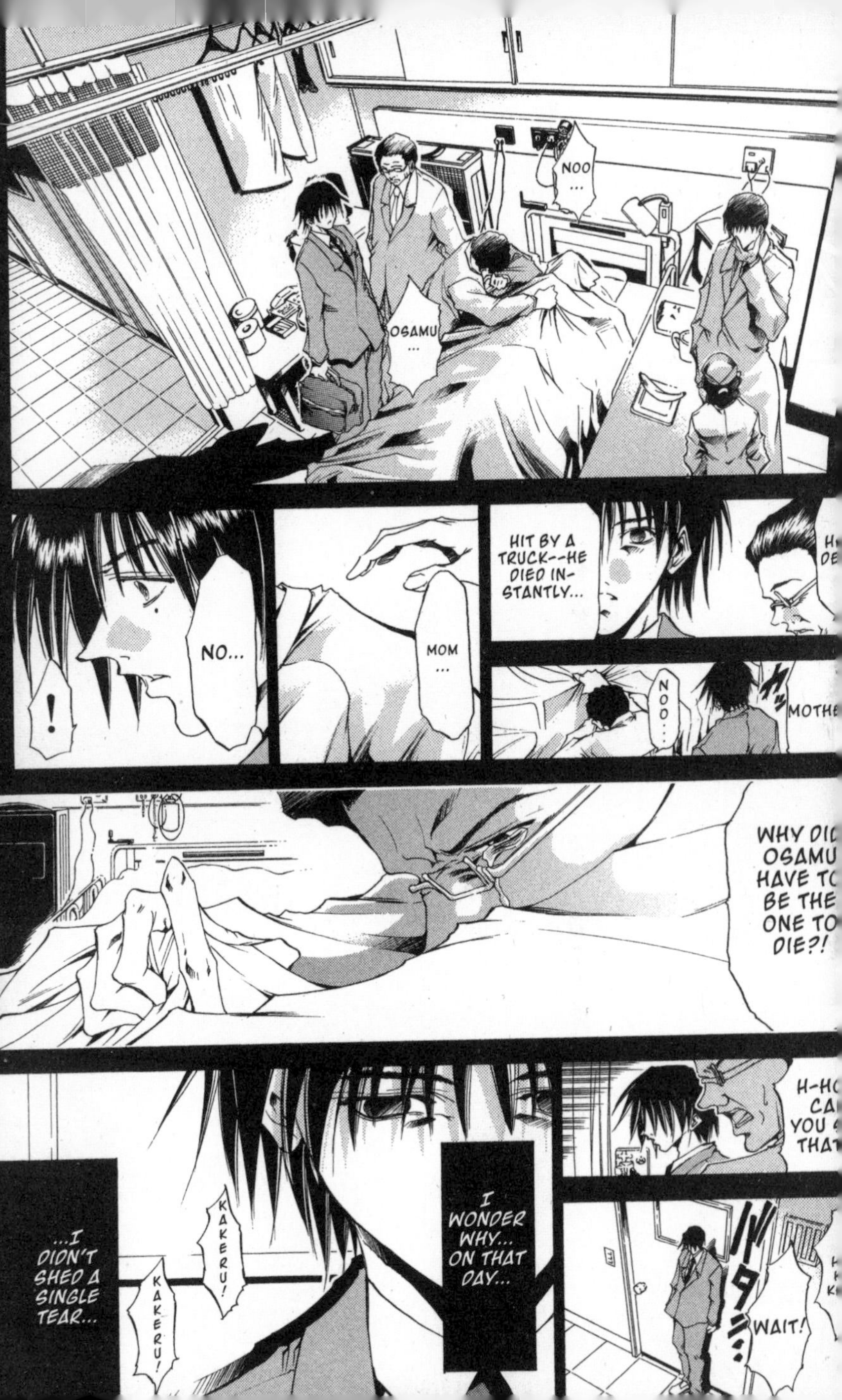
NOO ...
OSAMU ...
HIT BY A TRUCK--HE DIED INSTANTLY...
NOO...
MOM ...
NO...
!
WHY DID OSAMU HAVE TO BE THE ONE TO DIE?!
WAIT!
I WONDER WHY... ON THAT DAY...
KAKERU!
KAKERU!
...I DIDN'T SHED A SINGLE TEAR...

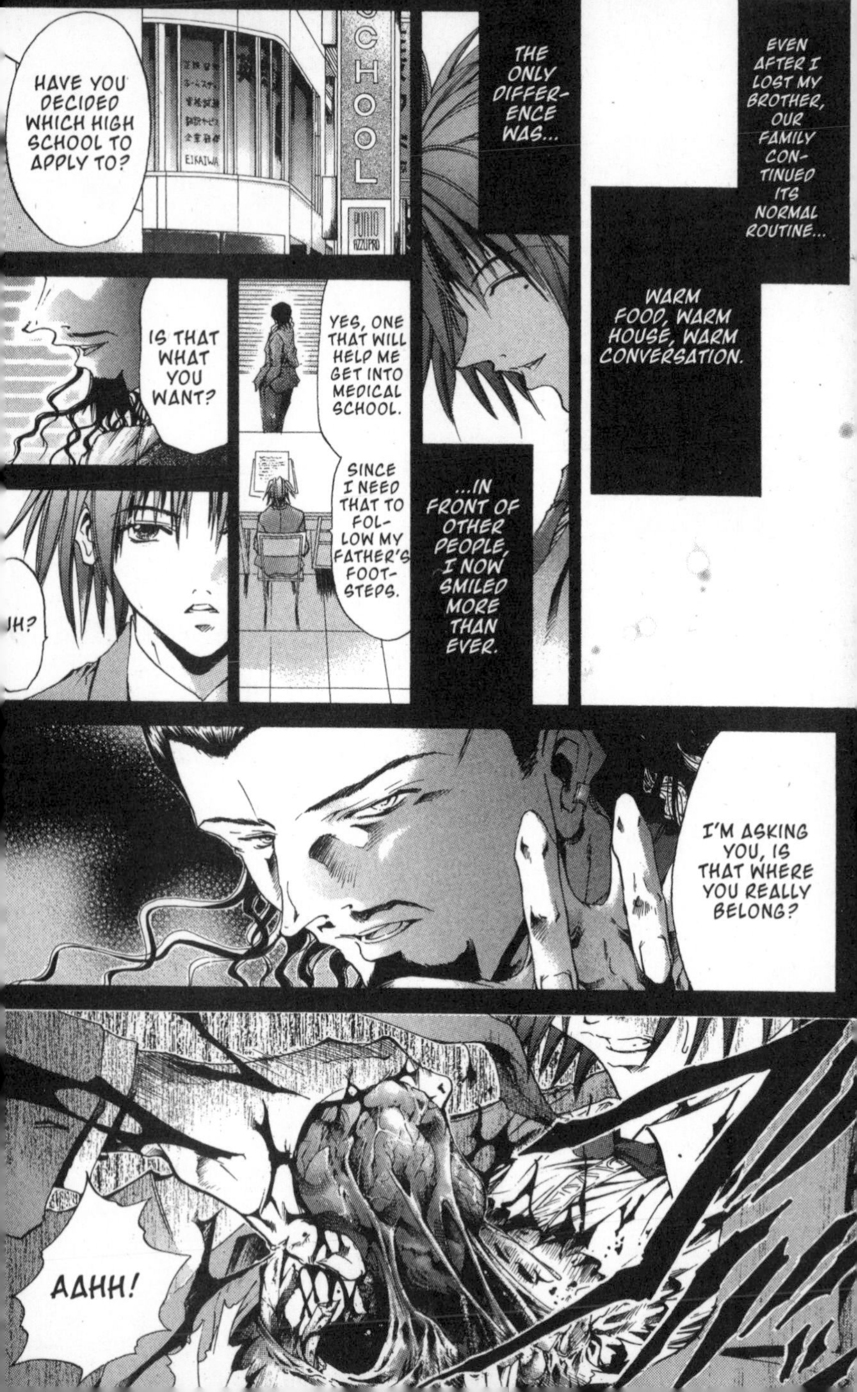
EVEN AFTER I LOST MY BROTHER, OUR FAMILY CONTINUED ITS NORMAL ROUTINE...
WARM FOOD, WARM HOUSE, WARM CONVERSATION.
THE ONLY DIFFERENCE WAS...
...IN FRONT OF OTHER PEOPLE, I NOW SMILED MORE THAN EVER.
SCHOOL
EIKAIWA
HAVE YOU DECIDED WHICH HIGH SCHOOL TO APPLY TO?
YES, ONE THAT WILL HELP ME GET INTO MEDICAL SCHOOL.
SINCE I NEED THAT TO FOLLOW MY FATHER'S FOOTSTEPS.
IS THAT WHAT YOU WANT?
H?
I'M ASKING YOU, IS THAT WHERE YOU REALLY BELONG?
AAHH!

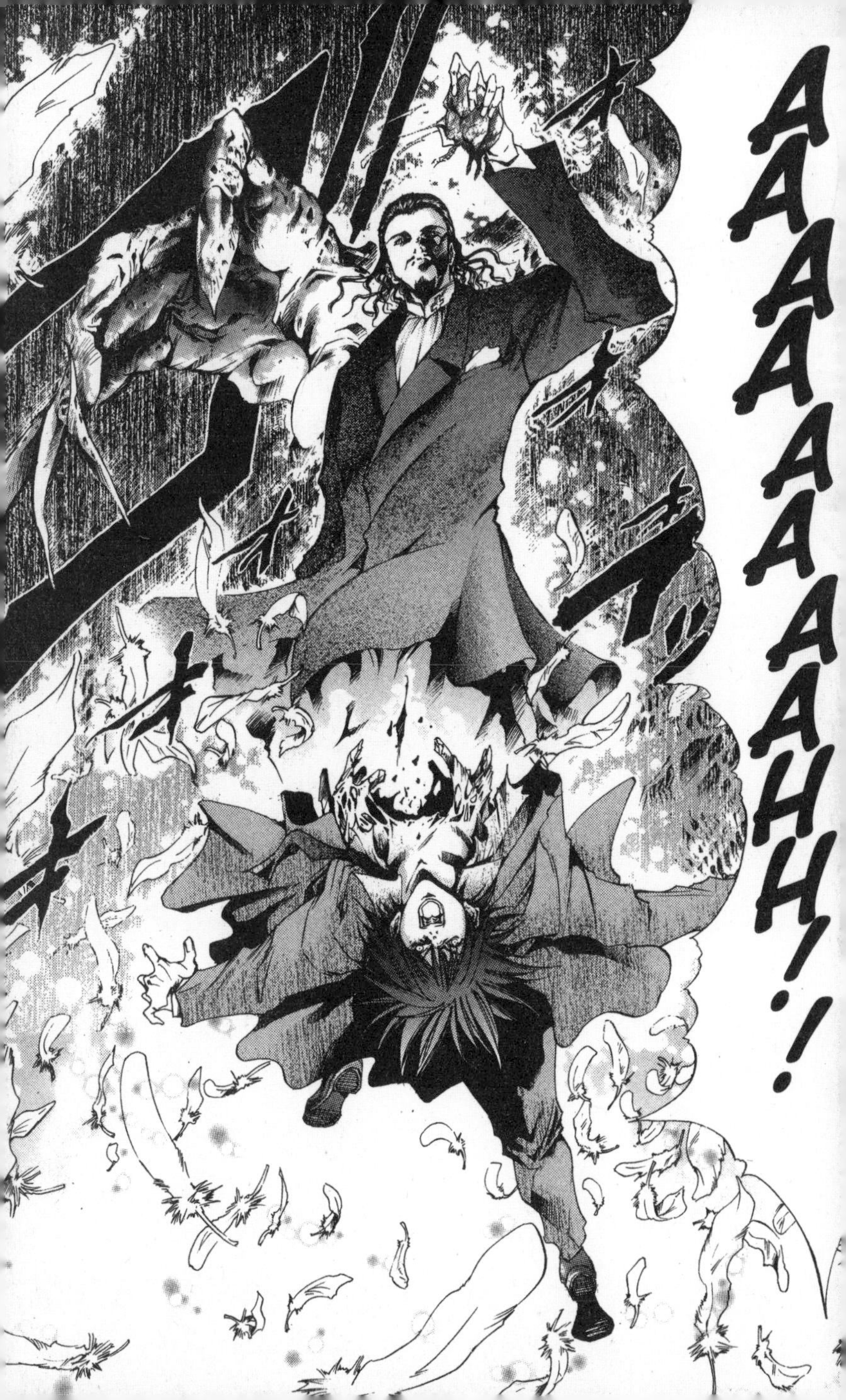
AAAAAAAAH!!!

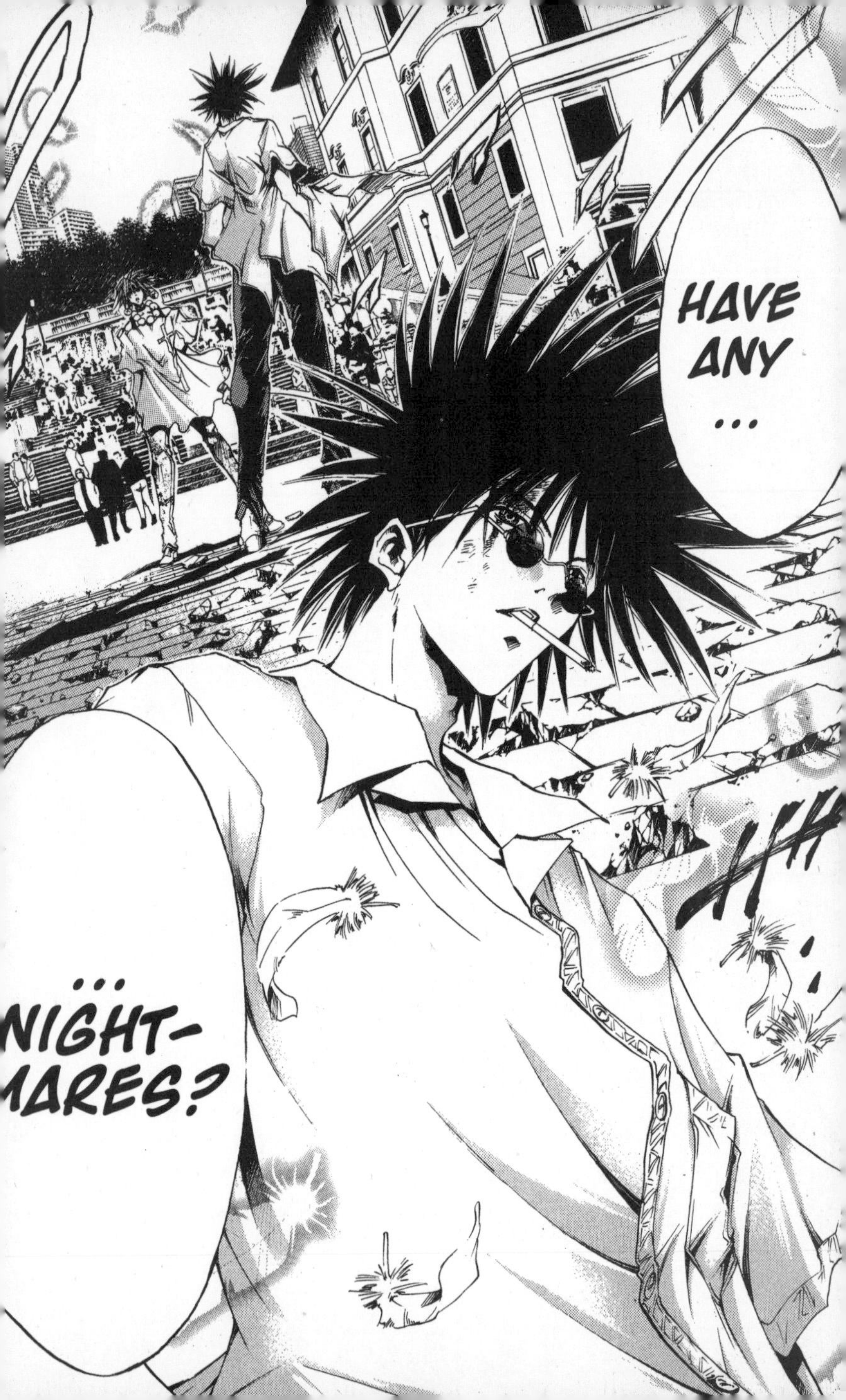
HAVE ANY ...
... NIGHT-MARES?

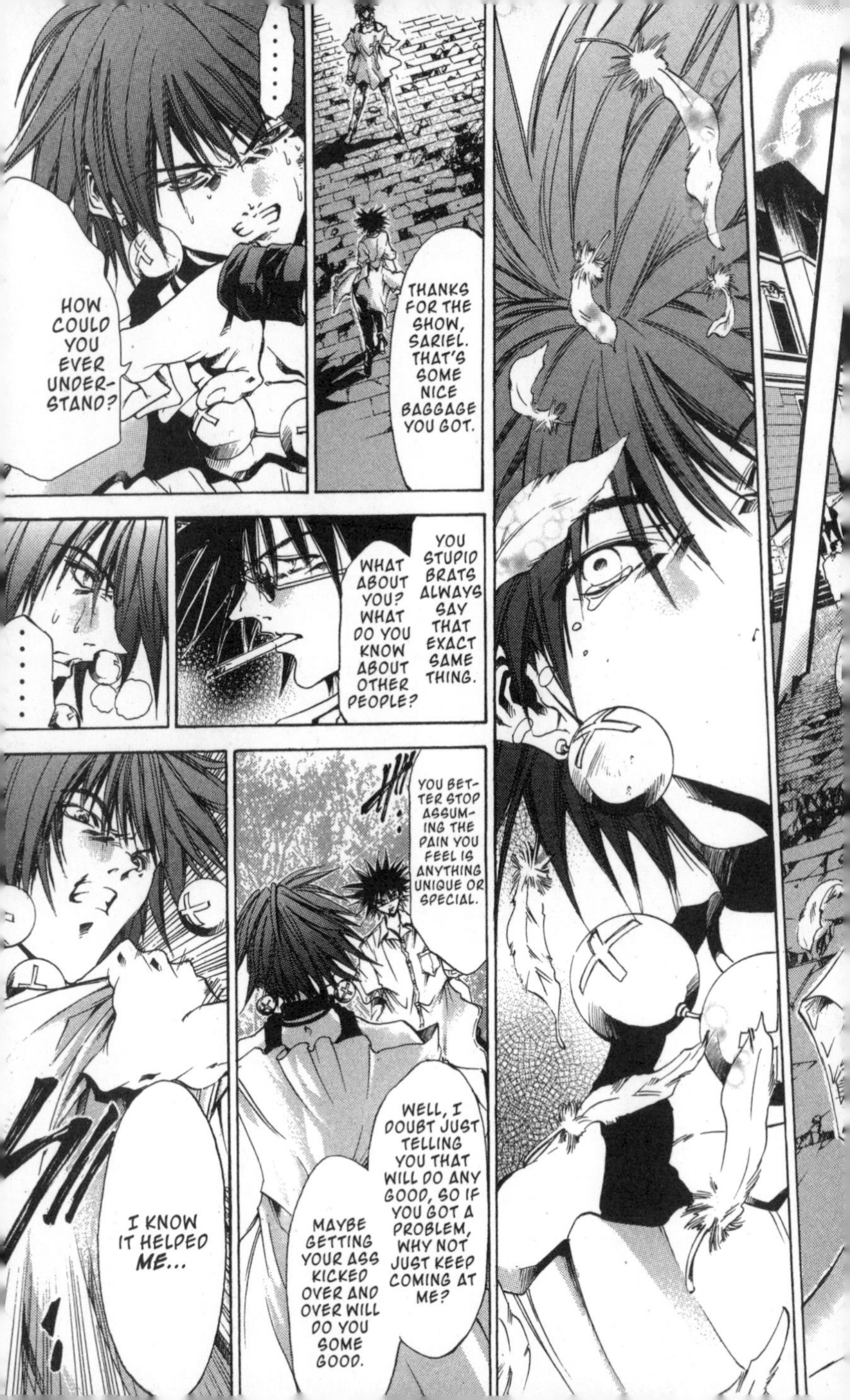
THANKS FOR THE SHOW, SARIEL. THAT'S SOME NICE BAGGAGE YOU GOT.
......
HOW COULD YOU EVER UNDER-STAND?
YOU STUPID BRATS ALWAYS SAY THAT EXACT SAME THING.
WHAT ABOUT YOU? WHAT DO YOU KNOW ABOUT OTHER PEOPLE?
......
YOU BET-TER STOP ASSUM-ING THE PAIN YOU FEEL IS ANYTHING UNIQUE OR SPECIAL.
WELL, I DOUBT JUST TELLING YOU THAT WILL DO ANY GOOD, SO IF YOU GOT A PROBLEM, WHY NOT JUST KEEP COMING AT ME?
MAYBE GETTING YOUR ASS KICKED OVER AND OVER WILL DO YOU SOME GOOD.
I KNOW IT HELPED ME...

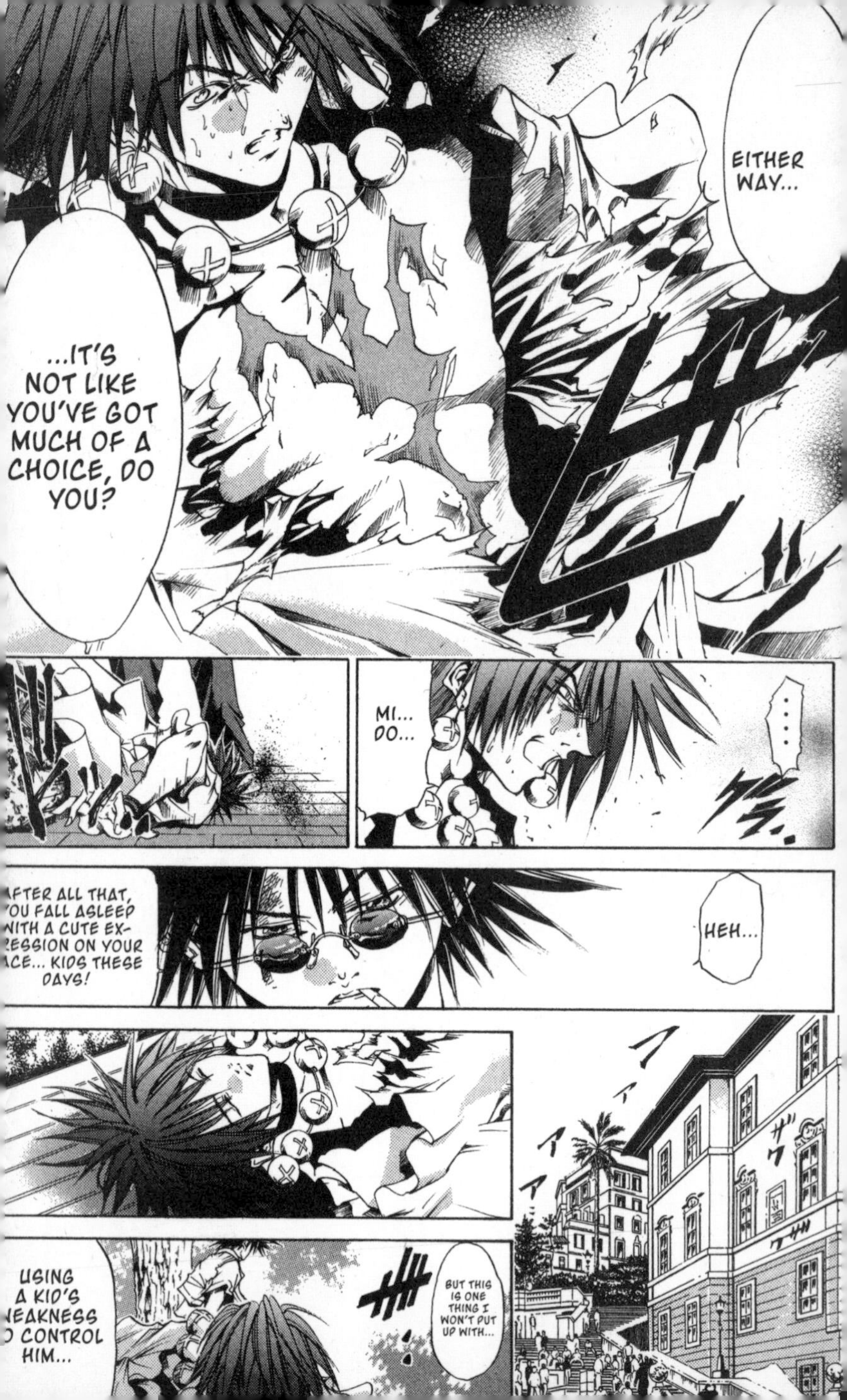
EITHER WAY...
...IT'S NOT LIKE YOU'VE GOT MUCH OF A CHOICE, DO YOU?
MI... DO...
....
HEH...
AFTER ALL THAT, YOU FALL ASLEEP WITH A CUTE EX-PRESSION ON YOUR FACE... KIDS THESE DAYS!
BUT THIS IS ONE THING I WON'T PUT UP WITH...
USING A KID'S WEAKNESS TO CONTROL HIM...

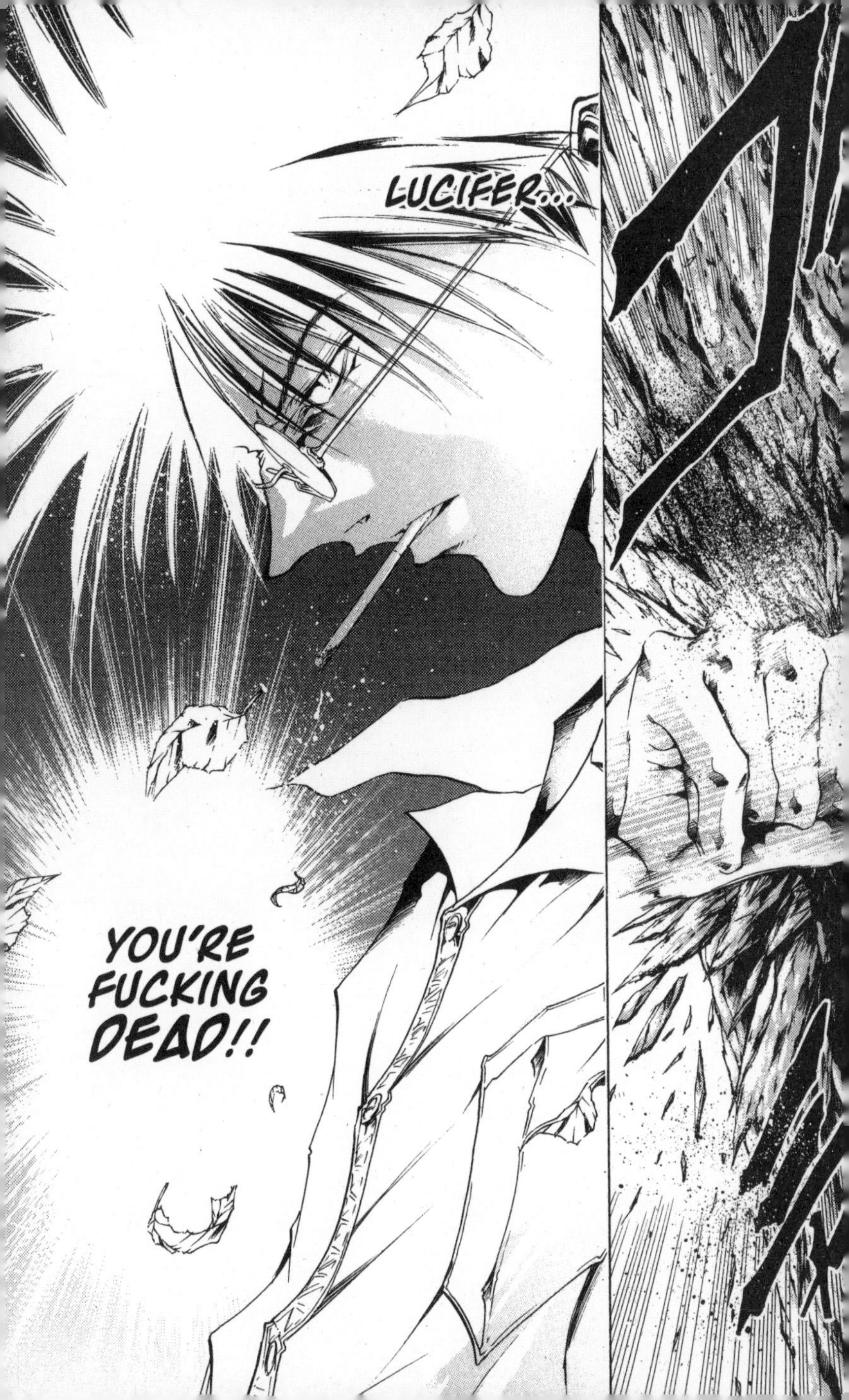
LUCIFER...
YOU'RE FUCKING DEAD!!

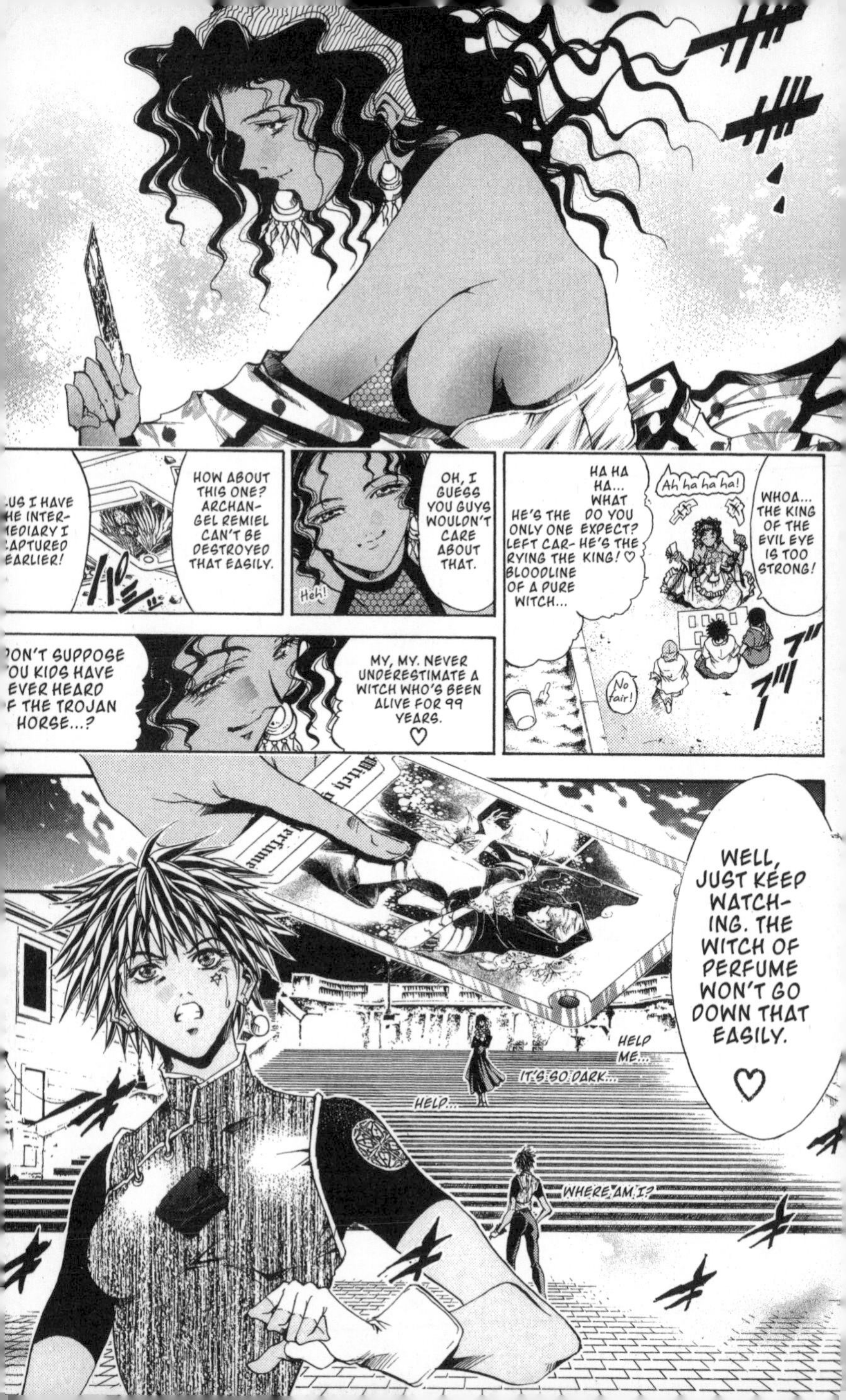
Ah ha ha ha!
WHOA... THE KING OF THE EVIL EYE IS TOO STRONG!
HA HA HA... WHAT DO YOU EXPECT? HE'S THE KING! ♡
HE'S THE ONLY ONE LEFT CAR-RYING THE BLOODLINE OF A PURE WITCH...
No fair!
OH, I GUESS YOU GUYS WOULDN'T CARE ABOUT THAT.
Heh!
HOW ABOUT THIS ONE? ARCHAN-GEL REMIEL CAN'T BE DESTROYED THAT EASILY.
LUS I HAVE HE INTER-MEDIARY I CAPTURED EARLIER!
MY, MY. NEVER UNDERESTIMATE A WITCH WHO'S BEEN ALIVE FOR 99 YEARS. ♡
ON'T SUPPOSE OU KIDS HAVE EVER HEARD F THE TROJAN HORSE...?
WELL, JUST KEEP WATCHING. THE WITCH OF PERFUME WON'T GO DOWN THAT EASILY. ♡
perfume
HELP ME...
IT'S SO DARK...
HELP...
WHERE AM I?

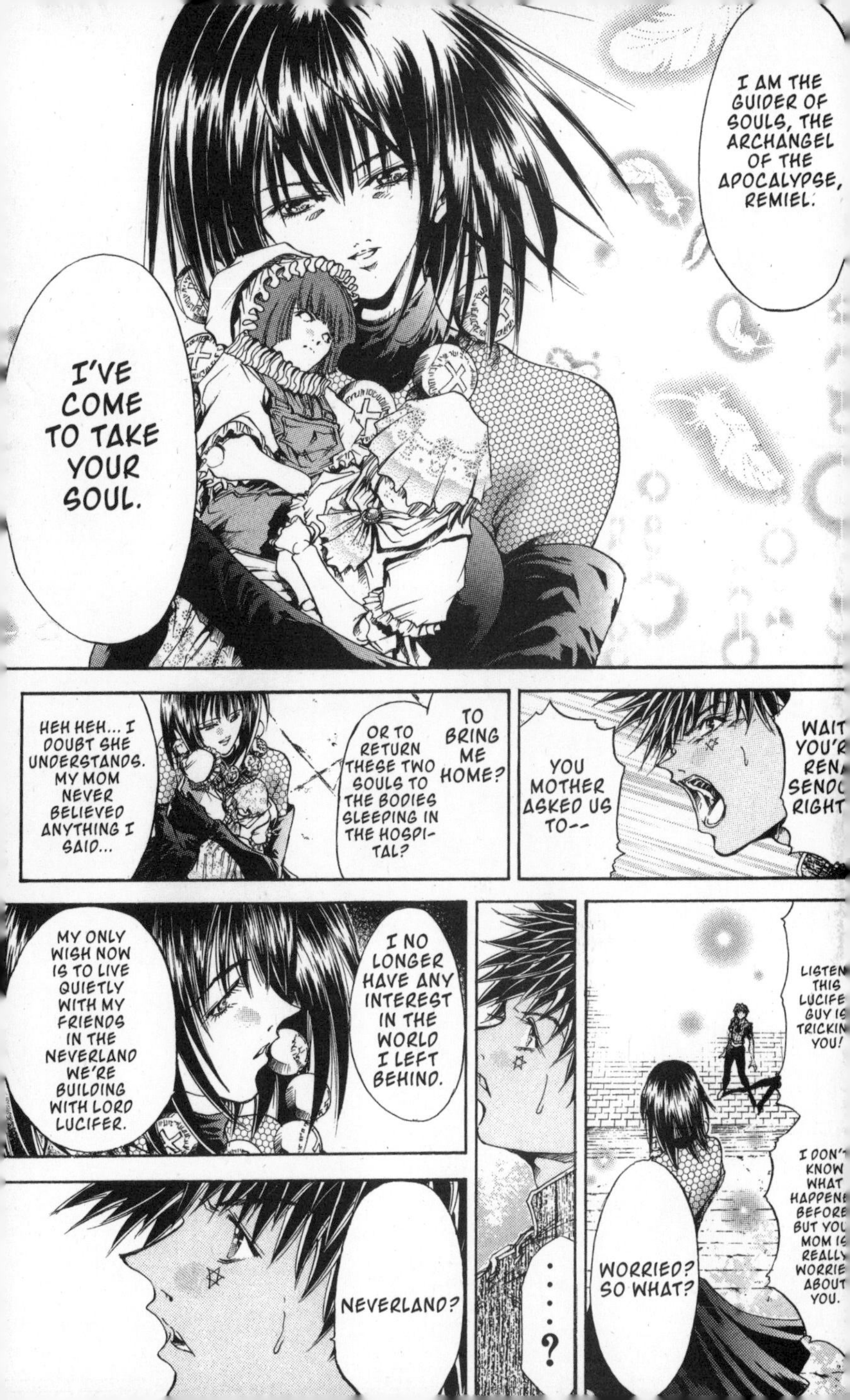
I AM THE GUIDER OF SOULS, THE ARCHANGEL OF THE APOCALYPSE, REMIEL.
I'VE COME TO TAKE YOUR SOUL.
WAIT YOU'R RENA SENDO RIGHT
YOU MOTHER ASKED US TO--
TO BRING ME HOME?
OR TO RETURN THESE TWO SOULS TO THE BODIES SLEEPING IN THE HOSPI- TAL?
HEH HEH... I DOUBT SHE UNDERSTANDS. MY MOM NEVER BELIEVED ANYTHING I SAID...
LISTEN THIS LUCIFE GUY IS TRICKIN YOU!
I DON'T KNOW WHAT HAPPENE BEFORE BUT YOU MOM IS REALLY WORRIE ABOUT YOU.
WORRIED? SO WHAT?
...?
I NO LONGER HAVE ANY INTEREST IN THE WORLD I LEFT BEHIND.
MY ONLY WISH NOW IS TO LIVE QUIETLY WITH MY FRIENDS IN THE NEVERLAND WE'RE BUILDING WITH LORD LUCIFER.
NEVERLAND?

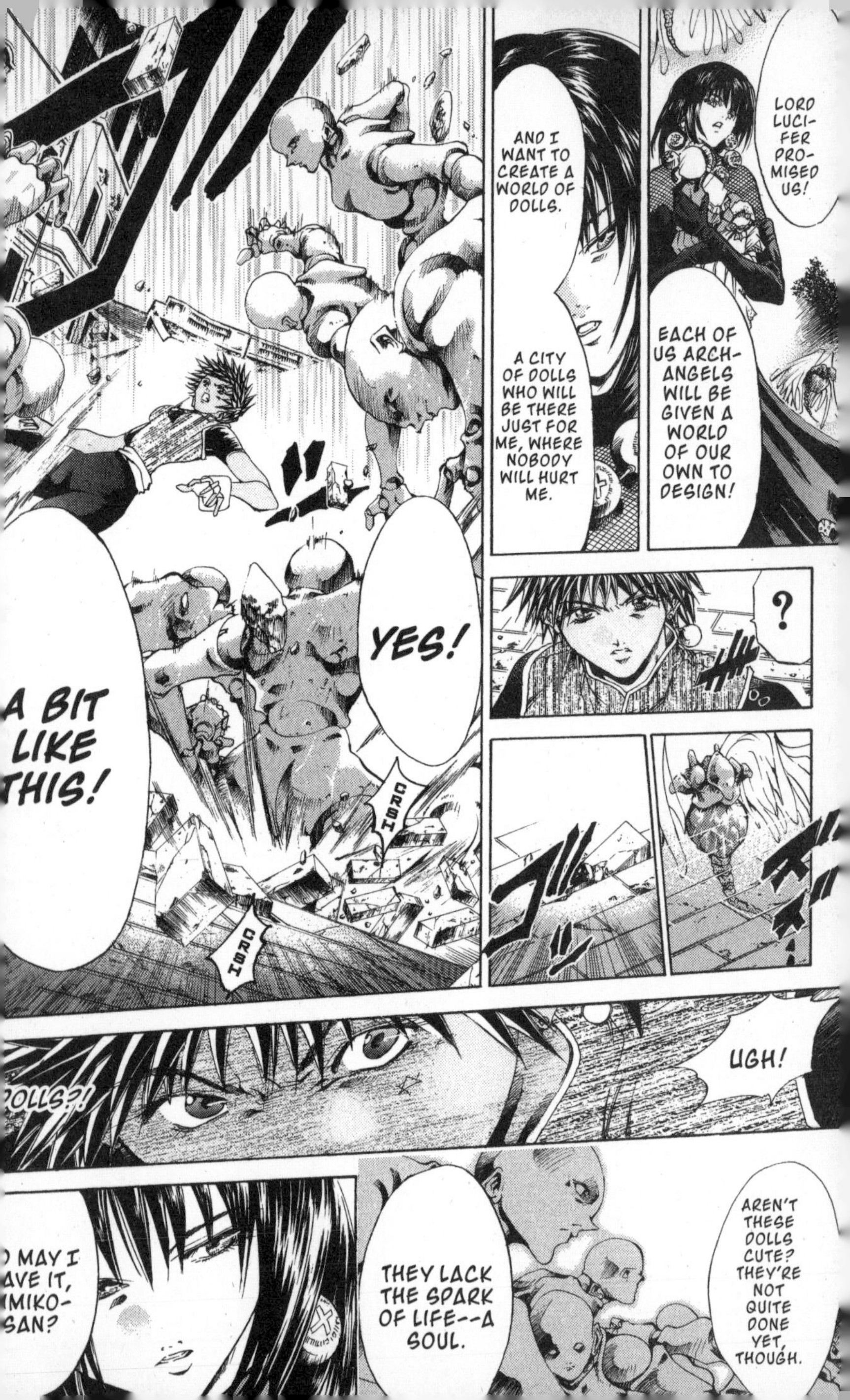
LORD LUCIFER PROMISED US!
EACH OF US ARCHANGELS WILL BE GIVEN A WORLD OF OUR OWN TO DESIGN!
AND I WANT TO CREATE A WORLD OF DOLLS.
A CITY OF DOLLS WHO WILL BE THERE JUST FOR ME, WHERE NOBODY WILL HURT ME.
?
YES!
A BIT LIKE THIS!
CRSH
CRSH
UGH!
OLLS?!
AREN'T THESE DOLLS CUTE? THEY'RE NOT QUITE DONE YET, THOUGH.
THEY LACK THE SPARK OF LIFE--A SOUL.
MAY I AVE IT, MIKO-SAN?

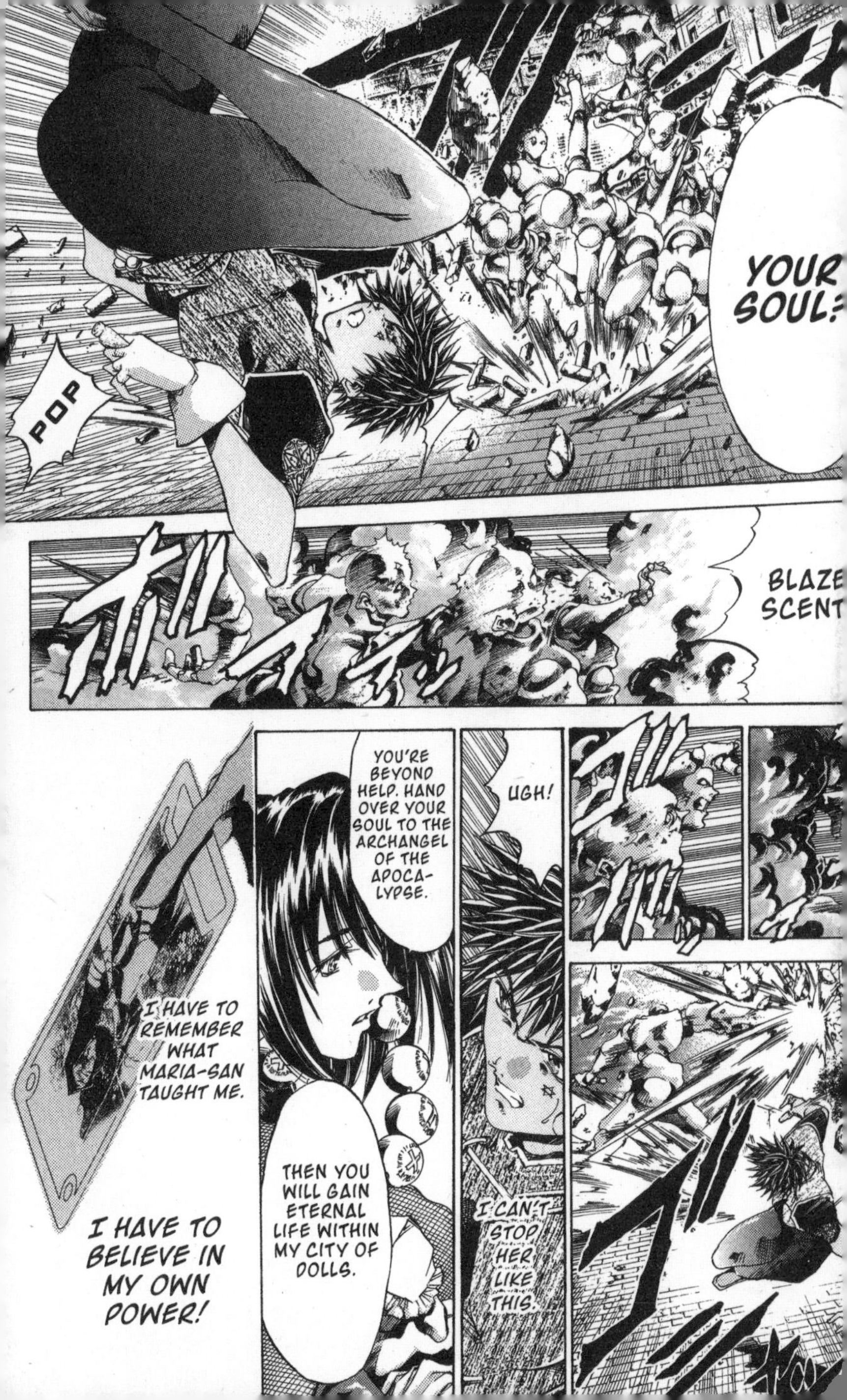
YOUR SOUL!?
POP
BLAZE SCENT
UGH!
I CAN'T STOP HER LIKE THIS.
YOU'RE BEYOND HELP. HAND OVER YOUR SOUL TO THE ARCHANGEL OF THE APOCALYPSE.
THEN YOU WILL GAIN ETERNAL LIFE WITHIN MY CITY OF DOLLS.
I HAVE TO REMEMBER WHAT MARIA-SAN TAUGHT ME.
I HAVE TO BELIEVE IN MY OWN POWER!

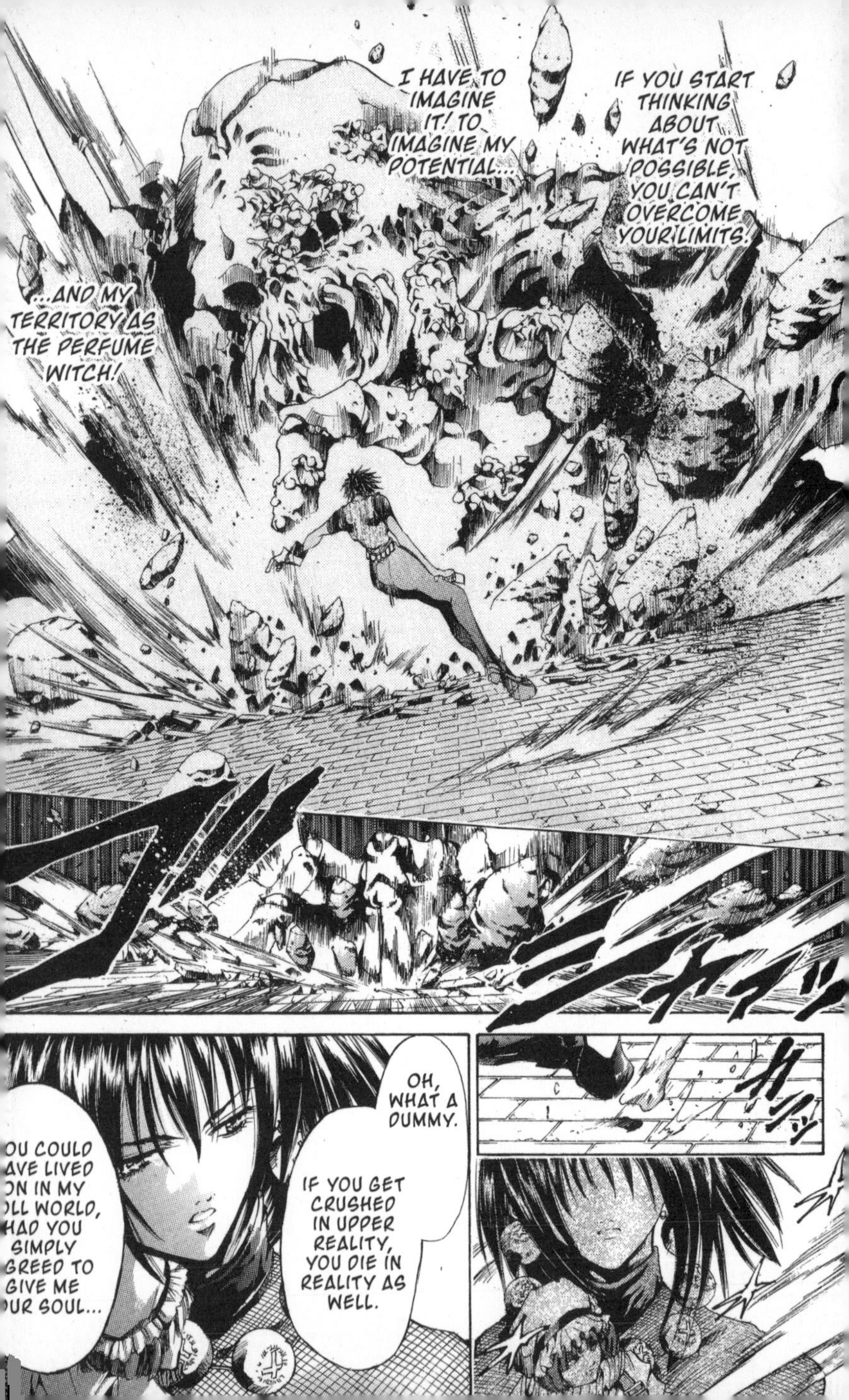
IF YOU START THINKING ABOUT WHAT'S NOT POSSIBLE, YOU CAN'T OVERCOME YOUR LIMITS!
I HAVE TO IMAGINE IT! TO IMAGINE MY POTENTIAL...
...AND MY TERRITORY AS THE PERFUME WITCH!
OH, WHAT A DUMMY.
IF YOU GET CRUSHED IN UPPER REALITY, YOU DIE IN REALITY AS WELL.
OU COULD AVE LIVED ON IN MY OLL WORLD, HAD YOU SIMPLY GREED TO GIVE ME OUR SOUL...

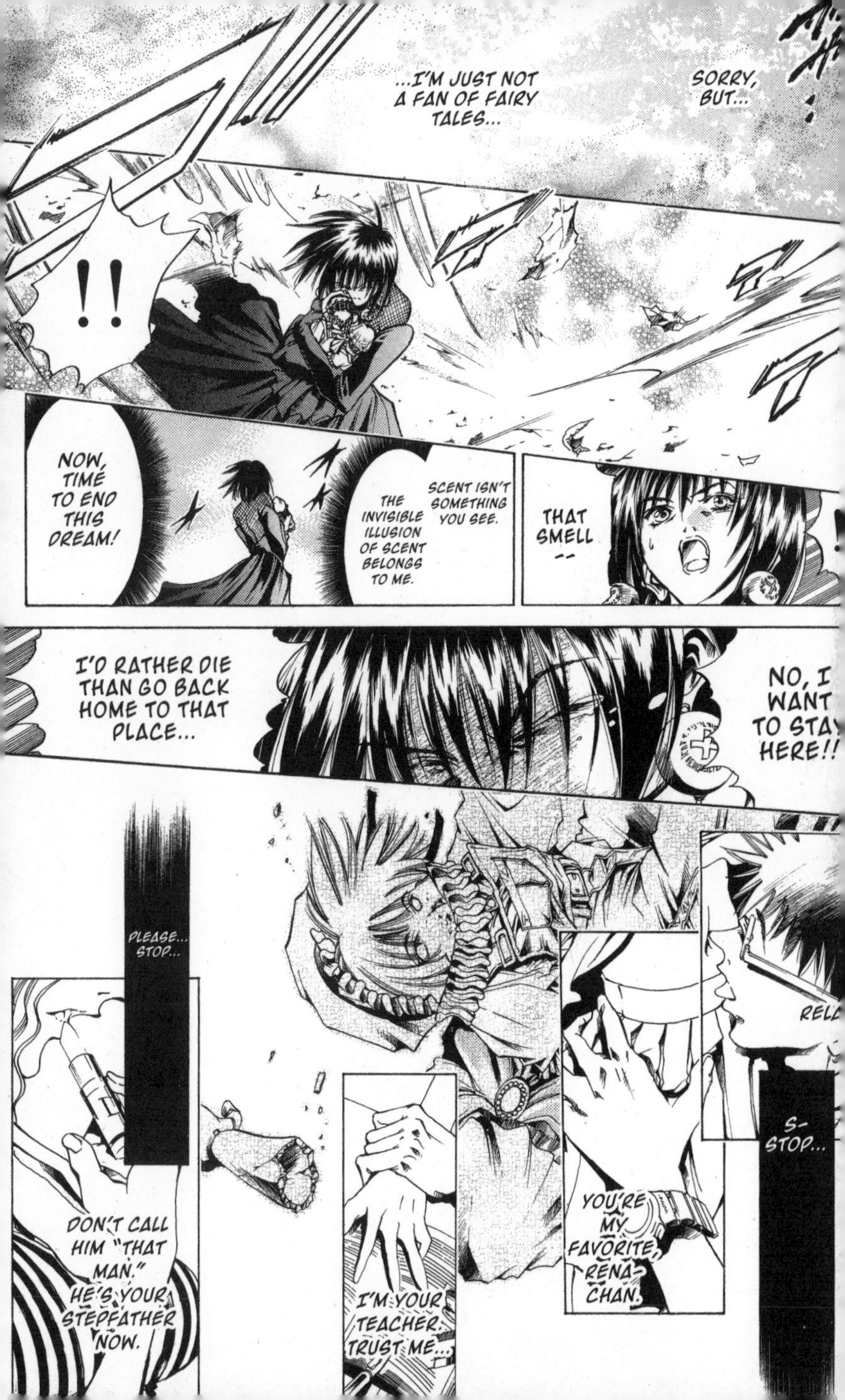
SORRY, BUT...
...I'M JUST NOT A FAN OF FAIRY TALES...
!!
THAT SMELL --
SCENT ISN'T SOMETHING YOU SEE.
THE INVISIBLE ILLUSION OF SCENT BELONGS TO ME.
NOW, TIME TO END THIS DREAM!
NO, I WANT TO STAY HERE!!
I'D RATHER DIE THAN GO BACK HOME TO THAT PLACE...
S-STOP...
YOU'RE MY FAVORITE, RENA-CHAN.
I'M YOUR TEACHER. TRUST ME...
PLEASE... STOP...
DON'T CALL HIM "THAT MAN." HE'S YOUR STEPFATHER NOW.

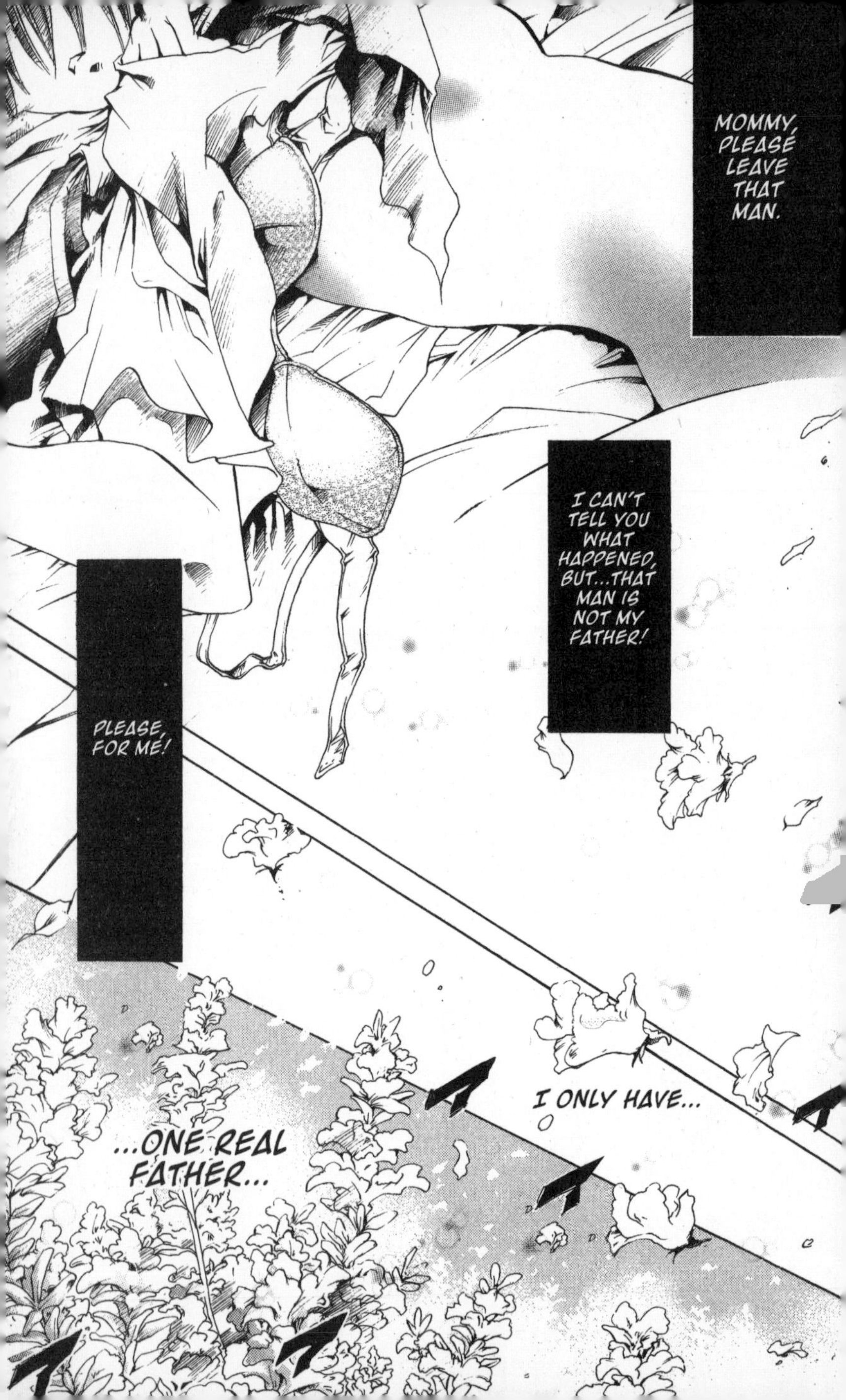
MOMMY, PLEASE LEAVE THAT MAN.
I CAN'T TELL YOU WHAT HAPPENED, BUT...THAT MAN IS NOT MY FATHER!
PLEASE, FOR ME!
I ONLY HAVE...
...ONE REAL FATHER...

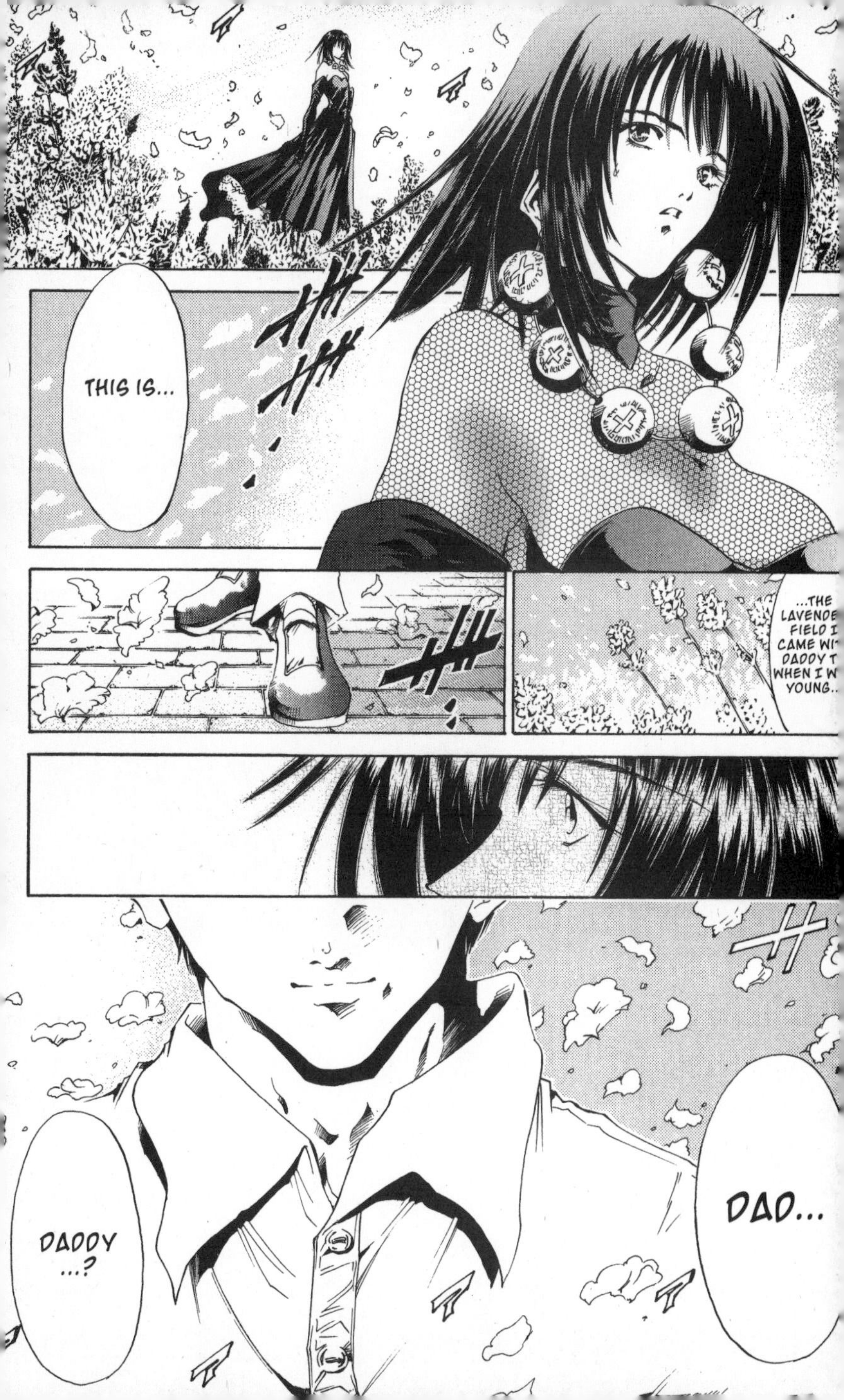
THIS IS...
...THE LAVENDE FIELD I CAME WI DADDY T WHEN I W YOUNG...
DAD...
DADDY ...?

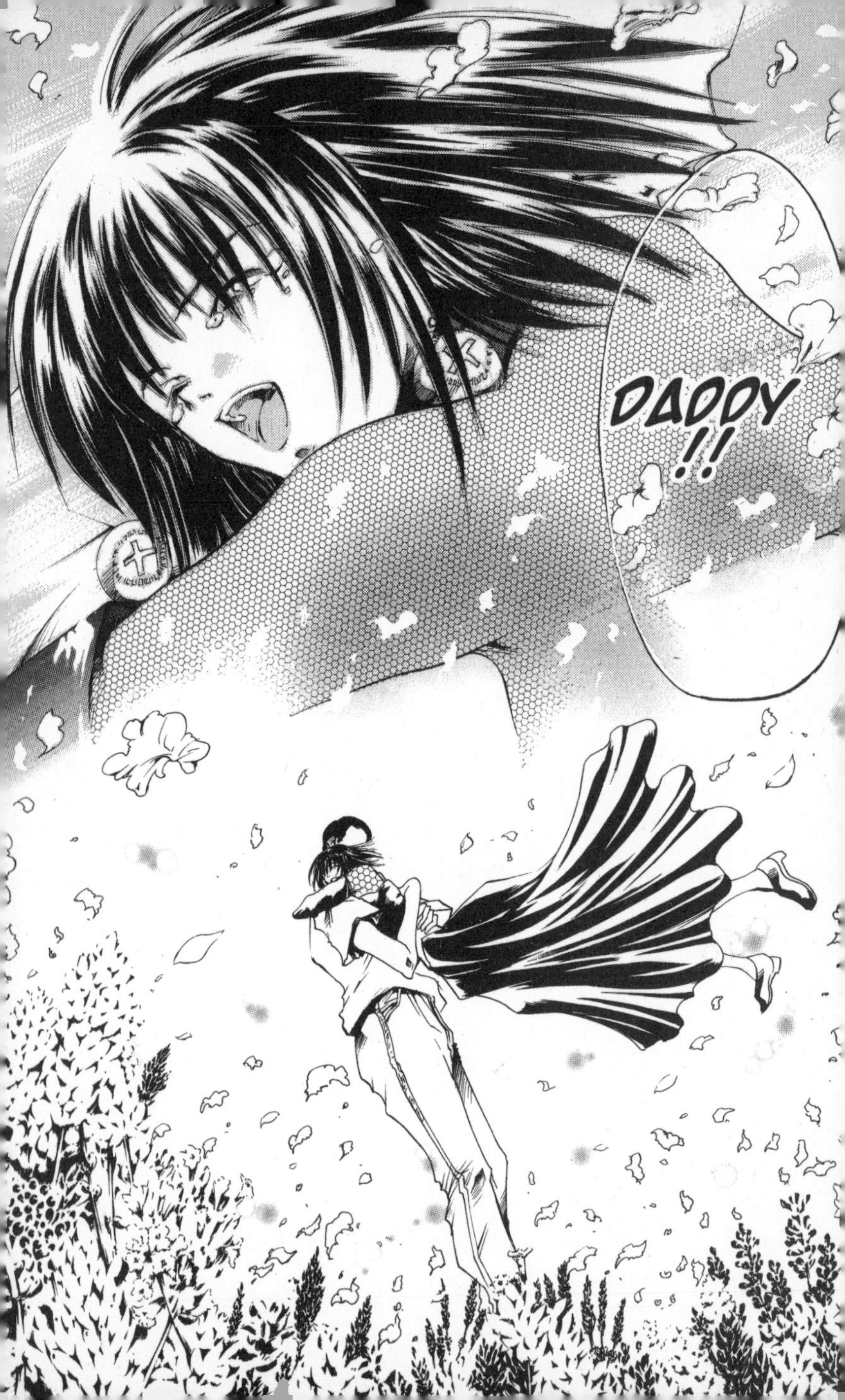
DADDY !!

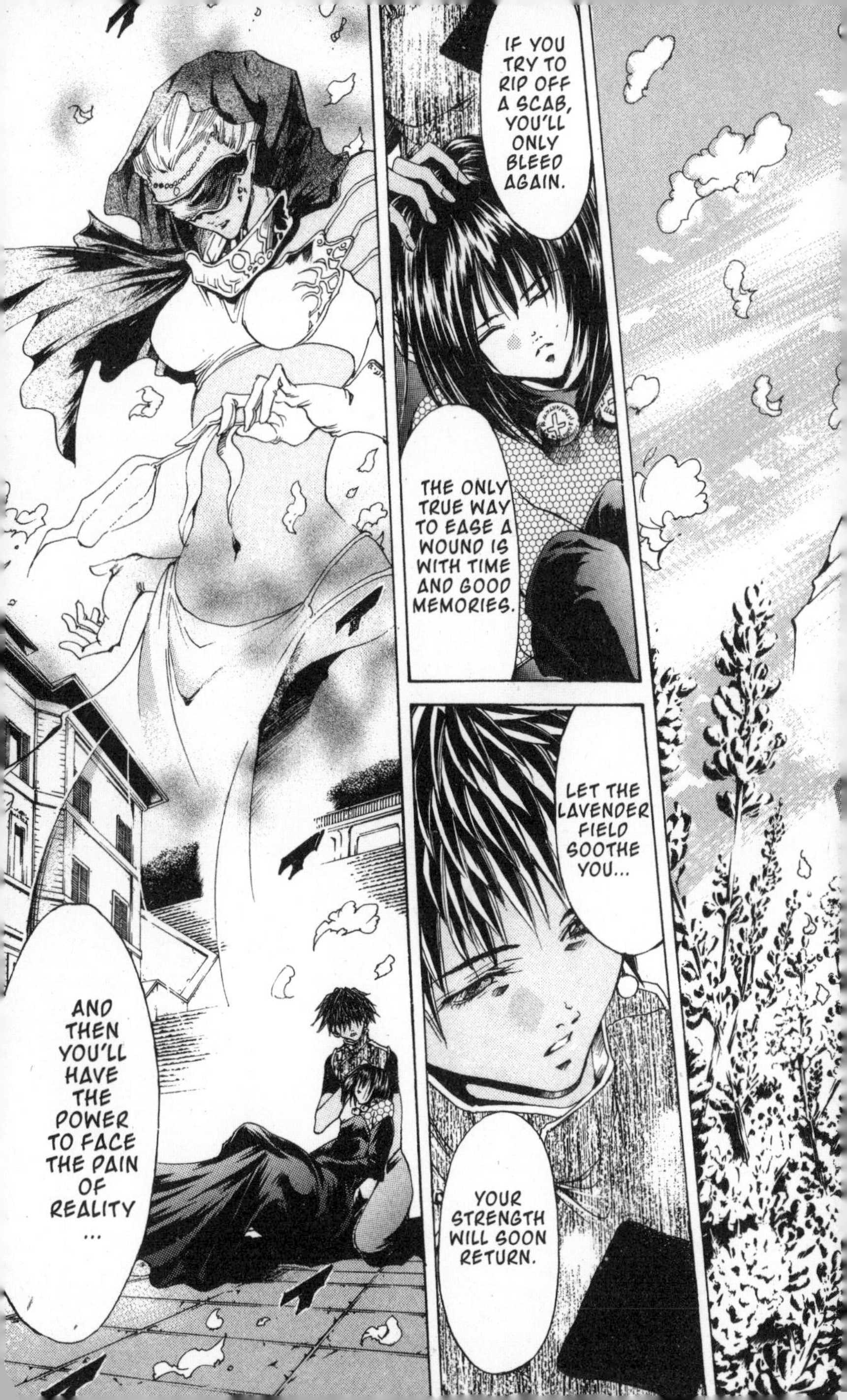
IF YOU TRY TO RIP OFF A SCAB, YOU'LL ONLY BLEED AGAIN.
THE ONLY TRUE WAY TO EASE A WOUND IS WITH TIME AND GOOD MEMORIES.
LET THE LAVENDER FIELD SOOTHE YOU...
YOUR STRENGTH WILL SOON RETURN.
AND THEN YOU'LL HAVE THE POWER TO FACE THE PAIN OF REALITY...

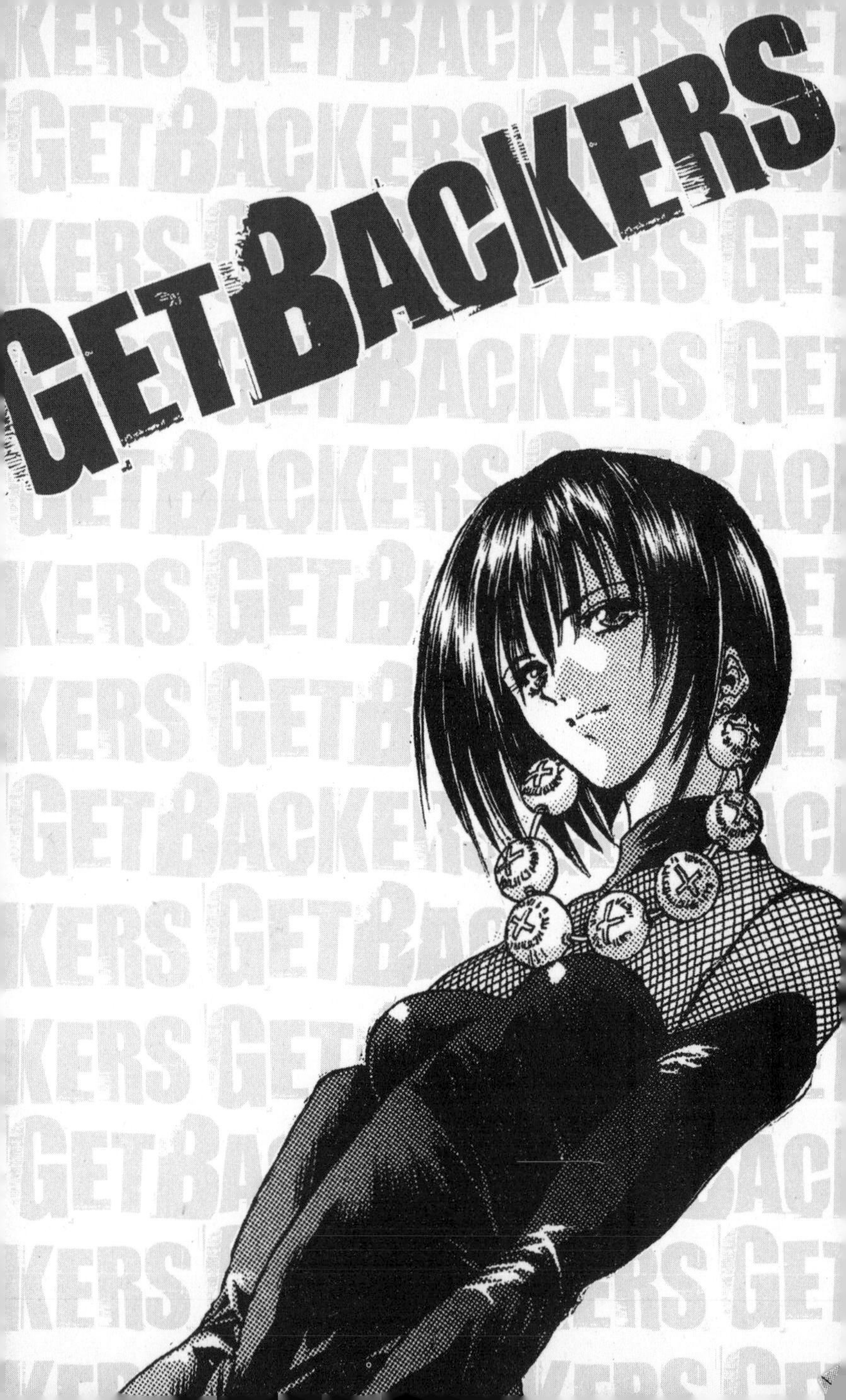
GETBACKERS

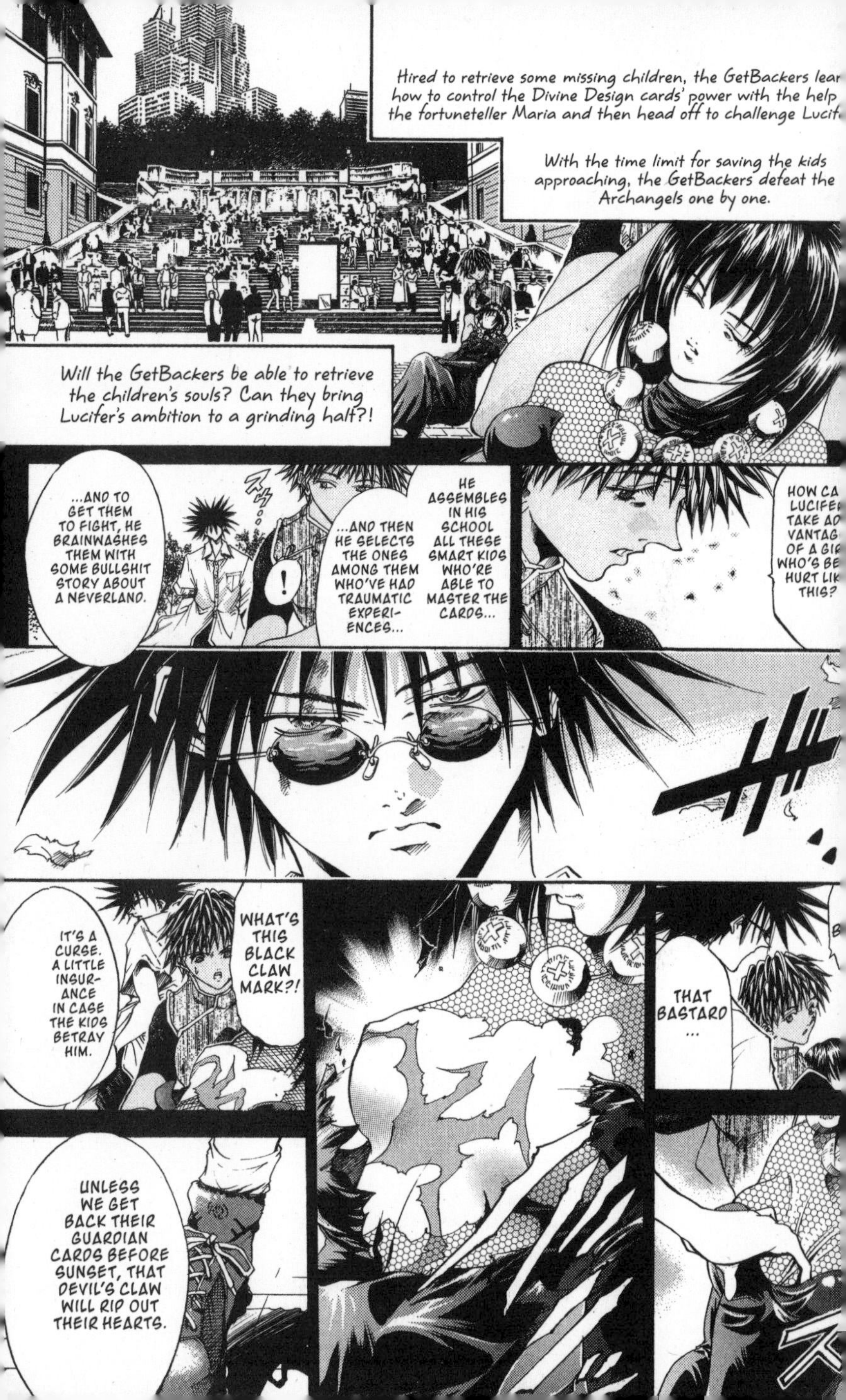
Hired to retrieve some missing children, the GetBackers lear how to control the Divine Design cards' power with the help the fortuneteller Maria and then head off to challenge Lucif
With the time limit for saving the kids approaching, the GetBackers defeat the Archangels one by one.
Will the GetBackers be able to retrieve the children's souls? Can they bring Lucifer's ambition to a grinding halt?!
HOW CA LUCIFER TAKE AD VANTAG OF A GIR WHO'S BE HURT LIK THIS?
HE ASSEMBLES IN HIS SCHOOL ALL THESE SMART KIDS WHO'RE ABLE TO MASTER THE CARDS...
...AND THEN HE SELECTS THE ONES AMONG THEM WHO'VE HAD TRAUMATIC EXPERI-ENCES...
!
...AND TO GET THEM TO FIGHT, HE BRAINWASHES THEM WITH SOME BULLSHIT STORY ABOUT A NEVERLAND.
THAT BASTARD ...
WHAT'S THIS BLACK CLAW MARK?!
IT'S A CURSE. A LITTLE INSUR-ANCE IN CASE THE KIDS BETRAY HIM.
UNLESS WE GET BACK THEIR GUARDIAN CARDS BEFORE SUNSET, THAT DEVIL'S CLAW WILL RIP OUT THEIR HEARTS.

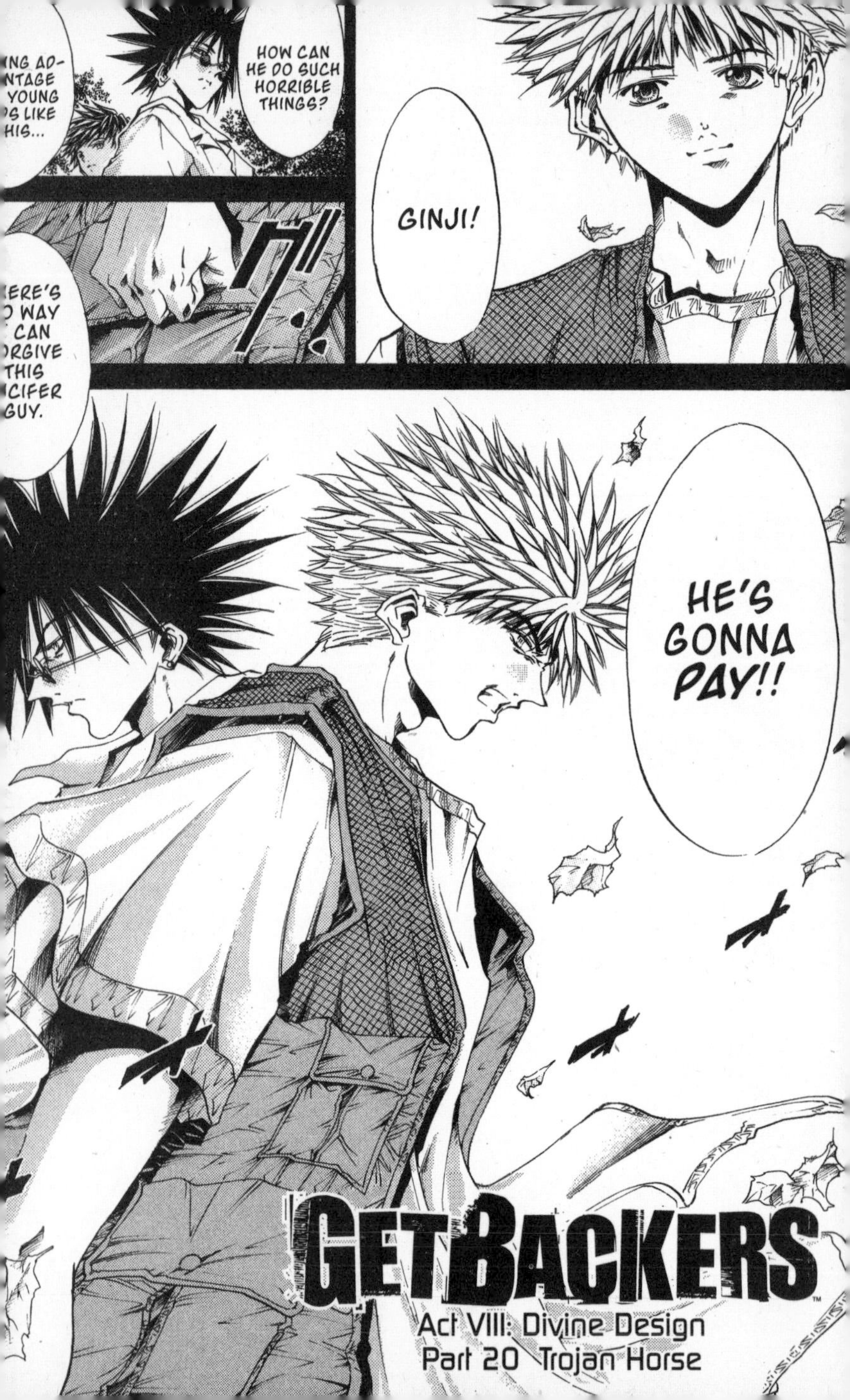
GINJI!
HOW CAN HE DO SUCH HORRIBLE THINGS?
...ING AD-...NTAGE ...YOUNG ...S LIKE ...HIS...
...ERE'S ...O WAY ...CAN ...ORGIVE THIS ...CIFER GUY.
HE'S GONNA PAY!!
GETBACKERS™
Act VIII: Divine Design
Part 20 Trojan Horse

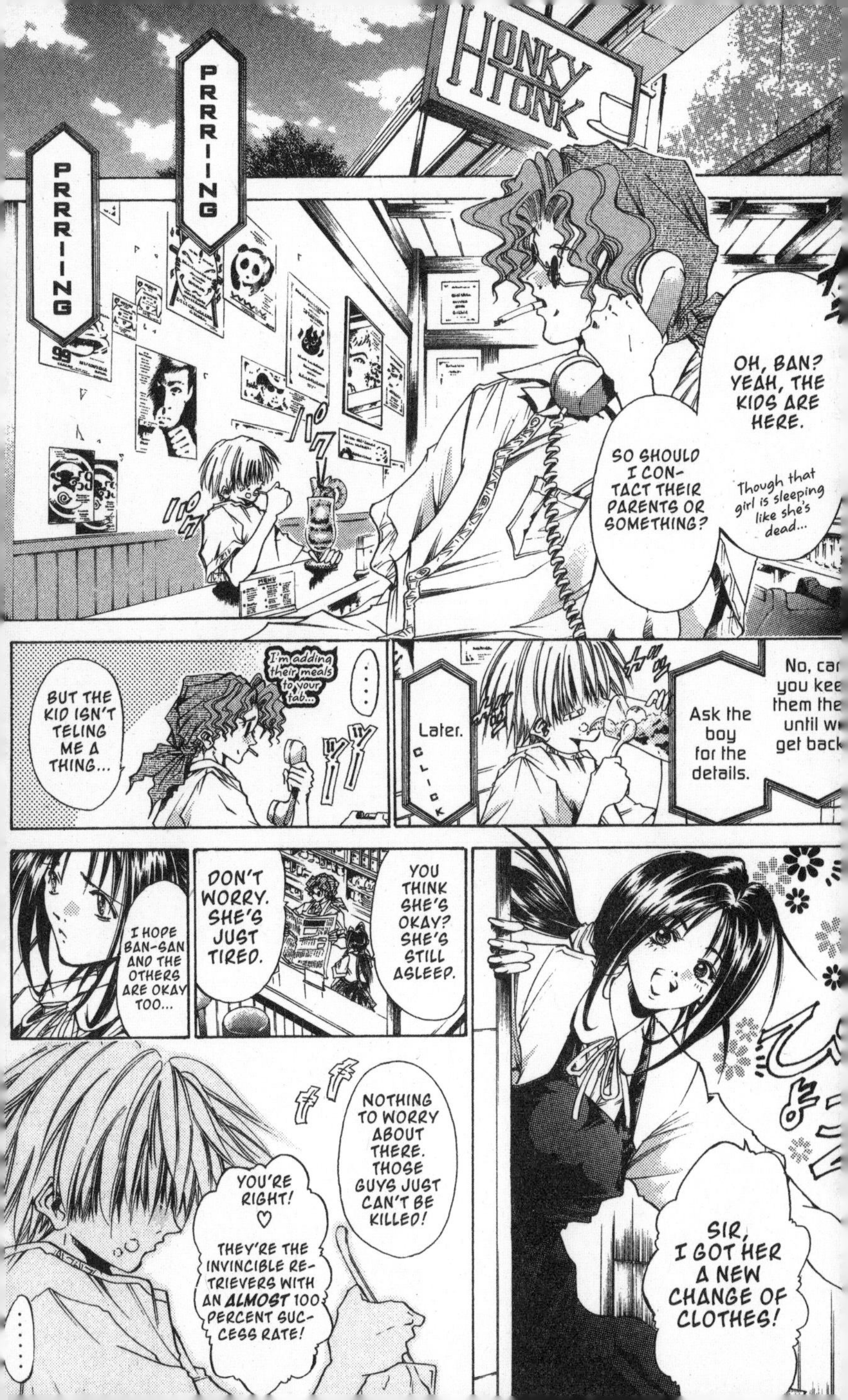
HONKY TONK
PRRRIING
PRRRIING
OH, BAN? YEAH, THE KIDS ARE HERE.
Though that girl is sleeping like she's dead...
SO SHOULD I CON-TACT THEIR PARENTS OR SOMETHING?
No, ca you kee them the until w get back
Ask the boy for the details.
Later.
CLICK
I'm adding their meals to your tab...
....
BUT THE KID ISN'T TELING ME A THING...
SIR, I GOT HER A NEW CHANGE OF CLOTHES!
YOU THINK SHE'S OKAY? SHE'S STILL ASLEEP.
DON'T WORRY. SHE'S JUST TIRED.
I HOPE BAN-SAN AND THE OTHERS ARE OKAY TOO...
NOTHING TO WORRY ABOUT THERE. THOSE GUYS JUST CAN'T BE KILLED!
YOU'RE RIGHT! ♡
THEY'RE THE INVINCIBLE RE-TRIEVERS WITH AN *ALMOST* 100 PERCENT SUC-CESS RATE!
......

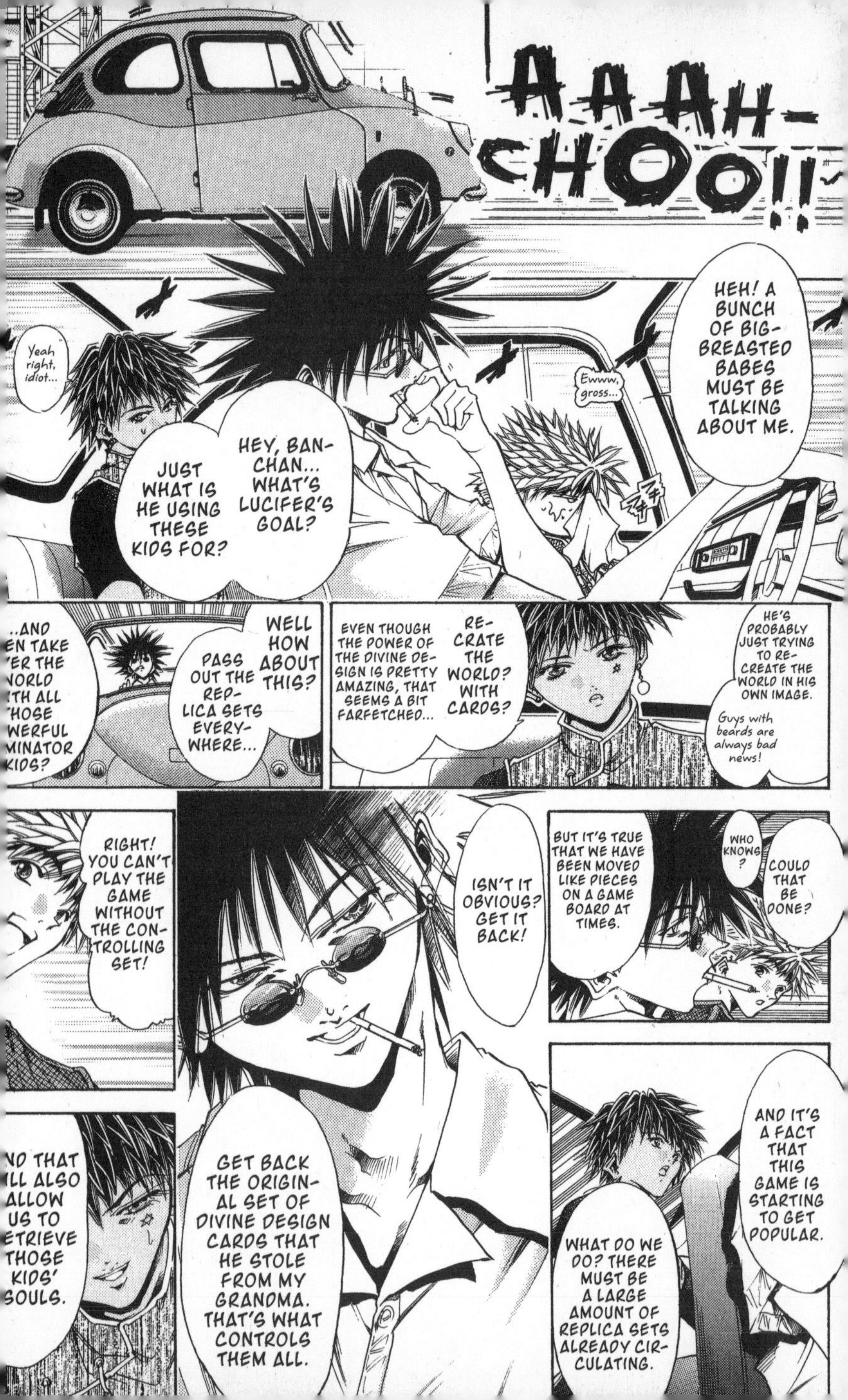
AAAH-CHOO!!
HEH! A BUNCH OF BIG-BREASTED BABES MUST BE TALKING ABOUT ME.
Ewww, gross...
HEY, BAN-CHAN... WHAT'S LUCIFER'S GOAL?
JUST WHAT IS HE USING THESE KIDS FOR?
Yeah right, idiot...
HE'S PROBABLY JUST TRYING TO RE-CREATE THE WORLD IN HIS OWN IMAGE.
Guys with beards are always bad news!
RE-CREATE THE WORLD? WITH CARDS?
EVEN THOUGH THE POWER OF THE DIVINE DESIGN IS PRETTY AMAZING, THAT SEEMS A BIT FARFETCHED...
WELL HOW ABOUT THIS?
PASS OUT THE REPLICA SETS EVERYWHERE...
..AND EN TAKE ER THE ORLD ITH ALL HOSE WERFUL MINATOR KIDS?
COULD THAT BE DONE?
WHO KNOWS?
BUT IT'S TRUE THAT WE HAVE BEEN MOVED LIKE PIECES ON A GAME BOARD AT TIMES.
ISN'T IT OBVIOUS? GET IT BACK!
RIGHT! YOU CAN'T PLAY THE GAME WITHOUT THE CONTROLLING SET!
AND IT'S A FACT THAT THIS GAME IS STARTING TO GET POPULAR.
WHAT DO WE DO? THERE MUST BE A LARGE AMOUNT OF REPLICA SETS ALREADY CIRCULATING.
GET BACK THE ORIGINAL SET OF DIVINE DESIGN CARDS THAT HE STOLE FROM MY GRANDMA. THAT'S WHAT CONTROLS THEM ALL.
NO THAT ILL ALSO ALLOW US TO ETRIEVE THOSE KIDS' SOULS.

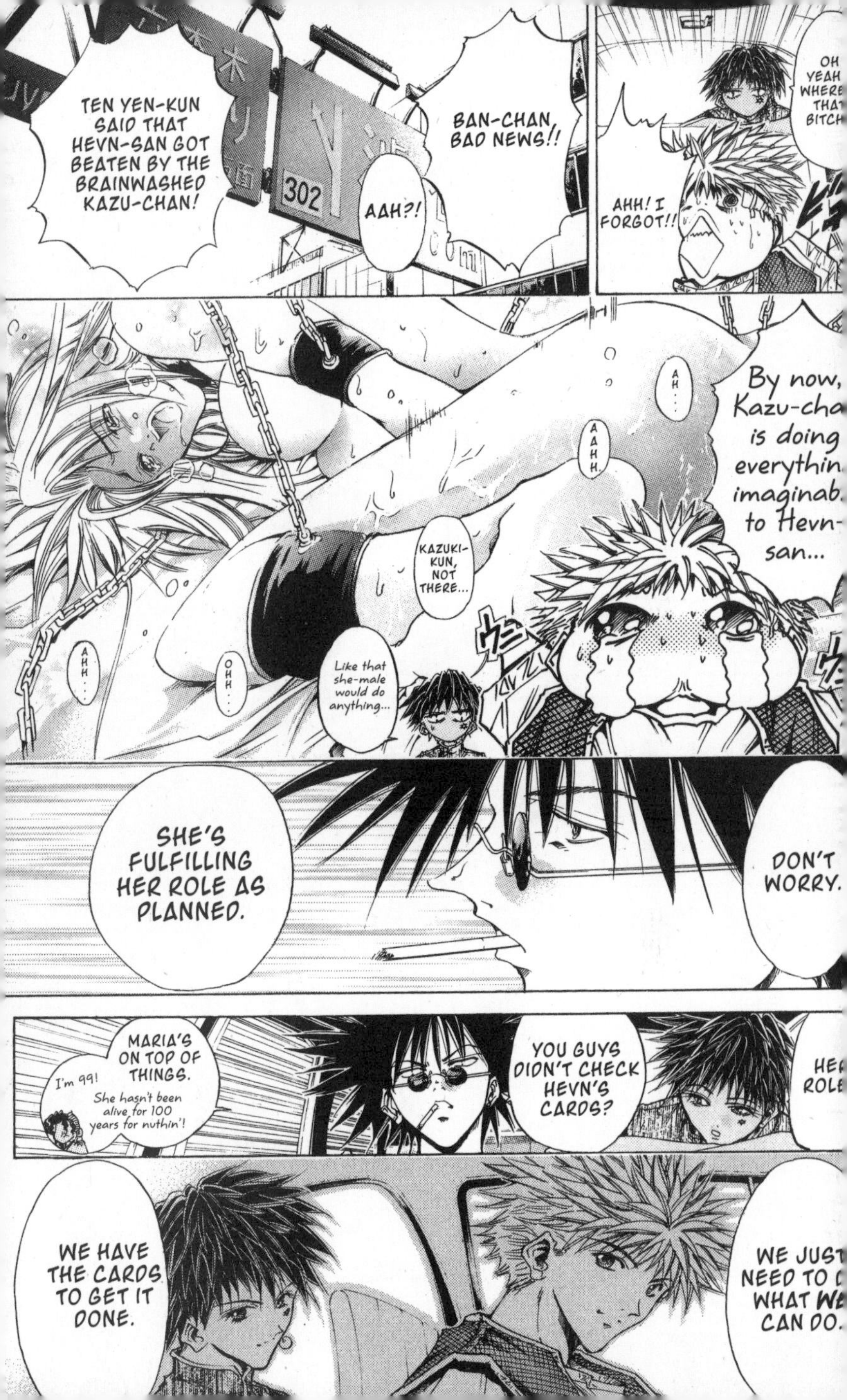
OH YEAH WHERE THA BITCH
AHH! I FORGOT!!
BAN-CHAN, BAD NEWS!!
TEN YEN-KUN SAID THAT HEVN-SAN GOT BEATEN BY THE BRAINWASHED KAZU-CHAN!
AAH?!
By now, Kazu-cha is doing everythin imaginab to Hevn-san...
AH...
AAHH.
KAZUKI-KUN, NOT THERE...
OHH...
AHH...
Like that she-male would do anything...
DON'T WORRY.
SHE'S FULFILLING HER ROLE AS PLANNED.
HE ROLE
YOU GUYS DIDN'T CHECK HEVN'S CARDS?
MARIA'S ON TOP OF THINGS.
I'm 99!
She hasn't been alive for 100 years for nuthin'!
WE JUST NEED TO D WHAT WE CAN DO.
WE HAVE THE CARDS TO GET IT DONE.

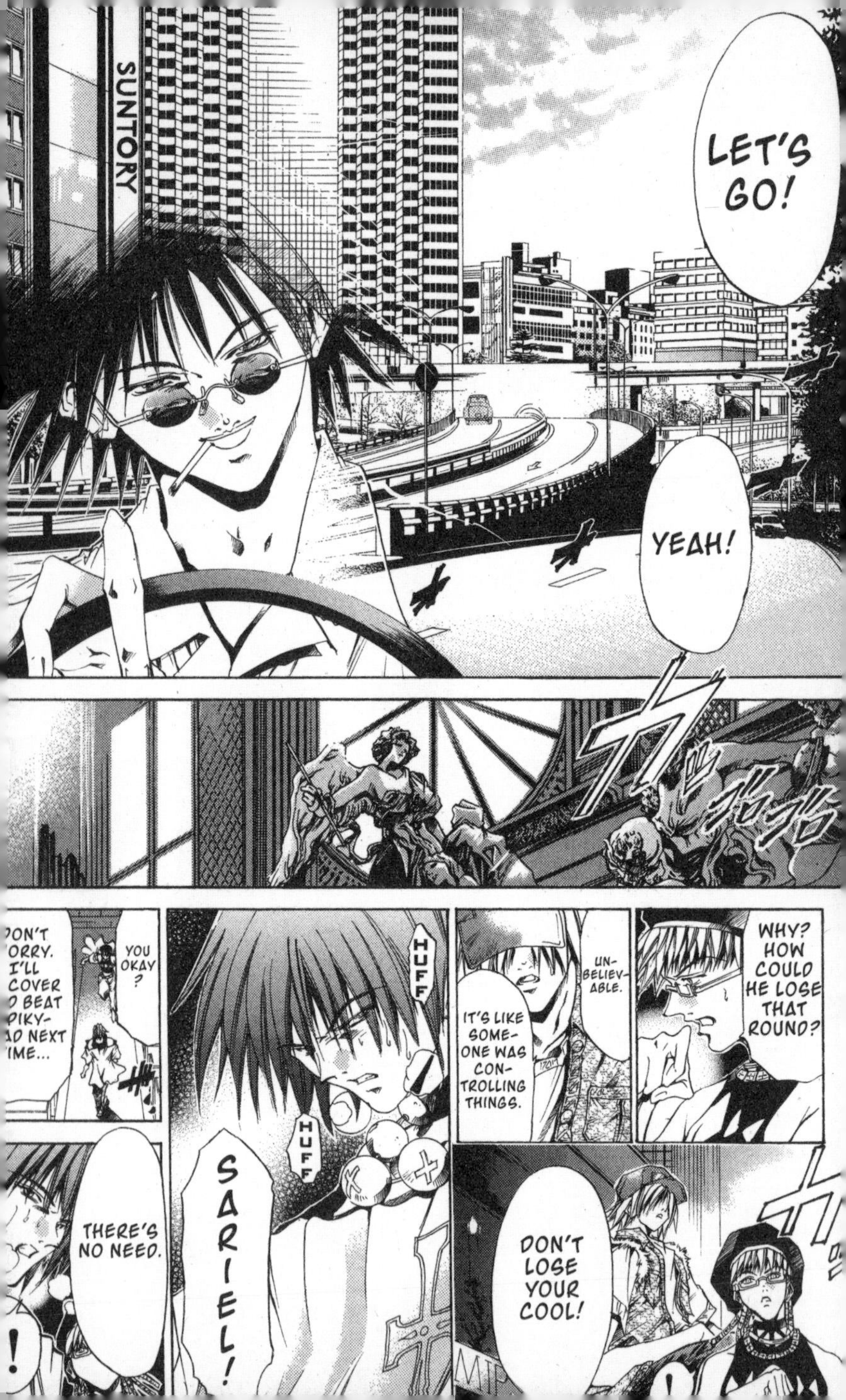
SUNTORY
LET'S GO!
YEAH!
WHY? HOW COULD HE LOSE THAT ROUND?
UN-BELIEVABLE.
IT'S LIKE SOME-ONE WAS CON-TROLLING THINGS.
HUFF
YOU OKAY?
ON'T ORRY. I'LL COVER O BEAT PIKY-AD NEXT IME...
DON'T LOSE YOUR COOL!
HUFF
SARIEL!
THERE'S NO NEED.
!

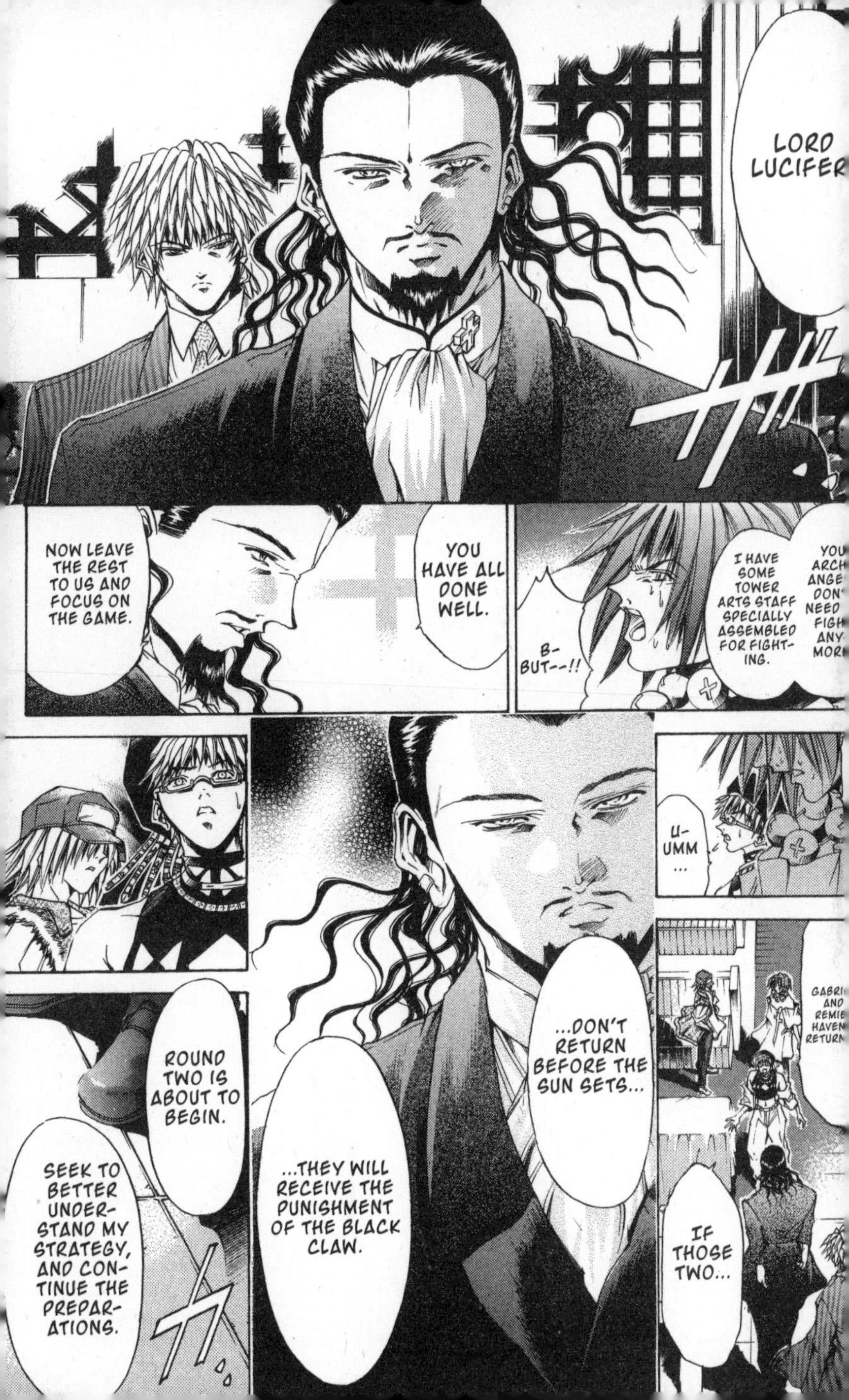
LORD LUCIFER
YOU ARCH ANGE DON' NEED FIGH ANY- MOR
I HAVE SOME TOWER ARTS STAFF SPECIALLY ASSEMBLED FOR FIGHTING.
B-BUT--!!
YOU HAVE ALL DONE WELL.
NOW LEAVE THE REST TO US AND FOCUS ON THE GAME.
U-UMM...
GABRI AND REMIE HAVEN RETURN
IF THOSE TWO...
...DON'T RETURN BEFORE THE SUN SETS...
...THEY WILL RECEIVE THE PUNISHMENT OF THE BLACK CLAW.
ROUND TWO IS ABOUT TO BEGIN.
SEEK TO BETTER UNDERSTAND MY STRATEGY, AND CONTINUE THE PREPARATIONS.

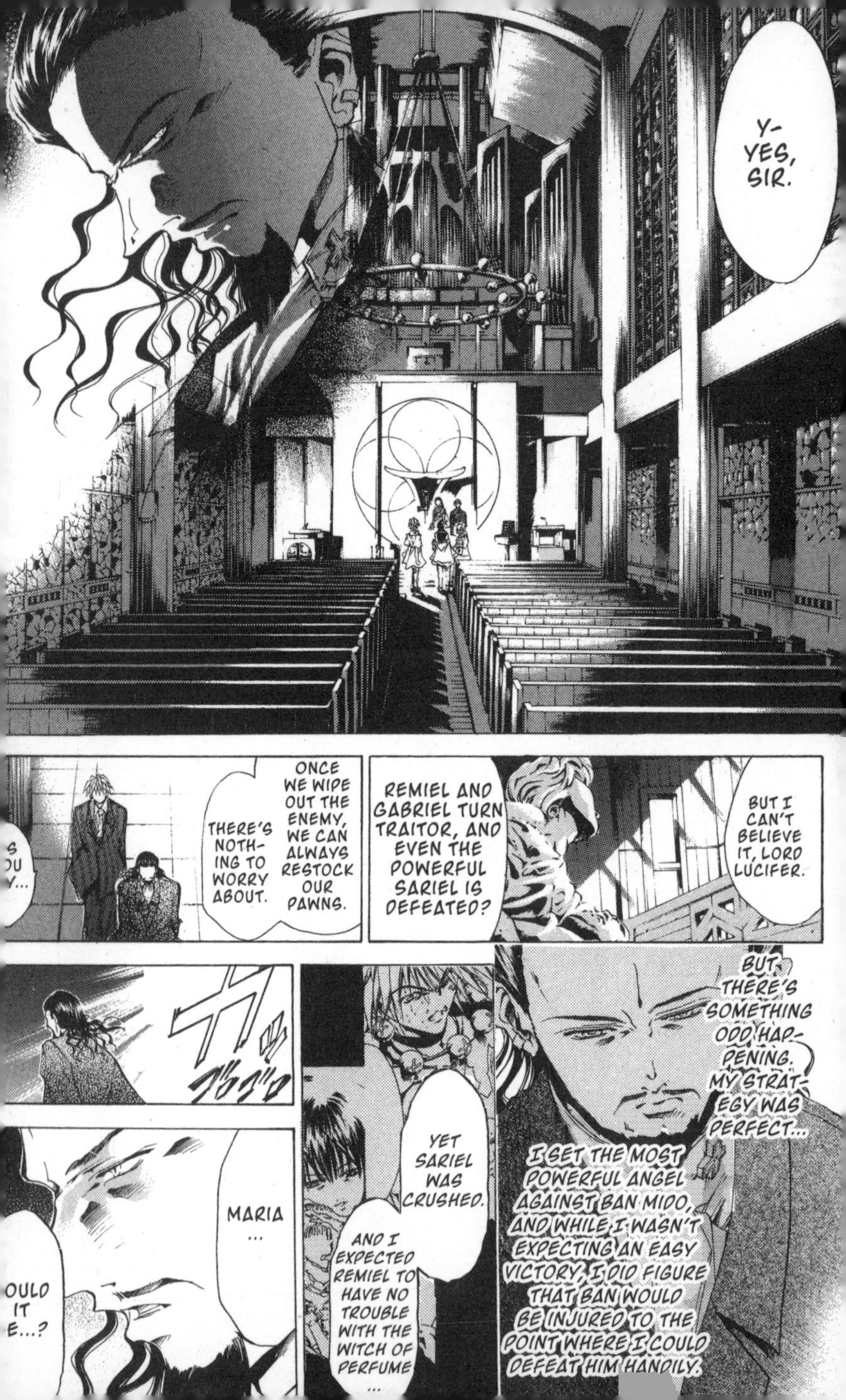
Y-YES, SIR.
BUT I CAN'T BELIEVE IT, LORD LUCIFER.
REMIEL AND GABRIEL TURN TRAITOR, AND EVEN THE POWERFUL SARIEL IS DEFEATED?
ONCE WE WIPE OUT THE ENEMY, WE CAN ALWAYS RESTOCK OUR PAWNS.
THERE'S NOTHING TO WORRY ABOUT.
BUT THERE'S SOMETHING ODD HAPPENING. MY STRATEGY WAS PERFECT...
I SET THE MOST POWERFUL ANGEL AGAINST BAN MIDO, AND WHILE I WASN'T EXPECTING AN EASY VICTORY, I DID FIGURE THAT BAN WOULD BE INJURED TO THE POINT WHERE I COULD DEFEAT HIM HANDILY.
YET SARIEL WAS CRUSHED.
AND I EXPECTED REMIEL TO HAVE NO TROUBLE WITH THE WITCH OF PERFUME...
MARIA...

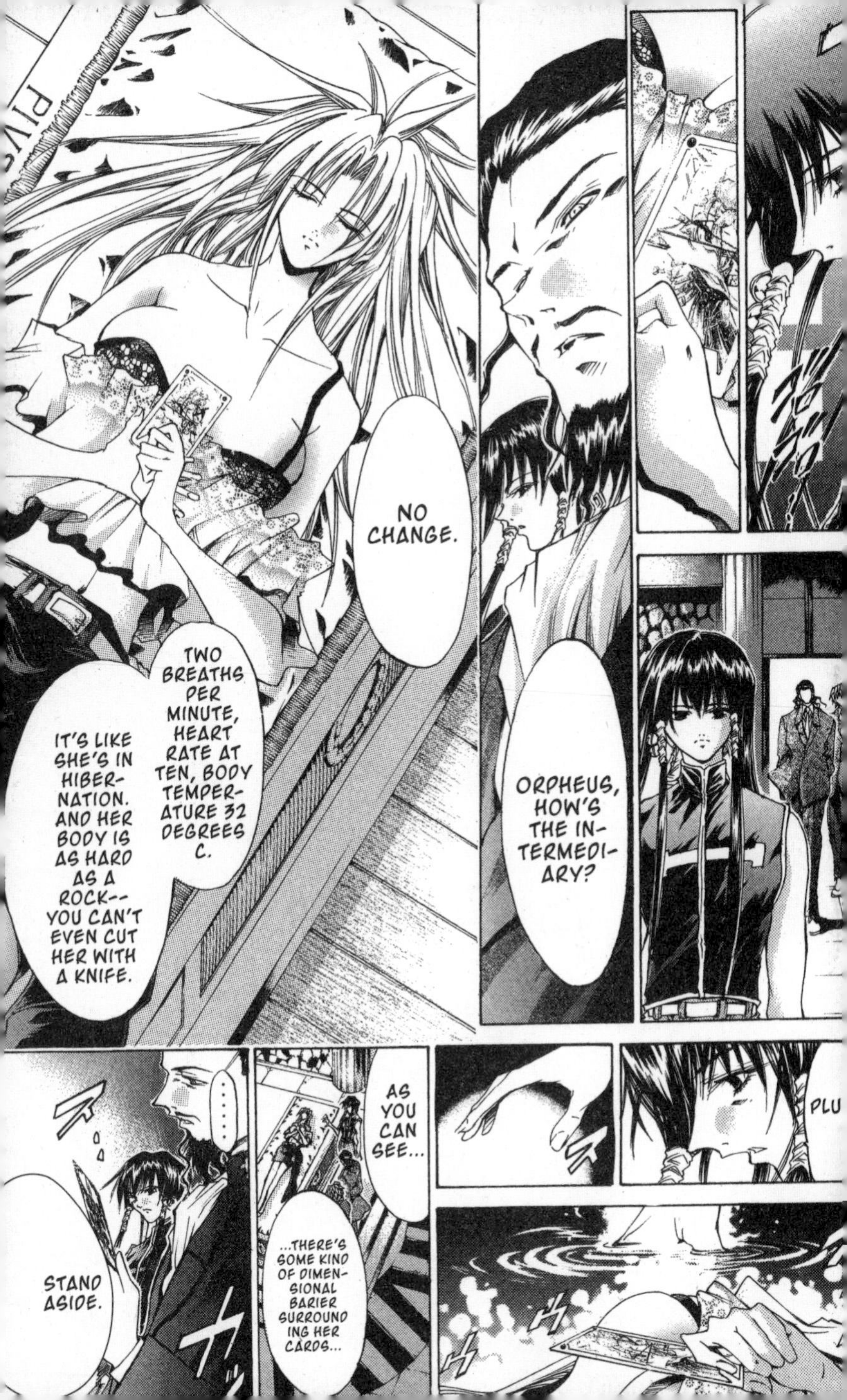
ORPHEUS, HOW'S THE INTERMEDIARY?
NO CHANGE.
TWO BREATHS PER MINUTE, HEART RATE AT TEN, BODY TEMPERATURE 32 DEGREES C.
IT'S LIKE SHE'S IN HIBERNATION. AND HER BODY IS AS HARD AS A ROCK--YOU CAN'T EVEN CUT HER WITH A KNIFE.
PLU
AS YOU CAN SEE...
...THERE'S SOME KIND OF DIMENSIONAL BARIER SURROUNDING HER CARDS...
......
STAND ASIDE.

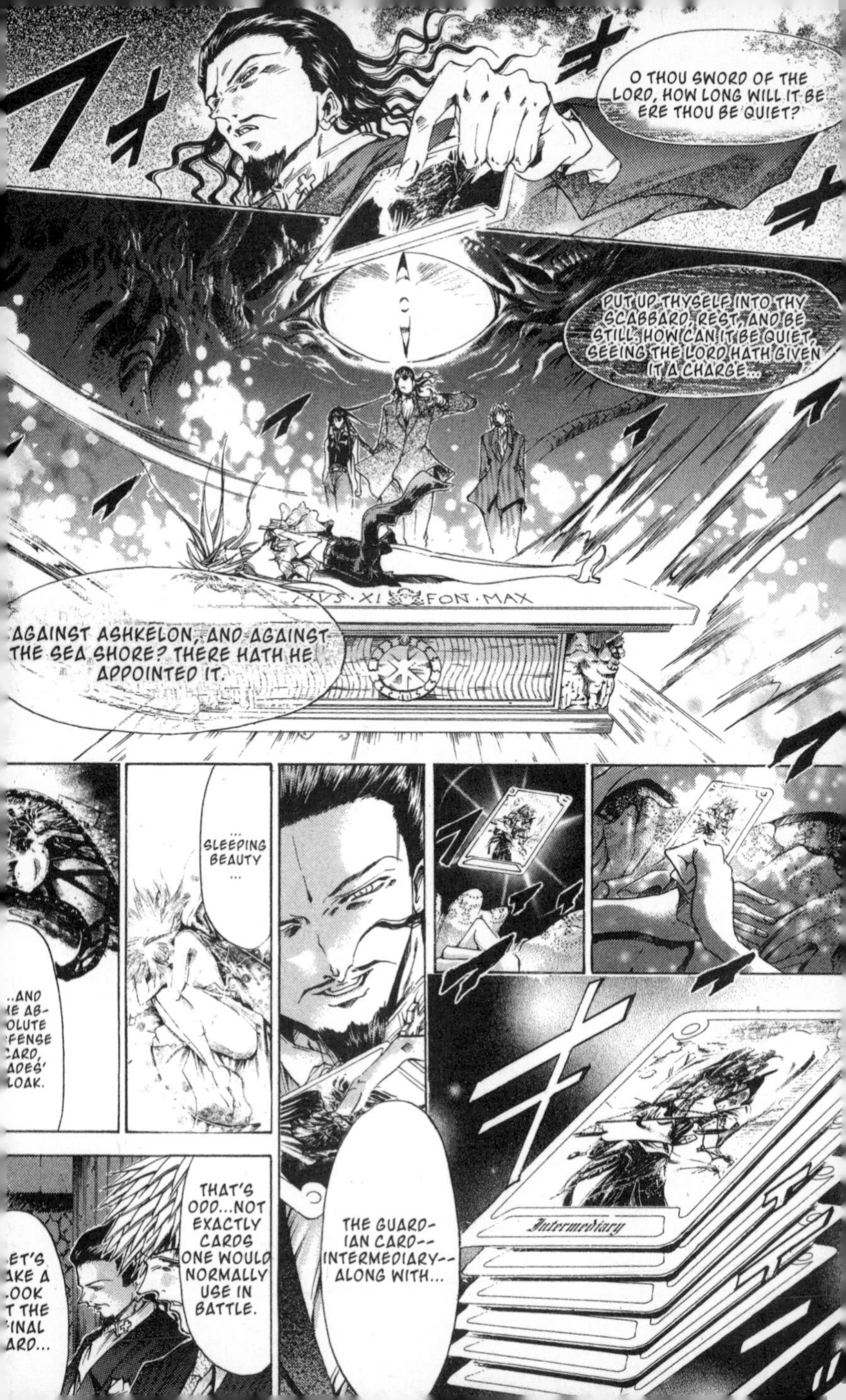
O THOU SWORD OF THE LORD, HOW LONG WILL IT BE ERE THOU BE QUIET?
PUT UP THYSELF INTO THY SCABBARD, REST, AND BE STILL. HOW CAN IT BE QUIET, SEEING THE LORD HATH GIVEN IT A CHARGE...
AGAINST ASHKELON, AND AGAINST THE SEA SHORE? THERE HATH HE APPOINTED IT.
... SLEEPING BEAUTY ...
..AND HE ABSOLUTE EFENSE CARD, ADES' LOAK.
Intermediary
THE GUARDIAN CARD--INTERMEDIARY--ALONG WITH...
THAT'S ODD...NOT EXACTLY CARDS ONE WOULD NORMALLY USE IN BATTLE.
ET'S AKE A LOOK T THE INAL ARD...

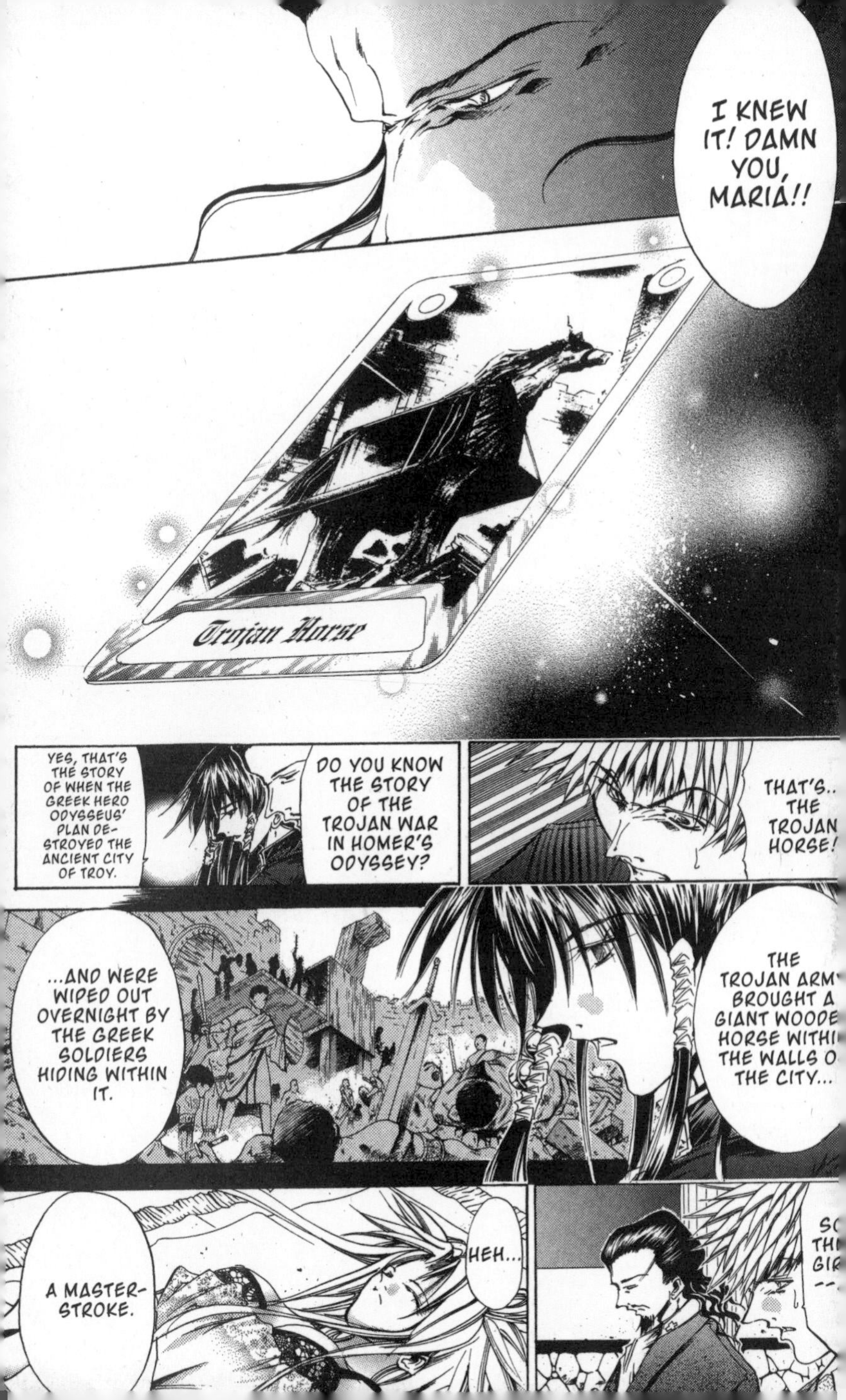
I KNEW IT! DAMN YOU, MARIA!!
Trojan Horse
THAT'S.. THE TROJAN HORSE!
DO YOU KNOW THE STORY OF THE TROJAN WAR IN HOMER'S ODYSSEY?
YES, THAT'S THE STORY OF WHEN THE GREEK HERO ODYSSEUS' PLAN DE-STROYED THE ANCIENT CITY OF TROY.
THE TROJAN ARM BROUGHT A GIANT WOODE HORSE WITHI THE WALLS O THE CITY...
...AND WERE WIPED OUT OVERNIGHT BY THE GREEK SOLDIERS HIDING WITHIN IT.
HEH...
A MASTER-STROKE.

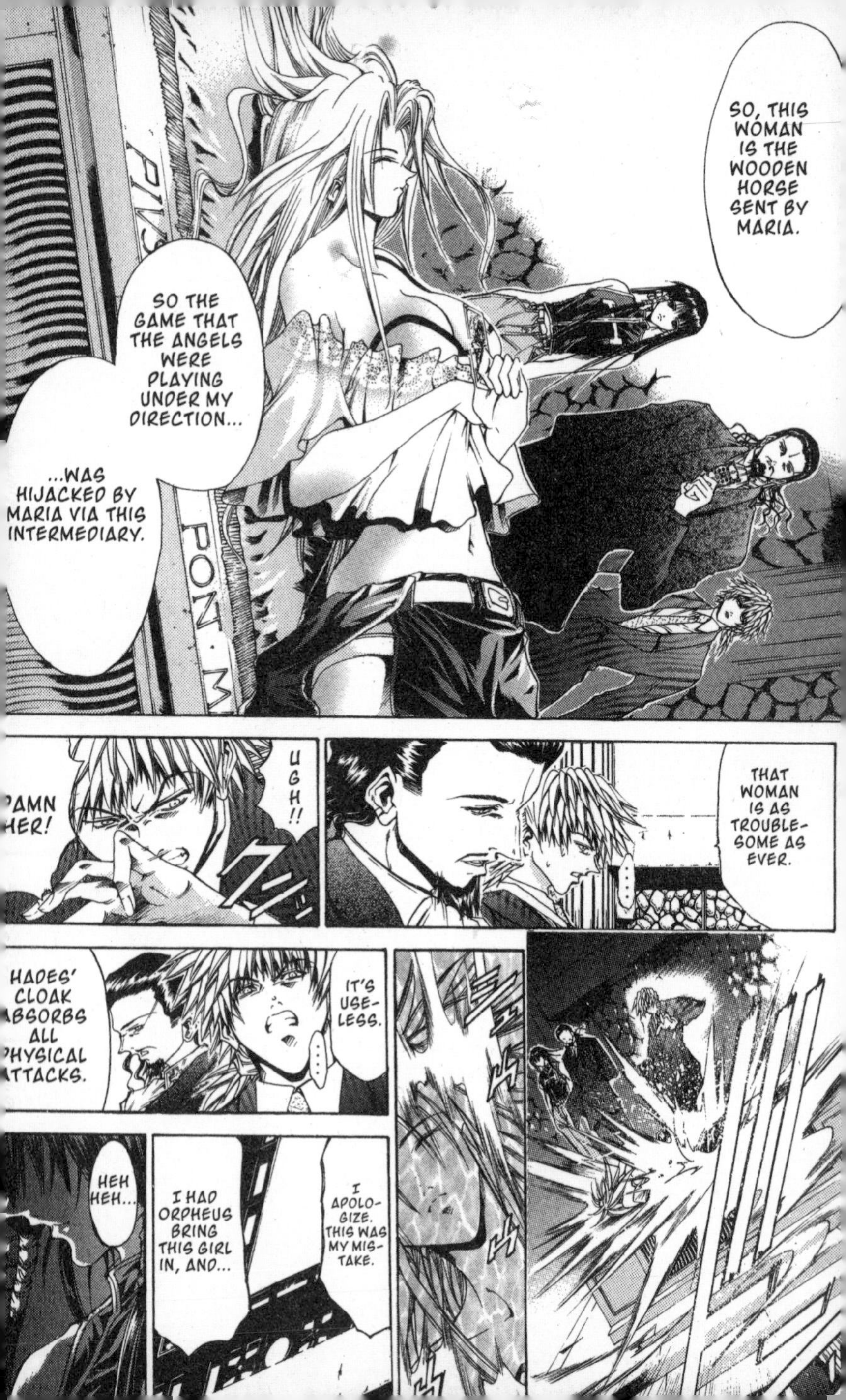
SO, THIS WOMAN IS THE WOODEN HORSE SENT BY MARIA.
SO THE GAME THAT THE ANGELS WERE PLAYING UNDER MY DIRECTION...
...WAS HIJACKED BY MARIA VIA THIS INTERMEDIARY.
THAT WOMAN IS AS TROUBLE-SOME AS EVER.
UGH!!
AMN HER!
I APOLO-GIZE. THIS WAS MY MIS-TAKE.
IT'S USE-LESS.
HADES' CLOAK BSORBS ALL HYSICAL TTACKS.
I HAD ORPHEUS BRING THIS GIRL IN, AND...
HEH HEH...

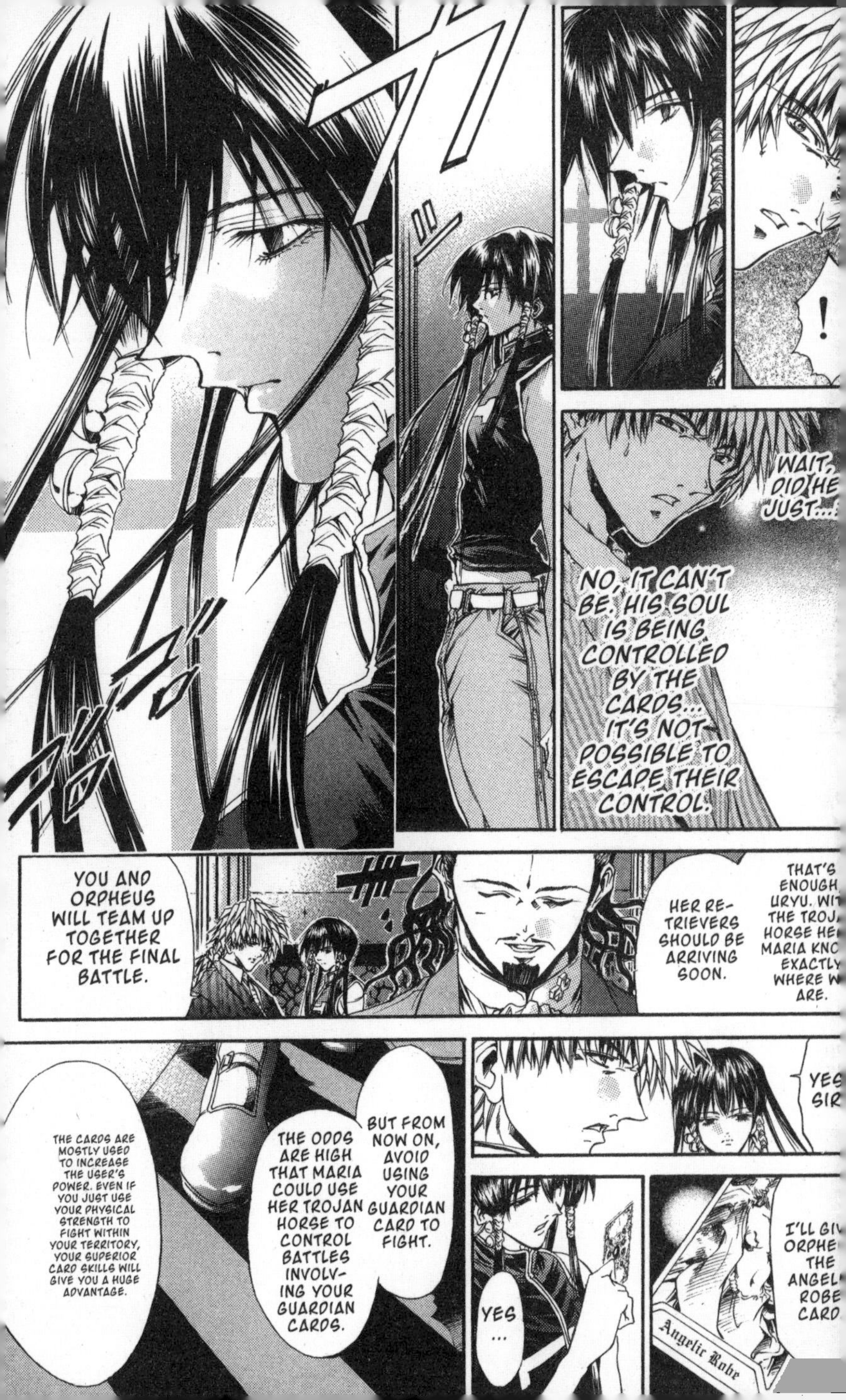
!
WAIT, DID HE JUST...!
NO, IT CAN'T BE. HIS SOUL IS BEING CONTROLLED BY THE CARDS... IT'S NOT POSSIBLE TO ESCAPE THEIR CONTROL.
THAT'S ENOUGH URYU. WIT THE TROJA HORSE HE MARIA KNO EXACTLY WHERE W ARE.
HER RE-TRIEVERS SHOULD BE ARRIVING SOON.
YOU AND ORPHEUS WILL TEAM UP TOGETHER FOR THE FINAL BATTLE.
YES SIR
I'LL GIV ORPHE THE ANGEL ROBE CARD
Angelic Robe
YES ...
BUT FROM NOW ON, AVOID USING YOUR GUARDIAN CARD TO FIGHT.
THE ODDS ARE HIGH THAT MARIA COULD USE HER TROJAN HORSE TO CONTROL BATTLES INVOLV-ING YOUR GUARDIAN CARDS.
THE CARDS ARE MOSTLY USED TO INCREASE THE USER'S POWER. EVEN IF YOU JUST USE YOUR PHYSICAL STRENGTH TO FIGHT WITHIN YOUR TERRITORY, YOUR SUPERIOR CARD SKILLS WILL GIVE YOU A HUGE ADVANTAGE.

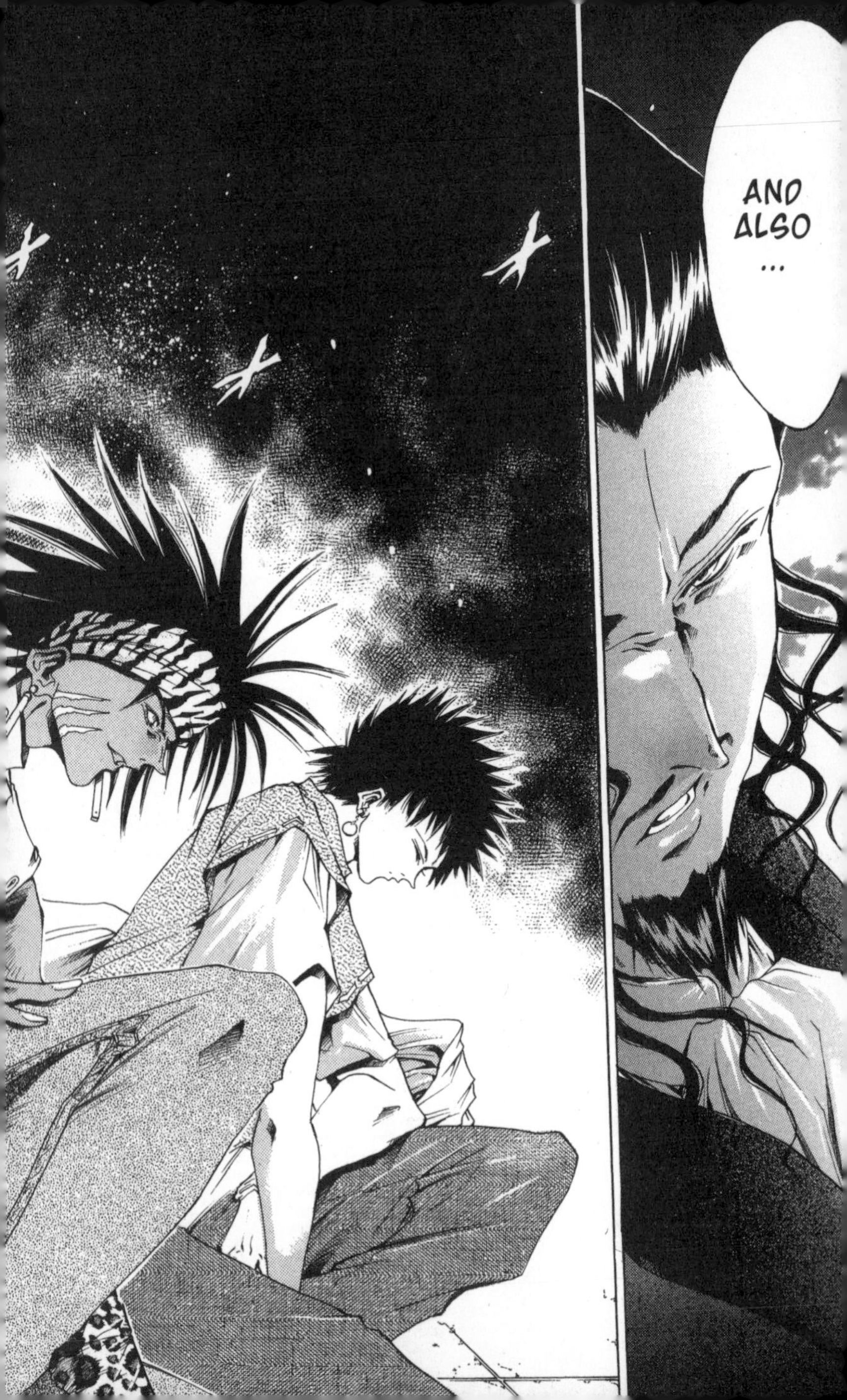
AND ALSO ...

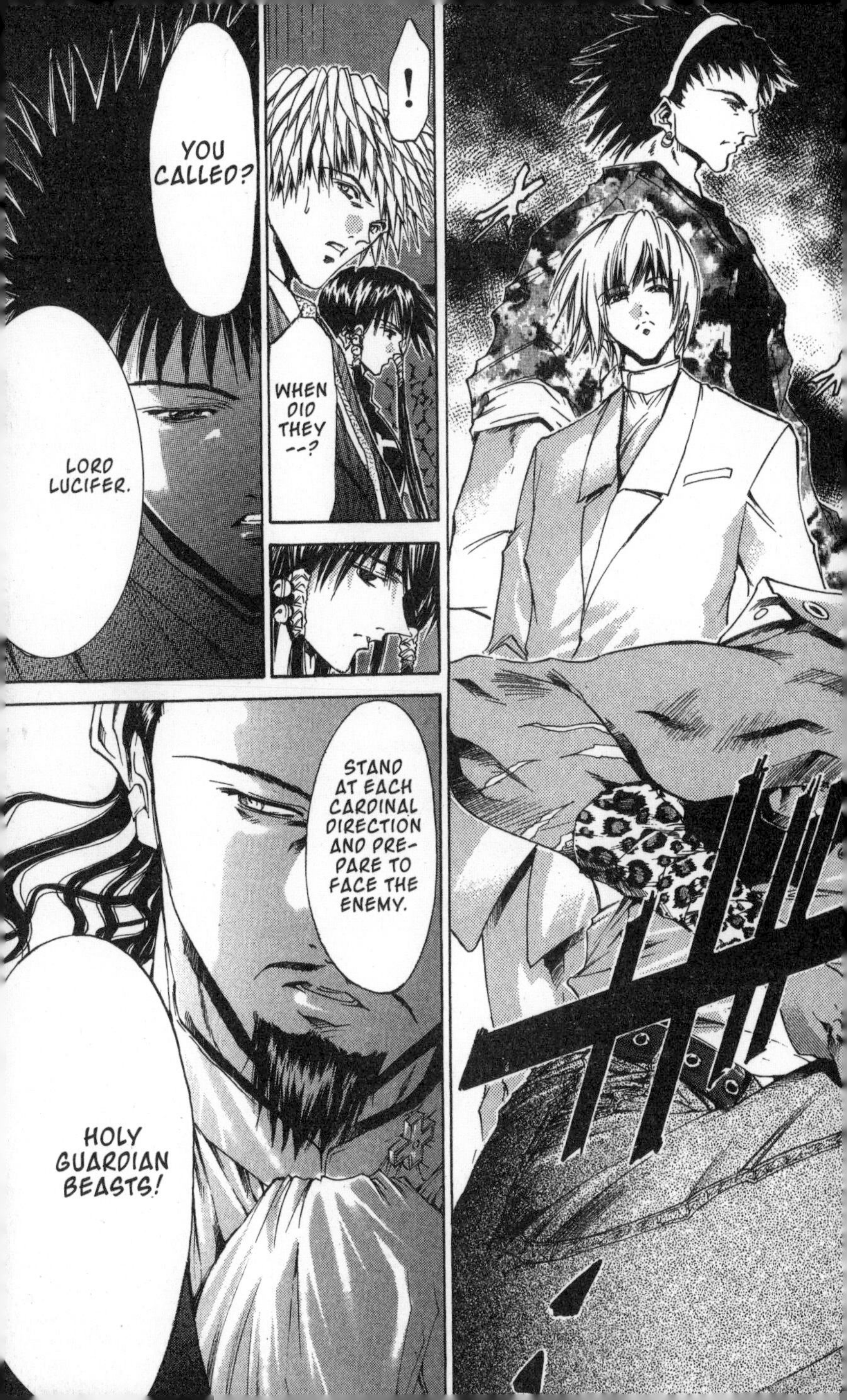
!
WHEN DID THEY --?
YOU CALLED?
LORD LUCIFER.
STAND AT EACH CARDINAL DIRECTION AND PRE-PARE TO FACE THE ENEMY.
HOLY GUARDIAN BEASTS!

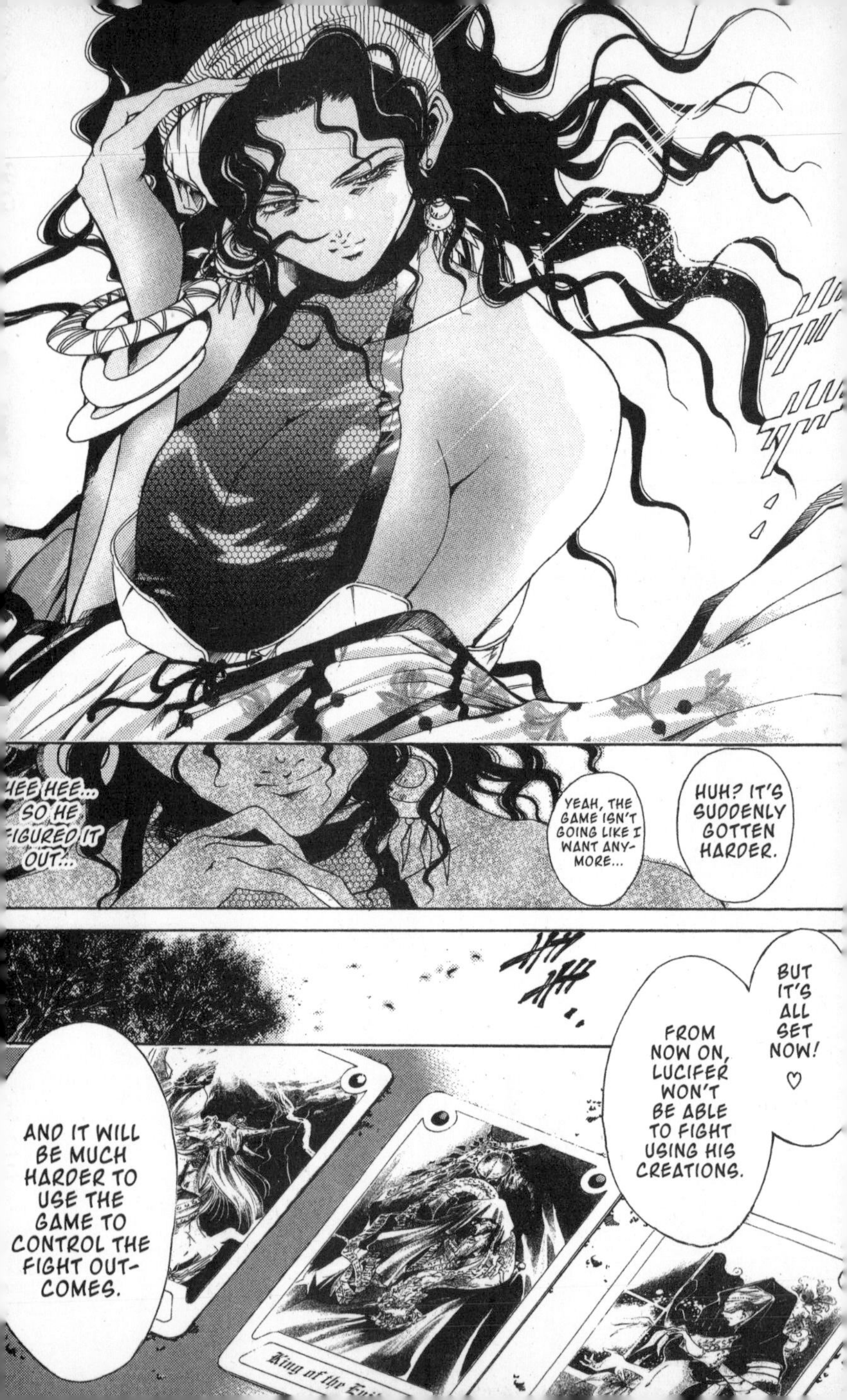
HUH? IT'S SUDDENLY GOTTEN HARDER.
YEAH, THE GAME ISN'T GOING LIKE I WANT ANY-MORE...
HEE HEE... SO HE FIGURED IT OUT...
BUT IT'S ALL SET NOW! ♡
FROM NOW ON, LUCIFER WON'T BE ABLE TO FIGHT USING HIS CREATIONS.
AND IT WILL BE MUCH HARDER TO USE THE GAME TO CONTROL THE FIGHT OUT-COMES.

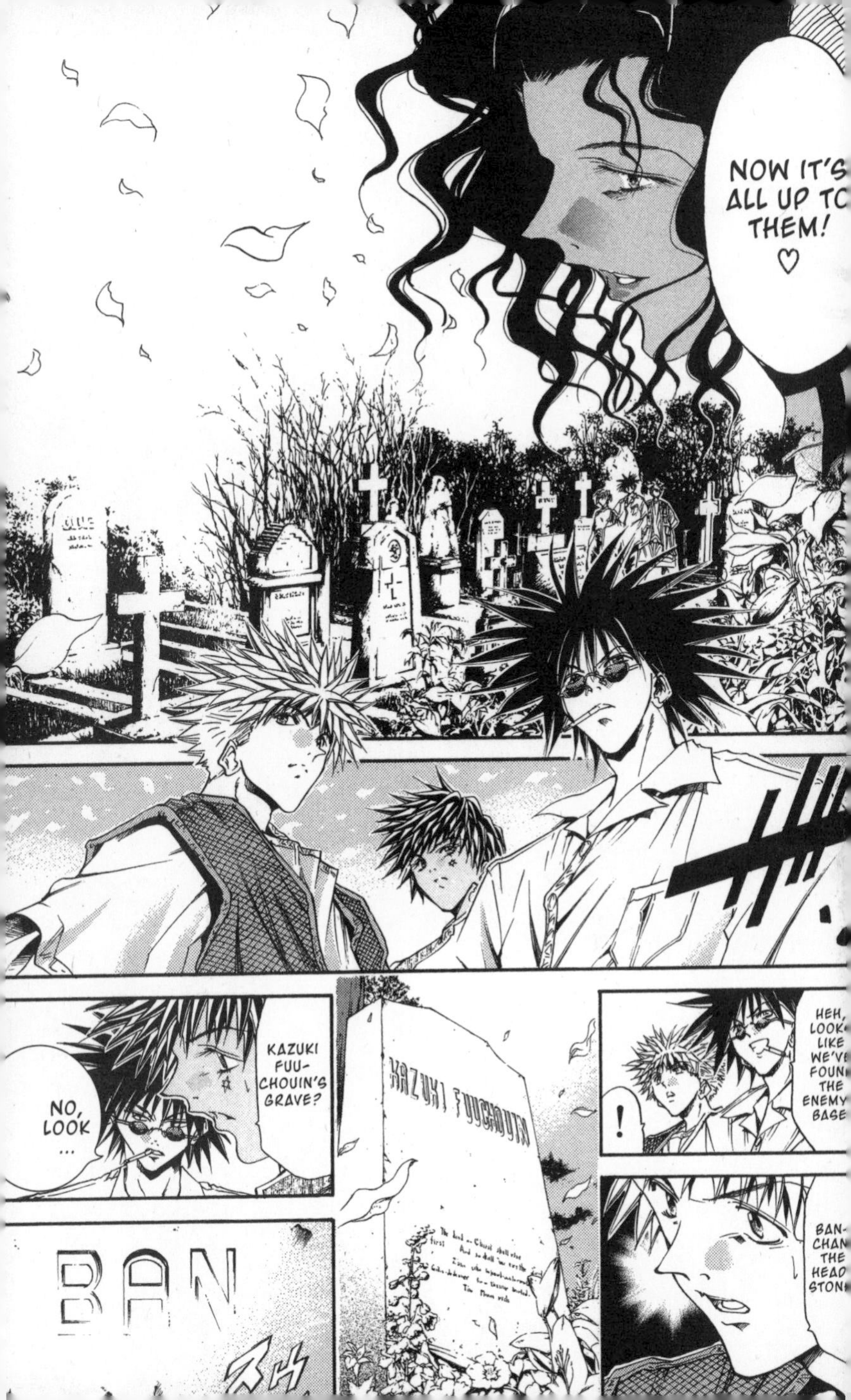
NOW IT'S ALL UP TO THEM! ♡
HEH, LOOK LIKE WE'VE FOUN THE ENEMY BASE
!
BAN-CHAN THE HEAD STON
KAZUKI FUUCHOUIN
KAZUKI FUU-CHOUIN'S GRAVE?
NO, LOOK ...
BAN

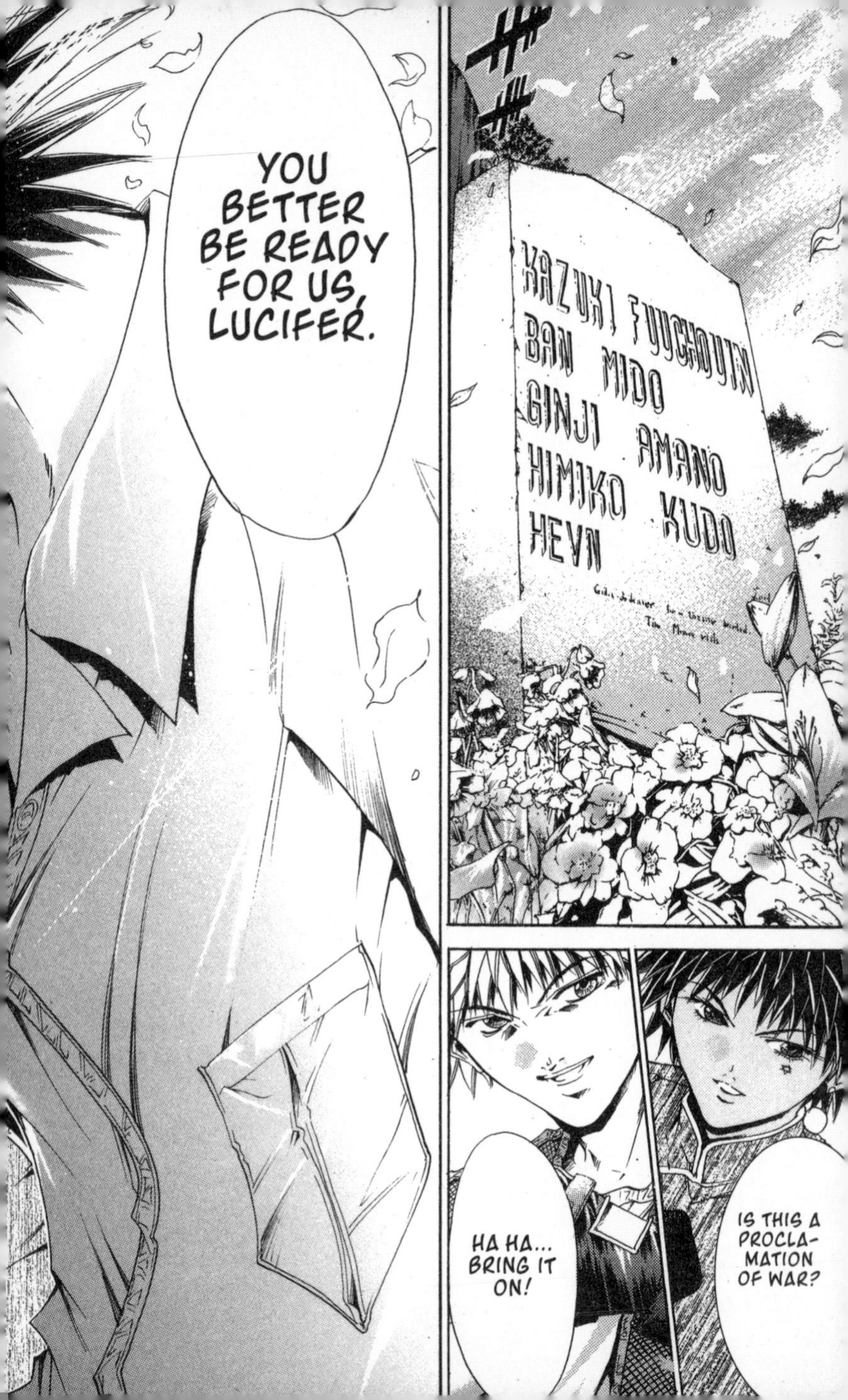
KAZUKI FUUCHOUIN
BAN MIDO
GINJI AMANO
HIMIKO KUDO
HEVN
IS THIS A PROCLAMATION OF WAR?
HA HA... BRING IT ON!
YOU BETTER BE READY FOR US, LUCIFER.

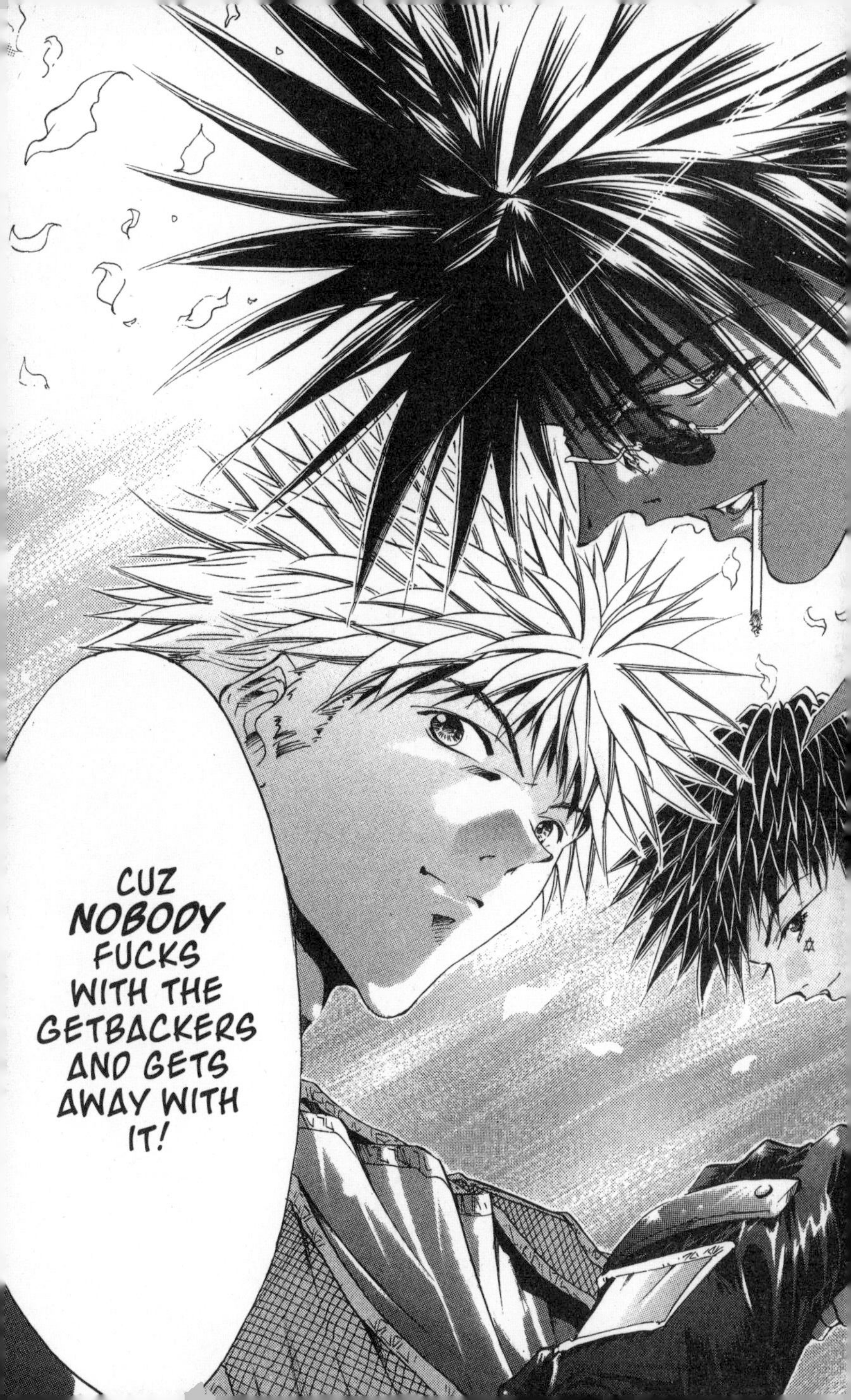
CUZ *NOBODY* FUCKS WITH THE GETBACKERS AND GETS AWAY WITH IT!

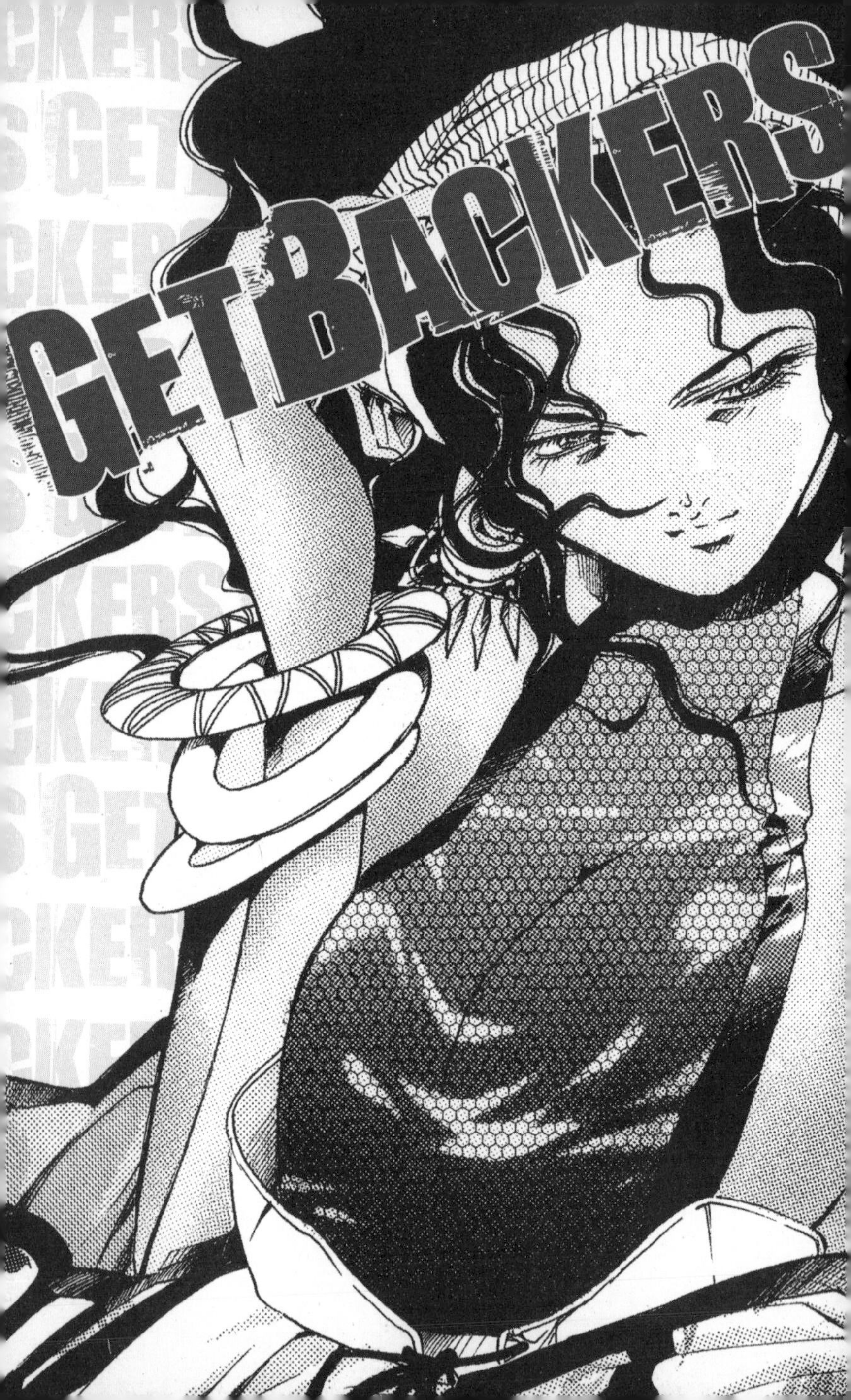
GETBACKERS

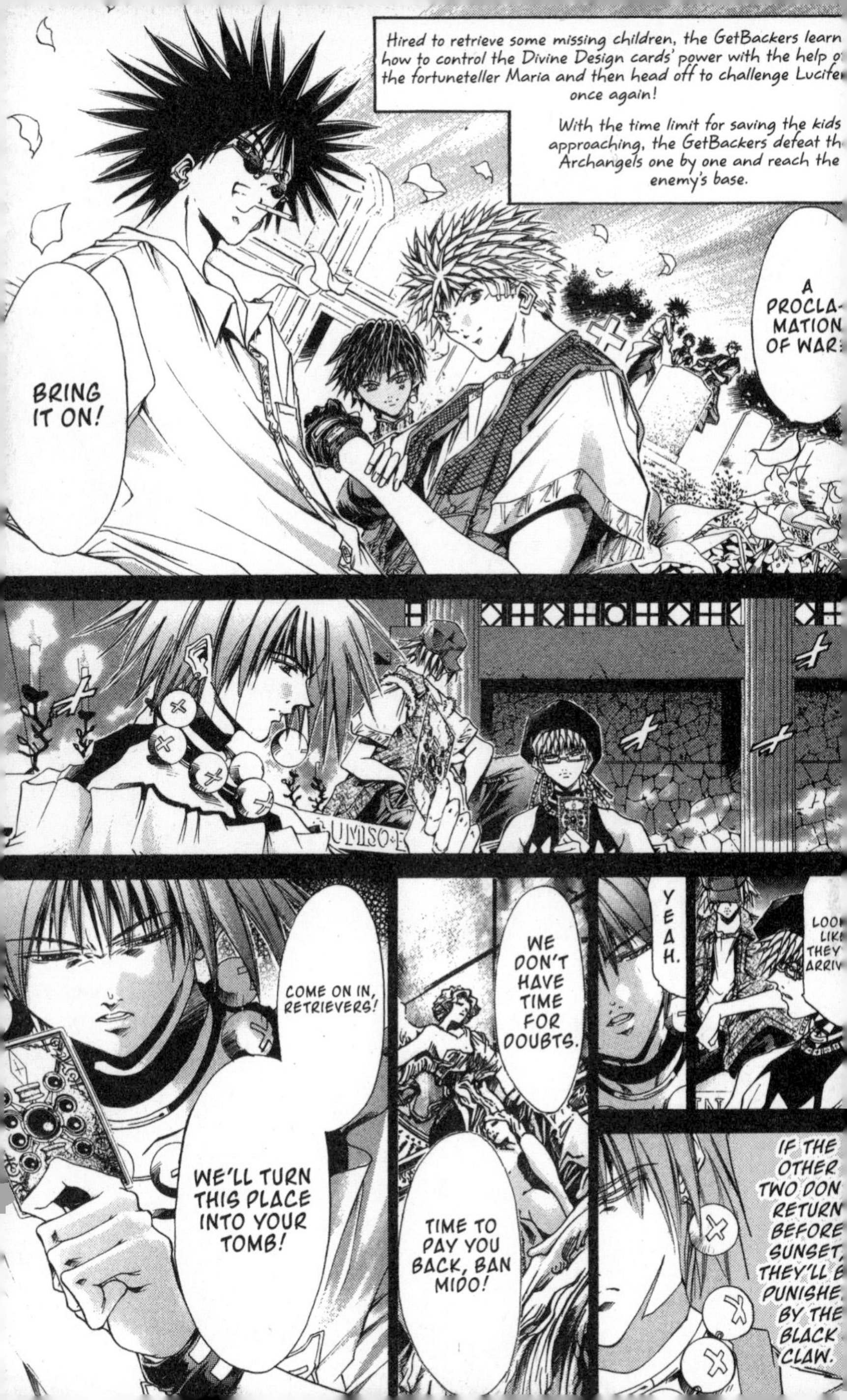

Hired to retrieve some missing children, the GetBackers learn how to control the Divine Design cards' power with the help o the fortuneteller Maria and then head off to challenge Lucife once again!
With the time limit for saving the kids approaching, the GetBackers defeat th Archangels one by one and reach the enemy's base.
A PROCLA-MATION OF WAR!
BRING IT ON!
LOO LIK THEY' ARRIV
YEAH.
IF THE OTHER TWO DON RETURN BEFORE SUNSET, THEY'LL B PUNISHE BY THE BLACK CLAW.
WE DON'T HAVE TIME FOR DOUBTS.
TIME TO PAY YOU BACK, BAN MIDO!
COME ON IN, RETRIEVERS!
WE'LL TURN THIS PLACE INTO YOUR TOMB!

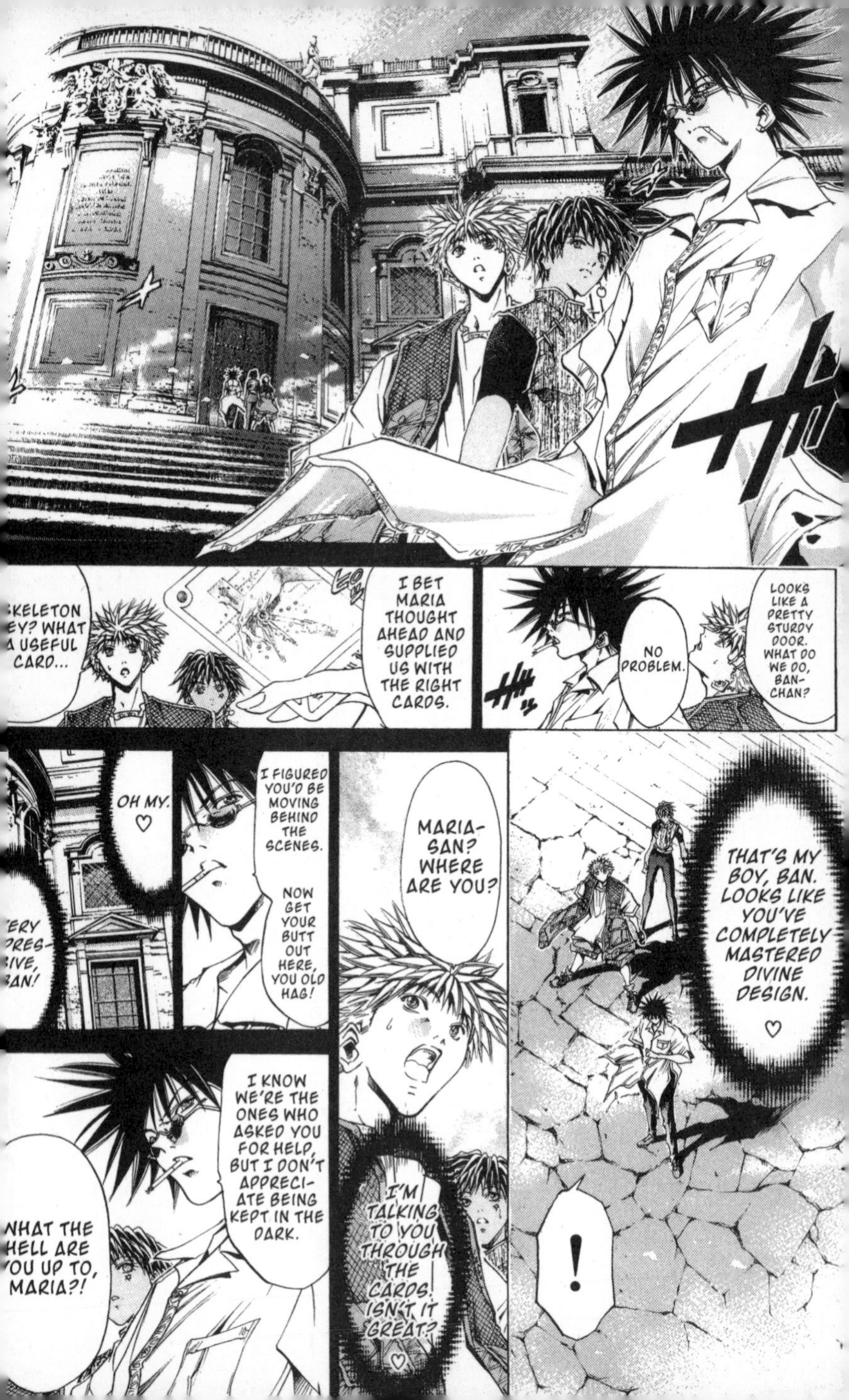
LOOKS LIKE A PRETTY STURDY DOOR. WHAT DO WE DO, BAN-CHAN?
NO PROBLEM.
I BET MARIA THOUGHT AHEAD AND SUPPLIED US WITH THE RIGHT CARDS.
KELETON EY? WHAT A USEFUL CARD...
THAT'S MY BOY, BAN. LOOKS LIKE YOU'VE COMPLETELY MASTERED DIVINE DESIGN. ♡
!
MARIA-SAN? WHERE ARE YOU?
I'M TALKING TO YOU THROUGH THE CARDS. ISN'T IT GREAT? ♡
I FIGURED YOU'D BE MOVING BEHIND THE SCENES.
NOW GET YOUR BUTT OUT HERE, YOU OLD HAG!
OH MY. ♡
ERY PRES-SIVE, AN!
I KNOW WE'RE THE ONES WHO ASKED YOU FOR HELP, BUT I DON'T APPRECIATE BEING KEPT IN THE DARK.
HAT THE HELL ARE OU UP TO, MARIA?!

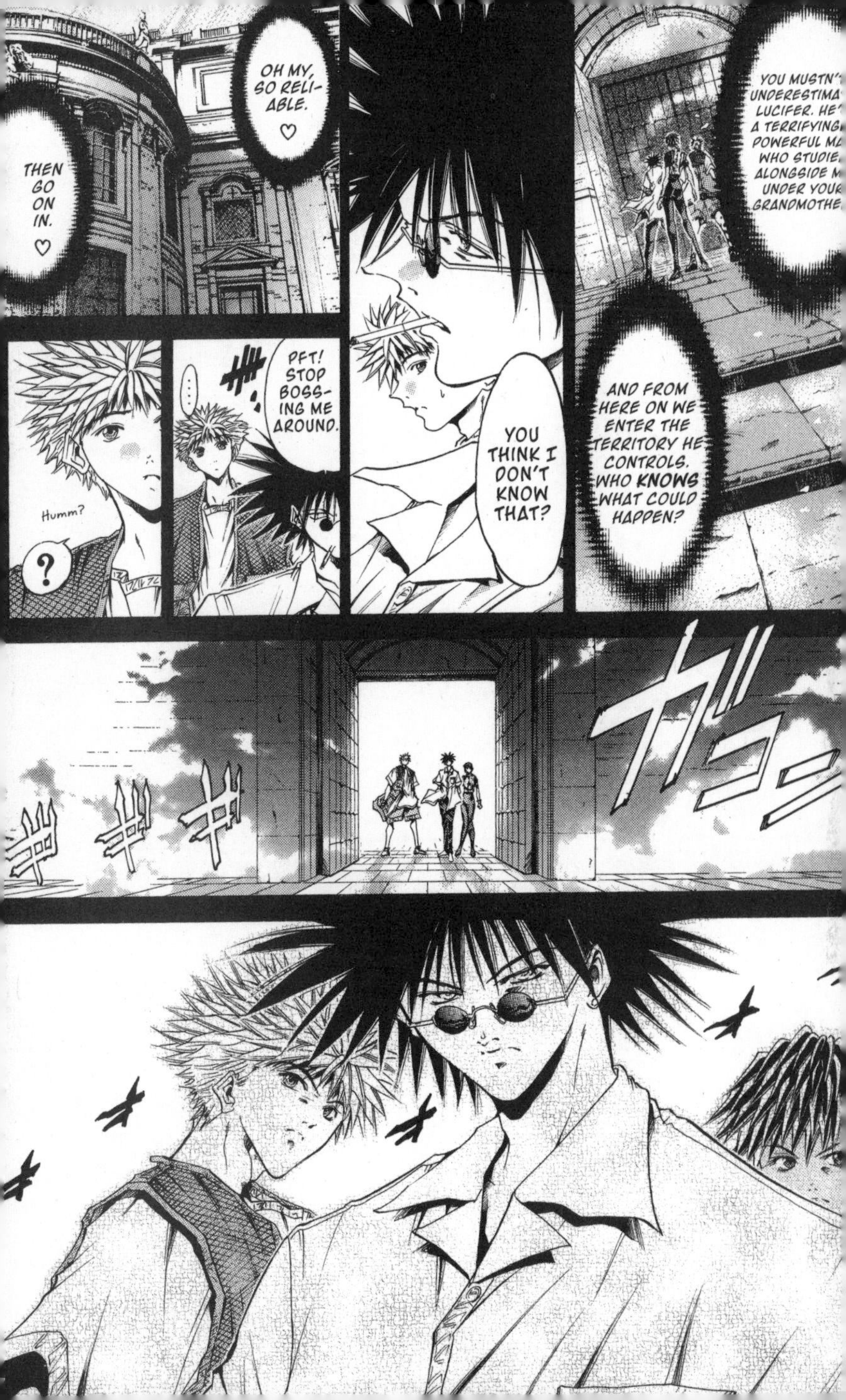
YOU MUSTN'T UNDERESTIMA LUCIFER. HE' A TERRIFYING POWERFUL MA WHO STUDIE ALONGSIDE M UNDER YOUR GRANDMOTHE
AND FROM HERE ON WE ENTER THE TERRITORY HE CONTROLS. WHO **KNOWS** WHAT COULD HAPPEN?
YOU THINK I DON'T KNOW THAT?
OH MY, SO RELI-ABLE. ♡
THEN GO ON IN. ♡
PFT! STOP BOSS-ING ME AROUND.
...
Humm?
?

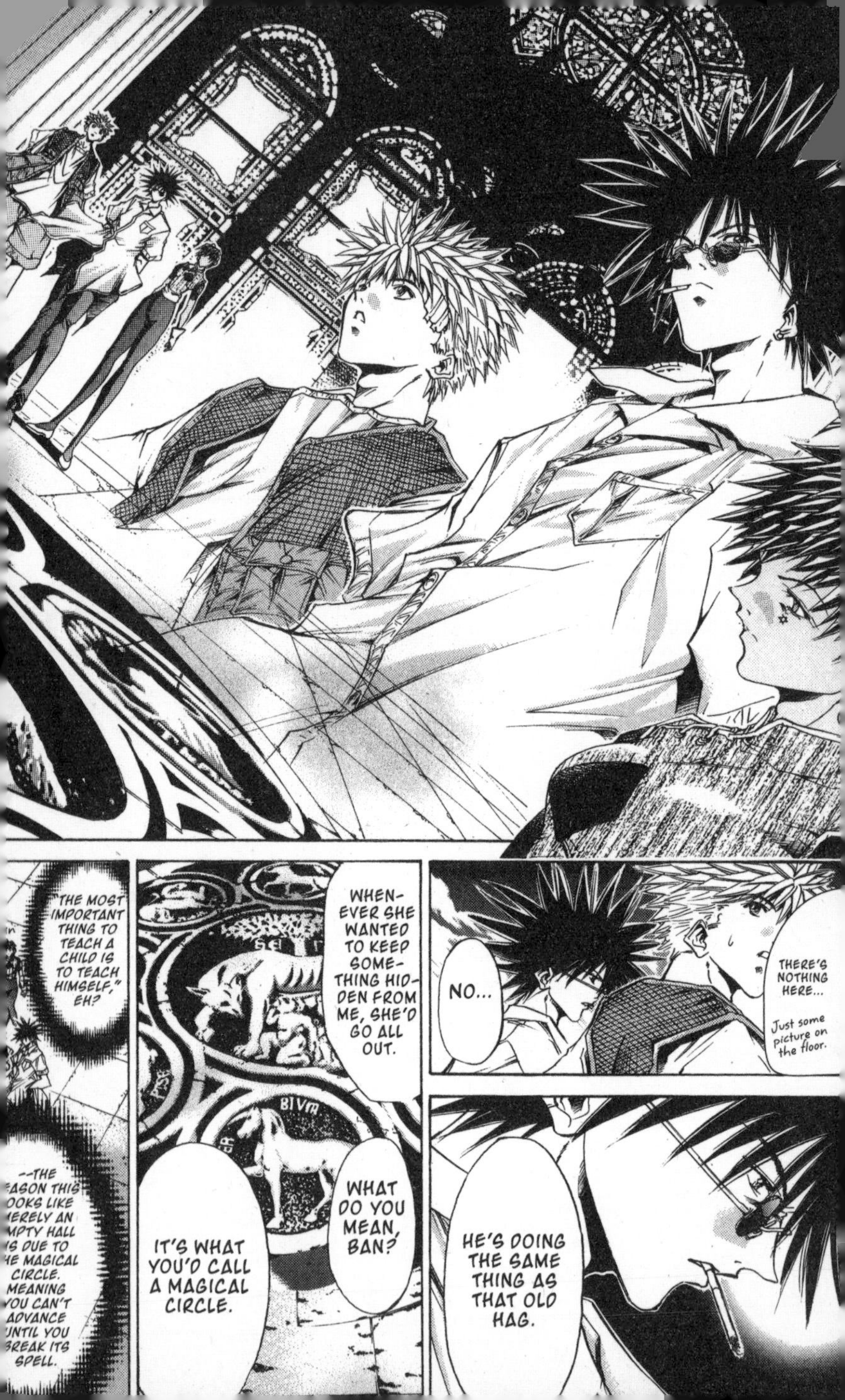

THERE'S NOTHING HERE...
Just some picture on the floor.
NO...
HE'S DOING THE SAME THING AS THAT OLD HAG.
WHEN-EVER SHE WANTED TO KEEP SOME-THING HID-DEN FROM ME, SHE'D GO ALL OUT.
WHAT DO YOU MEAN, BAN?
IT'S WHAT YOU'D CALL A MAGICAL CIRCLE.
"THE MOST IMPORTANT THING TO TEACH A CHILD IS TO TEACH HIMSELF," EH?
--THE EASON THIS OOKS LIKE IERELY AN MPTY HALL S DUE TO HE MAGICAL CIRCLE. MEANING YOU CAN'T ADVANCE UNTIL YOU REAK ITS SPELL.

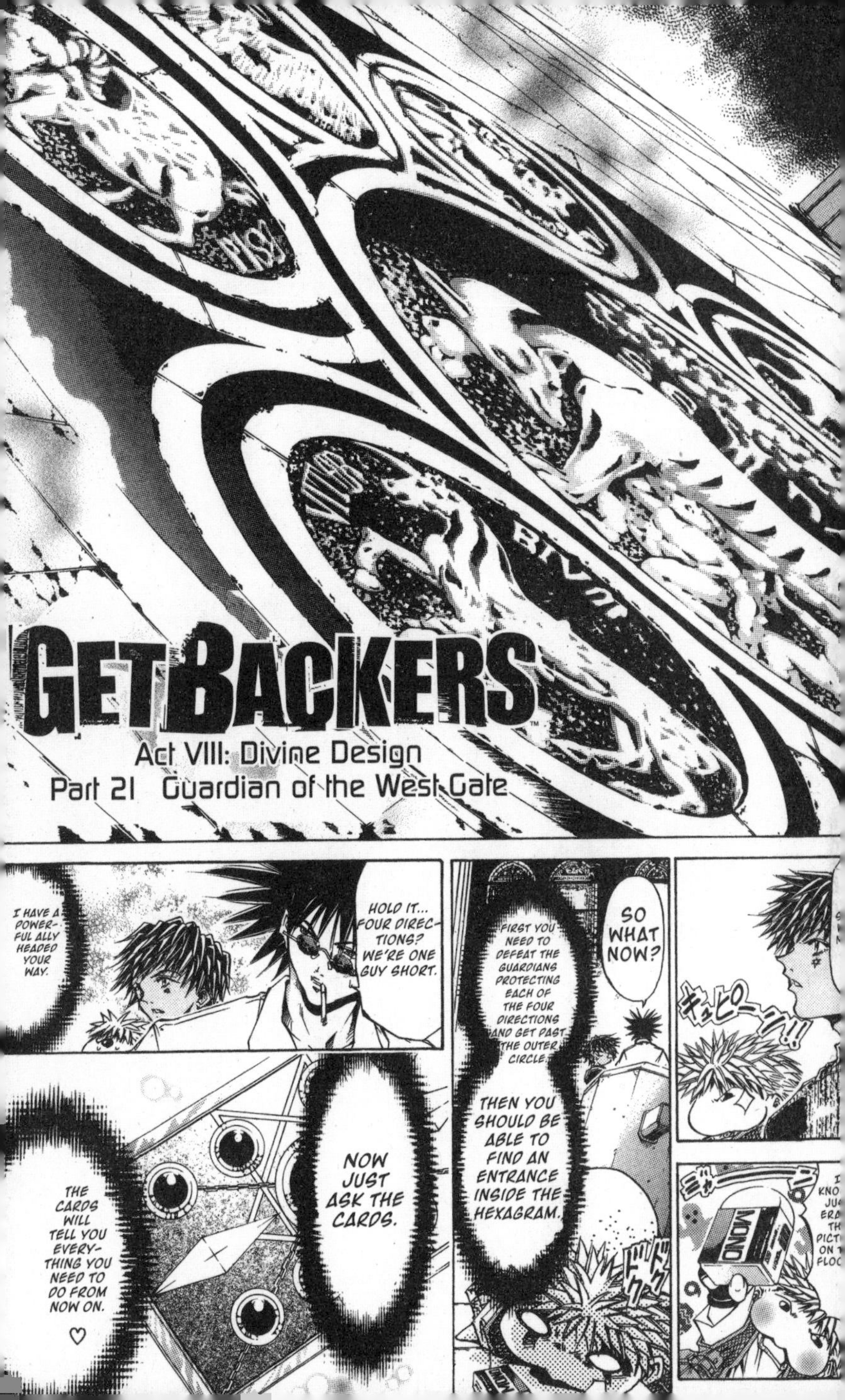

GETBACKERS
Act VIII: Divine Design
Part 21 Guardian of the West Gate
SO WHAT NOW?
FIRST YOU NEED TO DEFEAT THE GUARDIANS PROTECTING EACH OF THE FOUR DIRECTIONS AND GET PAST THE OUTER CIRCLE.
THEN YOU SHOULD BE ABLE TO FIND AN ENTRANCE INSIDE THE HEXAGRAM.
HOLD IT... FOUR DIRECTIONS? WE'RE ONE GUY SHORT.
I HAVE A POWERFUL ALLY HEADED YOUR WAY.
NOW JUST ASK THE CARDS.
THE CARDS WILL TELL YOU EVERYTHING YOU NEED TO DO FROM NOW ON. ♡

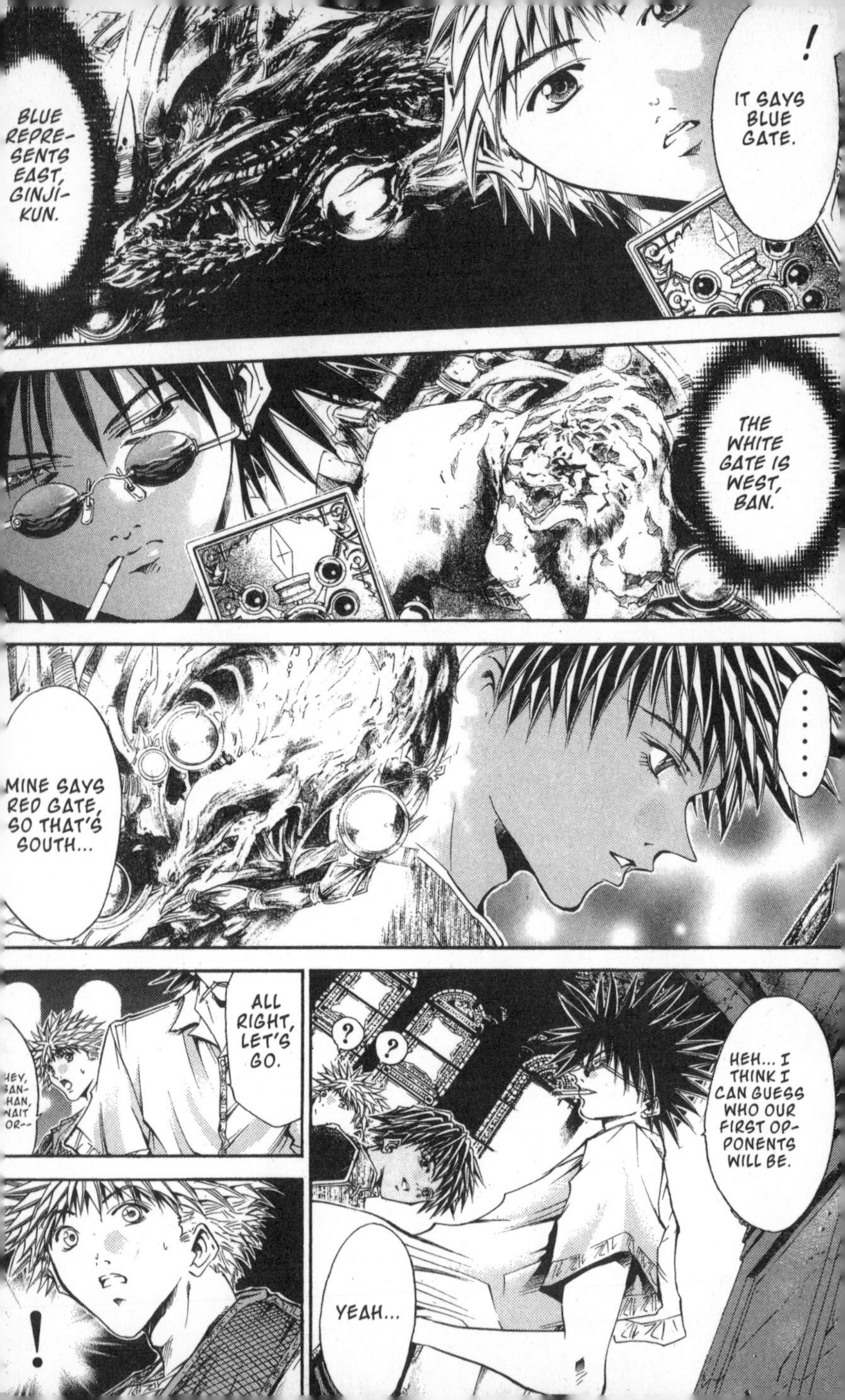

!
IT SAYS BLUE GATE.
BLUE REPRESENTS EAST, GINJI-KUN.
THE WHITE GATE IS WEST, BAN.
......
MINE SAYS RED GATE, SO THAT'S SOUTH...
HEH... I THINK I CAN GUESS WHO OUR FIRST OPPONENTS WILL BE.
?
?
YEAH...
ALL RIGHT, LET'S GO.
HEY, BAN-HAN, WAIT OR--
!

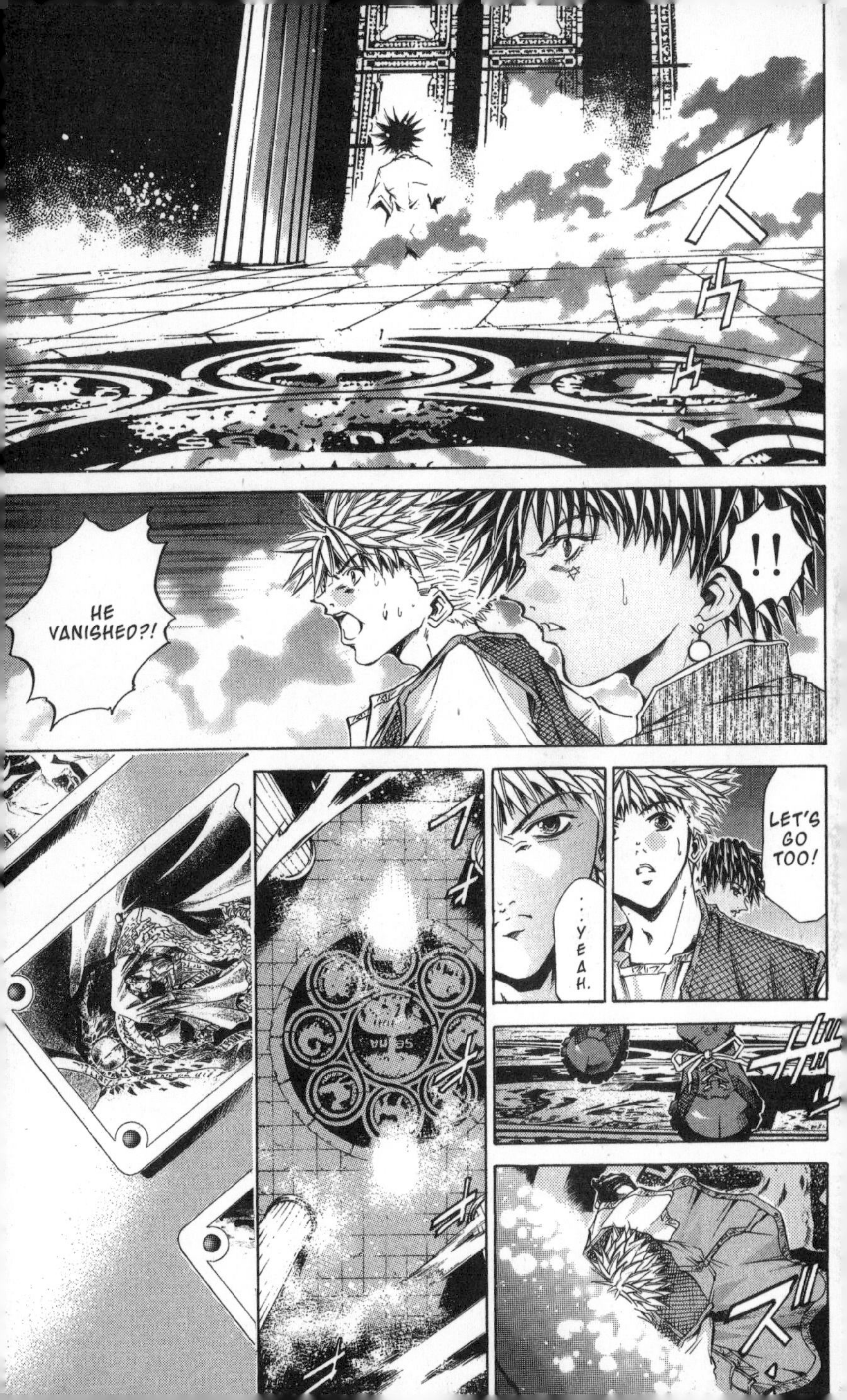
!!
HE VANISHED?!
LET'S GO TOO!
...YEAH.

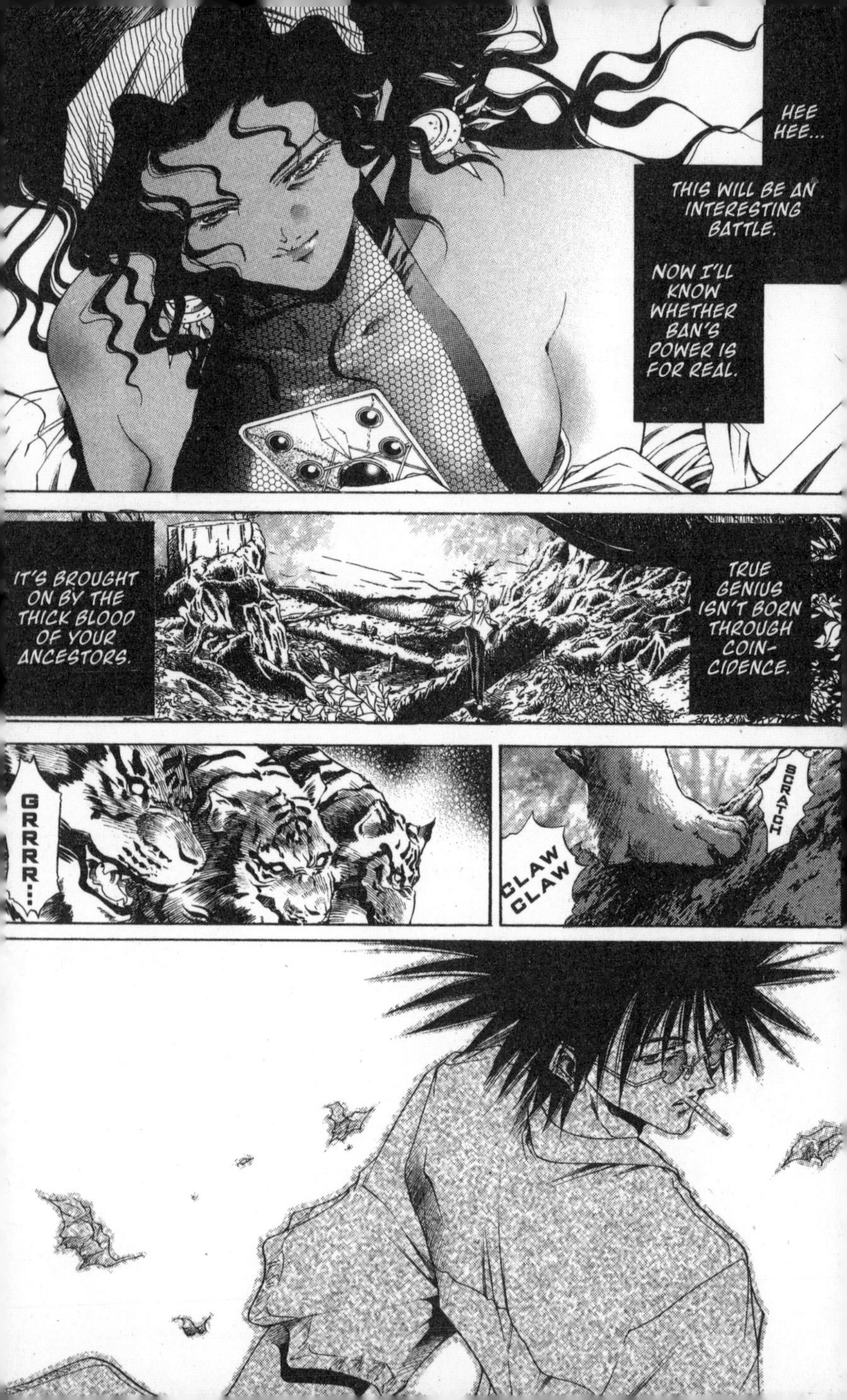
HEE HEE...
THIS WILL BE AN INTERESTING BATTLE.
NOW I'LL KNOW WHETHER BAN'S POWER IS FOR REAL.
TRUE GENIUS ISN'T BORN THROUGH COIN-CIDENCE.
IT'S BROUGHT ON BY THE THICK BLOOD OF YOUR ANCESTORS.
SCRATCH
CLAW CLAW
GRRRR...

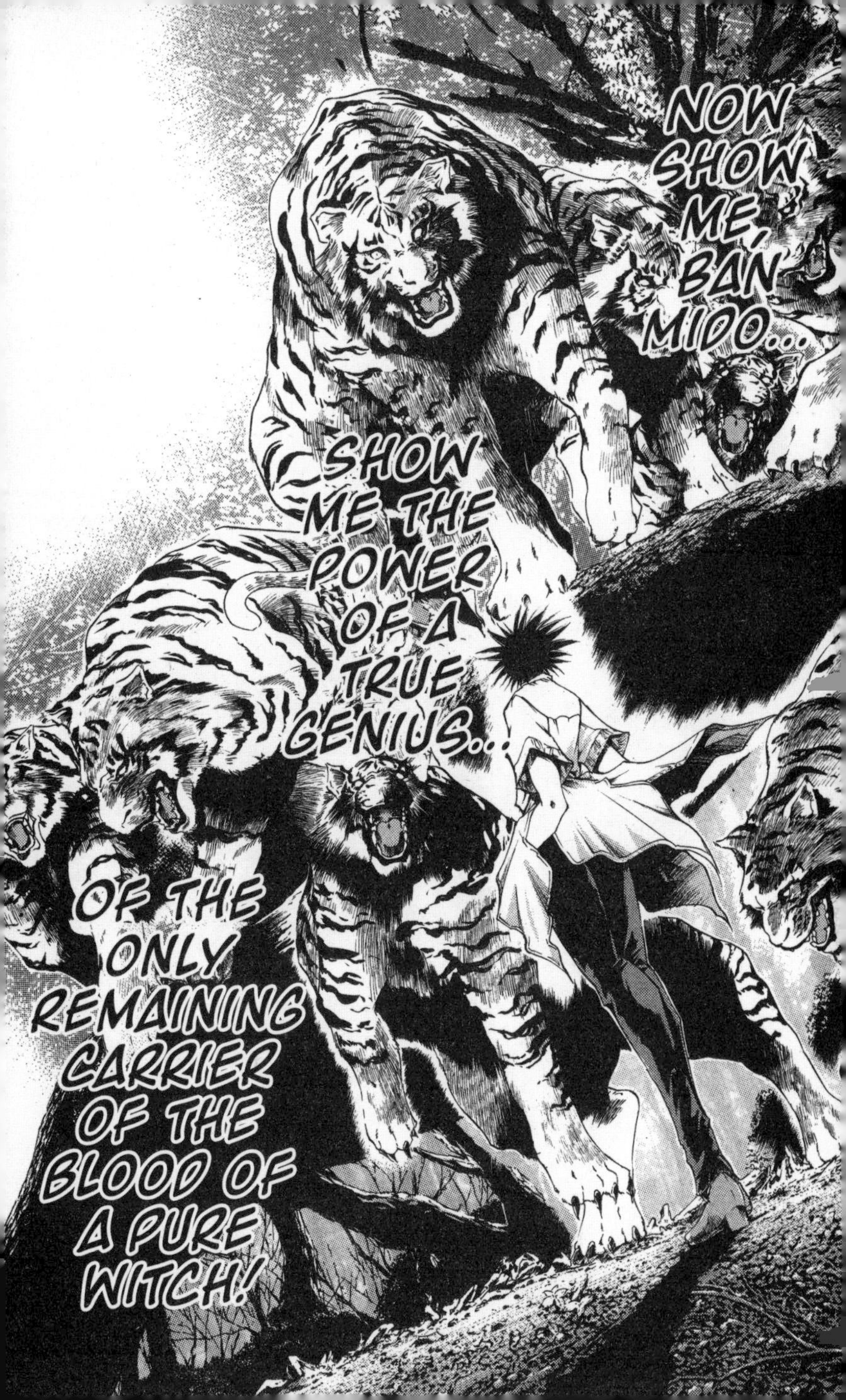
NOW SHOW ME, BAN MIDO...
SHOW ME THE POWER OF A TRUE GENIUS...
OF THE ONLY REMAINING CARRIER OF THE BLOOD OF A PURE WITCH!

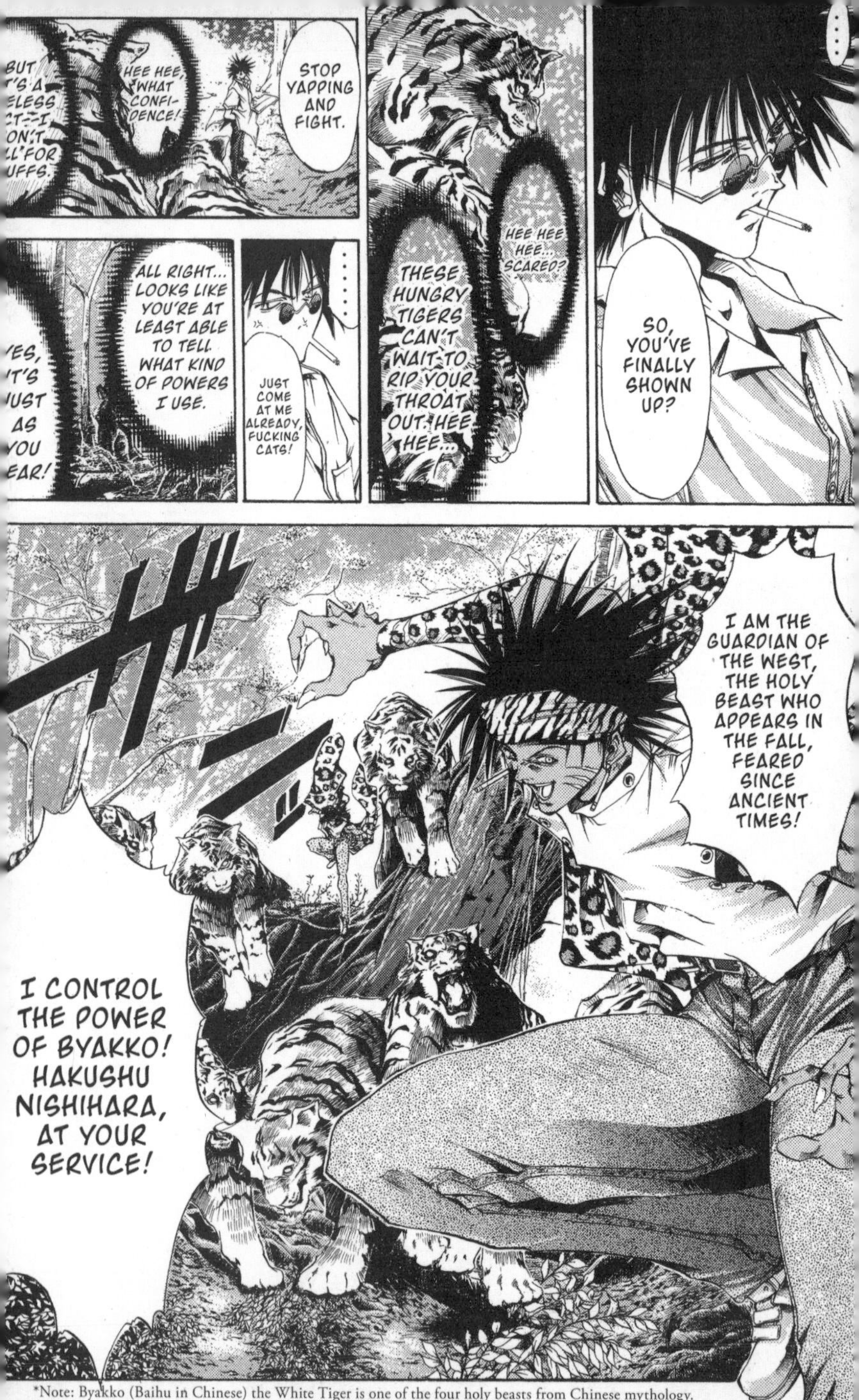
...
SO, YOU'VE FINALLY SHOWN UP?
HEE HEE HEE... SCARED?
THESE HUNGRY TIGERS CAN'T WAIT TO RIP YOUR THROAT OUT. HEE HEE...
STOP YAPPING AND FIGHT.
HEE HEE, WHAT CONFIDENCE!
BUT T'S A ELESS CT—I ON'T LL FOR UFFS.
...
JUST COME AT ME ALREADY, FUCKING CATS!
ALL RIGHT... LOOKS LIKE YOU'RE AT LEAST ABLE TO TELL WHAT KIND OF POWERS I USE.
YES, T'S UST AS YOU EAR!
I AM THE GUARDIAN OF THE WEST, THE HOLY BEAST WHO APPEARS IN THE FALL, FEARED SINCE ANCIENT TIMES!
I CONTROL THE POWER OF BYAKKO! HAKUSHU NISHIHARA, AT YOUR SERVICE!

*Note: Byakko (Baihu in Chinese) the White Tiger is one of the four holy beasts from Chinese mythology.

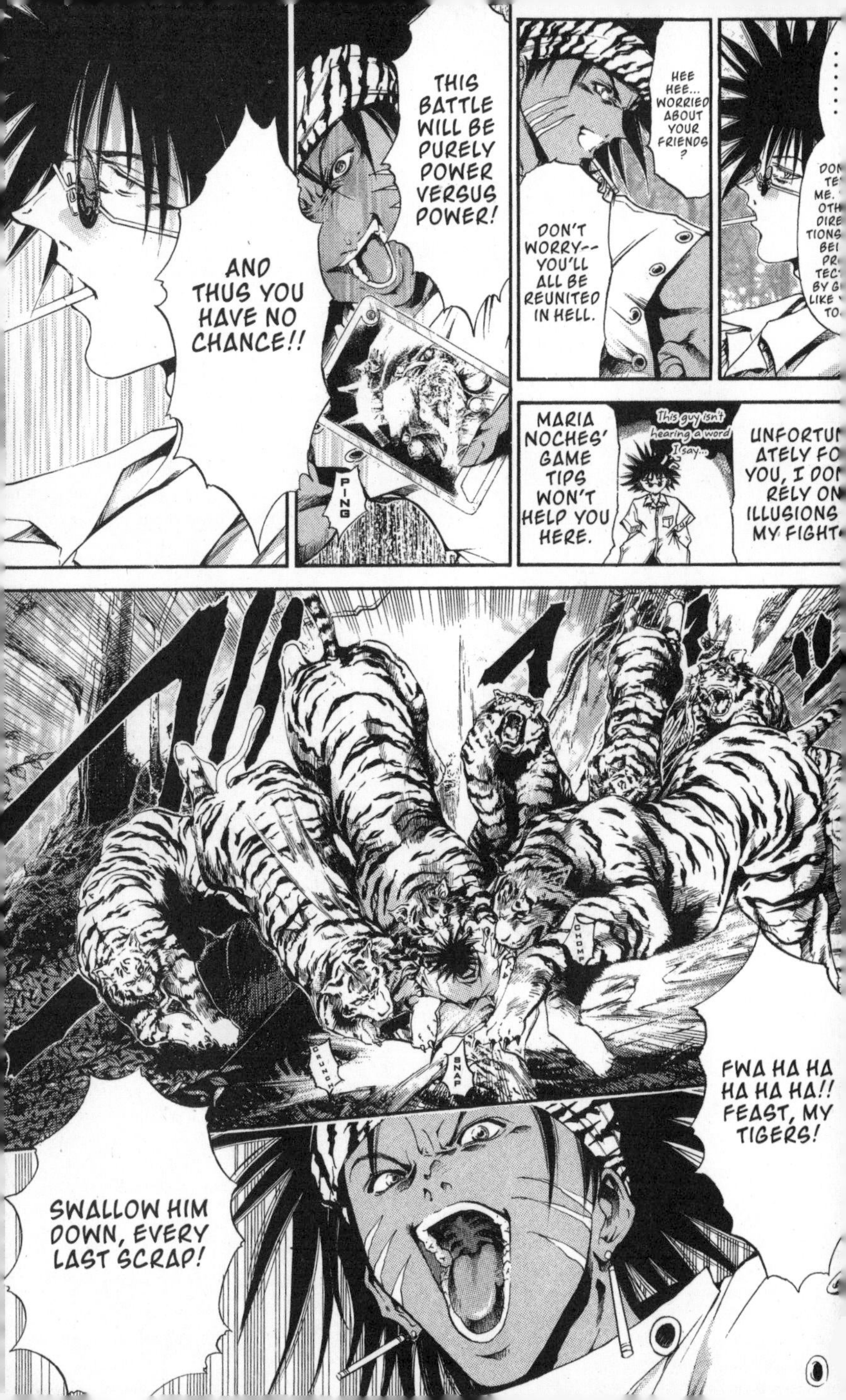
....
DON TE ME. OTH DIRE TIONS BEI PR TEC BY G LIKE Y TO.
HEE HEE... WORRIED ABOUT YOUR FRIENDS?
DON'T WORRY-- YOU'LL ALL BE REUNITED IN HELL.
THIS BATTLE WILL BE PURELY POWER VERSUS POWER!
PING
AND THUS YOU HAVE NO CHANCE!!
UNFORTUN ATELY FO YOU, I DON RELY ON ILLUSIONS MY FIGHT
This guy isn't hearing a word I say...
MARIA NOCHES' GAME TIPS WON'T HELP YOU HERE.
CHOMP
SNAP
CRUNCH
FWA HA HA HA HA HA!! FEAST, MY TIGERS!
SWALLOW HIM DOWN, EVERY LAST SCRAP!

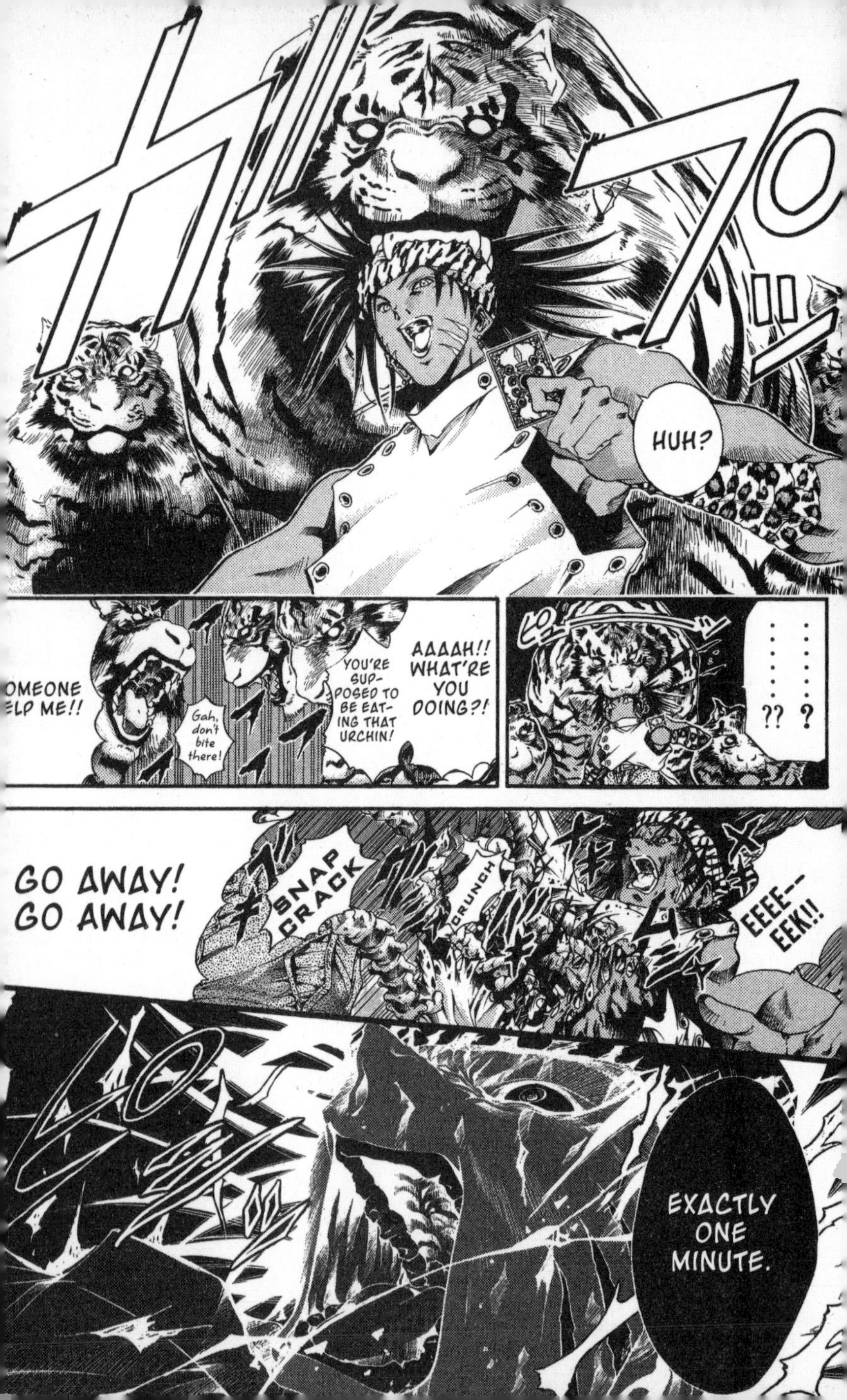
HUH?
......?
......??
AAAAH!! WHAT'RE YOU DOING?!
YOU'RE SUPPOSED TO BE EATING THAT URCHIN!
Gah, don't bite there!
OMEONE ELP ME!!
EEEE--EEK!!
CRUNCH
SNAP CRACK
GO AWAY! GO AWAY!
EXACTLY ONE MINUTE.

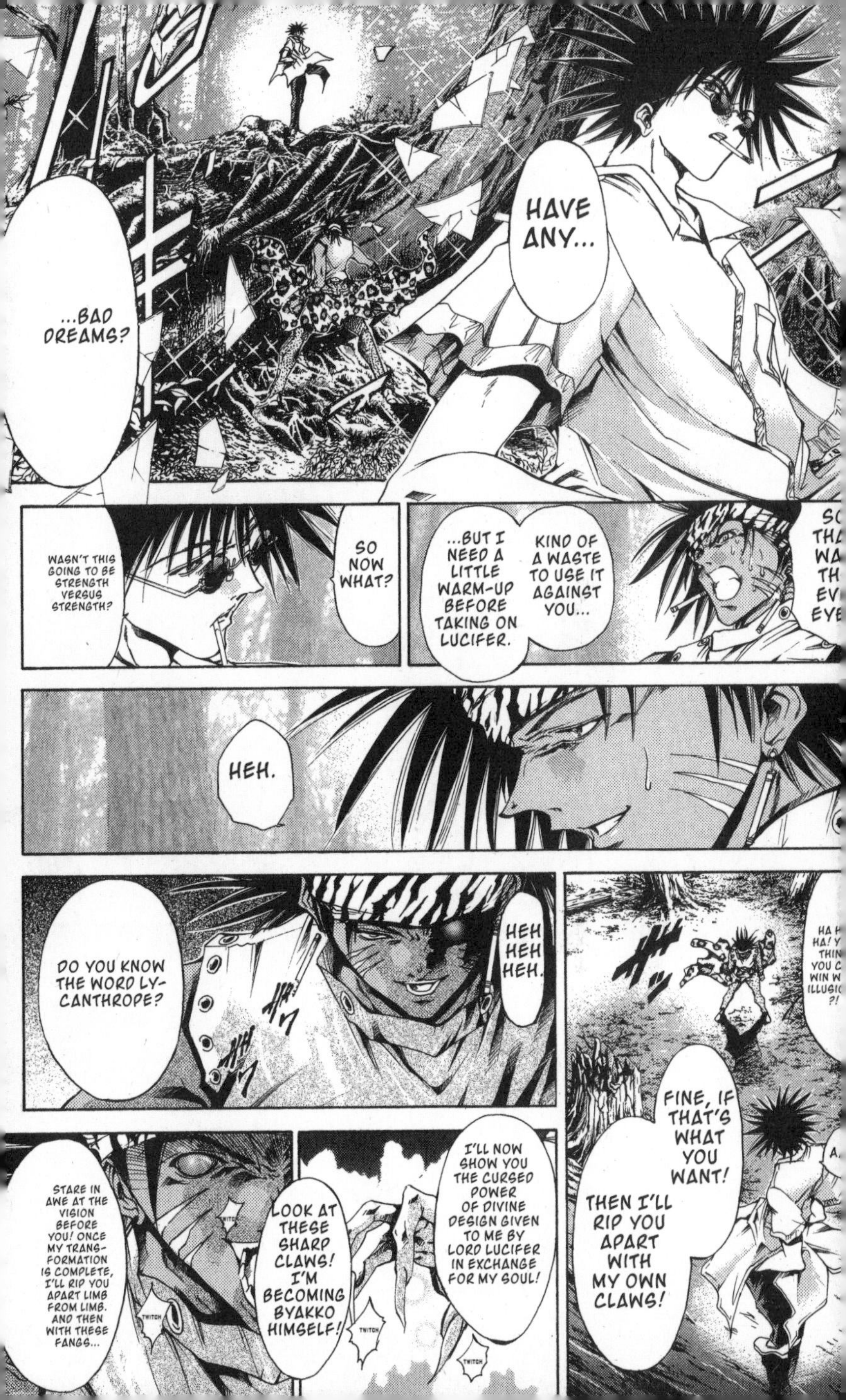
HAVE ANY...
...BAD DREAMS?
SO THA WA TH EV EYE
KIND OF A WASTE TO USE IT AGAINST YOU...
...BUT I NEED A LITTLE WARM-UP BEFORE TAKING ON LUCIFER.
SO NOW WHAT?
WASN'T THIS GOING TO BE STRENGTH VERSUS STRENGTH?
HEH.
HA H HA! Y THIN YOU C WIN W ILLUSIO ?!
A..
FINE, IF THAT'S WHAT YOU WANT!
THEN I'LL RIP YOU APART WITH MY OWN CLAWS!
HEH HEH HEH.
DO YOU KNOW THE WORD LY-CANTHROPE?
I'LL NOW SHOW YOU THE CURSED POWER OF DIVINE DESIGN GIVEN TO ME BY LORD LUCIFER IN EXCHANGE FOR MY SOUL!
TWITCH
LOOK AT THESE SHARP CLAWS! I'M BECOMING BYAKKO HIMSELF!
TWITCH
STARE IN AWE AT THE VISION BEFORE YOU! ONCE MY TRANS-FORMATION IS COMPLETE, I'LL RIP YOU APART LIMB FROM LIMB. AND THEN WITH THESE FANGS...
TWITCH
TWITCH

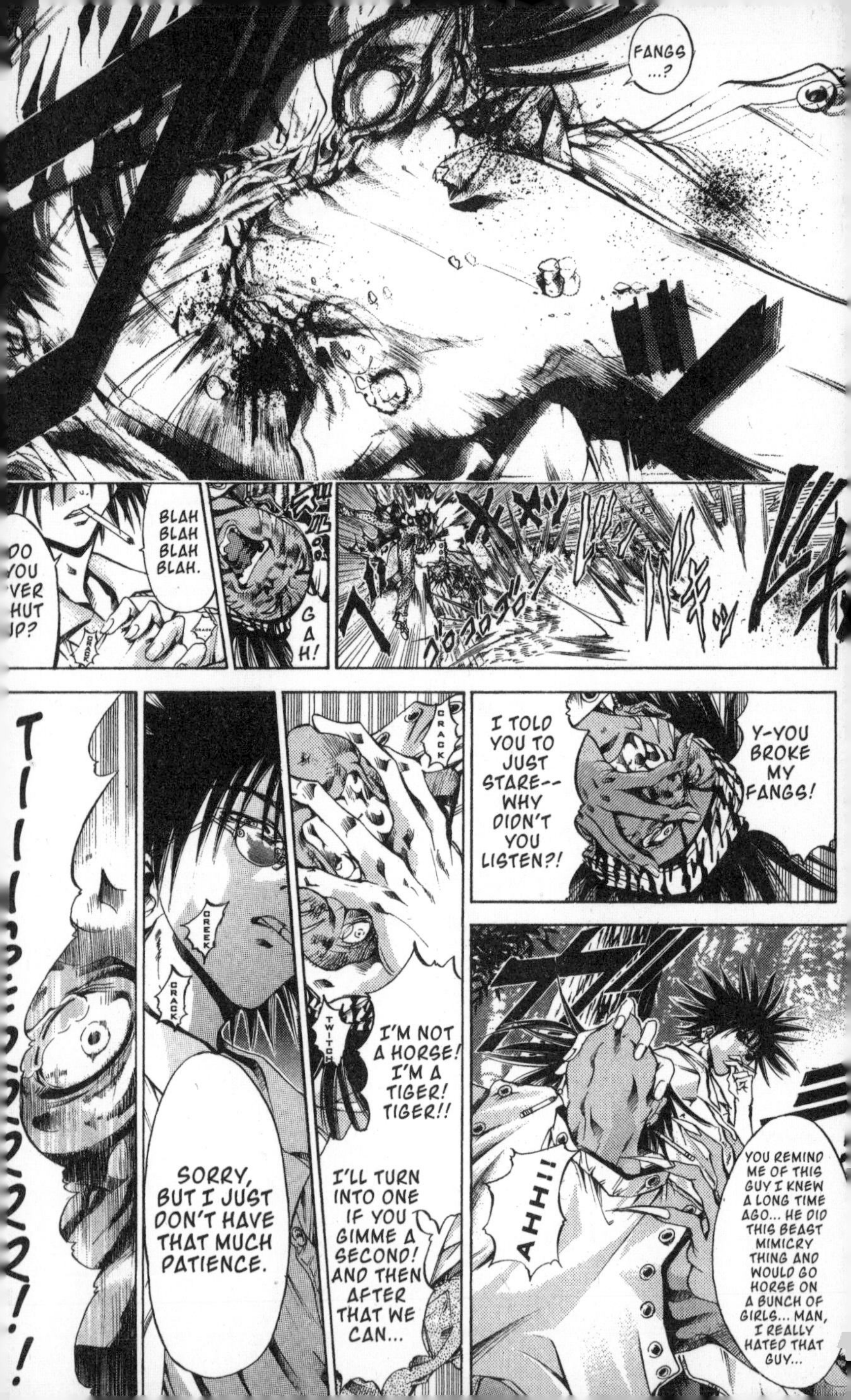

FANGS ...?
GAH!
BLAH BLAH BLAH BLAH.
CRACK
CRACK
DO YOU VER HUT UP?
Y-YOU BROKE MY FANGS!
I TOLD YOU TO JUST STARE-- WHY DIDN'T YOU LISTEN?!
YOU REMIND ME OF THIS GUY I KNEW A LONG TIME AGO... HE DID THIS BEAST MIMICRY THING AND WOULD GO HORSE ON A BUNCH OF GIRLS... MAN, I REALLY HATED THAT GUY...
AHH!!
CRACK
I'M NOT A HORSE! I'M A TIGER! TIGER!!
TWITCH
I'LL TURN INTO ONE IF YOU GIMME A SECOND! AND THEN AFTER THAT WE CAN...
CREEK
CRACK
SORRY, BUT I JUST DON'T HAVE THAT MUCH PATIENCE.

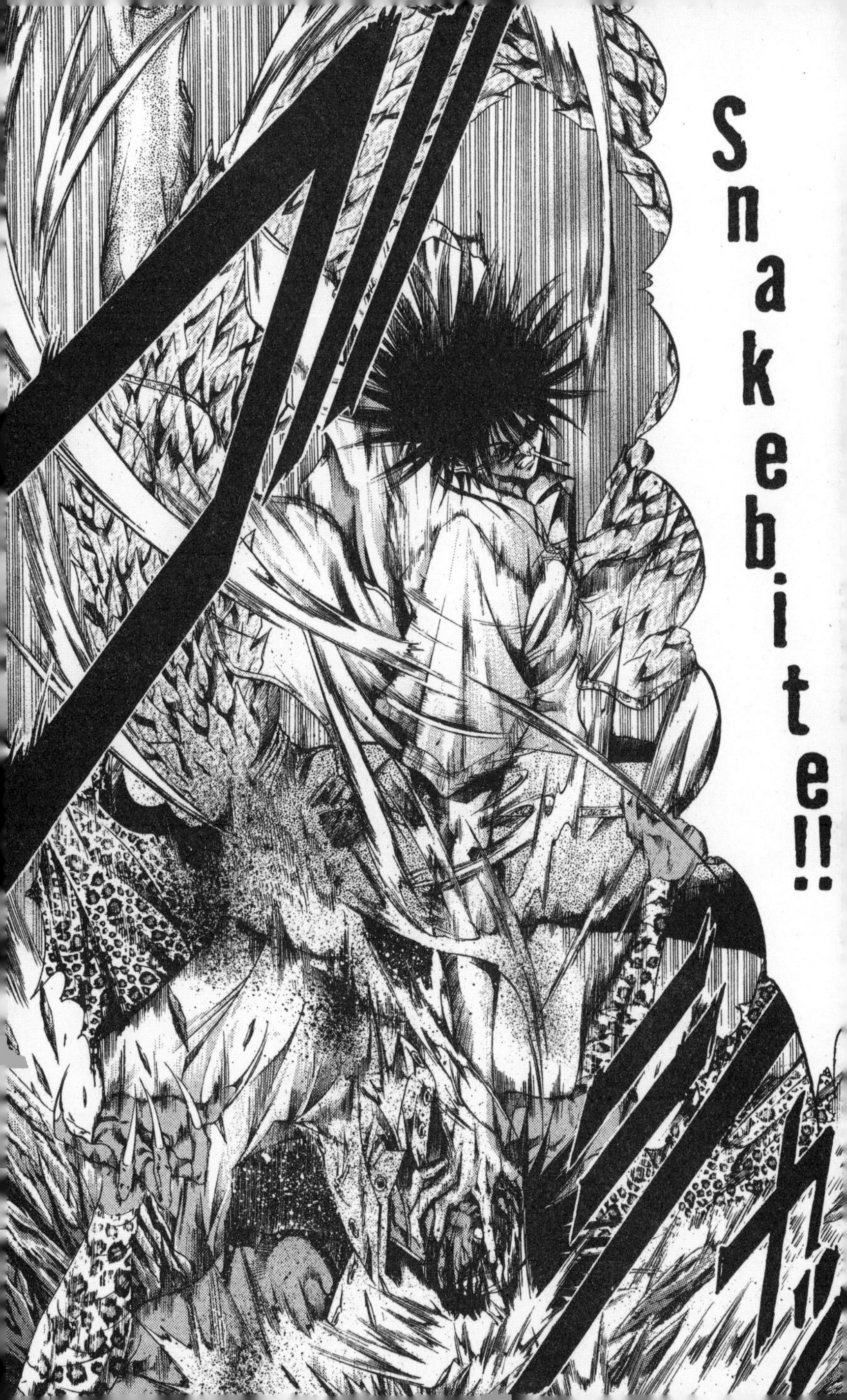
Snakebite!!

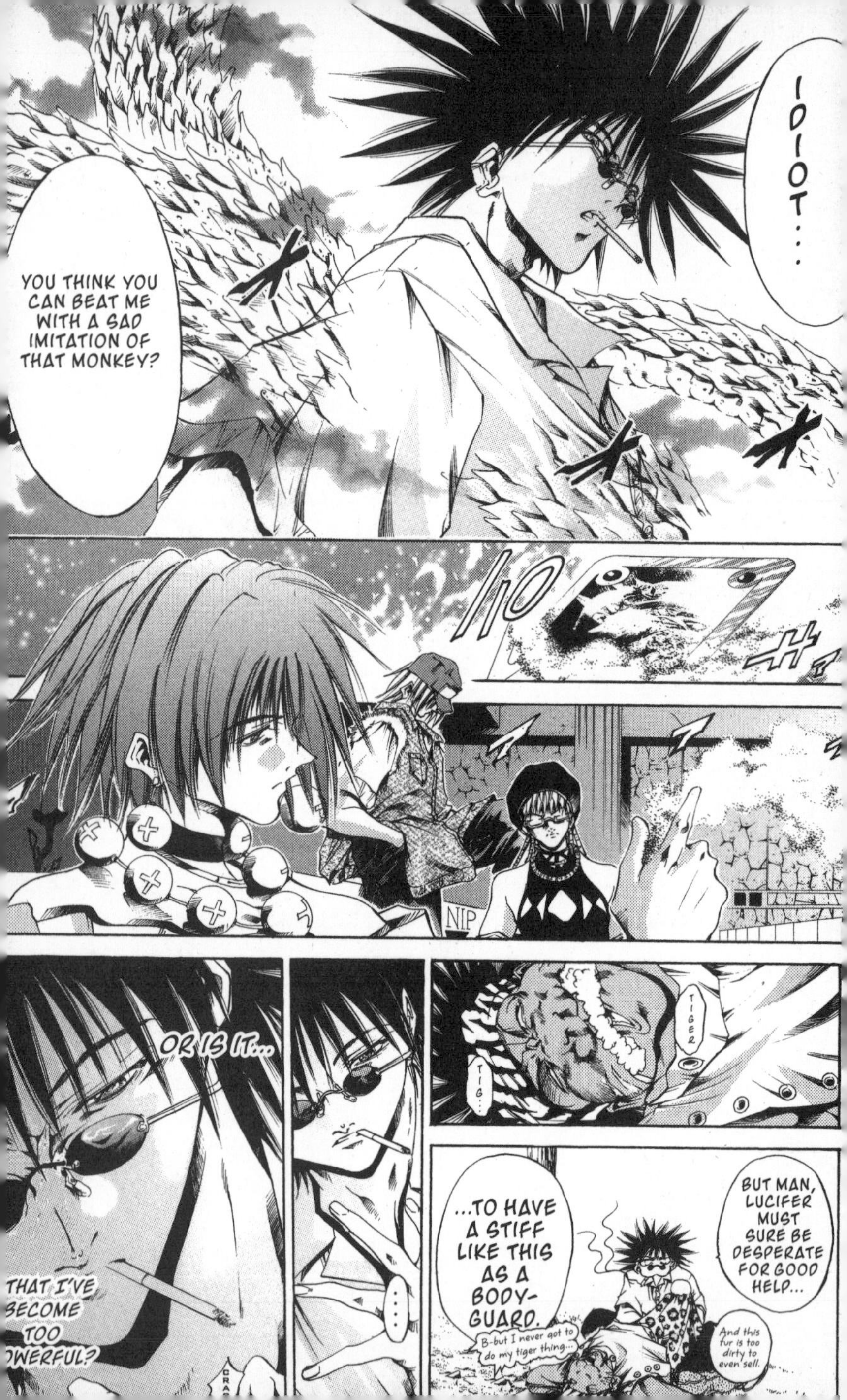
IDIOT...
YOU THINK YOU CAN BEAT ME WITH A SAD IMITATION OF THAT MONKEY?
TIGER
TIG...
BUT MAN, LUCIFER MUST SURE BE DESPERATE FOR GOOD HELP...
...TO HAVE A STIFF LIKE THIS AS A BODY-GUARD.
And this fur is too dirty to even sell.
B-but I never got to do my tiger thing...
...
OR IS IT...
THAT I'VE BECOME TOO OWERFUL?

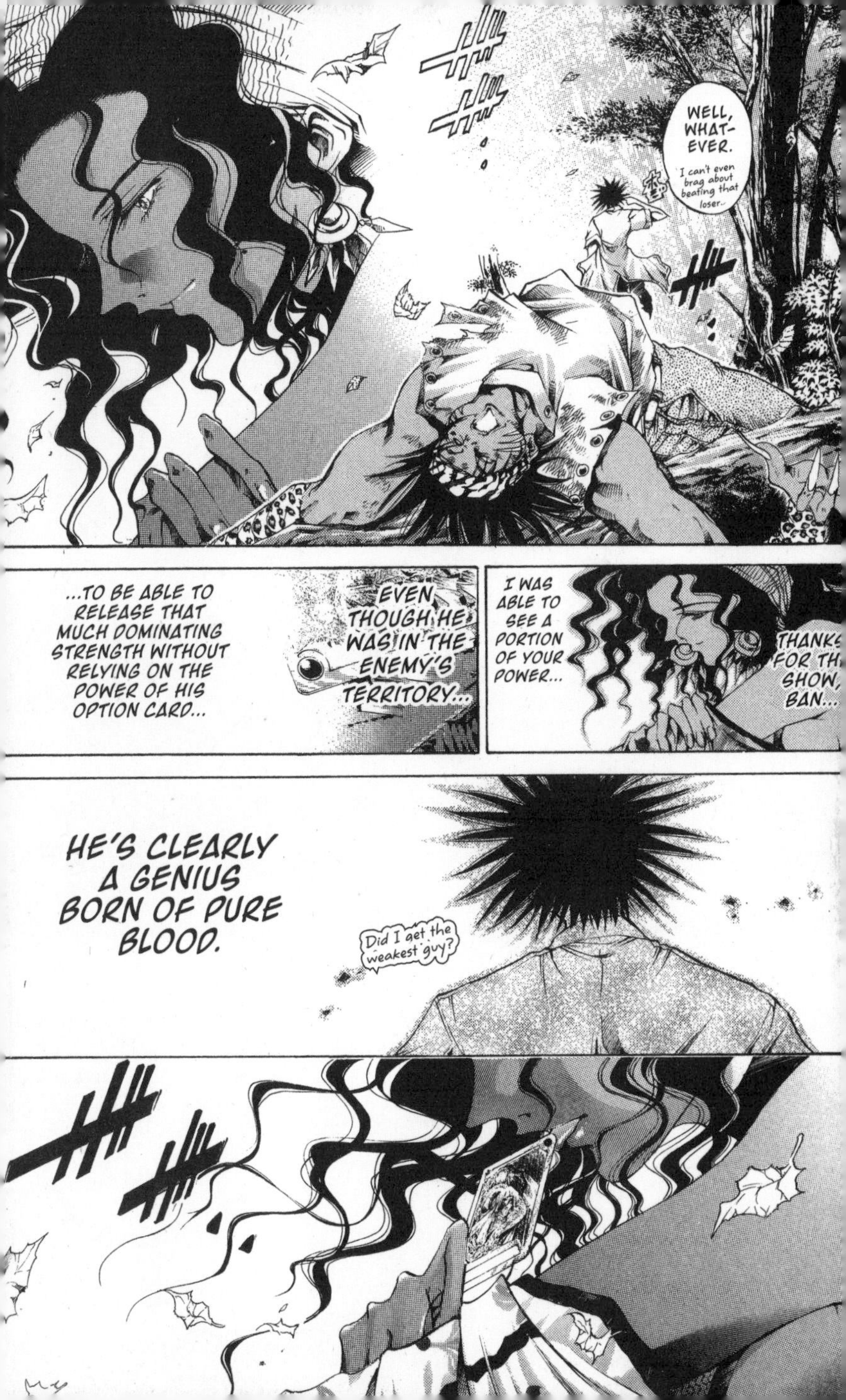
WELL, WHAT-EVER.
I can't even brag about beating that loser...
THANKS FOR TH SHOW, BAN...
I WAS ABLE TO SEE A PORTION OF YOUR POWER...
EVEN THOUGH HE WAS IN THE ENEMY'S TERRITORY...
...TO BE ABLE TO RELEASE THAT MUCH DOMINATING STRENGTH WITHOUT RELYING ON THE POWER OF HIS OPTION CARD...
HE'S CLEARLY A GENIUS BORN OF PURE BLOOD.
Did I get the weakest guy?

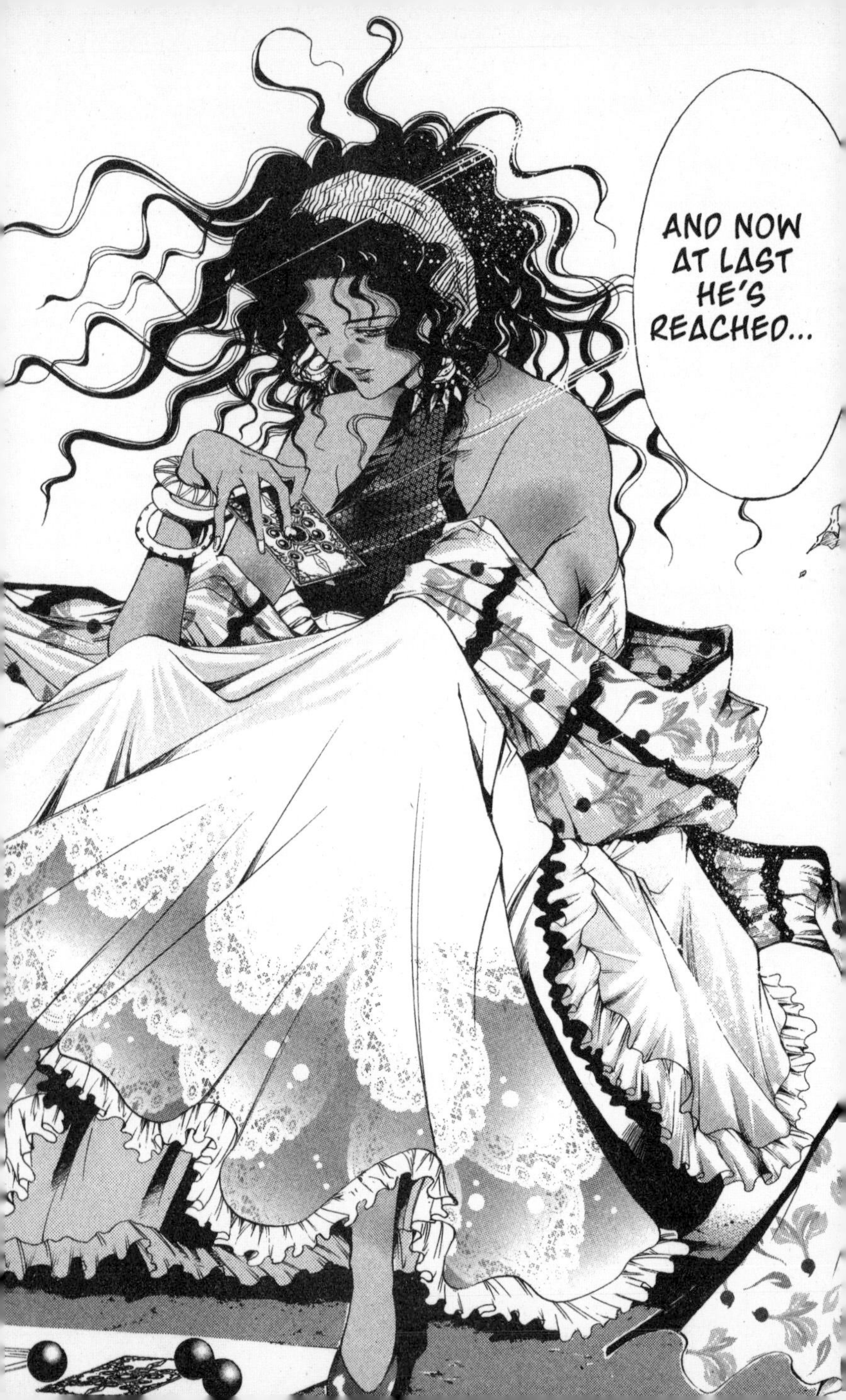
AND NOW AT LAST HE'S REACHED...

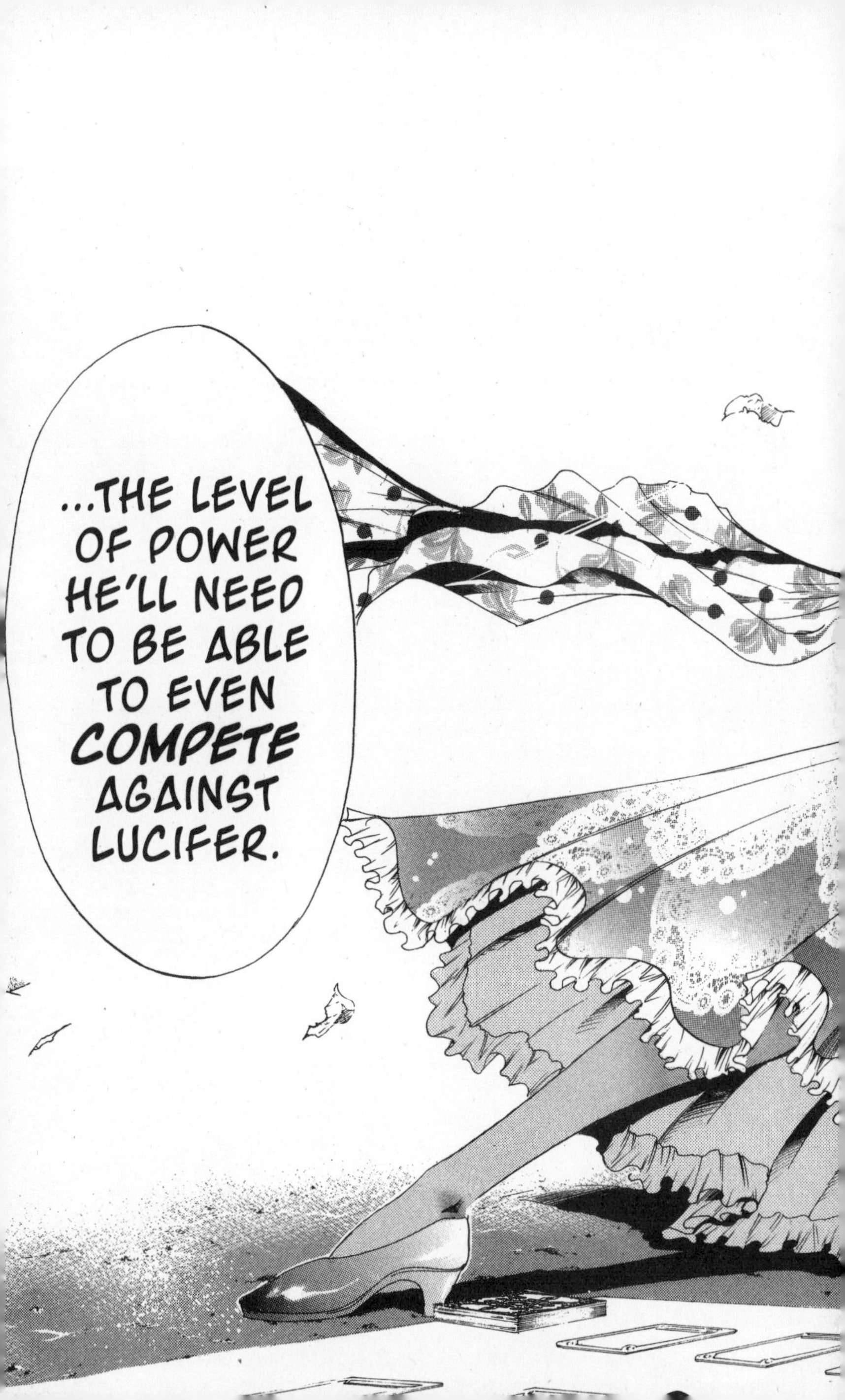
...THE LEVEL OF POWER HE'LL NEED TO BE ABLE TO EVEN **COMPETE** AGAINST LUCIFER.

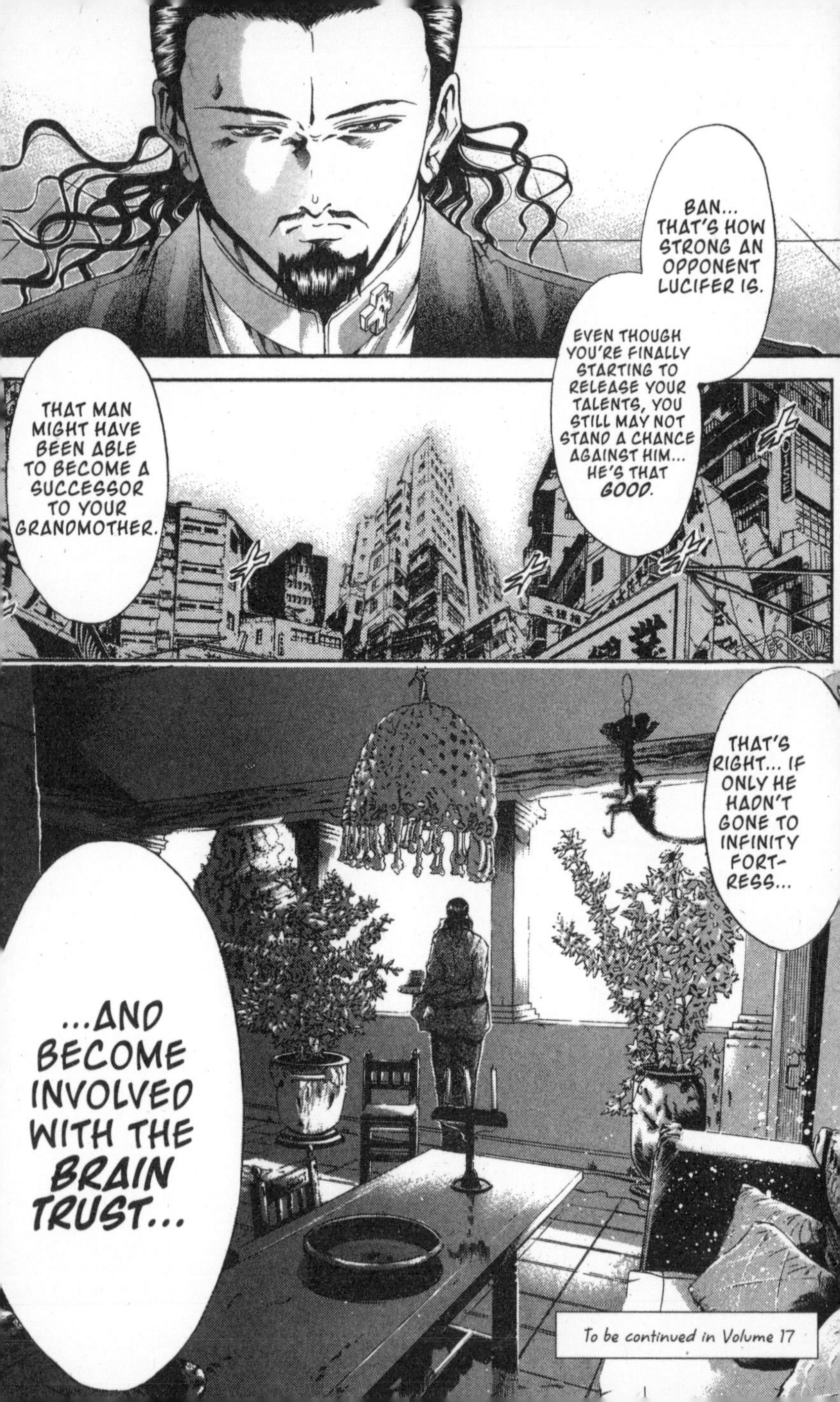
BAN... THAT'S HOW STRONG AN OPPONENT LUCIFER IS.
EVEN THOUGH YOU'RE FINALLY STARTING TO RELEASE YOUR TALENTS, YOU STILL MAY NOT STAND A CHANCE AGAINST HIM... HE'S THAT *GOOD*.
THAT MAN MIGHT HAVE BEEN ABLE TO BECOME A SUCCESSOR TO YOUR GRANDMOTHER.
THAT'S RIGHT... IF ONLY HE HADN'T GONE TO INFINITY FORT-RESS...
...AND BECOME INVOLVED WITH THE *BRAIN TRUST*...
To be continued in Volume 17

スタッフ紹介(しょうかい)

藤狗 知弥 CHIHIRO FUJIKOMA

加藤 亜季 AKI KATŌ

藍原 真樹 MASAKI AIHARA

大西 貴志 TAKASHI ŌNISHI

SPECIAL THANKS

伊川 良樹 YOSHIKI IKAWA

榎並 博昭 HIROAKI ENAMI

岡田 明典 AKINORI OKADA

岡田 有希 YUKI OKADA

為永 裕子 YŪKO TAMENAGA

EDITOR

TETSUYA NOZAKI

KIICHIRŌ SUGAWARA

YŪSUKE KIDO

The "Thank You for Buying this Volume" section!

Ve're now up to book 16 and it'll be
ntinuing for a long, long time. Many
ngs have happened and we've added
new staff members! There's always
oblems that crop up but I'm so happy
to have worked on GetBackers for so
ong and hope to continue for a while.
Thanks for all the support. And I'm so
sorry for that long break that I took, I
felt like I was betraying you guys. And
sorry to my editor as well!

Kinji-kun, congrats on the birth of your child!

I need to take better care of myself...

I read al the fan mail! Thanks to all of you, GetBackers is becoming an anime. I really appreciate all the support! I don't have time right now but I will respond to all those who sent mail eventually.

02.6.3

Shou-kun, I bought that game! It's awesome, thanks.
To the staff of the anime, please take good care of all my children.

Retrievers vs. Holy Beasts!

The man who stands in Ginji's way holds the ke

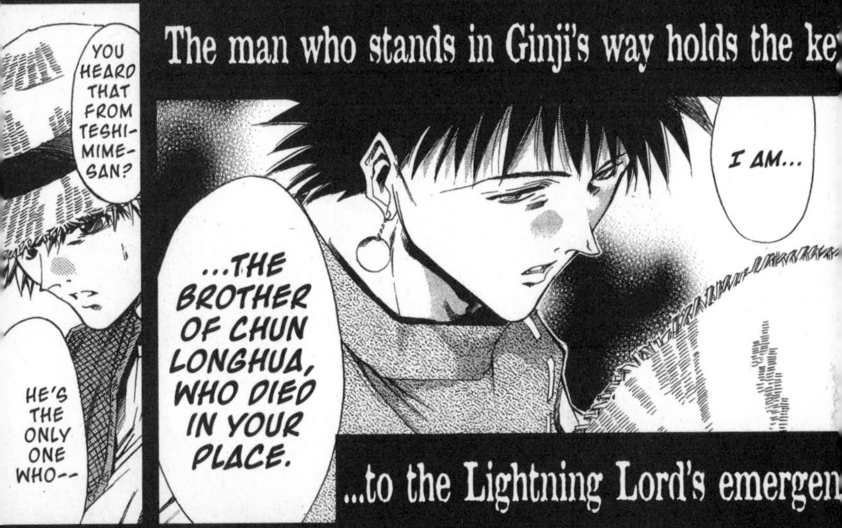
I AM...
...THE BROTHER OF CHUN LONGHUA, WHO DIED IN YOUR PLACE.
YOU HEARD THAT FROM TESHI-MIME-SAN?
HE'S THE ONLY ONE WHO--

...to the Lightning Lord's emergen

And...

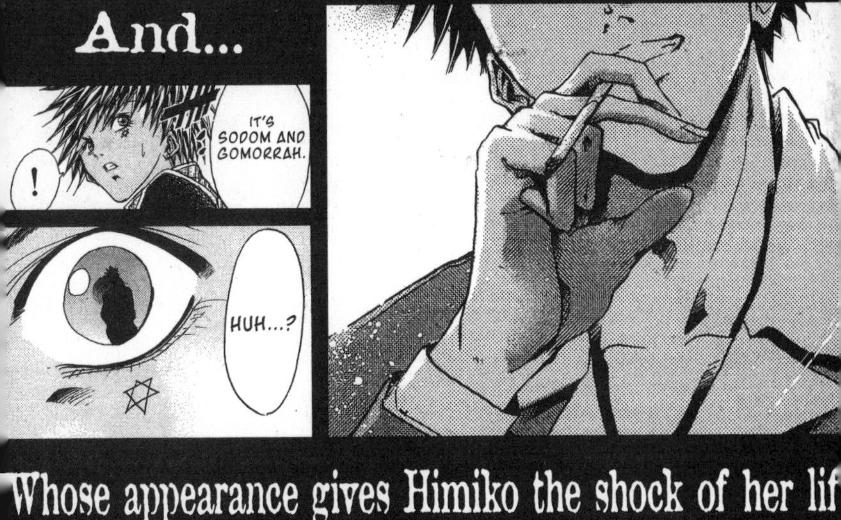
IT'S SODOM AND GOMORRAH.
!
HUH...?

Whose appearance gives Himiko the shock of her lif

In the next electri-
fying volume of **GETBACKERS**

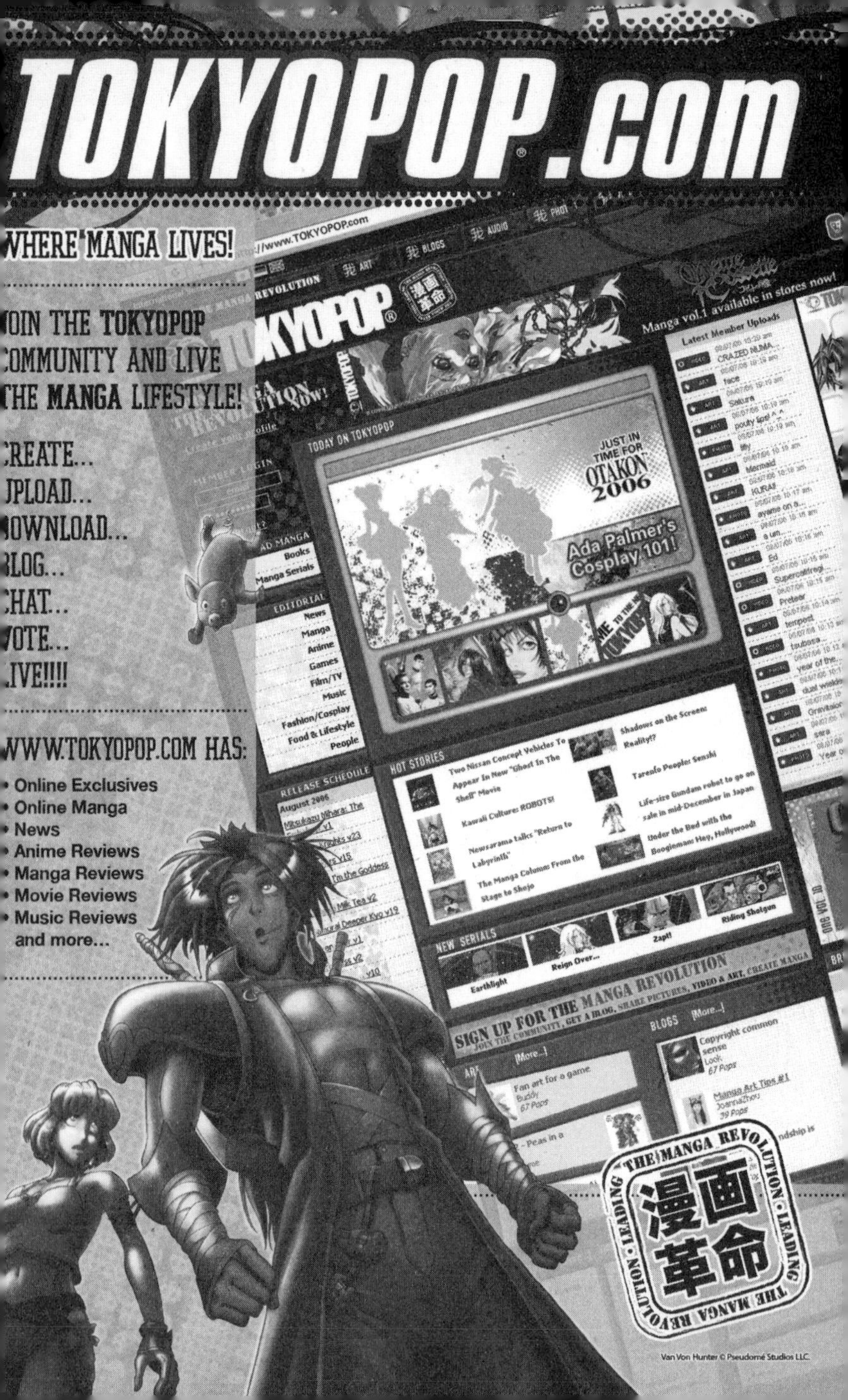
TOKYOPOP.com
WHERE MANGA LIVES!
JOIN THE TOKYOPOP COMMUNITY AND LIVE THE MANGA LIFESTYLE!
CREATE...
UPLOAD...
DOWNLOAD...
BLOG...
CHAT...
VOTE...
LIVE!!!!
WWW.TOKYOPOP.COM HAS:
• Online Exclusives
• Online Manga
• News
• Anime Reviews
• Manga Reviews
• Movie Reviews
• Music Reviews
and more...
http://www.TOKYOPOP.com
TODAY ON TOKYOPOP
JUST IN TIME FOR OTAKON 2006
Ada Palmer's Cosplay 101!
Latest Member Uploads
HOT STORIES
NEW SERIALS
SIGN UP FOR THE MANGA REVOLUTION
THE MANGA REVOLUTION · LEADING ·
漫画革命
Van Von Hunter © Pseudomé Studios LLC.

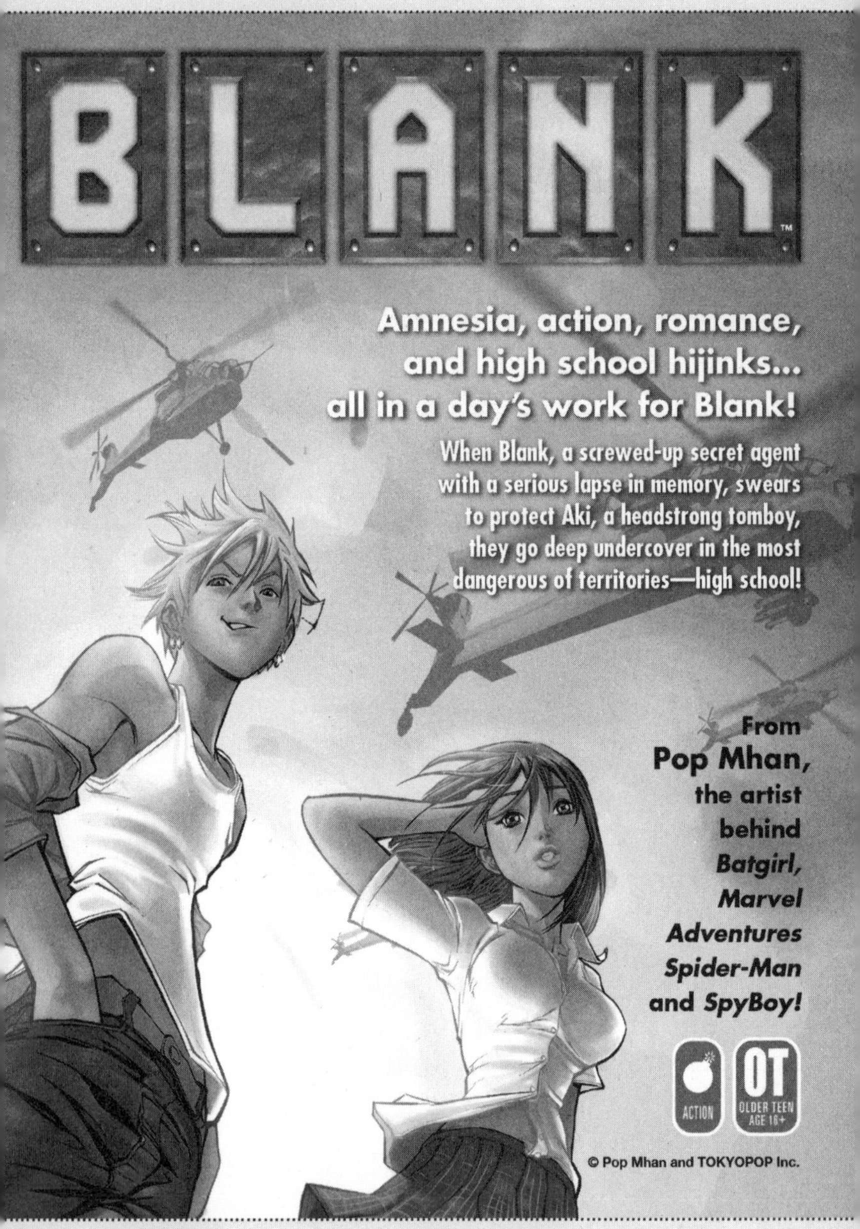
BLANK™
Amnesia, action, romance, and high school hijinks... all in a day's work for Blank!
When Blank, a screwed-up secret agent with a serious lapse in memory, swears to protect Aki, a headstrong tomboy, they go deep undercover in the most dangerous of territories—high school!
From Pop Mhan, the artist behind Batgirl, Marvel Adventures Spider-Man and SpyBoy!
ACTION
OT OLDER TEEN AGE 16+
© Pop Mhan and TOKYOPOP Inc.

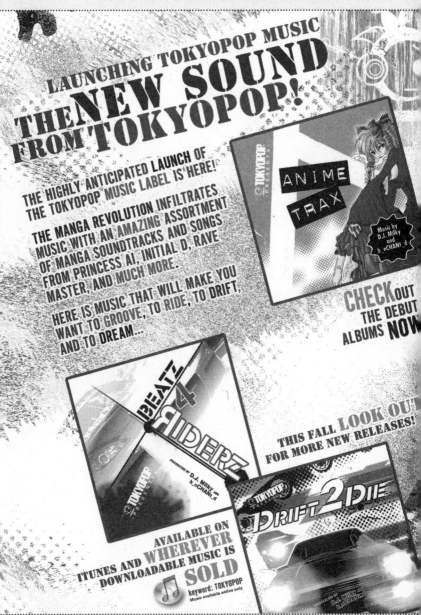

STOP!

This is the back of the book.
You wouldn't want to spoil a great ending!

This book is printed "manga-style," in the authentic Japanese right-to-left format. Since none of the artwork has been flipped or altered, readers get to experience the story just as the creator intended. You've been asking for it, so TOKYOPOP® delivered: authentic, hot-off-the-press, and far more fun!

DIRECTIONS

If this is your first time reading manga-style, here's a quick guide to help you understand how it works.

It's easy... just start in the top right panel and follow the numbers. Have fun, and look for more 100% authentic manga from TOKYOPOP®!